THE YOUNG AND THE VICIOUS

The innocence of youth is a sick joke to some perverted criminals. Obsessed by twisted desires and without any human feeling for their victims, they rob, rape, mutilate and kill at an age when most kids are playing baseball and going to the mall.

Now, from the authentic files of *True Detective* magazine, come the most savage cases of youthful violence ever reported, savage KILLER KIDS like North Carolina's April Barber, who killed her grandparents because they didn't approve of her 32-year old lover, and like Shawn Novak of Virginia, who brutally murdered two little boys. And from the pages of today's newspapers, KILLER KIDS like Luke Woodham, who allegedly murdered his mother before shooting his classmates in Mississippi, and Pennsylvania's Andrew Wurst, who is accused of killing a teacher and wounding three other people at a school dance.

KILLER KIDS

BOOK YOUR PLACE ON OUR WEBSITE AND MAKE THE READING CONNECTION!

We've created a customized website just for our very special readers, where you can get the inside scoop on everything that's going on with Zebra, Pinnacle and Kensington books.

When you come online, you'll have the exciting opportunity to:

- View covers of upcoming books
- Read sample chapters
- Learn about our future publishing schedule (listed by publication month *and author*)
- Find out when your favorite authors will be visiting a city near you
- Search for and order backlist books from our online catalog
- Check out author bios and background information
- Send e-mail to your favorite authors
- Meet the Kensington staff online
- Join us in weekly chats with authors, readers and other guests
- Get writing guidelines
- AND MUCH MORE!

**Visit our website at
http://www.pinnaclebooks.com**

KILLER KIDS

Updated by
Don Lasseter

Pinnacle Books
Kensington Publishing Corp.

http://www.pinnaclebooks.com

The editor wishes to express her sincerest thanks and appreciation to Stan Munro whose relentless efforts made this book possible, and who's a teen at heart with "killer looks."

Some names have been changed to protect the privacy of individuals connected to this story.

PINNACLE BOOKS are published by

Kensington Publishing Corp.
850 Third Avenue
New York, NY 10022

First Printing: September, 1998
10 9 8 7 6 5 4

Printed in the United States of America

CONTENTS

"SHOTGUN-TOTING
TEEN TERROR!"

by Charles W. Sasser

Two weeks before the police dragged the corpse from the Grand River, more than 100 angry residents of tiny Okay (population 554) in northeastern Oklahoma called a town meeting after work on Friday afternoon, February 16, 1990. Frayed tempers snapped. A fistfight broke out after one man cited the names of a handful of wild teenagers who he said had literally besieged the resort communities of Mallard Bay and Robin's Roost, two miles outside town at Lake Fort Gibson.

State Representative Jerry Hefner took the floor, announcing that Wagoner County Sheriff Elmer Shepherd and the district attorney were well aware of the crime wave that had engulfed the communities perched on the southwestern shores of the lake. Although the sheriff's department remained short-handed, with but a handful of deputies to patrol several hundred square miles encompassing a score of towns and small cities, Sheriff Shepherd promised to place a deputy on 24-hour standby for the Okay area and to ask the Oklahoma Highway Patrol for help.

"Everybody wants to do something," snapped someone from the crowd, "but juveniles just laugh in your face and say the law can't touch them."

Other townspeople hurled ominous suggestions of raw vigilantism at the law enforcement spokesmen.

"I ought to shoot them, but that's against the law," one man shouted.

Folks around Okay were fed up with the juvenile criminals, another man added. "Either something is done," he said, "or we'll have to take action ourselves."

Sheriff Shepherd agreed that the anger was well justified. Since the previous December, he said, juvenile crime in the region had "built up to a feverish pitch." Three teenagers had been arrested for rustling 58 head of cattle from Wagoner County ranches. Others had been arrested for, or named as suspects in, crimes such as arson, burglary, vandalism, fighting, and making threats. Invariably, most of the juveniles sought and found freedom in the custody of their parents and guardians. The crime wave continued, however, centered as it supposedly did on a loose-knit group of boys who lived spread out from Okay to Muskogee, eight miles away.

". . . There is nothing wrong with laws governing juvenile crime," proclaimed a Tulsa *Tribune* editorial, "but there is no place to lock up offenders, even temporarily. When we went through a great sentimental binge a few years ago over imprisoning children, juvenile detention facilities nearly vanished. High school corridors heard the triumphant sneer, 'They can't do nothin' to you,' and, sure enough, release to failed or uninterested parents became the normal order."

8

"These kids just drive around waiting for people to leave home so they can break in and steal," complained a Robin's Roost resident whose house had been burglarized three times.

"They're bold," put in another. "They have no fear of the law. If you call the police or try to prosecute them, you get telephone calls warning you that you'll never live to go to court."

During the past decade, the startling rise of violent crime among juveniles 14 to 17 years old had outraged Americans. Gang members as young as 10 or 11 routinely knocked each other off. Teenage dope dealers were the new dons of organized crime. In the larger cities, including nearby Tulsa, mobs of kids descended upon unsuspecting merchants and took whatever they wanted, looting with near impunity. Some sociologists suggested that Americans had failed to discipline their children and instill in them sound values and principles. The nation was now reaping the fruits of that neglect. Parents were afraid of their own children — and now the children were running wild.

"At the insistence of my wife," said a lakeside resident of Mallard Bay, "I keep a loaded .357, and I have been amazed at how many folks keep a gun loaded now."

"Citizens need to band together," said the state representative, "form some type of citizens alert group, and maybe even have some certified as deputies. Because we want this matter cleared up before someone is killed."

"Yes," came a muted response. "Before someone is killed."

While the unincorporated settlements of Wagoner

9

County suffered tremendously at the whims of juvenile criminals, Okay itself relied upon the reputation of its police chief Joe Reynolds, to stem the criminal tide.

Reynolds was known as a tough but fair lawman with over 30 years' experience in law enforcement. After retiring from California's Paloma Police Department, he migrated to Oklahoma, where he served two years as deputy and four years as undersheriff with the Wagoner County Sheriff's Department. He had been Okay's police chief—and sometimes its only police officer—for the past five years.

Okay's low crime rate suggested that criminals of whatever age group normally steered clear of the town. In late February and early March, while Wagoner County residents prepared petitions calling for a grand jury investigation of juvenile crime in the lake region, Chief Reynolds busied himself doing what he did best—chasing felons.

According to court documents, 18-year-old Eddie Simon, one of the young thieves who had allegedly plagued the Robin's Roost and Mallard Bay communities, had been identified in a Wagoner County arrest warrant charging him with burglary. After the Muskogee police chased Simon out of that city, Reynolds picked up his tracks in Okay. Informants slipped word to officers that the youthful fugitive was hiding out at the Okay residence of another teenager named Barry Belts.

Chief Reynolds kept close watch on the Belts house, waiting for Simon to make his presence known.

"If we could get a few of these troublemakers in

jail and keep them there," said Reynolds, "maybe we could break up the reign of terror."

A possible lead in the fugitive case broke on the morning of Saturday, March 3rd, when a citizen reported an unfamiliar vehicle parked on the street not far from the Simon boy's house. The complainant said that as he walked out to copy down the license plate number on the red-and-white pickup truck, a young stranger barged out of the Simon residence to confront him.

"We just parked it here while we're visiting," the stranger told him.

Reynolds requested a "10-28"—a vehicle owner's check—on the license number through the state Motor Vehicles Bureau. The information returned listing the number to a 1989 Ford Ranger pickup owned by Charles McMillin, who had a post office box in Fort Gibson, a small town northeast of Muskogee, east of Okay. The pickup showed a clean record—no wanteds, not reported stolen.

That didn't mean it wasn't somehow connected with the fugitive Simon. For the rest of that Saturday morning, Chief Reynolds maintained close surveillance on the vehicle, hoping it might eventually lead him to Simon.

Around noon, two teenagers left the Belts house and climbed into the pickup to drive off. Reynolds knew both of them. The passenger was Barry Belts, the driver was a 17-year-old named David Leon Wilson.

Wilson was a tall, muscular youth with long dark hair. Greasy-looking. Relatives politely referred to him as a hyperactive child with a learning disorder. Psychiatrists who'd examined him described him as

11

having a "borderline psychological disorder" and being of below average intelligence. Chief Reynolds bluntly countered that the boy was a bully and a known thief, wild, incorrigible, who lived in nearby Mallard Bay.

After red-lighting the pickup to a stop, Reynolds subtly questioned the two boys about Eddie Simon and asked to see the registration and insurance verification for the vehicle. Everything checked out. Wilson obligingly handed over papers showing that the pickup was registered to Charles McMillin.

"What are you doing, driving the pickup?" Chief Reynolds inquired.

"It belongs to my girlfriend, Sharon McMillin," one of the youths responded. "It's hers, but it's in her old man's name. She lives in Muskogee."

The chief later said that the boys could not convince him they did not know Eddie Simon's whereabouts, but he had no charges against them. He released the two teenagers.

That same night, Wagoner County deputies patrolling near the Muskogee County line also stopped the same boys in the red-and-white pickup. Wilson allegedly provided the deputies a story similar to the one he gave Chief Reynolds. The teenagers had a shotgun with them, the deputies said, but it was unloaded. Transporting an unloaded shotgun in a vehicle is not against the law in Oklahoma. Most farm trucks have rifle racks which are visible in their rear windows.

On Sunday, the pickup was back in Okay.

On Monday morning, March 5th, the matter of the red-and-white pickup unexpectedly assumed a new perspective. Chief Reynolds reportedly received a telephone call from a Muskogee girl who identified herself as Sharon Thomas. She said she was David Wilson's girlfriend.

"Sharon Thomas—not Sharon McMillin?" the Chief responded in surprise.

"I don't know any Sharon McMillin," the girl reportedly continued. "David has been telling everybody the truck he's driving is mine, but it's not. I don't know what's going down, but something is. Him and Barry Belts are getting ready to go to Texas. I think they're scared of something."

But of what?

Sharon said that she didn't know—but something.

Further questioning by Okay's top cop reportedly added more detail to Sharon Thomas' statement. She said she first saw Wilson driving the Ford pickup on Thursday, March 1st, when he came to her house in Muskogee. He told her that he bought the truck, a boat, and a TV set from his grandfather for a mere $500.

"That truck is almost new!" Sharon exclaimed. "He couldn't have bought it for that."

His suspicions piqued by the girl's revelations, Chief Reynolds requested that the Fort Gibson police check with the pickup's registered owner to determine if Charles McMillin had given Wilson permission to drive the vehicle. It didn't take long for officers to learn that while McMillin rented a post office box in Fort Gibson, he actually lived in Mallard Bay.

An Okay water department employee knew McMillin personally. At Chief Reynolds' request, the man hurried to Mallard Bay to find McMillin. In the meantime, Chief Reynolds staked out the pickup in question. It was parked, as usual, on the street near Barry Belts' house. At that point, Reynolds said, he was beginning to think that the Ford Ranger might be stolen.

The circumstances surrounding Wilson's possession of the pickup grew increasingly convoluted as the day passed, and as Sheriff Elmer Shepherd and his deputies, along with agents of the Oklahoma State Bureau of Investigation (OSBI), and Muskogee police detectives, were drawn into the probe. Together, they began picking up threads of a secret being kept by a small group of teenagers in Wagoner and Muskogee counties. It was a secret, the police said, that when exposed would prompt state legislators to consider new and stricter methods of dealing with youthful offenders.

The exposure of that secret began with Sharon Thomas' statement, then opened further when a second Muskogee juvenile admitted that David Wilson had visited him on Friday, March 2nd. Wilson was driving the red-and-white Ford, inside of which was a small arsenal—a .22 pistol, a 12-gauge shotgun, and a 20-gauge shotgun. But more disturbing than that, the youth said, were the bloodstains he'd noticed in the bed of the pickup.

According to later reports, Wilson explained away his possession of the vehicle by saying, "I bought it, a boat, and a TV from my grandpa for $1,500."

"You're full of it!" the juvenile said he retorted.

Later that same Friday, the Muskogee teenager reportedly telephoned Wilson's relatives in Mallard Bay and out of curiosity inquired about how Wilson might have obtained the mysterious Ford. Apparently, he was lying to everyone. While telling people in

Muskogee that he had bought the truck from his grandfather, he was allegedly telling Okay friends and relatives that the truck belonged to his Muskogee girlfriend, Sharon Thomas.

At Mallard Bay, a scattering of camper trailers, mobile homes, and smallish resort cottages on a gentle hill overlooking Fort Gibson Lake, the residents kept pretty much to themselves, especially during the winter. It was a mind-your-own-business neighborhood. The water department employee looking for Charles McMillin soon found that few people in the little community had noticed that one of their neighbors left home suddenly during the last week in February.

Charles McMillin was a fairly typical resident of the community. After retiring from the U.S. Navy, the 66-year-old man settled down in Mallard Bay, where he had lived quietly for the past 21 years. Some people said his wife had died; others believed that he might have been divorced. In any case, he lived modestly in a wooden cottage, painted red, at a bend in the gravel road. He had few visitors. He fished some, read, kept up his lawn, and spoke to his neighbors when they passed on the road.

His red-and-white Ford pickup, the neighbors believed, must have disappeared from his driveway at least five days earlier, sometime around the last day of February or the first of March.

"It was, like, maybe Wednesday or Thursday that I noticed it gone," one neighbor said. "I knocked on his door, but no one answered. The door was locked. I figured Charlie must have gone out of state visiting relatives or something."

Checking further, the water company man discovered that the living-room window on the west side of Charlie's little red cottage was missing from its frame. The window gaped open to the March weather, which in Oklahoma can still bring a freeze at night.

Even more puzzling was that no shattered glass lay on the floor below the opening for the missing window. Surely a burglar wouldn't have cleaned up after himself. Even more surely, Charlie himself would never have left home with his living room exposed to the blustering winds and rains of late winter.

"It doesn't make sense," the water man reported back to Chief Reynolds.

Reynolds agreed. Each new fact, he said, contributed to his growing concern that there was something ominous about the disappearance of Charlie McMillin. And the facts were mounting up—Charlie's disappearance, the broken window, David Wilson driving McMillin's pickup, bloodstains seen in the bed of the pickup, Wilson's lying about how he came in possession of the truck.

"I saw bloodstains outside Charlie's house, on the porch," the water man reported.

The mystery deepened. Chief Reynolds requested additional deputies from Sheriff Shepherd to help him fit together the pieces of the puzzle.

But even as the investigation took one step forward, it also took one step backward. Wagoner County deputies investigating the broken window soon concluded that the "bloodstains" on the porch were red paint. Had that also been red paint, then, in the bed of the pickup?

McMillin's home yielded little evidence to indicate that any crimes had been committed. Although his

TV was apparently missing, nothing inside the house appeared to have been disturbed otherwise. In fact, it looked as though housekeepers had gone through the residence, scouring and cleaning.

"No way would Charlie have given David Wilson the keys to his truck," said a neighbor questioned by police. "They were enemies, Charlie and that bully boy."

Another neighbor shook his head as he recalled that last conversation he'd had with Charlie McMillin. That would have been on Wednesday, February 28th, he said. He and Charlie were talking, passing the time of day, when the conversation naturally turned to the town hall meeting held in Okay and to the Grand Jury petitions being circulated to probe the problems of juvenile crime.

Charlie said that he'd had his own problems with juveniles. The Wilson boy, he said, had been harassing him, cutting across his property, yelling obscenities and threats at him.

"I guess I'm going to have to go to his parents about it," Charlie reportedly decided, "and see if that'll do any good."

No one in Mallard Bay remembered having seen Mr. McMillin since then.

Back in Muskogee, the police ferreted out information from a Wilson pal, suddenly enveloping the case in further intrigue and frightening possibilities.

"David told me that he killed this guy," the boy witness reportedly stated, "and that the truck belongs to this guy."

Was death, then, the secret behind Charlie McMillin's disappearance?

Chief Joe Reynolds shook his head in disbelief.

"No one would be stupid enough to kill a guy and then drive the guy's vehicle around the countryside for everyone to see."

Still, considering all the circumstances, Reynolds expressed confidence that he had more than enough probable cause to hold David Wilson for interrogation.

Shortly after noon on that Monday, March 5th, three teenagers emerged from Barry Belts' residence in Okay and climbed into the Ford Ranger. Watching and waiting, Chief Reynolds recognized the scraggly forms of Barry Belts and David Wilson. At first, the chief said, he thought the third boy might be the fugitive Eddie Simon, but he soon dismissed that thought.

Eddie Simon wasn't that important anymore, anyhow. The chief was now hunting bigger game.

Reserve Wagoner County Deputy Clifford Goad and Deputy Ron McKaig arrived as backup to help Reynolds take the three youngsters into custody on suspicion of auto theft. The lawmen seized a 12-gauge shotgun and a .22-caliber revolver from the Ford before they released the vehicle to crime scene search specialists. The experts immediately scoured the truck with chemicals and powders, attempting to detect traces of blood or other trace evidence.

If there was murder to add to the list of juvenile crimes in Wagoner County, the police still had no firm evidence of it.

But the detectives were still probing, still asking questions. Now in custody, David Leon Wilson received the full brunt of police attention. Subsequent reports described the long-haired youth as a sullen, evasive individual who flippantly attempted to explain away his possession of a missing person's pickup truck.

Yes, he said, he had indeed stolen the Ranger, but that did not mean he'd had anything to do with Mr. McMillin's disappearance. Undersheriff Johnny Cannon recorded the statements as Wilson drawled, "I was looking through Charlie's window and I saw the keys on the table. I climbed through the window and took them. I don't know what happened to Charlie, though."

Why, detectives wondered aloud, hadn't Charlie made a police theft report on his pickup when he discovered it gone?

Was it because Charlie McMillin was already dead?

There was still no evidence of that.

"With no more than we had to go on at that time," explained one detective, "we either had to have a corpse, or we didn't have a homicide. We couldn't really even file auto-theft charges without a complainant." That was true enough.

Sheriff Shepherd later said that he and OSBI Agent Dennis Francini questioned the Wilson boy on three separate occasions following his arrest. Although initially the boy reportedly denied all knowledge of any crimes except auto theft, remarks that he allegedly made to fellow inmates at the Wagoner County Jail soon meshed with interrogation results to form some discernible pattern of the suspect's activities within the previous week.

Two teenagers who shared a jail cell with Wilson offered sworn statements that Wilson entered one of their conversations by talking about the crimes he was accused of.

"He said he was walking through these people's backyards and dogs began barking," one teenager testified. "He went around to the back and saw a man sitting in his chair looking at a book. He pointed the [shotgun] at the window and shot him."

Afterwards, Wilson reportedly told his cellmates, he entered McMillin's house and rifled the dead man's body, taking $42 from his wallet. Then he fled the house, but returned shortly thereafter. He picked up the body and the chair it was in, loaded them and the deceased's TV into the back of the truck, and drove away. He planned to dispose of the body and return with other juveniles to steal more loot from the house. He later pawned the TV in Muskogee for $100.

The motive behind the callous murder and robbery?

"He said he was hot for some acid [drugs]," the witnesses concluded.

"It was the thing horror movies are made of," one Wagoner County lawman remarked about the crime. "Cold. Calculated. A man sitting in his living room, reading on a winter's evening. A young thug in the darkness outside peeping through his window. *Bam!* No warning—and the victim dies for forty-two dollars and a TV set."

The case file reveals that David Wilson apparently continued spinning his web of lies. While admitting to cellmates that a murder had indeed taken place and that it was he who killed the hapless old man at Mallard Bay, he soon confessed to authorities that, yes, there was a murder, but it was not he who shot Charlie McMillin. Barry Belts, Wilson said, was the triggerman.

According to later testimony, the accused youth said that he simply helped load the corpse into the pickup after Barry Belts blasted Charlie McMillin into the next world.

Then the two boys drove through the winter's night to nearby Fort Gibson Lake, where they tossed the old man's chair off the dam into the Grand River far below. The corpse, weighted with bricks tied around the ankles, soon followed the chair into the river.

Wilson agreed to show Sheriff Shepherd the location of Charlie McMillin's watery grave.

The body was there in the dark river, exactly in the spot where Wilson pointed. Police divers soon recovered it. Dr. Ronald Difaniao, the medical examiner, ruled that the victim died from a 12-gauge shotgun blast to the side of the neck.

"The right side," Sheriff Shepherd said in discussing the wound with the teenage suspect in custody.

"No," Wilson corrected immediately. "He was shot on the left side."

Officially, now that police had a corpse and suspects, what started off as a search for a fugitive teen burglar could now be classified as a homicide case. Detectives continued their relentless probe, drawing in the loose strings and knitting them into an escape-proof net.

The question of which of the two boys—Barry Belts or David Leon Wilson—actually pulled the trigger on the Naval retiree gradually resolved itself. Each claimed the other did it. Chief Reynolds said he personally believed that both were involved. However, the preponderance of facts and evidence soon weighed heavily against Wilson.

"It was Wilson, the detectives determined, who'd pawned Mr. McMillin's TV in Muskogee. It was Wilson who had possession of the dead man's truck. The murder weapon belonged to Wilson; police recovered it from the stolen pickup. It was Wilson who admitted to at least six other juveniles that he had shot the ex-Navy man.

"Wilson, I believe, actually shot the old man," said Chief Joe Reynolds. "But it would have taken two boys to load the body and get rid of it. I believe Barry Belts helped."

On March 6, 1990, David Leon Wilson was charged in Wagoner County District Court with first-degree murder, to be tried as an adult. Barry Belts was included in the indictment as a material witness.

After the arrest of the juveniles, the crime rate in the resort communities surrounding Okay began to drop until, a month afterward, someone remarked that parents seemed to have regained control of their delinquent offspring. The McMillin slaying had apparently shocked the community into taking responsibility for the behavior of its teenagers.

Still, life had changed around Mallard Bay and Robin's Roost. Life, someone observed, with a tinge of bitterness, would never again be quite okay around Okay.

"It's always been a quiet community," said a resident of Robin's Roost. "A lot of folks didn't even lock their doors at night because they had no reason. Now, it's imperative."

On March 5, 1992, after two years of legal wrangling, David Leon Wilson pleaded guilty to first-degree murder and was confined to the Oklahoma State Penitentiary to serve a 36-year sentence.

EDITOR'S NOTE:
Eddie Simon, Barry Belts and Sharon Thomas are not the real names of the persons so named in the foregoing story. Fictitious names have been used because there is no reason for public interest in the identities of these persons.

"HE TORCHED TOM
WITH KEROSENE!"

by Barbara Malenky

Homer Cantrell loved early mornings in Ellen-wood, Georgia. Breathing deeply of the sweet spring air on the morning of March 7, 1990, Homer leisurely walked the long driveway of his home to get his newspaper. The fact that a heavy, steady rain was falling didn't deter him. There was no wind, and it was a chilly but pleasant 53 degrees.

Living in Henry County had its advantages: freedom from the emotional toll of city living, a feel of small-town friendliness, and, of course, the fragrance of fresh air. Although Atlanta, Georgia, one of the nation's most crime-troubled cities, lay a mere 28 miles to the north, Henry County boasted a relatively low crime rate. It was a good place to live.

Homer picked up his paper and took a quick glance around, enjoying the tranquility of the neighborhood at 5:30 a.m. In the distance Homer heard the bark of a dog and the distinct song of a rooster announcing the dawn.

It was still dark, and for that reason, Homer's eye was drawn to an eerie illumination through the bare, skeletal trees. Standing motionless for a few moments, Homer peered steadily at the bright spot coming from a neighbor's house. Suddenly realizing what he was seeing, Homer rushed back up his driveway into his house and grabbed the telephone.

At 5:40 a.m., an emergency call was received and dispatched to the Henry County Fire Department. Within six minutes, a rescue squad vehicle arrived at the scene, quickly followed by four fire units. They found a brick house engulfed in flames. From the front it appeared one storied, but the firefighters quickly discovered a separate suite below, partially underground. The house had a total of 17 rooms.

Finding several automobiles parked in the driveway, a signal 77 was called in to indicate that human beings were possibly trapped inside.

Firefighters began the battle. Finding the front door ajar, they brought hose lines through the entrance. They were met by a hellish wall of fire thrusting down the hallway toward them. Lying to the left, inside the front door, was a heap of mattresses. The firefighters had to crawl back and forth over them to bring equipment inside. Fearlessly, they searched the residence for survivors. Despite the vehicles outside, the house seemed empty of human occupants.

As the firefighters fought to control the blaze, they made a gruesome discovery. A supine body lay concealed between the mattresses near the front door.

Jerry Mitchell, an investigator and inspector with the Henry County Fire Department as well as a police officer, received a call at 6:02 a.m. He listened carefully to the caller's voice and hastily dressed to drive out to the fire scene. It would be Mitchell's job to determine if the fire was set by accident, by an act of God, or by intention.

At the same time, Captain Kenny Smith, a 10-year law enforcement veteran of the Investigative Division of the Henry County Sheriff's Department, was notified by the fire department that a body had been found. He quickly dispatched Detective Sandi Graves to the scene. She would secure the area to preserve crucial evidence in case of a foul-play ruling.

Upon arriving, Investigator Mitchell found that the body had been moved outside the house into the front yard. He examined it. It was the partially burnt remains of a heavyset male. The victim wore only a pair of white socks and a blood-soaked white T-shirt. There were bedclothes wrapped partially around the victim's head. Fortunately, the mattress that had been on top of the body had protected it from the worst of the flames. The body wasn't badly burned. Investigator Mitchell could see there was a good bit of trauma around the head area. The victim's eyes were bruised blue and swollen. Mitchell felt there was an excessive amount of blood flowing from the body. Noticing an unusual odor wafting from the victim, Mitchell examined the mattress and found the same odor. He then entered the gutted house. Apparently, the rear bedrooms had taken the worst of the fire, which had burned around the walls and through the bed in one bedroom, causing the flooring underneath to fall into the room below.

To the knowledgeable investigator, the cause of this fire and the man's death appeared suspicious, but for legal reasons, the final conclusion would be determined by an autopsy on the victim and the clarification of samples taken and sent to the state crime lab.

Mitchell placed a call for state assistance. Soon, they would begin the fire investigation.

At a little past 7:00 a.m., the body was bagged and placed in an ambulance. It would be delivered to the Henry County General Hospital Morgue for autopsy. Until further notice, the name given to the victim was "John Doe." The detectives had little to go on.

In a fire death, there can be no more essential team work than that of the fire investigator, pathologist, and law enforcement agent. Together they can provide the ID for the victim, as well as the manner and cause of both the death and fire. Without the combined expertise of each individual force, the answers would be difficult to come by.

Investigating fire and arson is not a pretty job. Investigators put forth a team effort. They are a highly trained, specialized bunch whose attributes include more than intelligence—much more. Good attitude, determination to succeed, and ironclad patience are also important factors. A topnotch investigator will reconstruct the sequence of the fire by working backwards from what is still visible to its point of origin. The fire investigator must be thorough but cautious. The point and source of ignition are the key elements to be determined and are of primary importance in the investigation.

K.G. Davis is a 42-year-old veteran of fire and arson investigation. As the deputy state fire marshall in Georgia, assigned to the arson division since 1964, Davis is given credit for being *the* expert in his field. He has handled thousands of fire and arson cases during his career, with close to a 100 percent conviction record in cases he brought to court. Few law enforcers would disagree that when K.G. Davis states his opinion, there's no doubt it's the right one.

Davis arrived on the scene of the fire at 7:30 a.m. Although his habit was to examine the body at the scene, by the time he arrived, the victim had already been taken away. Davis began his investigation by walking carefully around the exterior of the house. He searched for the unusual. He photographed all sides. Not a detail would escape his trained eyes. It had been a nice house in a pleasant, quiet location, nestled high up a long curved driveway in a haven of trees. A double carport had been enclosed and used as a utility room. A large screened porch looked out into a backyard of trees. Now the roof area was burned out.

Davis walked into the interior. He began his examination in the least damaged areas, moving carefully toward the parts with the most damage. Davis believed in keeping an open mind. His rule of thumb was to eliminate all the accidental causes. He worked through the fire-ravaged rooms, photographing, sketching and observing.

By determining the burn pattern and heat level, Davis concluded that the fire had started in the back bedroom on the west side of the house. The flooring underneath the bed springs in the upstairs back bedroom had burned and fallen through on top of the kitchen stove and cabinets of the apartment below. All the bedroom furniture was incinerated.

The weather had been inclement for eight days prior to the morning of March 7th, and would not offer the investigators much relief now. Working with Investigator Mitchell, Detective Graves and firefighters trained in fire investigation, Davis would lead them in a painstaking search for evidence. Using their fingers, they would sift through two tons of charred debris collecting evidence to determine the cause and origin of the fire. In fog and light mist, they would spend the next 14 hours, nonstop, working at the difficult, tedious endeavor.

At 2:00 a.m. on March 7th, Dr. Gerald Gowitt of the Fulton County Medical Examiner's Office in Atlanta arrived to perform the preliminary autopsy. Also in attendance were Captain Smith and Detective Graves, who would soon begin the investigation into the victim's death.

Doctor Gowitt was quickly able to answer some important questions. "John Doe" was a Caucasian male, weighing 250 pounds. He was 68 inches in height. Gowitt found no carbon monoxide in the victim's blood. Finding no particles of soot or carbon in the moist surfaces of the victim's throat and lungs, Dr. Gowitt told his rapt audience that the victim had not died from the fire and had not been alive at the onset of it. His life had, however, ended in an unpleasant manner. The head trauma noticed earlier by Investigator Mitchell and thought to be caused by falling debris or blows around the head had actually been caused by multiple gunshots.

Apparently, someone had pumped five bullets, possibly from a small handgun, into the victim's head at close range. Three had actually pierced all the way through, leaving exit holes.

Receiving final word from the autopsy, K.G. Davis and his team increased their evidence search. Although some projectiles had been lodged in the victim's head, the investigators wanted to find the

29

others. It was nice, after all, to have a piece of confirmed evidence to look for. In the back bedroom, Davis recovered pieces of bedding. They were covered with blood. It became clear that the victim had been shot in the bedroom.

Meanwhile, Investigator Mitchell was busy. By running tag searches on the automobiles parked in the driveway, he'd been able to trace the occupant of the house and put a name with the body: Thomas Henry Patton, 60 years old, an auto salvager who was based in Henry County.

It was late in the afternoon when a relative of the victim's was located and notified of Patton's death. Arriving quickly on the scene of the fire, the relative was able to provide a possible motive for Patton's murder, one that would give the detectives a break and bring them rapidly to the door of a suspect.

There had been no jewelry found in the house, yet sleuths were told that Patton always wore two gold and diamond rings — one was a distinct horseshoe with a large stone in the middle — and a gold nugget watch. Because of the nature of his business in auto salvaging, he often carried a large denomination of currency on his person. No trace of money was located in the debris. One of the cars Patton had been driving most recently was a shiny black Monte Carlo. It, too, was missing.

Then Thomas Patton's relative looked at the detectives and asked, "Where is Billy Shane?"

The relationship between Billy Shane Willingham and Thomas Henry Patton was a confusing one at best. Although Billy Shane lived the first seven years of his life with the man whose last name he carried, his mother divorced Willingham while the boy was still an infant. She set up residence with Thomas Patton. When Billy Shane turned 13 years old, a secret was shared with him. He was told that Thomas Patton was his true biological daddy.

Opinions would vary greatly between Patton's legitimate children on this belief. Some would never accept it, others did grudgingly. As for Thomas Patton, he acknowledged it as fact and treated Billy Shane as his son. A relative of Billy Shane's remembered sadly that Billy Shane never seemed the same after learning the truth. He started having problems.

Investigators were told that Thomas Patton was a generous man who tried to provide Billy Shane with the necessities a teenager required. Even after the relationship between his mother and Patton soured and she'd moved out of Patton's house, Billy Shane continued to be provided for by Patton.

Billy Shane was beginning to show signs of being a troubled teen. He dropped out of high school halfway through his senior year. He hinted to his friends about drug dealings. While still a juvenile, Billy Shane got into trouble with the law. He was accused of stealing from his girlfriend's parents. Thomas Patton posted the boy's bond, getting him out of jail. Patton offered Billy Shane his basement apartment, free of charge. Some would say it was the only way Patton could keep tabs on him while waiting for trial. Others claimed it was done strictly out of the kindness of his heart. Whichever was the truth, Billy Shane set up housekeeping in the bottom part of Patton's house.

When it became possible to clear out enough debris from the basement living quarters, detectives discovered that Billy Shane's personal belongings were gone. Since personal belongings are the first thing an arsonist moves before lighting the match, the finger of suspicion pointed to the boy, making Billy Shane Willingham the first clear suspect in the death of Thomas Patton.

Upon learning that Billy Shane had relatives living in Alabama, Detective Graves quickly alerted the Jefferson County Sheriff's Department in Birmingham, with a description of Billy Shane and the car they thought he'd be driving. Then the relatives were notified to be on the lookout for the boy, who was wanted as a suspect in the death of Thomas Patton.

Late that night, good things started happening for the Henry County Sheriff's Department. A call was received from family members in Alabama. Yes, they told detectives, Billy Shane had been around during the day. And yes, he was traveling in a black Monte Carlo. The keen-acting Captain Smith chose two of his men and sent them immediately to Alabama. As often happens in their chosen profession, Detectives Randy Haynie and Mike Yates were dispatched so quickly, there wasn't enough time for them to go home and change clothes or say goodbye to their families. The sleuths didn't know it then, but they would not be back for three long days.

The Birmingham Sheriff's Department was also contacted and the search for Billy Shane intensified. By the time the two Georgia detectives arrived in Alabama, two new developments had been revealed. Upon learning that he was being actively sought by the sheriff's department and with the aid of an older relative, Billy Shane had rented a motel room. He'd used an alias name to register. And he wasn't alone.

It was late night when a motel room door opened

and a medium-built, dark-haired young man stepped out carrying an ice bucket. He jauntily made his way to the ice dispenser, looking like any other young man staying in a motel and thirsting for a cold drink. But this was different. Waiting patiently right outside the young man's door were sheriff's agents from Alabama and Henry County, Georgia.

On March 25, 1990, Billy Shane Willingham was bound over to a grand jury in Henry County. He was charged with murder, armed robbery, arson, and theft by taking. He pled not guilty.

Captain Smith and Detective Graves, along with a dozen of Smith's dedicated crew, worked long hours interviewing anyone who might shed light on the Patton homicide. They continued to dig through the debris of the smoldering house, searching for answers. Billy Shane continued to proclaim his innocence. The murder weapon could not be located. Sleuths still hoped to find the missing projectiles that had entered and exited the head of the sleeping Thomas Patton. Few if any details would escape the determined bunch. The probers would work nonstop until the case was airtight or they had collapsed trying to get it so.

One of the samples taken at the crime scene and sent to the state crime lab for determination of substance proved to be exactly what Investigator Mitchell had known it was the moment he smelled it on the body and mattress the morning of March 7th: It was unmistakably kerosene.

On March 19, 1990, Captain Smith sat in the living room of Billy Shane's relative's house in Alabama. He was anxious to interview Bobby Martin, another relative of Billy Shane's. Having learned the night before that Bobby had been taken into Billy Shane's confidence the morning of the murder of Thomas Patton, Smith knew the boy's testimony was crucial.

In the presence of his family, Bobby Martin listened quietly as Captain Smith explained the importance of the information that only Bobby could provide. Would he help? Would he let the burden of that knowledge fall onto Captain Smith's capable shoulders? It was the best way to help Billy Shane, the only way to help the people who loved him and Thomas Patton.

Bobby looked into Captain Smith's understanding eyes and began to talk about the tragic events Billy Shane had told him about, the events of the morning of March 7, 1990.

Billy Shane Willingham was in love, plain and simple. When Jeannie Allen looked at him with that cute little face and smiled the special smile reserved just for him, Billy Shane felt about 10 feet tall. And he felt strong, as though there wasn't a thing he couldn't accomplish. In Jeannie's eyes he wasn't just a punk, good-for-nothing kid, as some of the grownups referred to him. Jeannie looked up to Billy Shane, accepting his reasoning as fact.

Sure he'd made a few mistakes in his 18 years, but, hey, so what? His life was just beginning. No one could understand what his life had been like growing up. How could they? They weren't around to see.

The one thing clear in Billy Shane's mind was Jeannie Allen, and the place she belonged was in his life. He was in love with the girl. He'd given it little thought until seven months before. Until then Jeannie was simply a bratty kid, good for teasing. But now, she was his girl, and the thing to do was get hitched. Jeannie wanted it, too. She'd run away from home to be with Billy Shane. Unbeknownst to Thomas Patton, the 16-year-old Jeannie was living in the basement suite with Billy Shane, hiding out until the couple could put their wedding plans into gear.

Billy Shane had not made a secret of their plans. He'd told several people about his impending marriage. A family member, believing the young girl to be pregnant, even gave Billy Shane her own wedding band to place on Jeannie's finger on their marriage day. She also gave him some advice. She advised Billy Shane to sit Thomas Patton down, tell him the plan and offer to work for him. If Billy Shane was going to get married and have a baby, then Billy Shane needed to accept his responsibilities like a man.

The one thing he hadn't counted on was the man's stubbornness. Thomas Patton had thrown a fit, threatening to turn him in to the authorities, if he tried to leave town. After all, Patton had shouted, he'd put up the bond to get his butt out of jail. He wasn't about to lose that money just so the boy could take off on some jaunt to Alabama. Patton had then cut off Billy Shane's spending money.

To Billy Shane's way of thinking, Patton was standing in his way to becoming a man, to getting what he needed to be happy. With Jeannie by his side, Billy Shane would be somebody special. It was going to happen and nobody was going to stand in their way. Nobody! Thomas Patton was the problem. And the problem needed to be eliminated.

Thus began to grow the plan that had taken seed in Billy Shane's brain, a plan seemingly without ra-

35

tional consideration of future consequences. It wasn't a difficult plan, but one thing seemed sure. It would solve the problem. Billy Shane and Jeannie Allen could lead their lives without interference. Billy Shane knew if they could just leave the state of Georgia, he'd be free of the bond, free to go and live his own way.

The weather was bad during the early-morning hours of March 7, 1990. A cold heavy rain pounded the earth. Lightning streaked the sky followed by great booms of thunder.

In the basement apartment of Thomas Patton's home, Billy Shane Willingham and 16-year-old Jeannie Allen lay in bed. They waited.

Sometime after midnight, Thomas Patton arrived home. He moved about for a while and finally retired to bed. It grew quiet. Billy Shane rose and told Jeannie to start packing. They were going to Alabama that very night. It was 2:30 a.m.

Taking a gun with him, Billy Shane climbed the stairs to the upstairs hallway. He crept to the back bedroom where Thomas Patton was sleeping. Standing close to the bed, he aimed the gun and methodically pulled the trigger, emptying five shells into Patton's head.

Downstairs, Jeannie was sitting on the side of the bed. Hearing the sounds above, she ran upstairs. Billy Shane grabbed the keys to a 1988 black Monte Carlo, a car Patton had expressly refused to allow him to drive, and hurried outside to back it to the front door. As he guided it between a tree and another parked auto, Billy Shane scraped the driver's side against the tree, busting the side mirror. Running back inside the house, Billy Shane tried to pull the victim's corpse off the bed. The body was too heavy, so he called for Jeannie to help him. He pulled a mattress from another bed and together the couple managed to roll the body off the bed and onto the mattress. Not wanting to get blood on them, they wrapped Patton's head in a pillowcase and blanket. By inching the mattress, they were able to pull Patton's body down the hallway close to the front door, leaving a long streak of blood behind. Billy Shane had never seen so much blood before.

The plan was to load Patton's body into the car trunk. They would dump it over a bridge a quarter-mile away as they set off for a new life in Alabama. In life, Thomas Patton weighed 250 pounds, and the young couple found the victim's dead weight too strenuous for them. They abandoned the idea. After thinking a few minutes, Billy Shane ordered Jeannie to get the kerosene can. While she was gone, Billy Shane carried the mattress from Patton's bed and put it over the body. Moments before a place of rest, the mattress was to become a shroud of fire. Jeannie returned with a can of kerosene and watched as Billy Shane poured it over Patton's body, the mattress, and around the house.

Billy Shane ran back to Patton's bedroom. He pocketed two gold rings, a gold nugget watch, and a large roll of cash lying on top of a bureau. He then set the bed on fire. He and Jeannie loaded the Monte Carlo with their belongings, and while Jeannie sat in the car, Billy Shane took care of destroying evidence and set Thomas Patton's remains on fire.

As the couple drove down Highway 120 toward Alabama, Billy Shane threw the gun out the window. Jeannie, whose sneakers were stained red with Patton's blood, threw them out the window also. She would tell Bobby later that "it was gross."

Bobby Martin watched Billy Shane warily. He had been asleep when Billy Shane and Jeannie arrived and woke him up.

"Well, I done what I was talking about," Billy Shane told Bobby.

Since you never knew when Billy Shane was telling the truth or pulling your leg, Bobby suspected the story he was hearing now was a tall tale, but Bobby continued to nod as though he were hearing the gospel truth. Still it was odd, even for somebody wild like Bobby Shane, to drive all the way from Georgia to Alabama and show up on Bobby's doorstep at 7:00 a.m. And to top that, Billy Shane was weaving his story easy as pie, like he'd really done it.

Bobby's mind clicked back to a week before when Billy Shane last visited. At that time, he claimed that Patton was threatening to hire someone to kill him if he tried to leave the state before his trial, thereby forfeiting the bond money Patton had put up. That was hard for Bobby to believe. Everybody knew about Billy Shane's troubles with the law and how Patton had rescued him by posting bail. Just as well known was that Patton loved the boy and wanted the best for him, like he did for all his family. Patton had even allowed Billy Shane to live for free in his basement apartment. When Billy Shane told Bobby Martin that he was going to kill Patton, Bobby had just chalked it up as bravado and had forgotten it. Until now.

Although Billy Shane was normally evasive to others, he always told Bobby the truth. They were friends as well as relatives. They trusted each other.

Billy Shane showed Bobby the jewelry and told him he'd also taken a VCR. It was in the car trunk.

After having breakfast at Bobby's house, the three teens crawled into the Monte Carlo and headed for a relative's house to pay a visit. All the way over, Bobby sat waiting for the "joking" to end. Instead, in utter seriousness, Billy Shane recapped in detail the events of the morning.

It was quite a first day of freedom for Billy Shane. After visiting a while, he drove them all to a shopping mall. He pulled out a large wad of money from his pocket and counted it in front of Bobby's bulging eyes. There was close to $6,000 there. Bobby asked for a little loan. Billy Shane told him that he'd have to earn his own. This money was his own for doing his job.

Arriving at the mall, the trio spent several hours wandering around, playing video arcade games and shopping. Billy Shane bought Jeannie a pocketbook and a pair of pants.

Bobby had promised his family he'd be home by noon. He persuaded Billy Shane to hang around a while and help them work on a motorcycle. Then Billy Shane and Jeannie left, promising to come back at 5:00 p.m. for Bobby. They'd have a night out together, cruising and cutting up.

In the meantime, a close relative of Billy Shane's, having learned of Patton's death and of Billy Shane's possible involvement, frantically began telephoning Alabama relatives. She wanted to find him herself. She begged Bobby to help her find Billy Shane. She just wanted to look in his eyes and make him tell her that what she was hearing wasn't true. She knew that if she could only look in his eyes, she'd see the truth.

She felt it in her heart.

But the next time she would see Billy Shane, he'd be behind bars.

The Henry County Courthouse is an impressive structure of early American red-clay brick topped by a white-pointed dome. On the morning of October 16, 1990, down the polished hallway of this courthouse, the murder trial of Billy Shane Willingham began.

Henry County District Attorney Tommy K. Floyd revealed in his opening statement some of the facts he would present to the court to ensure the correct sentencing for the defendant. He told his audience how Billy Shane had shared his plans to kill Thomas Patton with people on several occasions before the actual murder.

Floyd gave the 12-member jury a brief summary of events during the early-morning hours of March 7th, how the victim was coldly assassinated and robbed by his own son, how his body was burned and his home destroyed.

On Tuesday, October 17, 1990, the court heard testimony from the accused. Billy Shane, looking boyish and younger than his 18 years, spoke for 40 minutes. He proclaimed his innocence and gave his own version of the events.

Billy Shane claimed he left the house at 1:30 a.m. and drove to his stepfather's home for a visit. When he left, Patton was still alive. Jeannie was also in the house. Several hours later, he returned to pick up his girlfriend, and together they left for a visit with his relative, Bobby Martin, in Alabama.

Billy Shane explained away the large amount of money the detectives found on him at the time of his arrest. He said he'd sold some cocaine to a man whose real name he didn't know. Painting himself as "frightened" when he heard that the authorities were looking for him, Billy Shane decided not to come forward. After all, he had left the state while out of jail on bond for other criminal charges. And the fact that he'd taken along his juvenile girlfriend, who was also a runaway, didn't help matters.

Billy Shane solemnly denied killing his father.

Defense attorney James P. Brown then called a relative of Billy Shane's to the witness stand. The relative testified that he'd seen Billy Shane in his home at 2:20 a.m. He'd talked with him for about 15 minutes, before he went to bed.

The confident district attorney next called Bobby Martin to the stand. Martin described the events that took place after Billy Shane dropped in on him on the morning of March 7th. He repeated what he'd been told what he had witnessed during that day.

Jeannie Allen was also called to the stand. She, herself, had been arrested and charged with arson, concealing a death, theft by taking, and motor vehicle theft. Since being arrested along with Billy Shane in March 1990, Jeannie had been held in a juvenile detention facility. She agreed to testify against Billy Shane. She would tell everything she knew to detectives and swear to the truth of her statements in court.

The pretty, blonde 16-year-old told the jury she did whatever Billy Shane told her to do. She placed total blame squarely on his shoulders. He'd told her to pack her bags, fetch the kerosene can, and put the gun and their clothes in the car's trunk. She did it all without question. She told the court how she'd refused to touch the victim's body and how she'd thrown her shoes out the car window afterward because "I didn't want blood on my shoes and the thought of ever having blood on my shoes was gross. It was a reminder."

When Jeannie Allen testified that she and Billy Shane had stopped at an all-night restaurant after the murder, loud groans of disgust were heard from Patton's family who sat in the courtroom. Superior Court Judge Hal Craig sent the jury out before sternly warning the audience that, "You're not going to distract the jury and you're not going to attempt to influence them with outbursts of emotion."

During the trial, testimony revealed that the day before the murder, Billy Shane rented a video movie called *Shocker* that depicts an execution by electric chair. While watching the tape, Billy Shane mentioned to his relatives that he was going to be there soon. Another relative remembered Billy Shane telling her that Thomas Patton may die soon, possibly of a heart attack, as if trying to prepare his relatives for Patton's demise. That was only a few days before the murder.

On October 18, 1990, after three hours and 15 minutes of deliberation, the jury returned guilty verdicts on charges of malice murder, arson, theft by taking, and armed robbery.

Defense Attorney James P. Brown asked the judge to have mercy on his client because he had come from a "rough upbringing."

Judge Craig replied, "It's apparent to the court that his upbringing wasn't the best in the world, but it's no excuse for the offenses."

He then sentenced Billy Shane Willingham to two

consecutive life sentences, plus another 40 years to run concurrently. He will be eligible for parole in 20 years.

EDITOR'S NOTE:
Homer Cantrell, Jeannie Allen, and Bobby Martin are not the real names of the persons so named in the foregoing story. Fictitious names have been used because there is no reason for public interest in the identities of these persons.

"THE YOUNG & THE WASTED"
by Arne Arntzen

When the burglar alarm went off at a private security company's headquarters in Des Moines, Iowa, at 4:14 a.m. on March 24, 1990, the message was relayed to the Des Moines Police Department, informing them that a crime was being committed at a convenience store on the 1400 block of Buchanan Street. The first officer arrived at the scene at 4:17. Three people, a newspaper delivery man and two shoppers, were standing near the form of a man who was lying face down on the floor. The officer checked for signs of life. There were none.

The witnesses told him they had called for an ambulance and identified the stricken man as the night-shift store clerk, David Conley Scott of Ankeny.

When the ambulance arrived, paramedics rushed the victim to the Iowa Lutheran Hospital. On their way there, they managed to restore a heartbeat.

Questioned by detectives, the three witnesses said they hadn't seen anyone in or near the store when they entered. Food, beer, and pop had been stolen, and other items had been knocked down from the shelves and lay scattered on the floor.

Sleuths searching the store found a hammer in back of the service counter. They theorized it could have been the weapon used in striking the store clerk and in prying open the drawers of the cash registers.

At the hospital, doctors worked on David Scott's head wound. His skull had been fractured and there was little doctors could do but place him on life support. Their examination showed that he was brain dead. On Sunday, when Scott's heart stopped beating, Polk County Medical Examiner R.C. Wooters pronounced him dead, and Des Moines police had another homicide on their hands.

A private forensic pathologist assigned to perform the autopsy said it would be done within a day or two. The results would be released after it was completed.

When Captain Nicholas Brown of the Des Moines Police Department arrived at the bloody crime scene, he asked, "What could the take be during the hours of a night like this? Certainly not enough to kill for."

The local manager of the store refused to comment to reporters regarding the murder of Scott or the robbery of the convenience store, saying it would be premature to say anything at this time. An official at the parent company in Hutchinson, Kansas, said their records showed that David Conley Scott had been in their employ since August and had an excellent work record.

"We've never experienced anything quite like this," the president said, pledging that tighter security measures would be taken to increase security at the store. The company had a silent alarm system in its stores. It appeared in this case that the alarm was activated when the cash registers were pried open.

45

When Detective Lieutenant William Fitzgerald arrived on the scene, he said every effort was being made "to apprehend the person or persons responsible for this vicious crime, but with little or no leads to go on we need public participation to help us solve this case. Anyone who was passing by the store Saturday between four o'clock and four-twenty a.m. should call the police," he urged.

David Scott's death marked the second homicide of a service employee in the area within a single month. Robert Duchene, 44, a Phillips service station attendant, was murdered while working on the company's books at their southside service station.

Referring to the Scott homicide, Detective Randy Dawson told reporters, "We have few leads, clues and no suspects. We don't know how many persons were involved in the slaying and robbery, if there was only one or if others were involved."

A background check on David Scott revealed he was a native of Chicago, Illinois, lived in Altoona most of his life, graduated from Southeast Polk County High School, and attended the Des Moines Area Community College. He was 32 years old at the time of his death.

"He was a good guy from anyone I've talked to," Detective Dawson said. "He was an excellent employee and never had any problems. He liked his job."

Meanwhile, the Des Moines Police Department had every available sleuth working on the case, questioning street people, snitches, and known drug addicts, probing for leads and information. Crime lab technicians were called in to check out the crime scene for possible clues or evidence, and a fingerprint expert dusted for prints. Friends, relatives, and acquaintances of the slain clerk were questioned in the hope they might reveal some information that could aid police in their search for David Scott's killer or killers. But they got nothing of value from their efforts.

In an attempt to encourage the public to come forward with any information, the police department set up a hot line, hoping this would bring in some worthwhile tips and leads.

On Tuesday, March 27th, the president of the chain of stores operating in the Midwest came to Des Moines to talk to the police. He also posted a $10,000 reward for anyone who had any information leading to the arrest and conviction of the person or persons responsible for the death of David Conley Scott. The president added that Scott was the first person to be killed in their 30 years of operating their stores. The company had 210 stores in Kansas, Nebraska, Iowa, Oklahoma, and Illinois.

Des Moines Chief of Police William Moulder said he was pleased with the reward offer, saying it "may smoke out" the killer.

Meanwhile, as the investigation was in progress, Officer John Thompson began hearing rumors on the street that three people were involved in the murder of David Conley Scott and the robbery of the convenience store. Thompson kept nosing around and picking up more information. He learned that the perpetrators of the crime were teenagers. Thompson kept on asking questions and following up leads. When he felt he had sufficient information, Thompson turned it over to Detectives Randy Dawson and John Shaver.

Checking out the information Thompson had given them looked promising. The two detectives began interrogating suspects. A number of teenagers were brought into custody and questioned, but they were released when their alibis checked out. Then a tip came in reporting that the youths lawmen were looking for belonged to a street gang who called themselves "The Young and the Wasted."

Checking out the gang's activities on March 24th, the detectives learned that the gang had a party that night. Three teenagers left the party to get beer about the time David Scott was murdered and returned with food and beer a short time later. Further investigation revealed they were the men the detectives were seeking.

Late Tuesday night, March 27, 1990, sleuths arrested Phillip Negrete, 19, and charged him with the murder of David Conley Scott. He was read his constitutional rights and held in the Polk County Jail without bail. Police refused to say whether the arrest was influenced by the reward money.

On Wednesday, another suspect was arrested. Jammi Reimier, 15, was taken into custody at his home on the 3000 block of Walnut Street and charged with first-degree murder in the death of David Scott. He was read his Miranda rights and held in the Polk County Jail without the opportunity to post bail.

On the same day, another suspect in the death of David Scott, Sam Archer, who lived on the 1100 block of Herold Avenue, was arrested and charged with the first-degree murder of the store clerk. He was read his constitutional rights and confined in the Polk County Jail, held without bail.

Lawmen checking on Phillip Negrete's criminal record learned he'd previously been arrested on an assault charge. The charge was reduced to simple assault, to which he pleaded guilty.

Sam Archer's record showed that he spent time at the State Training School at Eldora for stealing $475 and breaking 37 car windows. The theft charge had been dropped. However, he was found delinquent for breaking the car windows.

The police record showed that Jammi Reimier had never before been involved in any criminal activity and had a clean record.

Phillip Negrete's arrest shocked his relatives and friends. One told reporters, "I never thought he would kill anyone. He probably didn't either. I don't mean he's Mister Goody Two Shoes. He doesn't smoke or drink. He always treated me good.

"Only a short time ago," the relative continued, "a group of people in Ankeny beat him up so badly that he had to be taken to the University Hospital at Iowa City for treatment for a head injury."

She said an acquaintance had told her that when Phillip entered the store to buy a soft drink and when he saw David Scott, he struck out at him because he believed he was one of the men who had beaten him up in Ankeny.

But the Des Moines police had a different version of what Negrete's relative said. "We don't believe her story," one lawman said. Investigators said evidence proved the assault and robbery was well planned and executed.

In a surprise visit, the president of the chain of stores came to Des Moines to pay the reward money his company had posted. He said that one woman who had helped in the investigation would receive a portion of the reward money. Further discussion would be held to determine what should be done with the remainder of the money.

While the arrest of the three suspects served to allay the fears of other store clerks working the night shift, the fear still remained there, one of the clerks said.

The clerk said, "Of course I'm scared every time someone enters the store. You never know if he's a legitimate shopper or if he packs a gun in his pocket. I'd like to have one for my own protection, but it's against the company's policy, so I keep on hoping it will not happen during my shift."

Appearing before Associate District Court Judge L. Joel Pasternak on March 28th, Phillip Negrete's bond was set at $500,000, twice the amount recommended by the prosecuting attorney. While in the courtroom the judge was heard to say, "What we need is a firing squad." A few hours later when he was asked about the remark, the judge said, "I don't remember saying it." Others who were in the courtroom at the time, including reporters, said they had heard the judge make the statement.

The defense attorney refused to discuss the remark with reporters when questioned by them.

However, a Drake University professor who teaches a seminar in judicial ethics said that a remark like the one supposedly made by the judge was unlikely to be considered serious misconduct if it didn't affect how the judge handled the case.

"But," he added, "what it comes down to is, a judge shouldn't say something that brings discredit on the bench or indicates unfairness. I would hope that none of my students would make a remark like that publicly."

During the time of his interrogation, Phillip Negrete confessed to sleuths that he struck David Scott on the back of the head while the robbery was in progress. The loot, $61, was divided equally among the three suspects, Negrete said.

Court proceedings began in April to determine if Phillip Negrete's two accomplices, Jammi Reimier and Sam Archer, both 15 and both charged in juvenile court with David Scott's murder, should be tried in adult court.

Assistant Polk County Prosecutor William Thomas told the court that both suspects were members of a Des Moines street gang called The Young and the Wasted. Other evidence was introduced by the prosecutor that supported his case, which showed the youths should be tried as adults and not as juveniles.

On June 11, 1990, Polk County Juvenile Court Referee Larry Eisenhauer waived Sam Archer into adult court, charged with David Scott's murder. Jammi Reimier was also waived into adult court, despite urgent pleas from his relatives and friends that the two youths serve out their sentences, if convicted, in juvenile facilities.

Shocked at the referee's decision, many of the defendants' friends and relatives wept openly. If convicted as adults, the two teenagers would face mandatory life sentences without parole. Bail was set at $100,000 for each defendant. Unable to post the required bail bond, they were confined in a juvenile detention facility until their trial.

At their preliminary hearing, all three defendants

were bound over to Circuit Court. Phillip Negrete's trial date was scheduled to begin on July 11, 1990. No date was scheduled for Jammi Reimier or Sam Archer.

Faced with the prospect that he had only Phillip Negrete's confession, the prosecutor had serious doubts whether he would be able to secure convictions. Negrete's defense attorney had stated that he intended to challenge the validity of the confession, contending Negrete was coerced into making it by detectives while being interrogated.

One alternative Prosecutor Thomas had was to enter into plea bargain agreements with the other two defendants, but overtures in that direction had failed to produce any positive results.

On Monday, August 13th, Prosecutor Thomas entered into a plea bargain agreement with Jammi Reimier. Thomas agreed to reduce the first-degree murder charge to that of second degree in exchange for his truthful testimony at Phillip Negrete's trial.

Speaking to reporters, Thomas explained that second-degree murder carried a maximum sentence of 50 years in prison, but he said it was likely that Reimier would only serve about 10 years at the very most.

"From the evidence," Thomas said, "we are convinced that Jammi Reimier is not the person who actually did the killing of David Scott when he was struck in back of his head with the hammer."

After the completion of the plea bargain, Reimier was questioned by Polk County District Judge Ross Walters. During this questioning, Reimier stated that it was Phillip Negrete who had struck Scott on the head. He and Sam Archer broke open the cash registers with the hammer handed to them by Negrete and took the money amounting to $61.

On August 17th, Sam Archer agreed to plead guilty to a charge of second-degree murder in exchange for his testimony against Phillip Negrete at Negrete's trial. With these agreements from the two defendants, Prosecutor Thomas now felt he could get the conviction he desired.

As part of the plea agreement, Archer's attorney agreed not to ask the court for probation for his client at the time of his sentencing.

Phillip Negrete's trial was postponed again. This time it was rescheduled for October 1st.

After his plea bargain was resolved Sam Archer was questioned by Polk County District Judge Ross Walters. Archer told Walters that he was in the company of Phillip Negrete and Jammi Reimier early on the morning of March 24th. He said he watched Phillip Negrete strike David Scott with a hammer on the back of his head. Archer admitted he'd helped Reimier pry open the cash registers and take the money.

The Circuit Court trial of Phillip Negrete was finally scheduled to begin on February 5, 1991, at the Polk County Courthouse with Judge Ray Hanrahan presiding.

On Monday, February 4th, the day before the trial was to begin, Judge Hanrahan refused to admit into evidence the confession Negrete made to the police at the time he was arrested. The judge ruled that the confession could not be used because the police had arrested the defendant unlawfully.

In his ruling the judge said, "Though the court has determined Negrete's statements in this case were voluntarily made under the Fifth Amendment, the defendant's statements to the police must be suppressed because of the unlawful arrest."

Assistant Prosecutor James Ramey, while admitting that the ruling was a blow to the prosecution's case, told reporters it would not prevent him from continuing on with the trial. He said he was confident that the state had sufficient evidence to secure a conviction against Negrete.

"Obviously the defendant's statements in themselves won't make or break the case," the prosecutor said. "The police solved it without the defendant's statements."

However, there was no question that Negrete's attorney was pleased with the ruling, although he would make no comments concerning it.

In his ruling, Judge Hanrahan wrote that the police officers did not have a search or arrest warrant when they went to a house on the 1200 block of Fremont Street to question Negrete about the David Scott homicide. The resident of the house had come to the door to meet the police. Consent to enter the house was not voluntarily given to the officers, according to the judge, but rather their entry "was the result of the resident's acquiescence to the officers' claim of authority or physical ability to do so."

The prosecutor did not agree with the judge's ruling, saying he did not believe the police needed consent to enter the building because they were not looking for evidence against the resident.

"I don't think this is any sort of trend," Prosecutor Ramey said of Hanrahan's ruling. "I don't think the law enforcement officers acted unreasonably or in violation of the Constitution."

Phillip Negrete's trial convened on February 5, 1991, at the Polk County Courthouse with the selection of a panel of 12 jurors and 2 alternates.

In his opening statement, Prosecutor James Ramey told the court that the slaying of store clerk David Scott was one of the most brutal homicides ever committed in the city of Des Moines. The killing, Ramey asserted, was premeditated by the defendant and his two accomplices, who, like Negrete, belonged to a street gang called The Young and the Wasted. They lived up to their name and reputation when they "wasted" the life of a defenseless store clerk, the prosecutor charged.

"It's not a very pretty picture, this sequence of events that led up to the killing of David Scott," Ramey told the jury.

It began during the early-morning hours of March 24th when the street gang was having a party. When they ran out of beer, Phillip Negrete suggested that he leave for a convenience store and steal some. He said he needed help and Jammi Reimier and Sam Archer, both 15, volunteered to help him.

When the three left to steal the beer, the prosecutor continued, Negrete showed them a hammer he had brought from home. They agreed on the store they intended to rob, and when they arrived there, Negrete went inside and shoplifted some pop and food. Then, Ramey asserted, all three entered the store to rob it and pick up the beer.

Inside, the three youths found the storeclerk standing in the front aisle near the entrance door with his back turned toward them. With his hammer in his hand, Negrete approached the clerk quietly and struck him forcefully on the back of his head.

The clerk fell down to the floor unconscious. Negrete handed the hammer to one of the youths and told him to break open the cash registers and grab the money. They contained a total of $61.

On their way out, Prosecutor Ramey continued, the gang members picked up a supply of beer and fled. It was only when they arrived back at the party that they realized they had forgotten to take the hammer with them — and they had no way of getting it back, Ramey asserted. They realized that by this time customers would have come into the store and found the unconscious form of the store clerk lying on the floor.

"They counted the money down to the last penny," Prosecutor Ramey said, "and agreed that Negrete was entitled to an additional fifty cents as he was the one who struck the clerk."

None of the three young defendants showed any concern about the condition of the clerk they had struck down, Prosecutor Ramey argued.

At the conclusion of the prosecutor's statement, Defense Attorney James Whalen began his opening statement. Addressing the jury, he called their attention to the fact that there were only two witnesses to the slaying of David Scott, both of whom were members of a Des Moines street gang well known to the police for their criminal activities. Jammi Reimier and Sam Archer, because of their gang affiliation, were not to be considered as credible witnesses and their testimony had to be seriously questioned, Whalen argued.

Whalen also said the jury should note that the two suspects were "quick to agree to a plea-bargaining agreement with the prosecutor's office for reduced charges in exchange for their testimony at my client's trial.

"The defense contends," Whalen continued, "that while the two suspects, Jammi Reimier and Sam Archer, have pointed their fingers at my client as the slayer of the clerk, the fact remains [that] either of them should be considered suspect in the homicide. There are also mitigating circumstances that should be carefully considered by the jury concerning my client, namely, . . . that a few days before the assault on David Scott and the robbery of the convenience store, Phillip Negrete was badly beaten up by a group of people in Ankeny, suffering a severe head wound that required he be taken to the University Hospital in Iowa City. Friends and relatives will testify that since the beating, there has been a change in his mental attitude, which they assume can be [accounted for by] the beating he received in Ankeny.

"Testimony will also reveal that my client had only a vague idea of what happened at the time the homicide was committed, he being drunk at the time."

Defense Attorney Whalen also pointed out that many of the individuals questioned by the police made contradictory statements in subsequent interviews. Moreover, Negrete's confession, which, Whalen alleged, police obtained through coercion of his client, was thrown out by the judge because of improper arrest, Whalen said.

"These incidents," Whalen told the jury, "must be carefully weighed, plus other evidence that will be presented during the trial."

At the conclusion of the defense's opening statement, the prosecution began calling their witnesses to the witness stand.

The first witness to testify for the state said he entered the store minutes after David Scott had been struck down and lay unconscious on the store floor. Scott, he recalled, was bleeding from a head wound and did not respond when he talked to him. He immediately called for an ambulance.

The next witness to testify was a private pathologist who had performed the autopsy on David Scott. He testified that the victim died from a blow to the head with a blunt instrument, probably a hammer. The blow was struck with considerable force, crushing the victim's skull.

When John Thompson, a beat officer, took the stand, he testified that while making his rounds, he began picking up bits of information concerning the Scott homicide. He learned from various street informants that there were three people involved in the robbery and murder. He kept on nosing around asking questions, and when he felt he had enough information, he turned it over to Detectives Randy Dawson and John Shaver to check it out further. The information and leads proved promising and eventually led to the arrest of the three teenagers.

Sam Archer displayed considerable nervousness during his testimony, glancing occasionally at Phillip Negrete sitting alongside his attorney. When asked by Prosecutor Ramey to tell the court about the events that happened during the early-morning hours of March 24th, Archer responded by saying, "The three of us were at a party—Phillip Negrete, Jammi Reimier, and myself."

"Would you explain to the court what sort of party it was? Would you call it a street gang party?"

The youth hesitated a moment and replied, "Yeah,

I guess so."

"Then what happened?" questioned Ramey.

"We ran out of beer about four o'clock in the morning, and Phillip said he would go and rob a convenience store and get some. He said he needed help, and Jammi and I said we would go with him."

Archer paused for a moment, then continued, "On the way to the store, Phillip showed us a hammer he brought from his home with which 'he was going to do the thing,' and when we got there he went inside and shoplifted some food and pop.

"Then the three of us went inside," Archer continued. "The clerk was standing in the front aisle with his back to us. Phillip sneaked up behind him and, with the hammer in his hand, hit him hard on the back of his head. The clerk fell down. Then Phillip gave us the hammer and told us to break open the cash registers and take the money, which we did. It amounted to sixty-one dollars."

When Jammi Reimier began his testimony, he spoke in a clear, calm voice. At Prosecutor Ramey's request he pointed out Phillip Negrete, saying he was the person sitting next to attorney James Whalen.

The witness also testified that the hammer found in the store resembled the one used by Negrete to strike David Scott and the one used by him and Reimier in breaking open the two cash registers.

Several other police officers and crime technicians testified for the state before the prosecution rested their case and the defense began calling their witnesses to the stand.

Defense witnesses testified that the defendant was a conscientious and responsible person who didn't smoke, drink, or use drugs.

One of Negrete's relatives told the court that only a short time before David Scott's death, Phillip had been severely beaten in the head by a group of men. The wound was so bad, he was taken to the University Hospital in Iowa City for treatment. Ever since then, the relative said, Phillip hadn't been his "normal self, leading us to believe that the wound he suffered may have affected his mental state, and he wasn't aware of what he was doing if he was involved in the Scott slaying."

The defense then rested their case. The defense and state attorneys began presenting their closing arguments to the jury. In his closing statement, Prosecutor Ramey told the jury that David Conley Scott's murder was "premeditated, well planned and executed, and not done on the spur of the moment . . . a perfect example of what constitutes a case of first-degree murder."

Prosecutor Ramey called the court's attention to the fact that when the three defendants divided the stolen money, Phillip Negrete kept an additional 50 cents for himself, saying he deserved it because he was the one who struck the clerk with his hammer.

"As to the defense argument that the beating Negrete suffered in Ankeny [affected] his mental state, there is no evidence of that in his actions. Phillip Negrete was," the prosecutor insisted, "fully aware of what he was doing at the time he struck down David Scott in the convenience store."

Defense Attorney James Whalen in his closing argument told the jury that the statements of the two suspects, Jammi Reimier and Sam Archer, lacked credibility. He contended that they changed their stories so often, no one knew what to believe. "This must be carefully considered by the jury, as well as the mental state of my client after the beating he suffered in Ankeny that affected him mentally, as witnesses have testified."

Judge Ray Hanrahan then instructed the jury, who retired to their chamber, to consider the testimony and evidence presented to them during the trial. They returned to the courtroom after only two and a half hours of deliberation. They found Negrete guilty of intentional first-degree murder.

The defendant showed no emotion when the verdict was read. Friends and relatives broke out in tears, shocked at the verdict. Negrete had no comment to make to reporters as he was led to the Polk County Jail to be assigned to a state prison after sentencing. Judge Hanrahan scheduled sentencing for March 22, 1991. On that date, appearing before Hanrahan, Phillip Negrete was sentenced to life in prison without possibility of parole.

A close relative of the murdered clerk told reporters, "No matter what, he's not coming back. It's going to affect us for the remainder of our lives," she said.

Appearing before Judge Hanrahan on February 25th, Jammi Reimier was sentenced to 50 years in the Oakdale State Prison. The same sentence was imposed on Sam Archer on March 19th. Archer will also serve out his sentence in the Oakdale State Prison.

"THE HALF-NAKED TEEN WAS SLICED TO BITS!"

by Bud Ampolsk

A veteran New York City police sergeant, himself a college graduate who began his career as a beat patrolman in Harlem and rose through the ranks until he was assigned to the John Jay College of Criminal Justice as an instructor, got to talking about his special message to serious-minded criminologists recently.

Said the lawman-turned-educator, "The toughest job a cop has these days is getting to know the people on his beat. I don't care whether he's a member of the Sureté in Paris, the Metropolitan Police in London, or any jurisdiction in the states, he's got a bunch of new problems which can drive him right up a wall.

"Not the least of them is the mass movement of populations from one country to another. I'm not just talking about the difficulties of language differences posed by immigrants. I'm talking about the differences in customs and attitudes.

"The police officer who faces barriers represented by these factors must grow ever more sophisticated in his knowledge of where the strangers for whom he bears the responsibility of maintaining law and order come from, the language they speak, how and why they chose to leave their former homes, what portions of their origins remain very much a part of them, and how all these factors might influence a cop's success in dealing with the things which happen to them once they settle in his precinct."

The instructor went on to point out the mass migration of people from Asia as a prime example of his observation. He notes that the languages and dialects of those who have left such homelands as China, Korea, and Vietnam alone number in the thousands. Yet there are only eight Chinese-speaking detectives in the New York Police Department with enough expertise to understand and make themselves understood in even a few of these dialects.

Even where language problems can be mastered, much more is needed in the way of cross-cultural understanding, the instructor contends. A detective working a case involving a transplanted Asian must deal with such problems as the suspicion people from police states feel toward uniformed symbols of authority—even after they arrive in a land where their rights are protected by constitutional guarantees.

In developing theories about what transpired between victim and perp before an act of violence took place, detectives must be aware of what is acceptable or unacceptable behavior in another culture.

Says the faculty member, "There's no substitute for the knowledge of what makes people tick. I'd say it might be even more important to an officer than all the computer spreadsheets he or she uses, the .38 he packs, or any other piece of state-of-the-art equipment he employs on the job."

Duty officers of the Nassau County Police Department (NCPD) who were assigned to the well-kept streets of Herricks, Long Island, on the early spring evening of Friday, April 6, 1990, might not have been pondering what the New York City sergeant observed to his students. But by the time it was all over, the officers probably would have agreed whole-heartedly with everything their brother officer asserted.

As the NCPD cruisers made their way past opulent homes carrying price tags as high as $500,000 apiece, they were on the lookout for the usual problems facing officers: traffic violations, minor burglaries, and domestic disputes.

But Friday, April 6, 1990, was about to turn out to be anything but a routine tour in Herricks. The city's calm was about to be smashed.

The news came crackling over the 911 emergency number. It was given by a woman who was clearly upset. Gasping out the details to a police dispatcher, the woman recounted that something terrible had occurred in her Robby Lane home.

The dispatcher tried to calm down the caller and elicit the nature of the complaint. It appeared that a young girl had been discovered on the floor of a bedroom at a Robby Lane address. The youngster was unconscious and bleeding profusely from what appeared to be multiple knife wounds.

At approximately 8:20 p.m., the time, date, and address of the caller were logged, and the urgent news was broadcast over police radio bands. Minutes later, first on-scene cruisers were wheeling toward Robby Lane and the beautifully maintained home from which the 911 call had been made.

Car doors slammed and heavy feet moved through

the house's entrance as the uniformed officers followed the distraught caller into her home. The cops were immediately escorted to what had up until this evening been an immaculately kept bedroom.

The bedroom, however, was immaculate no longer. The spatter marks of blood were everywhere, besmirching furniture and floor coverings. Lying in a pool of blood that was spread across the floor was the slight form of a 12-year-old girl. Just how savagely she had been assaulted was readily apparent from even a cursory examination. The girl was in a deep coma, her breathing ragged and shallow. She was bleeding from a number of stab and slash wounds to her hands, arms, and torso. The most unnerving sight of all to the officers who knelt beside the stricken youngster was that of a kitchen knife that was still imbedded in the victim's head.

As the cops did what they could to give first aid, appropriate authorities at nearby Winthrop University Hospital in Mineola, Long Island, were contacted and informed about the girl's critical situation. Arrangements were hastily made to rush the girl to the facility where the desperate battle to save her life got under way.

Even as these steps were being taken, other officers now began a room-by-room search of the Robby Lane home. As they stepped into a second bedroom, the officers were hit with the sickening realization that as evil as the violence on the unconscious girl had been, worse things had occurred within the confines of the house.

The knowledge came with the discovery of the husky, half-naked body of a teenage boy, his face contorted by his death agonies, that lay under restraints on the floor. He, like his younger female relative, had been hacked and stabbed by a frenzied assailant. Unlike the girl, though, this victim was beyond all medical aid.

The sorting out of details was a slow and arduous task for those at the crime site. When he met with members of the press to give a preliminary briefing to reporters, Nassau County police spokesman Officer Howard Grandjean was not even prepared to divulge the names of the dead teenager or his wounded female relative.

Grandjean revealed only that the girl was undergoing surgery at Winthrop University Hospital and was listed in critical condition. The boy had been declared dead at the Robby Lane home where he had been found.

According to the police log, cops had been called to the address by the youngsters' mother shortly after 8:20 p.m., when the woman returned to her home and discovered the carnage.

From the very beginning of the intensive probe into the killings, it was apparent that the trail to the killer would be one that would test the skills and dedication of the 15 veteran detectives who had been assigned to the baffling case. The probe would involve a canvass of the Korean-American community, not only in Nassau County, but in Brooklyn and Queens. Sleuths would have to check into the activities of reputed Chinese and Vietnamese juvenile gangs, as well as the political affairs of Korean-American political leaders. The lawmen's investigation would necessitate probing discussions with faculty members at Herricks High School, where the slain boy had been a 10th grader.

The dead teenager was now identified by Nassau Homicide Squad Detective-Sergeant Robert Edwards as 15-year-old Chang Seok Ean. The son of a family that had immigrated to the United States from Korea in 1972, Chang Seok Ean had also been known to friends by the Americanized name of Steven.

By Palm Sunday, April 8, 1990, Edwards and the other detectives of the task force had made some slight progress in the investigation. They learned that the slain teenager and the severely wounded girl had last been seen prior to the knife attack at approximately 5:00 p.m., on Friday, April 6th.

Neighbors told detectives that they had heard no sounds of a struggle coming from the Robby Lane home despite the degree of violence that had taken place there.

The possibility that the stabbings were the work of somebody bent on burglarizing the comfortable home was soon discounted by the police. Exhaustive forensic studies of doors, windows, and other areas of the home had provided no signs of forced entry, nor was anything of value thought to be missing. Also, detectives were now theorizing that the killer or killers had not come to the house prepared to commit murder. On this point, Sergeant Edwards noted that the lethal weapon had been a kitchen knife belonging to the household. The knife was undergoing tests at a police laboratory.

Said Sergeant Edwards, "The weapon was one of convenience as opposed to one brought into the house by the killer or killers."

At that point, the homicide task force handling the case had yet to come up with anything to allow them to name a possible suspect. In reviewing the status of the mystery, Sergeant Edwards said that the detectives had interviewed the victims' family and classmates and would continue talking with school officials and other classmates.

"We feel the investigation is moving forward," said Edwards. He refused to elaborate beyond saying that the police were not looking for any specific person.

"We are still trying to put it together," said Edwards. "School is closed because of the holiday recess, and [detectives] haven't been able to reach school officials and some classmates."

Of the crime itself, it was reported that the surviving 12-year-old girl was still under a 24-hour police guard at Winthrop University Hospital. Thus far she had not regained consciousness and was in critical but stable condition, according to hospital spokespersons. Because of her physical condition, detectives had been unable to interview the girl about what she might recall of the knifings.

Sergeant Edwards inventoried the girl's injuries as being to her arms, hands, and torso. He added that the stabbing might have been so traumatic that she might not be able to remember much of the assault.

By April 9th, police felt their insights into the murder and assault cases were beginning to crystallize. They now believed the fatal stabbing had apparently climaxed a confrontation between Chang Seok Ean and someone known to him. They theorized that the younger female victim had then been attacked by Chang's slayer or slayers in an attempt to silence her as a witness.

Probers continued to maintain their 24-hour bedside guard of the girl, fearing that Chang's killer might find out she survived and could possibly identify him to detectives working the case.

Of particular interest to investigators was the need to construct a scenario for the attack. Their key questions were: How could a youngster who'd been a student of the martial arts, a wrestler, and an aspiring high school football player be so easily overpowered and tied up prior to his death? Why was the 12-year-old girl not bound as the boy had been? Had one killer or more than one taken part in the lethal assault?

The answer to the first question came with the release of the autopsy report by the Nassau County Medical Examiner's Office. In it, Dr. Daniel McCarthy had discovered what was probably the mortal wound from a deep knife thrust into Chang's back. The wound had caused massive internal bleeding and in all probability had prevented Chang from defending himself.

Elaborating on this theme, Sergeant Edwards noted, "It almost looks to me as if something was happening there, possibly an argument, and it escalated."

The detective-sergeant speculated that Chang had been stabbed first in the back when his assailant surprised him by moving on him from behind. After the primary attack, the killer had probably experienced no difficulty in binding the 15-year-old and continuing the stabbings and slashings.

Although Sergeant Edwards described the probable sequence of events, he refused to divulge any information about the type of restraints used to immobilize the victim, saying that this information bore on the ongoing murder probe.

As to why the girl had not been similarly tied up,

apparently, according to police sources, there had been no need to immobilize the slightly built and bespectacled youngster. From the nature of her wounds, it seemed obvious that she had made a valiant but pitifully futile attempt to protect herself from the assailant's thrusting knife. This was evidenced by the defensive wounds she had suffered to her hands.

The attack on the girl had been something of an afterthought, detectives reasoned. They believed that Chang had been either dead or dying as the murderer turned his attention to the lone witness who might link him to the crime.

Bolstering the argument that the knifing of the girl had no purpose other than to silence her, detectives reported that there was no evidence that the girl had been sexually molested by the killer.

There appeared to be a growing feeling among police that the perp had acted alone, although the possibility of him having had an accomplice could not be completely ruled out.

As cops continued their canvass of relatives, friends, and schoolmates of the slain 15-year-old, speculation arose as to whether the killing might have been gang-related and might have had its origins some two months before the actual slaying.

Some people who knew Chang reported that he had been recruited by a Korean crime gang operating out of Queens but that he had refused to join the group. His attitude had aroused the ire of reputed gang members, according to these sources. It was said that about two months before he was killed, Chang had been surrounded and beaten up by three other Koreans. The incident had taken place outside

70

the high school Chang attended.

Sources who held to the street assault theory described one of the alleged assailants as a man in his 20s, while a second perp had been approximately the same age as Chang. None of the trio was described further.

The Nassau County task force working the case now began checking out these rumors. They enlisted the aid of New York City authorities who specialized in working with Asian gang members. Exhaustive conversations with street people and others seemed to indicate that the February assault and the murder that followed two months later had not been gang-related. Sergeant Edwards pointed out that there was also no known Korean gang activity on Long Island.

Still, no possibility of a sinister plot against Chang or his relatives was going uninvestigated by those working around the clock to solve the murder. Now, detectives were moving through the Korean community attempting to get a line on whether there might have been some sort of a vendetta against Chang's adult relatives.

It was noted that the family had moved to Herricks, Long Island, from Queens only about three years before. Their reputation had been impeccable. Since their arrival on American shores, Chang's relatives had become a symbol of the dream held by all immigrants. They were living proof that hard work paid off.

After making a success of a retail dry cleaning establishment, adult family members had gone into the real estate business and had continued to prosper there. They had taken active roles in church and civic activities and were highly respected in Korean-

71

American circles. One family member was a leader in an all-purpose Korean-American community service association that numbered several hundred dues-paying members. The association was undergoing a hotly contested election campaign with the balloting date set for April 22nd. In connection with this, New York City police had received reports that one of the candidates had been briefly kidnapped in the Woodside-Elmhurst section of Queens and warned to pull out of the contest. He had been released later unharmed.

Sergeant Edwards discounted the possibility that community political activities had anything to do with Chang's murder.

One Korean-American community leader agreed whole-heartedly with the detective-sergeant. Said the man, "We don't want to even think it happened because of something political in the Korean community. I think it is Chinese or Korean gangs among the youngsters."

The adolescent gang theory was to surface once more when a close friend of the victim said, "I think the strongest possibility is that the boys from Queens would come over and do something like this."

Those who knew Chang best insisted that he had no known involvement with youth gangs. They said he was a sports enthusiast and a student of martial arts, including disciplines involving knives. But there was nothing aggressive or belligerent about him, according to faculty members at the high school.

Recalled one, "Though the boy claimed to have a black belt in karate, he wasn't a threatening kid. That was his problem in football. He was too nice." The faculty member said that Chang had been both an offensive and defensive lineman on the school's junior varsity team.

Chang had shown great courage in his refusal to tie in with those who had reportedly attempted to recruit him for membership in Asian youth gangs.

A newspaperman who knew of the earlier street attack upon the schoolboy athlete and was a close friend of the youngster stated that "Korean gang members, possibly from Queens, asked Chang for money and to join their activities. One time he refused to hand over money and was beaten," the reporter said.

Another source told how Korean and Chinese members of Asian-American gangs had been traveling to the Manhassat Hills area of Long Island from Queens to recruit new members from the growing enclave of Asian American students attending schools in Nassau County.

The faculty member who had discussed Chang's reticent personality acknowledged that there had been some activity by an alleged youth gang around the high school. He commented, "I heard about them last year but haven't really heard anything about it this year."

One youngster who had known about the winter beating suffered by Chang noted that when he had asked about it, Chang had replied, "Forget about it. It's over."

There were other possibilities that Chang had actually been shaken down by parties unknown. They revolved around a credit card discovered in his room after his death and $900 in cash that surfaced during an interview with school officials after the street altercation. The credit card belonged to an adult acquaintance and had been missing for some time. The $900 in cash was discovered by a school faculty member who was questioning Chang about his troubles with those who had accosted him. At one point, the faculty member reportedly had asked the boy to empty his pockets. Chang then produced the $900 and a star-shaped Ninja weapon.

When interrogated as to where the money had come from, the boy allegedly replied that one of his friends had been planning to buy a gun and had asked him to hold the money for him.

All of these happenings had now been reported to the police, and detectives were in the process of investigating whether the missing credit card, the $900, and the beating Chang had received had anything to do with his murder.

Meanwhile, Nassau County detectives began to look into what at first seemed to be an unrelated incident: a missing person's report filed by relatives of a 17-year-old youth, Yong Ho Han of New Hyde Park.

Perhaps the report would not have received as much priority attention from investigators had it not been for the fact that Yong Ho Han had been a classmate of Chang Seok Ean at Herricks High School. Moreover, he had vanished within days of Chang's murder.

Two months were to pass as Nassau County authorities went about the business of locating the missing student. Gradually the search widened until it encompassed the entire United States—from coast to coast.

Spurring probers on was that the 12-year-old girl who had lingered unconscious between life and death for so many days was now out of danger. She had regained some of her strength and was now able to give detectives limited but important information as to what had occurred in the bedrooms of the home on Robby Lane in the early-evening hours of Friday, April 6, 1990. This information was enough to change the police correspondence on Han from a "missing persons" to a "wanted" request.

Indeed, Yong Ho Han was now the prime suspect in the murder of Chang Seok Ean.

The effort and dedication of cooperating police paid off. On Sunday, June 3, 1990, acting on the Nassau County, New York, murder warrant, Los Angeles cops spotted Yong Ho Han at a self-service laundry and moved in. The capture was accomplished without incident and extradition proceedings were begun immediately. Details of the collar and of the case against the teenager were given by Nassau County Detective-Lieutenant John Nolan, head of the county's homicide bureau.

The motive for the murder, according to Nolan, was as simple as it was wanton. Nolan revealed that the suspect had gone to Chang's home to borrow something. Nolan declined to identify the object in question. However, the detective-lieutenant did note that Han had felt that Chang was "somewhat disrespectful in the way he talked to him. Han got angry and stabbed Chang in the back," Nolan added.

The homicide bureau chief pointed out that both the killer and his victim came from Korean backgrounds. "They come from a culture where people are supposed to be deferential to their elders—which could have been a factor in the killing—even though the boys were only two years apart in age," he stated.

"Han cuffed Chang's hands behind his back and stabbed him."

Lawmen learned that Yong Ho Han, who originally came from Seoul, Korea, immigrated to the United States in 1988.

Now, after conclusion of extradition hearings, he was brought back to Nassau County where he was charged with second-degree murder in the slaying of Chang Seok Ean and attempted murder in the stabbing of the 12-year-old girl.

Almost two years were to pass before a jury was convened in Nassau County Supreme Court to hear the case.

The jurors heard Prosecutor George Peck argue that Yong Ho Han had become enraged when Chang Seok Ean had ignored Han's orders to stop firing a BB gun in the Robby Lane home and thereby failed to respect Han, his elder.

Evidence was presented to show how Chang Seok Ean had paid with his life for that seemingly innocuous — by American standards — affront and how the innocent 12-year-old girl had been grievously wounded.

The jurors listened and then acted. On Thursday, March 26, 1992, they brought in their verdict. Yong Ho Han was declared guilty as charged on both counts.

On April 28th, Han was sentenced to 25 years to life for murder and 8$\frac{1}{3}$ years to life for attempted murder, the sentences to run consecutively.

" 'I'M GOING TO KILL THREE TONIGHT . . . THEN I'M GOING TO KILL MYSELF!' "

by Maryann Eidemiller

When Patrolman Randy Parfitt walked back into the Scottdale Police Station on that hot summer night, he had no idea that had he been starting his shift instead of finishing it, this might have been his last day alive. He completed his paperwork and went home to his wife and two children, unaware that someone wanted to kill him.

It was July 12, 1989, just a week after the Fourth of July. In another part of this southwestern Pennsylvania town, Madeline Obrenski turned on a fan before going to bed. Shortly after midnight she heard loud voices and popping noises and thought she was having a dream.

Madeline Obrenski sleepily realized that the sounds were coming from outside and might be left-over firecrackers. Then instinct jerked her fully awake. She jumped from bed and looked out the window toward the home of 27-year-old Michael Shelby, who lived alone since his father's recent death.

Just then, Obrenski observed a young man in a hurry come off the porch and walk to Shelby's 1986

Chevrolet Camaro, which was parked on the street. He obviously wasn't Shelby. This person was younger, had dark hair and a slight build, and appeared to be much shorter than Shelby. Obrenski watched him fumble at the car lock, then lean down, open the door, and get in. Starting the car, he quickly backed up and drove off.

Obrenski thought she heard moaning. She went into the bathroom to listen from a window there. It did sound like moaning. She returned to the bedroom to wake her husband from a deep sleep. "Did you hear that?" she asked. He said he didn't hear anything. "Come listen at the window," she urged.

Obrenski turned off the fan, but now the Shelby house was quiet. Obrenski and her husband debated what, if anything, to do. Obrenski would later tell the police, "I hear so much noise over there that I don't pay any attention to most of it. But it was just a feeling that I had—there was something wrong."

Madeline Obrenski went downstairs to look up Michael Shelby's phone number; if he answered, she'd know he was okay. Before she found it, headlights came down the street and a car slowed in front of Shelby's house. Obrenski thought it was the Camaro coming back, but it was a black car that went to the corner, paused, then parked along the curb. Obrenski could tell that the two men who got out were neither Shelby nor the person who had taken his car. The two men walked up to the front porch, but Obrenski couldn't hear if they knocked. They looked in the window, but then they hurried back to their car and drove away.

The Obrenskis decided to contact the police. They decided not to use the emergency number. They didn't want the incident broadcast over the radio and picked up by anyone who might be listening on a scanner. So Obrenski's husband got dressed and drove around town looking for a patrol car.

The borough of Scottdale, with about 6,000 residents, had a progressive seven-man police force headed by Chief Ralph M. Rich Jr., who has since retired. Rich was on the midnight patrol that Wednesday.

At about 12:30 a.m., Madeline Obrenski's husband pulled over to the side on Pittsburgh Street and waved down Patrolman Joseph J. Martin, who radioed for Chief Rich to meet him at Michael Shelby's house.

Moments later, the lawmen walked up to the front porch and looked inside the picture window. They saw a man lying on the floor, face up and covered with blood. Blood was also on the floor, on the couch, and on the coffee table.

The lawmen cautiously entered the front door, which was closed but not locked. Shelby, whom they knew, was obviously dead from multiple gunshot wounds in the head and chest. The officers quickly searched the house, but no one else was there. Chief Rich requested assistance from the coroner's office and from Records and Identification of the Pennsylvania State Police in Greensburg. He also called in other members of his department.

While Patrolman Mickey Thomas took the Obrenskis to the station for a taped interview, Assistant Chief Tony Martin (Patrolman Joseph Martin's brother who has since become chief) started looking for evidence. He found one spent .22-caliber casing on the ninth stair, two near the doorway leading to the bedroom, one in the bedroom near the south wall, two near the doorway leading to a sitting room at the head of the stairway, and one inside the sitting room doorway. There was also one casing behind the front door of the first floor.

The phone rang at 1:00 a.m. When Chief Rich answered, a woman asked, "Can I talk to Mike?"

"Who is this?" the chief asked.

"Judy," she replied. "Is Mike there?"

At this point the lawman didn't want to tell anyone that Michael Shelby was lying dead on the floor. Instead, he gave a reply that was truthful yet evasive. "No, he's gone," Chief Rich said, and the caller hung up.

At 1:15 a.m., the same dark car that Madeline Obrenski had seen earlier cruised by again. Chief Rich waved it over. The two young men inside said they had returned because they were concerned about Shelby. They'd stopped earlier after seeing someone driving his car. It was easily identifiable by its bright yellow paint and black vinyl "bra" (a protective cover over the front end), and like many people around town, they knew who owned it.

"As I was pulling out of the gas station," the driver said, "he was paused at the bridge, and as I was coming towards the bridge, that's when he pulled out in front of me and proceeded to go towards Alverton." The men couldn't see if it was Shelby behind the wheel, but they couldn't help but notice how carelessly the car was being handled.

"We just knew that the way Mike drove his car, it didn't seem like him," the other man said.

Shelby had purchased the used Camaro on June 16th for $11,700. He was so proud of it that it was unlikely he'd be hot-dogging around town. The witnesses also noticed that the right door was dented and the side mirror was dangling. This was so suspicious that they rode past Shelby's to see if the car was there.

"It was gone," the young man said, "I said maybe we should go knock on his door and tell him somebody might have stolen his car."

The men said that although they didn't see a body, they left when they saw blood in the house. The only sign of life was a cat sitting on top of the couch. They headed through Alverton, the same way the yellow car had gone. They slowed down to look at fresh skid marks in the road, speculated that there'd been an accident, and went to Frick Hospital in nearby Mount Pleasant. When they didn't see the Camaro anywhere, they drove to a fast-food restaurant in New Stanton and discussed what to do next. They returned to Mulberry Street and drove past two parked police cars. One of the men said, "Maybe we should go back there, you know, say what we saw and see if anything happened there."

Chief Rich drove the two men to Alverton, where they pointed out the skid marks.

"Looks like there's some more going out that road," Rich said. He continued following the streaks past the fire department and gas station. Black streaks marked the pavement up the hill, stopped at the top, and veered off at a fork in the road. Chief Rich followed the trail to Stone Road, to an area near a dump known as Cherry Hill. They continued onto a dirt road, but the way was blocked by tires, so they turned around and went another way.

At 1:34 a.m., they suddenly came upon a car,

81

stuck in a mud hole, that was engulfed in flames. Just as Chief Rich got out of his patrol car, the gas tank blew. The chief shrank back in case it blew again, but after a few minutes, it was obvious there would be no more explosions.

There was little doubt that the flaming wreck was Michael Shelby's beloved Camaro. The yellow paint was visible and a decal saying "IROC-Z" was visible on the bottom of the door. When it was safe enough to get closer, Chief Rich peered inside, but he saw nothing—no body or gun—of interest. Patrolman Mike Grimm came out to secure the scene while the car continued to burn.

"I took the two kids back because I didn't want to endanger them," Chief Rich later said. "I didn't know who was around. I knew a gun was involved, and this being a dark and desolate area, someone could be hiding in the bushes and start shooting.

"I later matched the vehicle identification numbers, and this was definitely Shelby's car."

Dog handlers from the Greensburg Volunteer Fire Department brought out a couple of bloodhounds. The dogs picked up a trail but were unable to follow it far from the Camaro.

In the meantime, Pennsylvania State Trooper Merrill D. Brant was collecting evidence from Shelby's home, including several .22-caliber casings, a slug from the arm of the couch, and three fragments on the floor beside the couch at the victim's feet. Two soda cans, one soda bottle, and four glasses were collected to be processed for latent fingerprints, but none of sufficient quality were developed on them. Trooper Brant processed numerous items and locations inside the house and found two good prints on the handrail of the stairway. They turned out to have been made by Shelby's left thumb.

Chief Rich also gave the state police blood samples from a telephone book, a coffee table, the victim's boot, carpet patches from the floor, the couch, and living-room wall.

The television had been on when the police arrived and it remained on through some of the investigation. Ironically, the old crime show *Dragnet,* with Jack Webb as Sergeant Joe Friday, was on the screen in the background while the Scottdale police photographed Michael Shelby's body lying on the living-room floor.

Back at the police station, Patrolman Mickey Thomas learned from a witness that Shelby had been getting phone calls from one Judy Larsen, whom he had taken for a ride after a recent party. Was that the Judy who had called Shelby while police were there? When his girlfriend saw them together, Shelby explained to her that Judy had only wanted to see his car. The witness didn't know of anyone who wanted to kill Shelby. The last he saw of him was sometime around 10:00 p.m., when Shelby was showering and getting ready to go out to a store.

Although Judy Larsen was separated, the lawmen wondered how jealous her husband might be. However, when Chief Rich contacted the relatives where the husband lived, they said he worked in Pittsburgh and didn't return until midnight.

"He'd have had to drive home, park his car somewhere, and walk to Shelby's," Chief Rich later said. "There just wasn't enough time for him to do this. We eliminated him as a suspect."

But Chief Rich still went to see the young wife.

She confirmed that she was the "Judy" who had called while the police were in Shelby's house. After hearing firecrackers or gunshots and seeing the police arrive, she feared something had happened to Shelby. Judy started crying and then said that three young men who were on her back porch at that moment knew something about the murder. Chief Rich called them in, then asked for assistance from Patrolman Mickey Thomas, Assistant District Attorney Al Bell, and Westmoreland County Detective Tom Horan.

The lawmen learned from one of the young men that earlier in the evening, Mark Grimm (no relation to Patrolman Grimm) was bragging to a couple of friends that he had a gun and was "going to kill three people tonight."

Grimm, 18, was no stranger to the Scottdale police. Patrolman Randy Parfitt had arrested him a couple of times, once for disorderly conduct and another time for underage drinking. The borough police were currently looking for Grimm to arrest him for recklessly endangering another person. Those charges were based on an incident at 8:30 p.m., just hours before Shelby's murder. At that time, Grimm was standing on South Broadway in the middle of the street. When the light changed, several cars went through without incident, but Grimm stepped in front of one car, taking short, slow steps and glaring at the driver.

When Grimm suddenly stopped moving, the driver had to veer to the left to avoid hitting him. The driver pulled over, got out of the car, and approached Grimm to ask him what the problem was. Grimm raised the front of his shirt, exposing the butt of a gun tucked down in his trousers. He took hold of the weapon with both hands and pointed it at the complainant's chest.

"Get back in your car!" he ordered.

The man obeyed and drove directly to a nearby fire station to call 911. He told Patrolman D. Barry Dunn that the weapon, which resembled a "German Ruger," appeared to be a semiautomatic .22-caliber pistol with brown grips and a dark blue or gray barrel.

None of the officers had seen Grimm to arrest him on those charges, but now they were interested in more than the incident at the intersection.

"From the time I saw the shell casings [at the murder scene], I felt that it could be Grimm," Chief Rich said. "We knew he had a twenty-two, and there was the fact that he was acting strange and that the [witness] who saw someone at Shelby's car described a thin youth with dark hair. It all fit in."

Then at 3:00 a.m., when the Scottdale police and county detectives were still at the scene, Grimm came walking up the street.

"I heard you guys were looking for me," he calmly told Chief Rich.

The lawman recalled, "It was a shock to me. I don't know what his thoughts were, if he was talking about both incidents or if he just assumed that we were looking for him for the earlier one."

Mark Grimm was taken to the police station. While Chief Rich left to talk to other witnesses, Patrolman Thomas and Westmoreland County Detective William Manning advised the teenager of his constitutional rights and started questioning him about the motorist's complaint.

Grimm said he was at a relative's home at 7:00 p.m. and got into a fight with a family member. He admitted that he also stole 11 of a relative's Percodan and took them all. Later, he said, he had a verbal confrontation with a driver who tried to run him over. Then he went to the apartment of a friend, Lorrie Blackley, at 8:00 p.m. and stayed there until 2:00 a.m.

Chief Rich, who'd just returned to the police station, knew better. "I saw Lorrie and her kids at around eleven-thirty p.m. and you weren't with them," he told Grimm.

"Do you think I did it?" Grimm asked.

"At this point," Chief Rich responded, "I wouldn't want to be in your shoes." No one had told Grimm that the Camaro had been burned, so the chief carefully chose his words: "We found Shelby's car, and it's ruined."

The teenager seemed to know more. "How can you find anything in a car that was burnt?" he asked.

"Where's the gun?" Chief Rich asked. Grimm denied that he had one, or that he ever had one.

Lorrie Blackley was questioned and she told the county detectives that she did *not* spend the evening with Mark Grimm. She was with her family until around midnight, she said. When she went to take out some trash at around 1:00 a.m., she saw Grimm walking up Pittsburgh Street. In her opinion, he "had an evil look about him" and was acting "strange."

When Patrolman Thomas asked Blackley if she felt uncomfortable in Grimm's presence, she answered, "Yes, I really don't like him."

Blackley also said that earlier in the evening, she

saw one of Grimm's relatives with a bump on his head. He told her that Mark had hit him with a pipe and wondered if he should get it stitched. She said they merely exchanged greetings, and she went back to her apartment.

When Detective Michael Paden confronted Grimm with Blackley's statement, Grimm changed his story and said he wasn't actually in her apartment but stayed in the hall.

"From eight p.m. until two a.m.?" Detective Paden asked.

"Yeah," Grimm responded.

"Do you mean you talked to Lorrie Blackley in the hallway for six hours?"

Grimm replied, "I don't know. Maybe not that long." He did not recant his alibi. "She's lying," he said. "I was with her from eight p.m. until two a.m."

Grimm voluntarily surrendered his canvas shoes to Detective Manning, who turned them over to Detective Paden. Grimm stated that if there was any blood on his shoes, it was from that relative. "We had a fight earlier, and I hit him in the head," he explained.

It was nearly 6:00 a.m. when the relative in question showed Detective Paden where Grimm had hit him with a pipe. It was more of a bruise and abrasion than a bleeding cut.

Detective Paden conducted an atomic absorption analysis on Grimm's hands. This test usually discloses traces of gunpowder residue. In this case, however, the suspected murder weapon was the type that wouldn't necessarily leave residue. Nevertheless, Paden sent the sample to the state police crime lab in Harrisburg.

The Scottdale police didn't have any probable cause to hold Grimm as a suspect in Shelby's murder, but they arrested him for the incident at the intersection. As he was being put into the jail cell, he told Detective Manning, "When this is all over, I'm going to blow my brains out."

Meanwhile, the lawmen were building evidence against Grimm in the homicide. From numerous witnesses that morning, they learned that the young suspect had spent the previous evening under the influence of drugs and alcohol, waving around a loaded shotgun, and threatening to kill people.

A girl who was with several others at the convenience store saw Grimm pull a gun on the motorist. Grimm then called out to her. She stopped her car and he got in the backseat. They went to a nearby restaurant where Grimm fired off a shot in the parking lot. The police would subsequently retrieve a .22-caliber shell casing from there.

The girl drove to Cherry Hill on Stone Road because Grimm said he was supposed to meet someone at the garbage dump. The group waited a few minutes, then got out of the car. Grimm pulled the gun from the waistband of his pants and started waving it around "like he was showing it off." He fired a few shots at an old sink and at a paint can, putting a hole right through the letter "P" on the label. The girl with him didn't know what kind of gun it was, but she remembered Grimm saying the word "Ruger" and that the bullets were "hollow." When later shown a picture of a Ruger Mark II, the girl replied, "That's it."

The party continued in the gravel pit. Grimm was lying down near the bottom of the pit while another young man stood above when some stones started rolling toward the bottom. Grimm stood up and aimed the gun right at the other teen.

"He said . . . if he didn't stop it, you know, he was going to get shot," the girl told police. "Then he said that if he would have shot him, he would have killed himself because there was no way he was going to jail."

The party left the pit to meet up with some other friends. They dropped Grimm off and promised to meet up with him later. In fact, the girl said, they had no intention of coming back for him. "He was getting, like, scary," the girl said.

The witness also related another incident on Sunday when Grimm told her he had a gun and was "on a mission."

"He was talking about this car that he liked, and he said that he could get [it] because he had this gun," the witness stated. "He said it was a TA, which apparently means Trans Am. That's the way he talks. He said that it was real fancy and that he could outrun the cops . . . if they tried to stop him."

One of the young men who'd also been at the gravel pit had more information on Grimm's bragging.

"He told me he was going to kill Parfitt," he said.

Scottdale Patrolman Thomas asked, "Parfitt being . . . ?"

"Police," the witness replied.

"Randy Parfitt from the department here?"

"Yeah."

The investigators weren't happy to learn that one of their own was allegedly the target for murder. But they didn't react and just let the witness continue.

89

He explained that Grimm said he was going to steal a car and entice Patrolman Parfitt into a high-speed chase.

"When he pulled over and pulled up and asked [Grimm] to step out of the car," the witness stated, "[Grimm] said he was going to blow him away."

The first thing that crossed Chief Rich's mind was the notorious "Kill for Thrill" murders that happened in Cleveland, Ohio, 10 years before. In that incident, two men on a random rampage killed four innocent persons, including a young mother who gave them a ride on a foggy night. The climax to their cold-blooded spree was when they sped past Apollo, Pennsylvania, Patrolman Leonard Miller in a stolen car and lured him into a pursuit. When Miller pulled them over and got out of his car, the driver leaned out the window and fatally shot him.

Patrolman Thomas continued with the questioning. "Did he mention getting Mike Shelby's car?"

"No, never. Never even mentioned his name."

This was not the first time the lawmen had talked to this witness, but it was the first time he'd mentioned that Grimm planned to kill a cop.

"Why did you hold back on the Parfitt incident?" Chief Rich asked him. "You thought you were going to get into trouble?"

"Yeah."

"Did he ask you to help him . . . to kill him?" Chief Rich asked.

"No, he never asked me." The witness also said that as far as he knew, Grimm didn't ask anyone else present, either. "We were all scared because he had the gun. . . . He was waving it around, and he pointed it right at [another person in the car], and he said, 'Don't worry, it's not loaded.' . . . I looked over at the gun—it *was* loaded."

When Chief Rich asked the witness why Grimm said he was going to kill Parfitt, the witness replied, "Because he was always arresting him. He didn't say why then, but that's the reason." The witness explained that Grimm told him after a hearing he had to attend for a disorderly conduct charge that "he was going to get him [Parfitt] back. He said he knew where he lived and he was going to get him."

The investigators later learned from witnesses that Grimm had seen Parfitt in a patrol car at around 11:00 p.m. and had assumed that he'd just come on duty. At that time, however, the police officer was ending his shift.

Randy Parfitt wasn't entirely surprised when Chief Rich told him of the alleged plot. He knew Mark Grimm didn't like him, and after one hearing, Grimm told him they were "running into each other too much" and that he was "going to take care of it."

Another witness told Westmoreland County Detective Thomas D. Horan that when he was with Grimm and several others at a gas station the previous evening, Grimm said he was going to "kill three people" that night, "then myself." The witness asked who Grimm was going to kill but could not understand Grimm's response. Grimm then asked another friend present, "What would you do if I pointed a gun to your head?"

"I would just stand there," the friend replied.

Another person told Detectives Horan and Manning that when he heard about the shooting at Michael Shelby's house, he suspected Grimm because he knew Grimm had a gun and was threatening people. The witness had driven to Grimm's house, where he found Grimm standing on the porch.

"What's going on up at Shelby's?" Grimm had asked the witness.

"Someone shot and killed him," the witness replied.

Grimm asked about the whereabouts of Lenny Gibson, one of his friends, then during the course of conversation stated, "Dead men don't talk!"

"He said it in a real cool and snickering manner," the witness told the police.

The bloodhound teams returned to Scottdale. Shortly after 3:00 p.m., a handler started his dog Cy at the corner of Pearl and Mulberry Streets, using an item of Grimm's clothing to track. Cy followed a trail to Shelby's home, put his nose to the front door, then immediately went inside when the door was opened.

Another dog named Ruthie was started on Grimm's scent at Homestead Avenue. The dog "casted" the area until a "hit" sent her toward the intersection of Homestead and Mulberry Street. She then led her handler to Shelby's home. She checked both sides of the house, then proceeded to the front porch. According to the handler's report, she "gave solid indications that the scent was in the front door by staying at the door and pressing her nose on the cracks of the door."

Inside, Ruth made a left turn to the living-room area and proceeded down the hallway trailing into the kitchen. She returned to the front door, then continued the trail up a set of steps leading to the second floor, stopped three-fourths of the way up, turned around, and went back and entered a bedroom near the bottom of the stairs. Ruthie retraced these same steps in the house two more times, then went out the front door and ended her trail.

Both canine sleuths showed that whoever had worn the scented articles—namely Mark Grimm—had entered Shelby's home. Both dogs indicated a similar path that Grimm had taken once inside, a path that took him through the kitchen, halfway up the stairs, in the downstairs bedroom, and out the front door.

That same day, Lorrie Blackley changed her original statement. Now she admitted to Detective Manning that when she saw Grimm at 1:00 a.m. on the street, he told her he needed an alibi. She refused, even when he became upset.

The investigators also placed Grimm behind the wheel of Shelby's stolen car. Grimm's friend Lenny Gibson told Chief Rich and Detectives Manning and Horan that at around 12:15 a.m., he saw the yellow Camaro at a traffic light.

"I stopped right beside it," Gibson said. "I thought it was Mike. I was going to ask him how his car was running. I hadn't seen him since he bought it. So I stopped, and Mark was in the car."

Gibson said he recognized the car because it had a license plate frame from the dealer who sold it to Shelby. "I said where did you get the car?" Gibson continued. "He said, 'It's a rental car.' Then he started smoking tires, and he pulled out."

Shortly after noon, Chief Rich and Detective Manning went to the Westmoreland County Detention Center to question Mark Grimm. Advised of his rights, he chose to remain silent and requested an attorney. The two lawmen left with no statement and headed for the office of A.D.A. Bell to compose an affidavit against Grimm on the charges of criminal homicide, burglary, theft, and receiving stolen property, the latter relevant to the theft of Shelby's car keys from his home and then the theft of his car.

Chief Rich thought it would be appropriate if Patrolman Parfitt was the one to bring Grimm in. Parfitt was glad to oblige.

Grimm was arraigned at 11:28 a.m. on Friday, July 14th, at the office of District Magistrate J. Bruce King and returned to jail without bond.

Minutes later at the police station, another young man started giving a taped statement to Patrolman Thomas and Detective Manning. He told them that he saw Grimm waving around a Ruger pistol and saying he was going to "blow away" someone who tried to run him over. Later, at about 2:45 a.m. on Wednesday, Grimm came into the witness' house and allegedly asked, "Did you hear the good news? Somebody blew Shelby away." The witness said Grimm mentioned something about a .22-caliber pistol being used and said the killer had been caught trying to steal Shelby's car.

"He said, 'Yeah, I did it,' " the young man added.

Grimm then asked the witness and another person present for a ride out to Stone Road so he could get the wheels off Shelby's car, but they declined. When they asked him what he did with the gun he replied, "Don't worry, I got rid of it."

The witness described Grimm's behavior as "real tense and real nervous . . . like he was really out of it . . . just off in a big daze. Spaced, like a zombie."

The other person who was there told Patrolmen Thomas and Dunn that Grimm went into detail about the murder.

"He said somebody shot him [Shelby] with a twenty-two seven times, and then he started pointing them out where they shot him," the second witness stated. "He said half of him was laying on the couch and half of him on the floor. He pointed like once at the top of the head, right above the ear, and then once below the ear and the neck, then in the bottom of the neck and in the shoulder."

The autopsy performed by Dr. Cyril H. Wecht, a renowned forensic pathologist from Pittsburgh, corroborated much of that information. Michael Shelby had been shot once in the head, twice in the chest, once in the shoulder, and once in the suprascapular region below the neck. There were also surface wounds on two fingers of the right hand. Dr. Wecht recovered four slugs and multiple bullet fragments.

Among other injuries, the gunshot wounds had perforated the victim's left lung, the pericardium and left ventricle of the heart, and the liver. Aside from the bullet wounds, Dr. Wecht found nothing else remarkable about the body. Toxicology reports showed no signs of any drugs, either prescription or illegal, in Shelby's blood.

The murder weapon was never recovered. At the home of one of Grimm's relatives, the investigators found an empty box for a Mark II automatic Ruger manufactured by Sturn, Ruger & Company, Incorporated. They ran a check on the serial number on the box and learned from records in Harrisburg that it was registered to a family member. When they showed a picture of it to the girl who'd been with the group at the gravel pit, she said, "That's it. That's the gun."

On July 24th, a jail inmate told Detectives Manning and Richard Kranitz that when Grimm came in on July 12th, he was telling everyone he was in for murder. The witness looked at Grimm's papers, noted that he was arrested for waving a gun, and figured Grimm was just trying to impress everyone. He said that the day after the police questioned Grimm in jail, Grimm claimed, "They don't have any evidence. They don't even have the gun I used."

Grimm allegedly told this witness that he killed Shelby and stole the car because Shelby was a cocaine dealer and had the drugs stashed in the Camaro. He also said, "They can't get me for a felony murder because all I did was burn the car." When the other inmate reminded Grimm that he could be sentenced to the electric chair, Grimm responded, "I will plead insanity."

On Monday, July 31st, Grimm, wearing a bandana to cover his shaved head, appeared before District Justice J. Bruce King. After five hours of witness testimony, Defense Attorney David Caruthers claimed there wasn't enough evidence to hold Grimm on anything more serious than receiving stolen property. "There's no way to identify who shot Michael Shelby," he said, "and there is no testimony to place Mr. Grimm in the Shelby home."

Assistant District Attorney Bell disagreed. "We have a statement that the defendant was in possession of a semi-automatic handgun, that he was in a bad frame of mind, that he needed a fast car because he planned to kill a police officer," Bell said. "It is clear from the evidence that the defendant went to Michael Shelby's house to get a fast car."

Judge King ordered Grimm to stand trial on all

charges and set court arraignment for September 1st.

Meanwhile, Mark Grimm just kept on talking. On August 8th, another inmate told Detective Manning that Grimm claimed he was "dropping acid" on the night of the murder. Grimm allegedly said he wanted to kill a police officer and "wanted him dead real bad." The witness further stated that Grimm wanted to escape to kill three witnesses who were going to testify against him—Lorrie Blackley and two friends who were with him the evening before the Shelby murder.

Because of overcrowding at the local jail, Grimm was sent to the detention center in nearby Cambria County. While there, he began dropping bits and pieces of information about the murder to a fellow inmate and finally divulged many details. The inmate contacted police in December, telling them about Grimm's talkative streak. On the 8th, Chief Rich and Detectives Manning and Paden went to see the jailhouse informant.

According to this inmate's statement, Grimm said Shelby owed him $17,000 for cocaine. Grimm had gone to Shelby's on the night of the murder to collect the debt. When Shelby said he didn't have the cash, Grimm suggested an insurance scheme: Grimm would take Shelby's car to a chop-shop where it would fetch a top price for parts resale. Shelby could claim the car was stolen and turn the loss over to his insurance company.

Grimm allegedly also planned to use the car to lure Patrolman Randy Parfitt into a high-speed chase, then kill him in the traffic stop.

Grimm's plan went astray when Shelby refused to become involved. Grimm then asked to use the bathroom, and while he was going up the steps, Shelby picked up the phone and started dialing. Grimm turned around and shot Shelby above one eye. The inmate said Grimm related that one shot in the head "blew out" a piece of Shelby's skull. When Shelby moaned and asked for help, Grimm "emptied the gun" into him. Grimm hung up the phone that Shelby had dropped, picked up the car keys, and left.

Grimm even drew a diagram of the murder scene and left it behind when he was transferred. The inmate turned it over to the investigators. There was also a drawing of a map showing where Grimm said he ran the victim's Camaro into a utility pole. It was the same place where a Scottdale patrolman recovered the vehicle's broken mirror.

Lenny Gibson didn't know how lucky he was that the light changed when he spotted Grimm in the stolen car. This witness said Grimm told him he had his hand on the gun and was going to kill Gibson, but Gibson drove away when the signal turned green. As for the whereabouts of the gun, Grimm claimed to have hidden it in a coal bin, then had a relative destroy it with a blowtorch and scatter the remaining parts. Grimm also said he didn't mean to burn the car, but that it caught on fire when he revved the engine while it was stuck in the mud.

"If Mark gets out," the witness added, "he's going to kill all the police officers. He shouldn't be out on the streets." He also claimed that Grimm told him he was going to try to pin the Shelby murder on Gibson.

In January 1990, the defendant's attorneys sought to have the charges dropped for what they claimed was lack of evidence. Defense Attorney Caruthers also wanted to suppress certain evidence, including the clothes Grimm wore at the time of the murder, the spent .22-caliber cartridges, and testimony from people who witnessed Grimm waving a loaded gun and threatening to kill people.

In February, Westmoreland County Common Pleas Judge Bernard Sherer ruled that the evidence in question could be included. Furthermore, he wrote, "The defendant's statements and actions throughout the evening define the defendant's violent state of mind. In addition, the charges involved one night's events and one weapon, thus creating a logical connection between the crimes."

A jury was selected on March 5th, with testimony beginning the following day in the courtroom of Westmoreland County Common Pleas Judge Donetta Ambrose.

Trooper Darrell Mayfield, a state police ballistics expert, was one of the first witnesses to testify for the prosecution. He told the jury that eight discarded .22-caliber shells found in Shelby's house matched the casing found in the parking lot where Grimm fired a shot just hours before Shelby was slain.

Robert Vislowsky, a forensic chemist from the troop's crime lab, testified that mud samples from Grimm's jeans matched mud taken from the Stone Road area, where the yellow Camaro burned.

One by one, witnesses took the stand against Mark Grimm. Through their testimony, they put the murder weapon in Grimm's hands hours before the shooting and placed him in the victim's car minutes after the incident. Some testified to his asking for an alibi, then bragging to friends, and later a cellmate, that he "did it."

The commonwealth's witnesses also related that Grimm had talked about stealing a car so he could kill Patrolman Parfitt. One of them said he saw Grimm at the town gazebo at around 6:00 or 7:00 p.m. on July 11th.

"He had a gun . . . and was waving it around," a witness testified. "He said he was looking for Randy Parfitt. He was out to get him, I guess. He said he was going to get Randy and then shoot himself."

On Wednesday, March 14th, Grimm took the stand and accused Lenny Gibson of being the killer. Looking pale and speaking quietly, Grimm told his version of the circumstances of the evening, beginning with his admission that he took seven to nine pills to help him "relax." He denied threatening the driver at the stoplight with a gun. He said that when the car almost struck him, he raised his arm in a shrugging gesture and muttered under his breath. Then when he pulled out a "target pistol" that "wasn't loaded," several bystanders yelled, "Shoot him! Shoot him!"

Grimm testified that he went to the dump to meet someone for a cocaine buy and to search for a measuring scale, which they didn't find. He said he later went with Lenny Gibson to a gas station. There, he said, Gibson devised a plot to get Shelby's car and take it to a chop-shop run by a friend, who at the time of the trial, was awaiting prosecution with three other men for dismantling four stolen cars, including three Camaros. Shelby was allegedly in on the plan because he wanted to collect insurance on his own car.

Grimm testified that before he went into the house, he saw Gibson slide his gun under the passenger seat.

"Mike wanted his car stole [sic], so I was going to ask him for it," Grimm said. For this, Gibson promised him $100 worth of cocaine. Grimm said before he went in, he placed his relative's gun under the car seat.

"I walked up to the house and Shelby waved me in," he continued. "I said, 'Lenny sent me here to pick your car up. Do you want it stolen?' He said, 'Tell Lenny I changed my mind. I don't want to do it.' "

Grimm said he went back to the car and relayed the message. Gibson angrily headed toward the house, then said, "I forgot something" and went back to the car. Grimm didn't say what he went back to the car for.

In the house, Gibson allegedly asked Shelby, "What's up? Didn't you tell me you wanted your car stolen? And now you're backing out of it?"

According to Grimm's testimony, Gibson said he was already paid for the car and offered Shelby first one ounce of cocaine, then two ounces, to go through with the deal. Shelby said, "Drop it. Let it go." While the other two argued about it, Grimm claimed he was going back and forth to the kitchen to get some soda. Then he heard Gibson curse and say, "I'll take the car!"

Shelby then told Gibson that he'd not only tell the police about it, but would also tell them that Gibson was involved with the theft of two other cars. While this was going on, Gibson allegedly asked Shelby if he could use the bathroom. While Gibson headed upstairs, Grimm went into the living room to talk to Shelby. Suddenly, there was a shot from the stairway.

"I seen Mike grabbing his head and he tried to stand up," Grimm testified. "Mike was making a lot of noise and asked me to help him. I could barely move. I ran for the door." Grimm said he heard more rapid fire and when he looked at the stairway, Gibson was pointing the gun at him. Frightened, he grabbed Shelby's car keys and drove off in the Camaro.

Grimm denied that he'd planned to kill Patrolman Parfitt. A.D.A. Bell asked him, "All of your friends — all of these witnesses — were mistaken about what you told them?"

Grimm replied, "To the best of my knowledge, yes."

The commonwealth called four witnesses who provided alibis for Lenny Gibson. According to their testimony, he arrived at a gas station between 11:00 and 11:30 p.m. and remained there until "a little after midnight." Two neighbors who also saw a thin young man leaving Shelby's house said that they had seen no one else, just that one person.

"I'm definitely sure I saw one man come out of the house," one woman testified. "I definitely would have seen anyone else coming out."

In his closing arguments, Defense Attorney Caruthers told the jury there was "plenty of reasonable doubt" in this case and that his client was guilty only of car theft and of recklessly endangering another person.

Prosecutor Bell reviewed the evidence and argued that on the evening in question, Grimm, under the influence of drugs, blamed "all his problems in the world" on the Scottdale patrolman. Bell argued that Grimm believed that by "eliminating Parfitt, he eliminates his problems."

Bell said that Grimm went to Shelby's house and after loitering there a while, he asked to borrow the Camaro. "But when Shelby refused to loan the car," he continued, "Mr. Grimm got agitated, upset, so he went upstairs, then aimed the gun at Shelby's head, and shot him. Shelby said, 'Help me.' And [Grimm] emptied the gun into him."

It took the jury just two and a half hours to return with a verdict. They found Mark Grimm guilty of first-degree murder, guilty of two counts each of theft and receiving stolen property for taking Shelby's car keys and his car, and guilty of recklessly endangering the motorist whom he had threatened with the gun.

Judge Ambrose sentenced Grimm to life in prison for the murder and imposed concurrent sentences for the other convictions.

Grimm's attorneys weren't pleased with the first-degree murder conviction. "The whole record is full of testimony [that] he was high on drugs throughout that day and night," Assistant Public Defender Gregory Cechitt said. After the trial, he shouted his opinion in the courthouse foyer and was reprimanded by a security guard.

Assistant District Attorney Bell denied that the issue of diminished capacity was even a consideration. "First of all, the defense claimed he didn't do it, so that made it real easy for the jury," he told a reporter. "Either he did it or he didn't do it. The defense drew those lines." Bell added that he didn't want "any n'er-do-well who ingests drugs to think he can go out and kill someone and be prosecuted for third-degree murder."

Mark Grimm smiled as he was being led out of the courtroom in handcuffs. His attorneys filed appeals on the conviction, which were denied in late 1992 and may be taken before a higher court. Mark Grimm is now serving his life sentence in one of Pennsylvania's maximum-security prisons.

EDITOR'S NOTE:
Madeline Obrenski, Judy Larsen, Lorrie Blackley, and Lenny Gibson are not the real names of the persons so named in the foregoing story. Fictitious names have been used because there is no reason for public interest in the identities of these persons.

"BULLET-RIDDLED BODIES IN THE RIVER!"

by Jack Heise

The call came in to the Miami County Sheriff's Office in Peru, Indiana, on Friday morning, November 23, 1990. Peru is a small town in the northeastern part of the state.

The caller said that while he and his buddy were hunting, they spotted a man floating in the Eel River, in the area of the Lost Bridge. The dispatcher said he knew where the Lost Bridge was located, about halfway between Denver and Chili, and someone would be there shortly. He told the caller to wait there.

Sheriff Don Howard, along with some deputies and the coroner, Dr. John Crashaw, responded to the call. The two hunters were waiting for them at the old steel bridge across a section of the river where the banks were steep.

One of the hunters pointed down to the far side of the river where a body was snagged on a log at the river bank.

"Looks like maybe he jumped or got pushed off the bridge," one of the persons present remarked.

"Don't think so," a deputy said.

"No. Why not?"

"Because it's upstream. If it came off the bridge, the current would have carried it downstream."

Some of the deputies were sent down to retrieve the corpse. They soon brought it up to the bridge deck. The corpse was a fully clothed young man. There was no wallet or any kind of identification in his clothing.

"Anybody recognize him?"

Looking at the body a deputy said, "He's about the same age as the guy we got a report on that's been missing in Shelbyville. They thought he might have committed suicide."

"This person didn't commit suicide," Dr. Crashaw said.

"How can you be sure?"

"Ever hear of a person jumping off a bridge, swimming upstream, and then shooting himself three times in the chest?"

If it was a murder, Sheriff Howard said, he was going to call the state police for assistance. Then he sent a deputy to call Shelbyville about the person they had reported missing.

Sergeants Fred Forbes, Bob Land and Bob Brisson came to the bridge with a mobile crime lab. There wasn't a great deal they could do other than make a video of the body and where it had been found in the river. It appeared obvious that the corpse must have been placed in the river somewhere upstream.

Meanwhile, the deputy who called Shelbyville came back and said that on October 10th, they had received a missing-person report on 17-year-old Jason Brown from a relative of his. The youth had left a note suggesting that he intended to commit suicide.

That was better than a month before the corpse was found in the river.

"Could he have been in the water that long?" one of the lawmen asked Dr. Crashaw.

The coroner said no. The river water was cold and might preserve the body for a time, but it couldn't have been in the water for more than a week, 10 days at the most.

Maybe it wasn't the Brown boy, after all. They'd have to get someone to make a positive identification. A deputy went to contact Shelbyville again for the name of the relative who had reported the teenager missing.

As the officers were about to wrap it up on the bridge and the coroner prepared to have the corpse transported to the hospital in Peru for a postmortem, someone came running upstream along the river bank, shouting.

When he reached the sheriff's group, the man said he had just found the body of a woman in the river downstream.

The deputies and state agents went down to check. What they saw was the body of a fully clothed young woman. She appeared to be older than the teenager found near the bridge.

No one recognized her.

"Maybe a suicide pact," one of the lawmen suggested. Since Brown had said he was going to kill himself, perhaps this woman shot him and then turned the gun on herself.

That wasn't possible, said Dr. Crashaw. He pointed out that the woman also had several gunshot wounds—not one—in her chest. No, this was definitely a double homicide.

Where and when the killings were done, and where the bodies had been dumped in the river, were among the puzzles to be solved. The first order of business, however, was to get the victims definitely identified.

Shelbyville reported that Jason Brown's relative told them Brown had lived in Shelbyville for only a short time. Before that, the youth had lived with a relative in Peru, and she could make the positive identification.

Brown's relative was located and brought to the hospital. There, she made a positive identification of the male as Jason Brown and a tentative identification of the female as Janice Scott.

She said that Brown had been going to school when he met Scott. The relative hadn't approved of the young man's relationship with an older woman who was divorced and tried to break it up by sending Brown to Shelbyville to live with the other relative.

"Let's get some information on this Scott woman," one of the state agents said. There was a possibility that the relationship itself could be what provided the motive for murder.

It didn't take the probers long to run a background check on the dead woman. She was soon positively identified as 23-year-old Nanette Scott, recently divorced from an airman at the Grissom Air Force Base. He said he had filed for a divorce in August. The dissolution hearing was held on November 15th and she had not been present.

The ex-husband told the investigators that he had learned she was using her maiden name. The last he had heard of her, she was living in Kokomo.

The airman was completely eliminated from consideration as a possible suspect in the murders.

The probers obtained more information on Jason Brown from the relative in Shelbyville. When Brown came to live there, he said, Nanette Scott followed him and went to work as a waitress. The relative tried to talk Brown out of the relationship with the older woman.

The last he had seen of Brown was on Monday morning, October 1st. That was when the relative found the note in Brown's room, indicating the teenager's intent to commit suicide.

A check at the restaurant where Nanette Scott was employed established that she had been at work on that Monday morning, but she'd left at two o'clock on a break and never returned to work, not even to pick up her paycheck.

To the sleuths, it now seemed obvious that the suicide note was a ruse by Brown to throw off the track anyone looking for him with Scott.

But why had the couple left so hurriedly that she had not picked up her paycheck? Where had they gone and what had they been doing between October 1st and November 23rd, when their bodies turned up in the river?

Brown had little money of his own, and Scott hadn't picked up her paycheck. Meanwhile, the investigators had picked up allegations that the woman had been associated with "undesirable persons." That led the probers to wonder whether the victims might have been involved with drugs.

"If they were—and were killed over some kind of a drug deal that went sour—it's going to be a tough case," one of the state agents said. "People involved in drugs aren't talkative."

In the meantime, Dr. Marvin Dzsiabis, a forensic pathologist, completed the postmortems on the bodies. He reported that death had been caused by gunshot wounds to the chests of both victims. Slugs from a .22-caliber weapon had been recovered. Tests established that neither victim had been under the influence of drugs or alcohol at the time of death. And there was no evidence that the female victim had been raped.

"Rule out robbery, rule out rape, and rule out jealousy, and what have we got?" a state agent asked.

"Narcotics?" suggested one of his colleagues in the investigation.

Peru and Shelbyville are relatively small Indiana towns. Everyone seems to know everyone else, and particularly the younger people. Jason Brown had been born and raised in Peru, so the persons he had associated with there were likely to know what he was involved in.

But the answers weren't forthcoming.

The persons who were interviewed by investigators said they knew Brown and knew about his relationship with Nanette Scott, but that was his business. They did not know where the couple could have gone after leaving Shelbyville, and had no idea who could have murdered them or for what reason.

A check was made at Maconaquish High School, which Brown had attended. His teachers said that Brown had been a serious student but had not engaged in social activities or sports. The other students knew of his relationship with Scott, but he hadn't openly talked to them about it.

Then a state detective who had been probing the murders along with the sheriff's team came to Sheriff Howard. He said that after checking with state and federal narcotics agents, he was reasonably certain that neither Brown nor Scott had been involved in drugs.

"They have informants," he said. "If their names had ever come up, someone would know about it."

The sheriff, too, said that neither Brown nor Scott had ever been mentioned in any of his department's investigations of drugs or any other criminal activities in the county.

With rape, robbery, jealousy, and drugs eliminated, what was left?

Even more perplexing was that Jason Brown and Nanette Scott were last seen in Shelbyville on October 1st. Their bodies weren't found in the river until November 23rd. The pathologists were certain that the couple could not have been slain and dumped in the river more than 10 days before they were found.

Brown had spent a lifetime in Peru. Scott wasn't as well known, but a significant number of persons did know her. Yet probers found no one in Shelbyville or Peru who could recall having seen either of the victims.

The sheriff had no answer for the mystery surrounding the slain pair. The detectives assigned to the case had questioned relatives and friends of Jason Brown. He had been sort of a loner, but if he and Nanette Scott had been around Peru, it would seem that someone would have seen them.

"In a town the size of Peru or Shelbyville— even the entire county of Miami—you can't move around without someone seeing you," the lawman said. "It isn't like a big city, where people can get lost."

The state detective agreed with the sheriff. But for some unfathomable reason, no one seemed to be willing to talk to investigators or become involved. It went on that way for days.

Then one of the deputies came in with a tip he'd just received. One of his informants, who insisted upon remaining anonymous, told him to check on three persons who'd left town hurriedly after the bodies were found in the river. The informant named them as 16-year-old Steven Pigg, 17-year-old Curtis Burke, and 19-year-old Carl Purvis.

The deputy said he checked out the lead and learned that Pigg had gone to Indianapolis to live with relatives. Purvis had also gone to Indianapolis. Burke had gone to relatives in Viper, Kentucky.

"What is their relationship with Brown and Scott?" one of the case investigators said.

The deputy said that he hadn't been able to get anything more from the informant. In questioning other persons about Pigg, Burke, and Purvis, all the deputy was able to find out was that they knew Jason Brown as a casual friend of the departed trio.

In the probers' view, it had to be more than coincidence that all three of them left town right after the bodies were found. If they were involved in the murders, though, what was it all about?

With the unwillingness encountered by the investigators in questioning persons in Peru, it didn't seem likely—even with the three names they had—that anyone would now be willing to say anything about why the trio had left town or for what reason.

The investigators took what information they had to Miami County Prosecutor Wil Siders. He told them that they could attempt to question the three persons, but they would have to advise them that they were being considered as suspects in the murders and inform them of their legal right to remain silent and be represented by an attorney.

If there wasn't sufficient cause to have a warrant issued for their arrest, the prosecutor said, the sleuths' best bet was to come up with additional information or evidence that they could use as a lever to get either the three suspects or someone else to reveal what this case was all about.

Siders suggested that the detectives pick up and quiz the informant who had told the deputy about Pigg, Burke, and Purvis. If he was reluctant, they could advise him that if he was withholding evidence in a murder case, he might be facing a serious charge, and if convicted, he could spend some time in jail.

It wasn't the way the lawmen liked to treat their informants, the prosecutor acknowledged, but it looked like the only way to get a handle on the case.

So the probers brought in the informant for questioning. When he refused to say anything more than he had told the deputy, they suggested that he ought to consider what withholding evidence in a murder case could lead to.

"Look," the informant protested. "This is a small town. If it gets out that I squealed on friends, I'm not going to be very popular around here."

The investigators assured him that unless he himself was involved in whatever had happened, his identity would remain confidential.

"I wasn't even there," the informant told the detectives. "All I know is what I heard from other people who know as much as I do about it."

"Then, I suggest you start talking," one of the lawmen told him.

The informant said he heard that Steven Pigg, who lived in a large, two-story brick house in a rural section, had invited some of his friends to a party while other members of the family were away on a visit and he was home alone.

Among those invited were Carl Purvis, Curtis Burke, Jason Brown, and Nanette Scott, along with several other friends. Everything went well until Sunday night, October 28th. Then, as the informant heard it, either Purvis or Burke—he wasn't sure which one—tried to become intimate with Nanette. Jason heard about it, became angry, and some kind of hassle resulted.

According to the informant, some individuals told him that there was a .22-caliber rifle in the house, and that Brown got it and threatened to kill either Burke or Purvis. There was a struggle and Brown was shot.

Nanette Scott became hysterical and threatened to go to the police.

According to what the informant had heard, Scott was slain to be silenced.

With two people dead in the house, the others had to figure out what to do with the bodies. Various plans were discussed. Pigg didn't want the bodies buried anywhere near the house for fear that they might be found and he would be implicated in the murders.

The killings had taken place Sunday night, October 28th. On Monday morning, the decision was made to put the bodies in a pickup truck, take them to the Eel River, and dump them.

All of the persons who attended the party took a solemn oath never to reveal what had happened or to talk to the police about it. That oath, however, concerned only the police. The friends themselves talked about what had taken place, but whenever it was mentioned by any outsiders, the persons kept mum, sworn to keep it secret.

After Jason Brown and Nanette Scott left Shelbyville, they'd come to Peru and stayed for short periods of time with persons they knew, including Curtis Burke and Carl Purvis. When the bodies were found, Pigg, Burke and Purvis de-

115

cided it would be best to leave town and avoid being questioned by the police.

On the basis of the informant's statement, the investigators obtained a search warrant for Steven Pigg's home. There they found a .22-caliber rifle and impounded a pickup truck. Ballistic experts checked the rifle against the slugs recovered from the bodies of the victims. Lab technicians analyzed bloodstains found in the bed of the pickup truck and other physical evidence.

Then prosecutor Siders filed murder charges against Steven Pigg, Curtis Burke and Carl Purvis.

Prosecutor Siders and State Agent Land went to Indianapolis and located Pigg and Purvis. The pair were brought back to Peru. Meanwhile, Kentucky authorities located Burke in Viper and took him into custody on the murder warrant. He waived his right to an extradition hearing and he, too, was brought back to Peru, where he was soon lodged in the county jail.

At a preliminary hearing before Judge Bruce Embrey, all three defendants entered pleas of not guilty. The court ordered that they be bound over for trial on the murder charges.

D.A. Siders announced that he would seek the death penalty when the defendants were brought to trial.

Lengthy legal delays followed. The juveniles had to be certified as adults to stand trial in adult court. There were more delays as defense attorneys requested a change of venue.

Curtis Burke's attorney was the first to come to Prosecutor Siders with an offer to plead his client guilty. Burke would testify against Pigg and Purvis in exchange for a promise that the state would not ask for the death penalty.

The defense lawyer alleged that Jason Brown was shot accidentally when he started a scuffle over the attention being paid to Scott, and it was Purvis and Pigg who decided to kill Scott to keep her from going to the police.

The court accepted the guilty plea and sentenced Curtis Burke to life in prison with the condition that he would be eligible for parole.

Following the plea bargaining for Burke, Carl Purvis' attorney asked for the same deal for his client. He said that Purvis would testify against Pigg. The plea was accepted and Purvis, too, was sentenced to life in prison with the condition that he would be eligible for parole.

Steven Pigg remained in jail for nearly a year before his trial was scheduled to start. The day before the jury was to be selected, Pigg's attorney appeared in court and said that his client would plead guilty in exchange for a life sentence with parole possible.

The judge considered the evidence in the case. Two of the defendants had already entered guilty pleas. The prosecution had only the word of witnesses as to who had actually premeditated and carried out the killing of Scott.

On November 18, 1991, the court accepted the guilty plea and sentenced Pigg to life in prison with the condition that he would be eligible for parole.

Following the sentencing, a state police detective was quoted as saying, "It is amazing, the loyalty friends have in a small town. At one point in the investigation, we had no idea where Brown and Scott went after they left Shelbyville, who had killed them, or for what reason. If one informant had not talked, we might still be trying to find answers."

Fortunately, the answers came, and three killers were brought to justice.

"LUST-CRAZED TEEN'S FLAMING VENGEANCE!"

by John Railey

The neighbors heard the thunderous explosion at a few minutes past 10:30 p.m. They ran outside and saw smoke pouring from the one-story, ranch-style brick house next door. Then they ran back home and called 911.

It was Wednesday night, September 4, 1991. When the Mulberry-Fairplains and Knotville volunteer firefighters received the call about a fire and persons possibly trapped, it was 10:53 p.m. Fire trucks raced to the scene on Fairplains Road in a rural community of Wilkes County, a region in the foothills of North Carolina's Blue Ridge Mountains.

Upon reaching the site, the firefighters found a severely burned elderly woman lying in the front yard of the home. As emergency workers began to administer first aid, she told them that her husband and granddaughter were still inside the burning house. She said that she'd been giving her physically disabled husband a bath when the fire broke out, and she'd jumped out a rear bedroom window to escape.

Two of the firefighters entered the modest home and fought through the dense smoke, hunting the two other residents. They found the man lying face down, stretched out across the bedroom doorway into the hall. Sweating from the heat and their own efforts, the firefighters carried the man outside, where emergency workers began performing CPR (cardiopulmonary resuscitation) on him.

The firefighters searched throughout the house, but they couldn't find the granddaughter. A few minutes later, the 15-year-old girl showed up unharmed outside the house.

Meanwhile, an ambulance team took the woman and her husband to the Wilkes Regional Medical Center in the nearby county seat of Wilkesboro. There, the man was examined and pronounced dead. County Coroner Howard Laney believed that the death had been caused by soot and smoke inhalation, but he ordered the body sent to a state medical examiner's office for autopsy to be sure. Pathologists there would later confirm Laney's initial conclusions.

Emergency workers loaded the victim's wife onto a helicopter and flew her to the N.C. Baptist Hospital in nearby Winston-Salem for treatment. The woman identified herself as 77-year-old Lillie Turner Barber and her husband as 83-year-old Aaron Anul Barber. The neighbors who'd gathered outside the burning home confirmed that identification.

By early Thursday, the firefighters had the fire squelched. Then fire investigators went through the house to determine what caused the inferno. Poking their way through the hot, smoky gloom, they found that the firefighters had contained most of the blaze in the living room, but the damage there had been intense. The flames had been so hot that a TV set and a telephone had melted.

A strong smell of gasoline hung over the house. The fire investigators established that a flammable substance, probably gas, had been poured on the carpet covering the floor of the living room and hallway, and then set afire.

By now, Detective Bob Benfield of the Wilkes County Sheriff's Department was on the scene. A night-shift sleuth at that time, Benfield had raced to the scene after he heard radio traffic about a fire fatality. He consulted with the fire investigators, who told him they believed that the fire was intentionally set. That information meant Benfield was facing a homicide investigation.

Who would want to harm the elderly Barbers? Their neighbors and friends at the scene had remarked to firefighters that they were such a kindly couple.

Detective Benfield quickly understood that his one possible witness was the 15-year-old granddaughter, who was the adopted ward of the Barbers. She'd already left the scene with other relatives, but they had left their address with the fire officials. Benfield drove to their home, which was nearby, and talked to the girl.

She wasn't much help. She said she didn't know how the fire had started. She'd run outside right after it began.

Benfield, a man in his early 30s who'd earned his detective's spot relatively recently by solid work as a crime scene technician, decided that he'd better call his supervisor. After all, the only potential witness was barely of any value. He would need some help in finding the pieces of this puzzle.

Benfield's supervisor, Lieutenant Bobby Walsh, was sleeping soundly that warm summer night when his phone rang at 5:30 a.m. Walsh, a tall, bearded, soft-spoken man of 38, didn't mind the call. He'd logged 13 years with the 50-member department under Sheriff Dane Mastin—five of those years in investigations.

So Walsh was used to midnight calls. Wilkes County investigators usually investigate only about four to five murders a year, but the annual handful of homicides have sometimes contained a couple of real whodunits.

Wilkes is a picturesque county of rolling hillsides with a rich history. National stock-car racing has its roots here, where local legend holds that the first race drivers cut their teeth by running moonshine in their hopped-up cars down the treacherous mountain roads to the cities in the valleys below.

Lieutenant Walsh was about to hop into a case that would shock the rugged inhabitants of Wilkes County. He would later describe the case as one of the more tragic he'd ever worked. The Barbers, who'd moved to Wilkes from Pennsylvania about 25 years earlier, were good people, he'd quickly learn.

Walsh met Detective Benfield at the relatives' home where the granddaughter was staying. With her relatives' consent, the teenager agreed to go back to headquarters in Wilkesboro and make a formal statement.

Meanwhile, Walsh had called an old law enforcement buddy, Agent Steve Cabe of the State Bureau of Investigation (SBI), to meet him at headquarters. Cabe, a veteran sleuth who often lends a hand in felony cases in the Wilkes County area, is a short, stocky man with curly brown hair and glasses. As he entered the case, Cabe called up a fellow SBI agent, Tom Rasmussen, and asked him to go check out the crime scene. Rasmussen specializes in arson cases.

The girl had mentioned that she had called her boyfriend after she escaped from the fire. Figuring that it wouldn't hurt to check out her story with the boyfriend, Lieutenant Walsh told Detective Benfield to go to the man's house and ask him to come down to headquarters to give his own statement. At this point, Walsh wasn't suspicious of the girl or her boyfriend. With the girl as the only witness, however, he just wanted to make damn sure he got her story straight.

By now, the girl's grandmother, Lillie Barber, was in critical condition in the burn unit at the Winston-Salem hospital. She had sustained second-degree burns over her arms, chest, neck and back—40 percent of her body. Doctors did not expect her to live, much less tell who started the fire.

Lieutenant Walsh already had one murder to solve on his hands, and if the elderly woman didn't survive, it looked like it would soon become a double-murder probe.

In an interview room at headquarters, as Thursday morning pushed toward noon, Lieutenant Walsh and Agent Cabe began to interview the girl, 15-year-old April Leigh Barber. Her grandparents had adopted her at birth and raised her as their own.

The investigators quickly saw holes in her story. The way she said the fire had just blazed up didn't make sense. Why hadn't she been burned, as well?

The attractive teenager could have passed for a 30-year-old. A few minutes into the interview, as she chatted pleasantly with the detectives, they realized that not only was April Barber quite mature, but she was also very intelligent. They'd have to play their hand carefully. She was just too cool, strangely calm about the whole thing. When Cabe and Walsh left the room, Barber, an excellent artist, started to sketch as she sat by herself.

Was the girl protecting someone?

From other witnesses, the sleuths had learned that

April Barber was an aloof yet promising high school sophomore who frequently made the honor roll and won academic awards. They also learned that the teen, a usually quiet girl who rarely talked of her emotions or her family, was in constant need of attention.

As the investigators continued their interview of Barber, Detective Benfield brought her boyfriend to headquarters and deposited him in another interview room. Clinton Lawrence "C.L." Johnson was a 32-year-old logger, recently separated from his wife and family.

Agent Cabe and Lieutenant Walsh left Barber alone and went in to talk to Johnson. He said he didn't know anything about the fire. Ironically, the stocky logger was very nervous — in striking contrast to his cool young girlfriend.

Johnson said he wanted to talk to Barber. Lieutenant Walsh told him he could talk to her — after Walsh and Cabe were through interviewing her.

A records check had showed the teen girl's slate to be spotless, and her boyfriend had virtually no criminal history.

As Lieutenant Walsh and Agent Cabe continued questioning April Barber, Agent Rasmussen got back to headquarters. Walsh and Cabe excused themselves from the interview room again to confer with Rasmussen. He confirmed the local fire marshal's ruling — the blaze had been arson. And Rasmussen had a detailed idea of how the fire had started.

Walsh and Cabe decided to tip their hand and let Rasmussen explain what they knew about the fire to the girl. They hoped their gamble might prod her into talking more freely about what they suspected she knew. The sleuths' suspicions about the girl's involvement were growing by the minute. What they also wondered was, had her boyfriend been involved, too?

Agent Rasmussen went into the interview room and drew for Barber a sketch of the burn pattern — how the gasoline had apparently been poured from a hallway, on the living-room carpet, and all the way out to a back door in the kitchen. Someone must have lit the blaze at the rear door, causing the gas to explode.

The lawmen's gamble worked.

April Barber said she had set the fire accidentally. Investigators Cabe and Walsh pressed her to explain that point. Finally, she said that she had set it intentionally.

Under careful questioning by the probers, April went on to say that her grandparents had forbidden her to date Johnson, disapproving because he was twice her age. For months, she had fought with them, especially with her grandfather, about the issue.

Two weeks before the fire, April found out that she was pregnant by Johnson. She concealed her condition from her grandparents, whom she described as being "too strict." She just wanted them "to get off her back," and said they would be "better off dead." But she also said she had figured that "if something happened, it would bring them [her and her grandparents] closer together."

She said that she and Johnson had planned the crime. Shortly before the fire, Johnson brought April a plastic, gallon-size milk jug with a red, snap-on top, full of gasoline. She knocked it over minutes before the crime occurred and just decided to go ahead with the plan. She poured a gas trail from the hall, across the living room, and to the back door of the kitchen. At the back door, she lit a newspaper

125

with a black butane lighter, dropped it on the trail of gas, and stepped outside.

Walsh asked Barber if she and Johnson had made previous attempts on her grandparents' lives. She told the sleuth that they had.

After several fights, April said, she and her boyfriend had plotted ways to kill her grandparents. Once, they took her grandfather's service pistol from his bedroom. Johnson came over to the Barber home with the concealed pistol to kill the elderly couple, but he couldn't bring himself to do it. He never even pulled out the gun.

Another time, they planned to kill her grandparents with poison. Johnson gave April some "pest stuff" to put in their food. She put the poison in an old purse in her grandmother's closet. Her grandmother found the poison, however, and April told her it was for killing rats. Her grandmother kept the poison.

Finally, several days before the fire, April and her boyfriend hatched the plan for the blaze. Five days before the crime, Johnson brought the gas over to the Barber house. The previous day, April had called Johnson several times, saying she wanted to get rid of her grandparents that night.

"Tonight is as good as any," April said she told her boyfriend.

The sleuths ended the interview, which had lasted several hours. Then they went into the other interview room and confronted Clinton Johnson with his girlfriend's statement. The logger immediately broke down and gave a statement that essentially corroborated April Barber's.

He confirmed that, beginning about three months before, he and April had discussed several ways of killing the elderly Barbers as April's arguments with them escalated. April came up with all the plans, Johnson said, and the pair believed that killing her grandparents would end all their problems.

"April's ideas were not very good, but they had merit," Johnson told the sleuths. "I had to try it."

Johnson said he never thought they'd really carry out the final plan. When April called him only hours earlier to tell him what had happened, he said, he couldn't believe it.

While April had said that her grandparents didn't know about her pregnancy, Johnson said that they did know, and they were furious. He and April had been going together for about 14 or 15 months. They'd sought counselors to help them deal with her grandparents, Johnson said, but their efforts had been in vain.

After they took Johnson's statement, Agent Cabe and Lieutenant Walsh conferred outside the interview room. They decided to go ahead and charge April Barber, whom they saw as the instigator. But, given what Johnson had said about never thinking they'd actually go through with it, the sleuths felt they ought to confer with District Attorney Michael A. "Mike" Ashburn about what the proper charges for Johnson should be.

The lawmen felt that Johnson wouldn't run, so they released him—for the time being. They charged April Barber with first-degree murder, first-degree arson, and conspiracy to commit murder in connection with the death of her grandfather. She was held in a juvenile detention center without bond.

Later that Thursday, the investigators conferred with D.A. Ashburn, a gentle but deadly prosecutor. Based on Ashburn's advice, the lawmen picked up Johnson that night and charged him, too, with first-degree murder, arson, and conspiracy. Then he was placed in the Wilkesboro jail under $500,000 bond.

In the days ahead, Lillie Barber regained consciousness, but never her speech, due to her burned throat. She was unable to communicate any details about the blaze. Then, eight days after the fire, she died in the Winston-Salem hospital of the complications from her injuries.

As a result, Lieutenant Walsh tacked another first-degree murder count on the charges against April Barber and Clinton Johnson.

The tragedy of the case was that the grandparents had loved April Barber so much. A family friend later remarked, "She was their heart—that's all. Anything she wanted, she got."

The case was a twisted version of the Romeo and Juliet story—a classic example of how easy love blended with other volatile emotions can create a deadly cocktail.

Since April Barber had been 15 at the time the crime was committed, the prosecutors could not pursue the death penalty against her, under North Carolina law. In the Tarheel State, the law considers only those who are 16 and older as adults. But the state would seek the death penalty against Johnson.

April Barber was the first slated to go to trial. On Monday, August 3, 1992, she appeared in Wilkes Superior Court in Wilkesboro. Courthouse observers quickly learned that her lawyer, William F. Brooks, had reached a plea agreement with D.A. Ashburn: there would be no trial.

Barber pleaded guilty to the two counts of first-degree murder. In return for her guilty pleas, Ashburn dropped the arson and conspiracy charges. Now it would be up to Judge James A. Beaty Jr. to sentence the teen. First, however, he would allow the attorneys to present relevant evidence.

Defense Attorney Brooks, a dapper, sharp barrister, called teachers and friends of Barber's who testified that the girl seemed to want affection, but had problems with attachment and discussing her feelings.

D.A. Ashburn called witnesses who said the grandparents were wonderful parents who had doted on April since her birth.

In his closing argument, Defense Attorney Brooks sought as light a sentence as possible for April as he told the judge, "I would urge you that April Barber is not a monster. Here we have a girl who was searching, who searched and searched and searched, but never found. And then along came this older person [Johnson]."

In his closing, D.A. Ashburn worked to counter that argument by depicting April Barber as a calculating young woman who killed the two people who cared most about her, then showed little remorse about it.

The next day, Tuesday, spectators filled the country courtroom up to the gallery as Judge Beaty prepared to pass sentence. When the judge was ready, April Barber, dressed in a plaid jumper and white shirt, stood silently at the defense table, her eyes cast downward.

The judge began to ponder his decision aloud. "I see before me a young woman who seemed to have everything [she] could have wanted in life," the judge said. "And yet two lives have been destroyed."

Judge Beaty then sentenced April Barber to the maximum—two life terms, to be served consecutively.

Clinton Johnson's trial began in late November 1992. The state's case went well. Agent Cabe presented strong testimony that held up well under cross-examination. On Friday, November 21st, after winning a battle with Defense Attorney Mitchell "Mitch" McLean, Assistant District Attorney Randy Lyon—who was prosecuting the case for his boss, Ashburn—showed the jury photos of the victims' burned bodies. One juror looked at the photos briefly and then cast her eyes downward.

Also on that Friday, bailiffs brought April Barber into the courtroom. The state had subpoenaed her to testify against her boyfriend. Johnson, seated at the defense table, at first avoided looking at April. But when he glanced at her after a few minutes, April flashed him a quick smile.

Once on the witness stand, however, April wasn't so pleasant. She refused to testify against Johnson, exercising her Fifth Amendment right of not having to give testimony that might incriminate her, even though she already stood convicted. Bailiffs took her out of the courtroom and back to prison.

Defense Attorney McLean did not present any evidence, nor did Johnson himself choose to take the stand. In his closing argument, McLean said that Johnson had not wanted April's grandparents to be killed, and he hadn't thought that April was serious about the plan.

"For there to be a conspiracy, there has to be a meeting of the minds," the lawyer argued. "There was no meeting of the minds here. Her [Barber's] ideas were to shoot, to poison, to kill. His [Johnson's] ideas were to talk to the minister, to counselors, to the Barbers."

In his closing, Prosecutor Lyon conceded that Johnson didn't set the fire, but he maintained that Johnson had just as much to do with the crime as Barber.

"If there was no intent to harm these people,

ladies and gentlemen, what in the world was going on . . . with the gun and the poison and the gas?" the prosecutor demanded. "There is no reasonable person who carries on like this without intending to do harm."

The jury deliberated for three and a half hours before coming back with their verdict on Tuesday, November 24th. Johnson retained the passive expression he had worn throughout the trial as the court clerk read the verdict: Johnson was found guilty of two counts of first-degree murder, and of first-degree arson, conspiracy to commit murder, and conspiracy to commit arson.

On the next day, Wednesday, November 25, 1992, the lawyers came back to argue for and against the death penalty.

Testifying for the defense, a psychologist said that Johnson had allowed himself to be dominated and manipulated easily. "He's immature . . . and he's self-defeating," the doctor said. "He puts himself in situations where he sets himself up. He sets himself up to mess up."

The psychologist contended that Clinton Johnson had latched on to April Barber as a source of love and support. Ironically, the doctor said, Johnson apparently believed that the younger Barber was stronger and more mature than he was. Maybe, in a sense, that was true.

In his closing argument, Defense Attorney McLean, seeking life sentences for his client, quoted the Bible. "Blessed are the merciful, for they shall obtain mercy," the lawyer declared. He argued that his client had played a minor role in the crime, which had actually been carried out by Barber herself. The lawyer maintained that the teenager had manipulated her older lover into helping her.

In his closing arguments, Prosecutor Lyon said that Johnson deserved death because he acted with his girlfriend, all the time knowing that he was placing the elderly couple at great risk.

The jury came back that afternoon, after about an hour of deliberations, with their decision. This time, Clinton Johnson, dressed in a gray-and-white shirt, dress pants, and black shoes, did show some emotion as he heard the clerk read the decision. Johnson let out a deep sigh. The jurors had spared him, sentencing him to two life terms in prison instead of the gas chamber or lethal injection.

The sobs of Johnson's family and friends broke the courtroom silence.

Then Judge Beaty meted out an additional 30 years to Johnson for the arson and conspiracy convictions.

Thus, the curtain dropped on the twisted Romeo and Juliet drama.

"SHORTCUT TO A DEADLY RUN-IN!"

by Nelson Andreu

Coconut Grove, located in the southernmost part of Miami, is a bustling section of the city. The lavish homes of many of the town's most affluent citizens sit hidden away beneath tall trees. The business district is lined with bars and open-air cafes and filled with street performers. Every night the five-block district comes alive with crowds who have come to have a festive, fun-filled time, visiting the fancy restaurants and specialty shops, enjoying the live music. From white-collar professionals to blue-collar workers, they all come to eat, drink, and be merry.

Friday night, November 22, 1991, was no different from any other night that began a weekend in "The Grove." Fun-seekers swarmed on the streets like a steady stream of ants as music blared out of the local shops. Extra officers hired by the Miami Police Department patrolled the area, making sure that the thousands of weekend revelers enjoyed themselves with maximum security and that the traffic kept flowing without any major jam-ups.

Among the throng of pleasure-seekers that night were two friends—41-year-old Allan David Terrell and

25-year-old John Mcguire. Having visited several bars earlier in the evening, they decided to hit the Grove. Terrell, who had recently relocated to Miami, was currently trying to get his new business off the ground. His friend, Mcguire, was visiting from Canada as a tourist who'd heard about Miami's Coconut Grove and was eager to experience its delights.

The two friends drove around until it was past midnight, seeing what sights they could. By one o'clock in the morning — it was now Saturday, November 23rd — they decided to call it a night. As they tried to head homeward, however, they found that the area traffic was a bit heavy and moving at a crawl — not unusual for a weekend night. Figuring on bypassing the busy streets, Terrell looked for a shortcut. Unfortunately, he was still unfamiliar with the Miami streets, having been a resident of the city for only a few months, so when he made a turn onto Florida Avenue, he never suspected how wrong a turn it would turn out to be.

Where Florida Avenue intersects Douglas Road is a section of Coconut Grove that stands in great contrast to the glitter and glamor of the business district. This is the darker, seamier side of the Grove, a high-crime area infested with drug dealers, junkies, robbers, and other street hoods. The intersection of Florida Avenue and Douglas Road is not a very safe place to be in at 1:00 a.m.

As Allan Terrell eased his 1991 Mercury Capri to the stop sign and braked, a young man approached the car. The young stranger walked to the passenger side, where John Mcguire was sitting. The youth started talking to him, but Mcguire, a Canadian, was unaccustomed to what might be described as Miami "street talk," so he couldn't understand what the young man was saying.

Then the stranger walked around to the driver's side

and started talking to Terrell. A brief conversation between the youth and Terrell followed, but Mcguire still couldn't grasp what was being said. Later, he recalled that the exchange was not argumentative, although what was said seemed unintelligible to him.

Within seconds, two other men walked up to Terrell's side of the car and the talking continued. Mcguire managed to understand only what Terrell said to the three men, which sounded like, "It's not for me," or, "It's not me." Those were the only intelligible words Mcguire gleaned from the entire exchange, which lasted just under two minutes.

Feeling uneasy and suspecting that something wasn't right, Mcguire suggested to Terrell that it would be better if they left the area. A moment after Mcguire urged Terrell to leave, a gunshot rang out. Terrell, suddenly dazed and in pain, turned to Mcguire, gasping, "I've been shot!" Reacting quickly, Mcguire pushed on Terrell's right leg, forcing his foot down on the accelerator. The car lurched away, skidding as the assailants ran off. Desperately trying to control the rapidly accelerating vehicle, Mcguire reached over and grabbed the steering wheel. The car jumped onto the sidewalk before Mcguire was able to gain control and turn it south on Douglas Road.

Several blocks later, Mcguire turned the careening car east on the South Dixie Highway (U.S. 1). He struggled to pull Terrell's foot off the accelerator, but by now Terrell had lost consciousness and gone limp, his foot still on the gas pedal. Mcguire now faced the double task of trying to control the speeding car and trying to lift Terrell's foot off the accelerator. Mcguire switched gears into park position, but the car continued moving, partially out of control. It coasted and finally slowed when Mcguire succeeded in lifting Terrell's foot off the gas pedal. He also yanked the emergency brake lever, which was located in the center console, in a last-ditch effort to stop the car. After traveling a few hundred more feet, the car stopped with an abrupt jerk as the gearshift finally caught hold in the park position.

Aware that Terrell was seriously wounded, Mcguire jumped from the Capri and flagged down a passing car. He frantically begged the two young men inside that car to call the police and the rescue squad. As it turned out, these two men had also heard the shots and seen the car driving erratically down the street. They drove to a pay phone and called 911.

Not knowing for sure if the two men were actually going to call for help, Mcguire himself ran to a nearby pay phone and called 911. Terrified and a stranger to this type of incident, Mcguire waited anxiously for help to arrive. South Dixie Highway is a heavily traveled road which joins the Florida Keys with the mainland. It's an eight-lane highway at the intersection where Mcguire was standing. With cars whizzing by at high speed, Mcguire waited nervously for help to arrive. Within minutes the wail of police and rescue sirens pierced the air, until they finally arrived at the site where Allan Terrell was slumped over in the front seat of his car, mortally wounded.

The paramedics raced from their emergency vehicle carrying an array of life-saving equipment. They checked Terrell for vital signs, but found none. They tried every life-saving technique they knew, but to no avail. Behind the wheel of his fancy new sports car, Allan David Terrell appeared to be merely asleep, with very little blood or other evidence of having been shot, but his life had been extinguished by a ruthless gunman's bullet.

The first Miami PD uniformed officers on the scene, having arrived shortly after the paramedics, tried to calm down John Mcguire. As they brought him over to their police car, the full effect of what he had just witnessed hit him hard. His friend had been shot to death only inches away from him just a few minutes earlier. Mcguire began shaking as the officers sat him down in their vehicle.

The officers then got to work — they secured the scene, questioned the two men flagged down by Mcguire, and radioed headquarters for a team of homicide detectives. The flares they set up on the road protected the apparent crime scene as well as the officers themselves from the cars that continued to speed by, northbound on U.S. Route 1.

Meanwhile, once the paramedics had informed the officers that the man in the Capri was dead, the wheels were set in motion for the homicide investigation that would follow. There were two homicide sleuths working the midnight shift — Sergeant Luis Albuerne and Detective Jorge Gil. They arrived at the scene within minutes of getting the call.

For some reason, during the past few weeks, the homicide midnight shift had been bombarded with an ample share of murders. No one knows why it happens, but at any given time, any one of the three homicide shifts can get a dozen murders, while the other two shifts get only a few. In an effort to spread out the numbers and give the midnight-shift sleuths a chance to catch up on their own recent cases, it was decided to call in the day shift early to handle this latest case.

I was home asleep when the phone rang at about 2:00 a.m. "Nelson, this is Albuerne," said the voice on the line. "We're holding a murder scene for you at Dixie Highway and Douglas Road. I called Spear [my partner] and he is en route, as well."

It was a rude awakening — but the kind that I had grown accustomed to over the last 10 years as a Miami homicide detective. With the usual complaints from my wife, I got up, took a quick shower, got dressed, and headed for the Coconut Grove murder scene. I arrived before my partner, Jon Spear, and met with Albuerne and Gil. They gave me a quick rundown, mostly based on John Mcguire's testimony. This scenario sounded like an armed robbery gone bad. Ralph Garcia, assigned to this case as the lead crime scene technician, had almost finished photographing and processing the car when I arrived. With little physical evidence available, Spear—who had now arrived—and I got to work.

I went over to the police car in which Mcguire was sitting and tried to console him. The terrified man couldn't understand why Terrell had been shot. Neither man had done anything to provoke the shooting. All they'd been trying to do was take a shortcut to avoid the heavy traffic. My interview of Mcguire provided no additional information.

With the scene photographed and processed exactly as it had been found, and with all the known witnesses interviewed, it was now time for the medical examiner to examine the body. At 3:24 a.m., Dr. Bruce Hyma arrived at the scene. With our help, Allan Terrell's corpse was removed from the car. The victim was wearing casual clothing—black jeans, a black T-shirt, and black boots.

We saw a small hole in the front upper portion of the T-shirt, which, upon removal of the shirt, corresponded with the entrance wound. The bullet had entered the victim's left upper chest, approximately two inches from the left nipple. There was no exit wound, but an apparently insignificant detail was found on the T-shirt. There was "stippling," a technical term for the burns caused by the escaping gases and still-burning powder that follow the lead portion of a bullet as it leaves the barrel of a gun.

The stippling indicated that Terrell's arm had been down when the lethal shot was fired. After the stippling was photographed, Terrell's shirt was removed and sent to the crime lab. At that time, we had no idea that those minute particles of powder which had burned Terrell's shirt and skin would be the single greatest factor to dispute the killer's version of events.

Once Dr. Hyma had completed his work—examining the body, checking for other injuries, taking his own set of photographs and documenting the body—he had the body put into the medical examiner's van and taken to the morgue. Detective Spear and I made sure that the crime scene technicians had completed their duties and that the witness, John Mcguire, was being transported to the homicide office. With everything at the scene completed, we drove to headquarters ourselves.

At the homicide office, we needed a little caffeine to get us going. Having had only a few hours of sleep before Sergeant Albuerne called us in, we'd been operating on pure adrenaline and training. Between the two of us, Spear and I have over 25 years of experience in homicide, and we've been called in dozens of times with only a couple of hours' sleep. After a few cups of coffee and a short strategy-planning session, we were ready to re-interview our only eyewitness to the murder.

When Spear and I walked into the interview room where John Mcguire was seated, we brought him a cup of coffee. Understandably, he was still visibly shaken. We talked to him for a while, just trying to get his nerves settled. After about 10 minutes, Mcguire had finished his coffee and was becoming more at ease.

Then Detective Spear and I began going over the tragic events of just several hours earlier. As gently as possible, we drew out every detail we could from Mcguire. We went over every aspect of the night — before, during, and after the shooting. Once Spear and I were convinced that we had established all the details, we brought in a tape recorder and went over everything again. The whole process took us about two hours. Afterwards, we had to carry out one of the most difficult duties involved in any death investigation, be it murder or natural death. The notification of the deceased's next-of-kin is always tough.

We learned that the car in which Terrell and Mcguire had been riding was not actually registered to Terrell himself. According to the registration, it belonged to Ben Wheeler, a friend of Terrell's whose address was an apartment building just a few blocks from our police station. Accompanied by John Mcguire, Detective Spear and I went to Wheeler's apartment. When we knocked on the door, no one answered. As it turned out, the keys we'd found in Terrell's possession included the key to this apartment. We used it to unlock the door and entered. Inside, we found Wheeler in a deep sleep. We woke him up gently, identified ourselves, and told him about Terrell's murder.

Wheeler could not believe that his close friend was dead. He went on to inform us that Terrell had no family in Florida. Terrell's kin, including two brothers in law enforcement, lived in Michigan. Wheeler agreed to make the calls to inform Terrell's family of the slaying.

Grief-stricken and still disbelieving, Wheeler wanted to hear as much as possible about his friend's death. In asking us for details, he also wanted to know the name of the killer. That, of course, was something we couldn't tell him yet.

Spear, Mcguire and I returned to the stationhouse, where Mcguire was then picked up by his relatives from Fort Lauderdale.

Then Detective Spear and I went back to the Grove and canvassed the area of the shooting. By now the sun had risen, and the streets were beginning to crawl with people. We handed out our own business cards and dozens of "Crimestoppers" cards. We hoped that the offer of a $1,000 reward would stir things up and bring forward the information we urgently needed to find the killer. We failed to turn up anything useful during that canvass.

Back at the homicide office, we ran dozens of computer checks on other robberies, arrests, and incidents in the area where the Terrell murder had taken place. Still no answers. There had many other similar cases in the area of Florida Avenue and Douglas Road. We had many possible suspects, but no firm leads. Once we felt that we were out of answers, we called it a day.

For the next several days, Detective Spear and I went back into the Grove area and questioned person after person, hoping to catch a break. Nothing cropped up for the next couple of weeks.

I was in Philadelphia on another unrelated murder case when the phone call came in. Detective Spear was in the homicide office when it came. Crimestoppers called with some information that they had received from an anonymous caller. That caller had identified the killer as a black male named "Terrance" or "George." The caller gave an address for the suspect as well as a physical description.

Spear went right to work. After running a few computer checks, he came up with a photo of the person he thought the anonymous caller was referring to.

Detective Spear called my hotel room in Philly while I was out and left a message for me to call him. When I called him back, Spear gave me the good news. I couldn't wait to get back to Miami to pick up the Terrell case.

A couple of days later, when I got back, Spear gave me all the information he had gathered, including a photographic lineup that included the person described by the anonymous caller. The first thing I did was to submit the suspect's fingerprints to the latent fingerprint detail for comparison with the latent prints lifted from Allan Terrell's car.

Latent fingerprint technician Guillermo Martin later told me that the suspect's prints didn't match. That information didn't faze me, since it was possible that the perp had never touched the car. I called John Mcguire, who was now back in Canada, and verified that he would be available to view the photographs. He believed strongly that he would be able to identify the killer if he saw a photo.

The Crimestoppers information was reinforced by a report that Patrol Officer J. Soccorro sent me about some "street talk" he had gotten through the grapevine while working the streets of Coconut Grove. That information indicated that the perp who killed Terrell had also been responsible for another unrelated armed robbery just a few days earlier. I researched the other case and found out that an arrest had been made, but the person arrested was not the perp who killed Terrell. Attached to Officer Soccorro's report was a photograph of a black male whose name was completely different from the one provided to Crimestoppers by the anonymous caller.

When I looked at both photographs—the one obtained by Detective Spear and the one provided by Officer Soccorro—they looked as though they were of two different people. One subject had short hair, the other had long dreadlocks. I sat and stared at both photos, feeling somewhat frustrated. Then I began to notice distinct similarities between the facial features of the subjects. The harder I looked, the more I felt that both photos were of the same person, even though the facial hair and hairstyle were quite different. To make sure, I took the photos to other investigators and asked them to compare the two faces. Everyone else felt the same way. They thought both pictures were of the same person.

I obtained photographs of two other suspects involved in the previously unrelated robberies and met with Assistant State Attorney Jackie Scola. When I ran the case by her, she advised me that it was appropriate for me to mail the three photographic lineups to Canada and have the authorities up there show the lineups to John Mcguire.

I called the Montreal authorities and spoke to Investigator Jacques Paquim. I explained the entire case to him, adding my request to have him show the lineups to Mcguire. Investigator Paquim was more than willing to help. I sent the photos via certified mail.

Since the photo lineups would take several days to get to Montreal, I continued working the case from my end. I went to the Metro-Dade Police Department's record section and did some research on the best suspect we had. I made copies of his previous arrest history, wrote down the names of his family members, and checked out every aspect of his past life. One interesting fact in the file was that one of the suspect's listed family members was Taryn Lagrome. Then, in a precious police report, I learned that another relative had been the victim of a burglary. I spoke to the burglary detectives who had handled that prior case. Both addresses were the same — the one in the Crimestoppers report, and the one on the prior burglary report.

On Thursday, December 19, 1991, I went to that address and pretended to be re-investigating that prior burglary. I spoke to a young woman who told me that she was the girlfriend of one of the other relatives of

Taryn Lagrome. When I asked where Taryn Lagrome was, she said that he was in school. I had checked the school for the past several days and learned that young Lagrome had missed class every day since the Terrell murder.

After leaving the apartment, I went back to the school and checked with the resource police officer assigned there. I explained to the officer what help I needed and gave him my business card and beeper number. I asked him to call me if and when Lagrome returned to school. The youth apparently never returned, since the officer never called me.

At this point, Taryn Lagrome was beginning to look better and better as a suspect than our original suspect. Lagrome's age, height, facial description — and the fact that the pronunciation of Taryn and Terrance was almost the same — supported my feeling.

Delving deeper, I located one of the offenders in a previous robbery committed in the area of the Terrell murder. That perp was in custody, so I paid him a visit at the jail. He wanted help in facing the robbery charges and I wanted help in my murder investigation. He told me that he had been in contact with his family, from the jail, and learned that Terrance or Taryn was Allan Terrell's killer. The word on the street was that Taryn killed Terrell during a botched robbery attempt.

The case was now beginning to come together. Next, I tried to turn up a photograph of Taryn Lagrome, but I kept hitting dead ends. I researched the high school yearbooks and found that Lagrome had apparently missed the photo session, so he wasn't in the 1990 yearbook. I called the school and learned that they had already taken the photos for the 1991 yearbook, but it hadn't been printed yet. The school office personnel hand-searched the actual photos for a picture of Taryn Lagrome, but he had again apparently missed that year's photo-shoot day, too.

I ran a few more computer checks and came up with a Florida driver's license for Taryn Antwan Lagrome; without the middle name the computer won't make a match on a Florida driver's license. I ordered the driver's license photo. When I got it a few days later, I shipped it off to Montreal. Some days after that, I got a call from the Montreal cops. The news wasn't very good. Apparently, they had shown all the lineups to John Mcguire, but he had failed to identify anyone from the photographs.

There were two uniformed officers who assisted me immensely in this case. These officers, Robert Brown and Luis Vargas, work the Grove area exclusively and know most of the ins and outs there, as well as the bad guys. I gave them photographs of Taryn Lagrome and George, and asked their help.

It was another big break when Officers Brown and Vargas caught up with George driving a car in the Grove. Aware that he had a suspended driver's license and a couple of traffic-related bench warrants, they arrested him and advised me of it over the police radio. I asked them to bring him down to the homicide office.

Within 20 minutes, I was in an interview room at the homicide office interviewing George. I told him about the case I was investigating and he denied any knowledge of, or involvement in it. He maintained that he didn't know anything about it, or about any involvement by his relative, Taryn Lagrome.

After a few minutes, he asked to use the phone. I thought of a plan and agreed to let him make his call. I kept him in the interview room and set up a lawful recording device on the same line that George was using. George's first call was to his girlfriend. He told her to have Taryn stay away from the apartment because the cops were looking for him. The second call he made

145

was to an unknown male. This other male asked George where he was. George told him that he was at the police department and that the homicide detectives were questioning him about Taryn's involvement in the murder of a man in the Grove. The unknown male on the other end of the phone line asked George if Taryn had or had not killed the guy. George's answer would be a big key in the case. He said to the caller that Taryn had told him "he killed a cracker."

With the tape-recorded conversation in hand, I went back to the interview room and played it back to George. He was shocked and refused to continue talking about the case. He was subsequently escorted to the prisoner processing area and booked on the traffic-violation charges.

For several more weeks, Detective Spear and I tried to locate Taryn Lagrome, but without success. We sought out the woman who had been robbed several days before the murder by a trio we thought included Lagrome. She told us how three black males had walked up to her as she was sitting in her car. Two of them were armed and they took her car and her jewelry. When I showed her the photographic lineup, which included Lagrome's photo, she positively identified him as one of the two armed robbers.

We now had probable cause to arrest Taryn Lagrome for this other armed robbery — if and when we ever found him. Even though Lagrome was only 15 years old, he was doing a good job of eluding us. Then, on Saturday, January 11, 1992, Detective Spear and I decided that we would just walk up to the apartment where Taryn Lagrome lived and knock on the door. We might find him at home, or maybe we could convince some of his relatives to turn him in. As we were pulling our unmarked car into the apartment building parking lot, I saw a young black male walking down the stairs.

Before we were able to park and get out, he reached the bottom of the steps. As we got closer, I recognized him. It was Taryn Lagrome.

"Hey, come here a minute," Detective Spear called to him. But when Lagrome saw us, he took off running. With his young legs and headstart, he outdistanced us, and we lost him. We quickly radioed for assistance, but even with other officers coming to the area, our attempt to find and apprehend Lagrome had failed. He'd gotten away—at least for now.

Nothing happened for the next few weeks—until Sunday, February 2, 1992. At 11:00 p.m., I got a call at home from Detective Ronald Ilhardt, who told me that Officer Robert Brown had found Taryn Lagrome in the Grove. Officer Brown knew that we had probable cause to arrest Lagrome for the previous unrelated robbery involving the young woman. Brown had been off-duty when he spotted Lagrome on the street. Since Brown didn't have a police radio available, he ran to a pay phone and called our complaint room to request that a uniformed officer come out to help him make the collar.

Taryn Lagrome continued walking, unaware that Officer Brown was keeping an eye on him. Brown went from one pay phone to another, updating the complaint room on where the perp was. Within a few minutes, other officers arrived and arrested Lagrome. After hearing from Detective Ilhardt, I got dressed and headed for the homicide office.

Since Taryn Lagrome was a juvenile, I had to follow certain legal procedures required by our department in the interviewing of juvenile suspects. First, I tried to call a family member of Lagrome's. She told me she was sleeping and since she had to work in the morning, she wouldn't come in to be with him. Next I tried to get a juvenile officer to sit in on the interview, but that plan fell through, too.

Finally, I decided to ask one of the female homicide detectives to help me out. At 12:19 a.m., Detective Eunice Cooper and I advised Taryn Lagrome of his Miranda rights and he agreed to speak to us. For the first 10 minutes, he denied any involvement in the Terrell shooting. Then I told him that I had a tape-recording of George in which he told someone over the telephone that Taryn had shot "a cracker in the Grove."

When Lagrome heard this, he looked shocked. He asked to hear the tape-recording and then sat in disbelief as he heard the words coming from the tiny speaker of the cassette recorder. Hearing George's voice was all that Lagrome needed to change his mind. Now he admitted being the shooter in the Terrell murder. Although his story didn't exactly fit with the way the shooting took place, it was an admission, albeit self-serving. Lagrome related that he was handed a gun by one of his other accomplices and was told to hold the gun on the driver—Terrell. As Lagrome was holding the gun, the driver grabbed the barrel and the gun went off.

That part we knew was impossible, contradicted by the stippling found on Terrell's arm and clothing. Had Terrell grabbed the gun, all the stippling would have been on the inside of his hand, none on the areas where we found it. Once we realized that Lagrome would stick to his self-serving confession, Detective Eunice Cooper and I took a taped statement from him. He told the same story, but at least he admitted that he had pulled the trigger.

After completing the necessary paperwork for his arrest, we had Taryn Lagrome charged and booked for the attempted robbery and murder of Allan Terrell.

Over the next few months the case was prepared for court. A.S.A. William "Bill" Howell was assigned to it and did an outstanding job with the case preparation, grand jury presentation, and all the other pretrial procedures. We knew who the other two perps were, but we lacked sufficient evidence to charge them with the robbery or murder. We settled for the shooter, Taryn Lagrome, who was the only one armed during the incident.

A.S.A. Howell and I thought that we should give witness John Mcguire one more shot at identifying the assailants. We put together three more lineups, using not still photographs, but color videotapes. In the past, our police department used to videotape all persons arrested on felony charges. The process was unfortunately discontinued several years ago. Those videotaped mug files had been a great asset to many criminal investigations.

Since Taryn Lagrome had never been videotaped, A.S.A. Howell had to get a court order to have Lagrome stand before the camera. Once the videotapes were completed, we were ready to show them to John Mcguire.

In July, A.S.A. Howell and I traveled to Montreal and showed the video lineup to Mcguire. Again, he was unable to identify Lagrome or either of the other two suspects. We weren't surprised; not only had he seen the three assailants for less than two minutes, but at the time, the lighting had been poor and the shock of the gunshot had terrified him.

The trial began on Wednesday, October 7, 1992, when I appeared to testify during a motion to suppress the only real evidence we had against Taryn Lagrome—his confession. Lagrome's defense attorney tried to convince Judge Michael Chavies that the police—specifically me—had acted improperly when we interviewed Lagrome and obtained his confession. After hearing hours of testimony, Judge Chavies ruled

149

that I had acted properly and had not violated the suspect's rights during the reading of Miranda.

The only evidence we had against Lagrome was his confession, and since it had been a self-serving statement, the state attorney's office offered Lagrome and his attorney a plea offer. Lagrome was facing the possibility of being sentenced to the ultimate penalty — death by electrocution — if he was found guilty of first-degree murder. Lagrome's attorney got him to agree to plead guilty to second-degree murder and accept a 30-year sentence, thereby sparing Lagrome the possibility of the electric chair. A.S.A. Howell had been faced with the possibility of the jury believing the only evidence we had, that being Lagrome's self-serving confession. The state, Terrell's family and I agreed that the 30-year sentence was an appropriate one. On October 8, 1992, Taryn Lagrome accepted the plea offer of second-degree murder and 30 years.

The book was finally closed on this difficult and time-consuming murder probe. The next 30 years behind bars will keep Taryn Lagrome from hurting anyone else. But that is still no comfort to Allan Terrell's family, who will never get their loved one back.

EDITOR'S NOTE:
John Mcguire, Ben Wheeler and George are not the real names of the persons so named in the foregoing story. Fictitious names have been used because there is no reason for public interest in the identities of these persons.

"BLONDE WAS BATHED IN BLOOD AT ZUMA BEACH!"

by Bruce Gibney

Pretty, Paris-born Jacqueline Kirkham, 43, had mixed feelings about Los Angeles. She loved the near-perfect weather, the beautiful beaches, the international flavor. The excitement of the place made bearable the endless traffic jams, poisonous air, and fast-food mentality of America's second largest city.

But the one thing that horrified Jacqueline and other expatriates living the good life in the Big Orange was the city's explosive, violent crime rate. L.A. was the most violent place Jacqueline had ever lived in—worse than Paris, worse even than the Middle Eastern countries she had visited.

Jacqueline tried to protect herself by renting a home in Northridge, a middle-class neighborhood in the San Fernando Valley, and by shying away from such trendy but high-crime neighborhoods as West Hollywood and Venice.

For a while, anyway, it worked.

Tuesday, May 28, 1991, was warm and sunny. At noon, Jacqueline hopped in her red Nissan 240SX sports car and headed for the beach. Her favorite spot was Malibu. Just over the Santa Monica mountains, Malibu was home to celebrities and some of the best surf in Southern California. On this day, Jacqueline selected Zuma, a less crowded beach just north of glittery Malibu.

Jacqueline parked in the nearly empty lot, took a lengthy walk along the shoreline, and plopped down on the beach. For the next few hours, she lay undisturbed on the white sand, relaxing and reading a trashy novel.

At 4:00 p.m., Jacqueline closed her book and walked to the public rest room to change out of her swimsuit. It was just another day at the beach.

Shortly thereafter, an elderly couple was headed toward the parking lot. They had spent a good chuck of the afternoon at the beach, and despite their wide-brimmed hats, they were burned to a crisp. As they passed the rest rooms, a woman suddenly staggered out and fell in front of them. Her clothing was ripped, and she was covered with blood.

The lifeguard toward is a short distance from the rest rooms. A guard was watching surfers bopping in the water past the shore break when the frightened couple told him about the wounded woman. He ran to help.

The woman was curled up in a ball outside the rest room entrance. She was holding her side. Blood oozed from between her fingers.

She was still alive when paramedics arrived. They placed compresses against the wounds, and gently lifted her into the waiting ambulance.

Los Angeles County Sheriff's deputies arrived, followed by a supervisor. They stretched crime scene tape in front of the washroom and lined up witnesses, who now clogged the parking lot.

Downtown, at the Hall of Justice, Sheriff's Detective William Newman was bulldozing through paperwork when the call about the Zuma Beach stabbing came through.

It was rush hour, and the freeways were jammed. Newman said to hell with it and took the sheriff department's helicopter. Detectives joined Newman from the Lennox substation.

The rest room facility was cordoned off by yellow crime scene tape. Tan-shirted patrol officers protected the crime scene, mostly from news photographers and cameramen, who saw the stabbing as a "big story."

The elderly couple who had alerted the lifeguard had remained at the scene. "She just kind of spilled out the door and fell down," they told Detective Newman.

The bathroom was a cold, square cinder-block building with a cement floor and six stalls. One of the stall doors had been pushed in, breaking the wood around the hinge. A search by sleuths turned up a broken fingernail, an earring torn from the victim's earlobe, and pinpoint blood splatters on the wall opposite the stalls.

The victim was taken to a nearby hospital and admitted to the emergency room, suffering from stab wounds. She was admitted, police learned, without any identification.

The lifeguard who administered first-aid to the victim said he did not know her, and neither did anyone else who was clustered around the crime scene like gawkers at a Hollywood movie opening.

Detectives got a break when a woman handed them a scrap of paper she found pushed under her car's windshield wiper. Apparently, an anonymous witness had seen a car racing from the parking lot and had written down the license number.

A Department of Motor Vehicles check showed

the car's registrant was Jacqueline Kirkham, 43, of Northridge. Investigators went to the address on the registration slip, a condo in suburban Northridge. A man in his mid-40s, dark-haired and handsome, answered the door.

Did he know Jacqueline Kirkham? he was asked.

"Yes," he said crisply, with a strong Australian accent. "That's my girlfriend."

Jacqueline worked at Robinson's, an expensive, West Coast department store chain. She had taken the day off to go to the beach, something she did frequently.

"Why?" the man asked. "Is something wrong?"

Something was very, very wrong, the man was told.

Meanwhile, at the hospital, Jacqueline Kirkham had lapsed into a coma. Shortly before 10:00 p.m., she died without regaining consciousness. The official cause of death was massive blood loss due to stab wounds.

The shocking daytime beach murder became a media sensation, a signature in blood about what Los Angeles inhabitants have known for years — that the city of dreams had become a river of blood.

"Jacqueline Kirkham's violent death was not terribly unusual for Los Angeles County," the *Albuquerque Journal* noted, one of several out-of-state newspapers to carry the story and take a stab at the Big Orange in the process. "In the land of lasting summer and beautiful people, more than eleven hundred people were murdered in 1991."

Jacqueline Kirkham became a symbol for everything that was wrong with L.A.

At Robinson's, where the victim worked, Jacqueline had been more than a name on the payroll. "She was so alive, so full of excitement, you could

154

just feel it," recalled one shaken employee at Robinson's. "She was a fashion plate who loved to wear high heels. My God, she was born to wear high heels."

Jacqueline's boyfriend was stunned and angry. The couple had met in 1987 at a Sherman Oaks, California, restaurant. "We were both foreigners in a foreign land," the Australian said about his French lover. "We were inseparable. We were best friends, really."

The Australian realtor and French saleswoman had clicked like a Swiss watch. On weekdays, they enjoyed their adopted city. On weekends, they traveled to cities like San Francisco or Las Vegas. "She liked to fly. It gave her the feeling she was leaving for somewhere," her boyfriend said. "She was always happy when we were going somewhere different."

No place made Jacqueline happier than the beach, her boyfriend told police. The ocean invigorated her, made her feel alive and that anything was possible.

And anything was possible at the beach—even death.

Initially, detectives had few leads. Massive media coverage changed that, however. Three women from Kansas, visiting a friend in North Hollywood, told detectives that they had been at Zuma Beach on Tuesday morning and saw two men hanging around the women's rest room. "They were creeps," one of the witnesses told detectives. "They were hanging around making lewd remarks. Real jerks."

One of the witnesses described them as Latinos, mid-to-late teens, with short haircuts and wearing baggy pants and white T-shirts. "They were really badly dressed. They looked like they slept on the beach."

Probers were told that three men matching the

same description were seen on the same Tuesday morning at the mini shopping mall across from Zuma Beach. A pizza shop manager told detectives that she saw the youths early that morning "shaking and shivering."

"They looked mighty hungry," the pizza manager said. "They told me they had not eaten in three days. I said, 'You have now,' and gave them pizza and root beer."

The strangers had wolfed down the food like hungry dogs. "They told me they were from Arizona," the manager told police. "They said they slept in the bathrooms at night and left in the morning before security came around. They said they were sick and tired of California and wanted to get the hell back home."

To beach people, it was a familiar story.

The manager met with a police artist, and sketches of the three teenagers were released to the media.

On June 5th, sleuths got a hit when New Mexico State Police contacted Los Angeles sheriff's detectives to report that they had recovered the victim's stolen Nissan 240SX.

A New Mexico state police officer had discovered the car abandoned off the highway near Pojoaque, a small town north of Santa Fe. The car, bearing California plates, had rolled over several times and hit a tree before coming to a stop.

Suspecting the vehicle was stolen, the officer ran a check on the license plate and discovered to his surprise not only that it was stolen, but that it was wanted in a homicide.

Pojoaque? Detective Newman had never heard of the place. And no one from New Mexico had surfaced in the investigation. Still, that's where the car was.

The Santa Fe County Sheriff's Office was handling the stolen car investigation. Newman faxed investigators sketches of the three men spotted at the shopping mall on the morning of the stabbing. That evening, the sketches were shown on the evening news.

The next morning a man called the Santa Fe County Sheriff's Office and told detectives, "I think I know who the driver of that stolen car is."

The man met with detectives later that day. He said the hot car driver was Tony Dominguez, 18. "I saw him driving the car around yesterday," the witness told police. "Tony doesn't have enough money to buy a taco, but here he was driving this hotshot car. I knew something wasn't right."

Stolen or not, the man decided to let things slide—until he learned that the mangled car had been linked to the murder of a Los Angeles woman. After all, joyriding was one thing, but murder was something else.

"Tony has been in trouble, but he is basically a good kid," the man said. "I find it real hard to believe he would kill a woman and take her car. But he had to get it some way, right?"

Dominguez was a wild kid, all right. On May 10th, burglars broke into the El Rancho Bar and stole $2,600 in cash and enough beer to keep themselves drunk for a week. Detective Bill Martinez, of the Santa Fe County Sheriff's Office, spearheaded the investigation and focused on three suspects: Guillermo Bustos, 16, Michael Loretto, 17, and Tony Dominguez, 18, all of Pojoaque.

Bustos and Loretto had extensive juvenile records, and all three were known troublemakers. None of them worked, and they were always scrounging around for beer money. Martinez learned that immediately after the burglary of the popular neighborhood bar, the trio flashed wallets stuffed with cash and went on a buying binge, gobbling up new CDs, car stereos, and clothes.

Martinez said he was ready to make an arrest when the troublesome trio disappeared. Now they were back — and in plenty of hot water.

Bustos, Loretto, and Dominguez were arrested in connection with the car theft. Mugshots were faxed to Los Angeles.

The manager of the pizzeria quickly identified the trio as the three youngsters she'd fed pizza and Cokes to on the Tuesday morning of the murder.

Detectives Newman and Crowley flew to New Mexico and met with Detective Martinez. That same day, they questioned the three youngsters about the slaying.

If Newman and Crowley harbored doubts about the killing, Guillermo Bustos cleared them up in a hurry. "We did it," the macho teen told Newman. "We killed her."

Bustos, Loretto, and Dominguez grew up in Pojoaque, an isolated Indian reservation outside Santa Fe. Dominguez had dropped out of high school, and Bustos and Loretto were just about to. They spent most of their time playing basketball in front of Bustos' trailer.

The kids had reputations as "bad hombres." Classic outsiders, they wore heavy-metal T-shirts, got drunk on beer, and fought often.

One thing they didn't have, though, was cash. So on May 4th, Bustos said, they broke into the El Rancho Bar and cleaned out the safe.

With full wallets, they headed for California. "Tony had a [relative] who lived near Los Angeles," Bustos said. "We thought we would go live with him until this burglary thing cooled down."

The El Rancho Bar burglary had netted them $2,600. But they blew most of it on marijuana, clothes, and compact discs, and had barely enough left to buy one-way bus tickets to Los Angeles. But they decided to go anyway. Once in Los Angeles, they figured they could get jobs, or maybe pull another burglary.

They arrived in Los Angeles on May 26th. Dominguez tried to call his relative only to learn that he had left for Germany and would not be back until the end of the summer.

"That really screwed us," Bustos said. "We only had a dollar ten apiece after paying for the bus tickets. We didn't know where to go or what to do."

The trio considered staying in downtown Los Angeles. But a drifter at the bus station told them the downtown area was too violent and suggested they go to Santa Monica.

With the last of their cash—$1.10 each—they took a bus to Santa Monica. But once there they learned that Santa Monica wasn't safe either.

"We were flat broke," Bustos told Detective Newman.

A homeless person took pity on them and paid their bus fare as far as Zuma Beach. The little runaways from Pojoaque, New Mexico, had realized their dream—only to see it blow up in their faces.

"We were cold, broke, and hungry," Bustos admitted.

For the next three days they slept on the beach in public rest rooms at the shopping centers across from Zuma Beach. Bustos said they got in by picking the lock with the tip of the eight-inch knife he wore on his belt.

On the third day of their adventure, a woman saw

them at the shopping center and fed them pizza and soft drinks. By then, the trio was sick of California.

"We were hungry all the time," Bustos admitted. "We were sleeping in bathrooms and living on the beach in the day. No one would talk to us. They were too stuck up. It was like we didn't exist."

Taking the bus was out of the question—they were still flat broke. So they decided to steal a car. The teens said they focused on a van. Two of the teens hid in the bathroom, while the third one approached the driver and complained that he was sick. The idea was to lure the man into the bathroom, take his keys and money, and then split. But it didn't work out because the van driver got suspicious and took off.

The trio next considered targeting a teenage girl who worked in a yogurt shop at the Zuma Beach mall. The idea was to push the woman into her car when she got off work, leave her in the desert, then continue on to New Mexico. The problem was that the trio couldn't agree on how to do it.

Bustos said they were still arguing when an attractive blonde in a red Nissan sports car pulled into the parking lot.

The driver was Jacqueline Kirkham.

"We knew it was going to be her," Bustos said.

Bustos said he went to sleep on the beach while his cohort Loretto watched the woman. When she got up three hours later, Loretto woke up Bustos and they followed the woman into the rest room. With Bustos waiting outside, Loretto went into the bathroom, punched Kirkham in the face and grabbed her purse.

Kirkham surprised Loretto and fought back. Loretto then yelled for Bustos, who ran into the rest room.

"The two were really going at it," Bustos said.

160

"The woman was some wildcat. Micky told me to, 'Do her, do her.' "

Bustos said he pulled the knife from the sheath strapped to his belt and stabbed Kirkham in the right kidney. He pulled the knife out when she screamed, then stabbed her again. Kirkham fell to the floor and they grabbed her purse and fled in Kirkham's car.

In Barstow, 120 miles east of Los Angeles, the trio stopped to pawn Kirkham's jewelry found in the purse, but they were turned away because of their age.

"We found this guy," Bustos said. "He looked like a bum, so we asked him if he would pawn the stuff for us. He said, 'Sure.' "

They got $100 for the jewelry. Bustos gave the man $20 for his trouble and used the rest to buy food and gas.

Bustos said their next stop was Laughlin, Nevada, where he tossed the bloodied knife into the Colorado River. They continued on to New Mexico, where Bustos was left off at a relative's house. "I told them to get rid of the car once they got home," Bustos told Detective Newman. "But Dominguez called me two days later and said they had kept the car and he had wrecked it outside of town. He said it was cool and not to worry. But I told him no, we were dead."

Bustos, Loretto and Dominguez were held at the Santa Fe County Jail, charged with the murder of Jacqueline Kirkham.

Bustos and Loretto were extradited to Los Angeles on August 1st and charged with murder. The district attorney's office did not file charges against Tony Dominguez after investigators determined that Dominguez had not participated in the stabbing and had not known about it until they fled in Kirkham's car.

Bustos went to trial in October 1992, before

With the suspects behind bars, Detectives Newman and Crowley conducted a search for the stolen
jewelry and eight-inch knife used in the stabbing.

Using Bustos' instructions, the sleuths found the
pawnshop, east of downtown Barstow. They recovered the pawned rings, and using the pawn ticket,
they located the stranger the three teens had stopped.

He remembered the transaction. "Only twenty
bucks," he said remorsefully. He identified the three
suspects, and later, at the trial, he was flown round
trip to Los Angeles, put up in a hotel and given
spending money in return for his testimony.

Finding the murder weapon proved to be more difficult than recovering the jewelry. Bustos said he had
secured the bloody knife in the sheath and tossed it
into the Colorado River after they entered Laughlin,
Nevada. Using a map hand-drawn by Bustos, detectives located the spot, north of the Riverboat Ca-
sino. Nevada authorities ordered Hoover Dam partly
shut down, reducing the amount of water flowing on
the river. Vacationers waking up the next morning
were stunned to see muddy beach where the night
before there had been water.

Divers walking nine abreast searched the river
bottom—and found the knife. It was encased in the
leather sheath and lay in about one foot of water 50
feet from shore.

Guillermo Bustos and Michael Loretto appeared at
their preliminary hearing on February 3, 1992. After
two days of testimony, Judge Lawrence Mirea ruled
there was sufficient cause to believe that Bustos lay
in wait for his victim and killed her during the commission of a robbery and that he should stand trial
as an adult. Loretto was bound over for trial on similar charges.

162

Bustos went to trial in October 1992, before Judge David Perez, one and a half years after the murder. His court-appointed lawyer argued that Bustos did not want to murder Jacqueline Kirkham and that he wasn't "thinking about anything more than helping his friend, who was asking him to 'do it.' "

Deputy District Attorney Harvey Giss argued that Bustos had showed no hesitation in stabbing the victim in order to get her car, and he added that he found the defendant's actions appalling. "The idea that there's no sanctity in the privacy of the women's room," Giss said, shaking his head. "Nothing is sacred.

"This is a forty-three-year-old woman who was spending her single day off at the beach," he told the judge, at the non-jury trial. "You know what upset me? The coroner's photos of the stab wounds on her body. She couldn't even die with dignity."

D.A. Giss urged the judge to sentence Bustos to the most severe sentence, life in prison without the possibility of parole. California has the death sentence, but it does not apply to juveniles. Giss said both Bustos and Loretto were on probation for burglary at the time of the attack, that they stalked the victim for hours, attacked her when she was at her most vulnerable, stole her purse, car keys, and jewelry, and left her for dead.

Judge Perez found Guillermo Bustos guilty of first-degree murder. He also found him guilty of special allegations of murder while lying in wait and during the commission of a felony.

Bustos, who had been in jail for the past 18 months, showed little emotion. At his sentencing, he stood ramrod straight and told the judge, "I want leniency, judge, but I am ready to accept whatever punishment comes my way. I am willing to pay for what I did."

Judge Perez sentenced Bustos to life in prison without the possibility of parole. "You are a young man with a lot of potential," the judge told Bustos before sentencing. "But I could not find any way to balance the mitigating circumstance of your young age with the violent nature of the attack on the victim."

Michael Loretto, now 18, who set the murder in motion but did not actually participate in the stabbing, was sentenced to 25 years to life in state prison. By law, he must serve at least 15 years before he becomes eligible for parole.

The youths are currently serving their sentences in the California prison system.

EDITOR'S NOTE:
Tony Dominguez is not the real name of the person so named in the foregoing story. A fictitious name has been used because there is no reason for public interest in the identity of this person.

"RAMPAGE OF THE TEENAGE BONNIE & CLYDE"

by Charles W. Sasser

Understandably, relatives and colleagues of Timothy McClellan of Churubasco, Indiana, near Fort Wayne, assumed something dreadful had befallen the 38-year-old assistant store manager when he failed to show up for work on Saturday, September 29, 1990.

"Tim is always punctual, always on time," complainants advised authorities in Allen County, Indiana. "Something has happened to him. He just wouldn't leave without a word to anyone."

Police issued a routine missing person's report on the man described as uniformly average — average brown hair, average medium height, average weight. According to reports, McClellan was last seen at his store on Friday. He left in his late-model, silver-gray Ford Probe.

"I assumed he was going home," McClellan's employer informed police.

McClellan's bed had apparently not been used. The door to his residence remained locked. Neighbors did not recall having seen him during the past day or so. Apparently, the middle-aged man and his vehicle simply disappeared somewhere between store and home, leaving no clue as to where.

"We can't automatically assume he's met with a bad end at this point," explained an Allen County deputy. "It is not unusual for people to get fed up suddenly with their lives and take off. It happens thousands of times every year to people who have no spouses and no real roots. They just chuck everything and point their noses toward greener pastures."

"Not Tim," relatives insisted. "Not Tim."

The search for the missing Timothy McClellan occupied the last two days of September and used up a big chunk of October's first week. Nothing developed. McClellan had vanished as surely as a dust devil in an Indiana cornfield.

In the meantime, however, events that were unfolding 600 miles southwest of Fort Wayne would hurl Indiana and Oklahoma into one of the most disturbing investigations since Bonnie and Clyde cut their bloody swatch across the nation earlier in the century.

Near noon on Thursday, October 4th, Sheriff Therl Whittle in Miami, Oklahoma, the government seat of Ottawa County in the extreme northeastern corner of the state, received a phone call from Caddo County Undersheriff Walt Brown. Caddo County lay another 300 miles toward Texas in southwestern Oklahoma.

"Have you had any reports of a robbery-homicide in your jurisdiction within the past week or two?" Brown wanted to know.

Ottawa County had remained relatively quiet for almost a month, Whittle responded. There were the usual things — burglaries, cattle thefts, larcenies. But no murders.

"We have word there's supposed to be two bodies

somewhere in Oklahoma, somewhere around Miami," Brown continued. "People named Granger, something like that."

Whittle said he was in the dark about any bodies.

Shortly after he hung up, the sheriff overheard agents of the OSBI (Oklahoma State Bureau of Investigation) discussing murder over the multi-band police radio. The agents were prowling about in the Narcissa and Fairland communities a few miles south of Miami, searching for a family with an unusually spelled name beginning with the letter "G." Sheriff's Lieutenant David McCracken also overheard the transmission. He contacted the sheriff.

"The letter 'G,' the name Granger . . ." he mused. "That could be the Greningers. They live over there."

The Greningers' nephew was an Oklahoma Highway Patrol trooper stationed on the Pryor beat.

Less than an hour later, Sheriff Whittle and Lieutenant McCracken met OSBI Senior Agent Cary Thurman at a farm off the Will Rogers Turnpike between the tiny settlements of Fairland and Narcissa. The large, older-styled farmhouse faced a county road near State Highway 125. The moment detectives stepped from their cars onto the wide lawn, they knew they had found the right place. The stench of putrefying flesh hung in the air. The sleuths gagged, covering their mouths and noses.

OSBI agents and sheriff's deputies advanced into the house, noting as they went that the porch light was still shining, the front door was unlocked, and the TV in the living room was playing.

Beyond the living room, sprawled face down in the short hallway, lay the first badly decomposed body. Police identified it as that of Ira Greninger, 65, still fully clothed. His wife Vivian, 63, wearing only a nightgown, lay on her back in the bedroom at the foot of the bed.

Medical examiners and forensic experts who arrived to photograph, measure, fingerprint, and record the crime scene soon determined that the retired couple had been dead approximately one week, each shot to death by a .38-caliber weapon.

Ira Greninger had been shot twice, once in the back between his shoulder blades and a second time at the base of the skull. Dr. Ronald Distefano of the state medical examiner's office reported finding powder burns and lead tattooing on Ira Greninger's head, leading him to conclude that the bullet in the victim's brain had been fired at point-blank range.

"In other words," a detective prompted, "Mr. Greninger was executed?"

"Yes," came the reply. "He was executed."

Sheriff Therl Whittle, with nearly 30 years' experience in law enforcement, used available evidence to re-create the crime. The shining porch light, the unlocked front door, the still-playing TV, and the fact that Greninger was fully clothed, he said, suggested that the old man was watching television in the evening after dark when someone apparently came to the door. Something about the caller—a drawn gun perhaps—caused Ira to attempt to flee. The intruder shot him in the back, then walked over and finished the job with a second bullet to the brain.

The bullet into the old man's back had ripped its way completely through his body. Police found it spent on the carpet.

The assailant then charged to the bedroom, where the gunshots had awakened Vivian Greninger. A third shot presumably missed her, since police found the bullet, unbloodied, lodged in a mattress. The fourth shot, however, had struck Vivian in the forehead just above the right eye and felled her.

168

"She died shortly after being shot," Dr. Distefano decided.

The house did not seem to have been ransacked, nor was anything obviously missing. Ira Greninger's wallet containing $22 remained in his pocket. Vivian Greninger's purse in the bedroom had $80 in it.

So if it was not robbery, what, then, was the motive for the murders? The Greningers simply had no known enemies, sleuths were told.

"He was a good person," said a friend of Ira's. "The best thing I can say about him is that he was a consistent, good person. He was kind of a do-right guy."

Detectives canvassing the surrounding countryside asked neighbors if they had noticed anything unusual at the Greninger farm during the past week. Only one, the nearest, recalled seeing anything. On both Sunday and Monday, the neighbor said, he saw a white male with dark hair down to his shoulders. The man drove up to the farm in a small car and "was sitting on the hood, and he was messing with our fence and looking at their [the Greningers'] mailbox."

"Was that all he was doing?" a sleuth asked.

"That's all I saw," the neighbor replied.

The neighbor added that later on Monday night, he saw Ira outside his house. That was three days before.

"He must have his dates mixed up or something," the medical examiner reportedly informed detectives. "Ira Greninger could not have still been alive Monday night. The Greningers were slain, I'd say, no later than Saturday."

That estimation coincided with verifiable facts.

"All the newspapers were in the Greningers' mailbox since Sunday and the mail had not been disturbed since Saturday," Sheriff Whittle noted.

Further information about the Greninger homicide kept sifting out of Anadarko, the county seat of Caddo County, where a young couple on their way to California had been detained by police. According to this information, sketchy in the beginning, the Greningers had probably met their end on Saturday night, September 29th.

That was the evening of the day police in distant Churubasco, Indiana, learned of Timothy McClellan's disappearance.

Gradually, as the afternoon of October 4th wore on, authorities penciled in the connections between the dead Greningers in Narcissa, the missing McClellan in Indiana, and the mystery couple in Caddo County.

Shortly after Sheriff Whittle in Miami received his telephone call from Undersheriff Walt Brown, Deputy Chief Joseph Squadrito of Indiana's Fort Wayne Police Department, reportedly received a similar call. Undersheriff Brown asked him if Indiana lawmen were investigating the murder of man named Timothy McClellan.

"Not a murder. A missing persons—unless you know something we don't know," came the response.

Undersheriff Brown did know something.

"At first," Chief Squadrito said, "they told us to look on the wrong side of Hamilton Road off Indiana Route Fourteen. That put us a mile from the scene, but then we got clarification that led us right to the spot."

The "spot" was an isolated cornfield about 40 feet off Hamilton Road near Churubasco. There, police discovered Timothy McClellan's badly decomposed remains lying face up with a .38-caliber bullet shot point-blank into the back of his skull. Medical ex-

170

aminers established his time of death as Thursday, September 27th or Friday, September 28th. That meant the body had lain there staring sightlessly into the autumn sky for at least six days.

Chief Squadrito said there were no signs of a struggle around the corpse. "From the condition of the corn around him, he was killed there. There would have been more of the field disturbed if his body had been dragged there."

Detective specialists photographed, collected, and processed evidence from the crime scene. Clues proved scant. Police canvassing the flat farmland for several miles in every direction failed to turn up any witnesses. No one had apparently seen McClellan's silver-gray Probe parked next to the cornfield where its owner was summarily executed. No one saw his slayer then escaping in the dead man's car.

While detectives in Churubasco and in Miami worked to build their respective homicide cases, Anadarko authorities continued their grilling of a 17-year-old girl and her 19-year-old boyfriend, both being held in the Caddo County Jail. The couple had languished there for four days while OSBI agents and sheriff's deputies delved into the teenagers' background.

According to detectives and subsequent press reports, Christopher Alan Carrion, 19, claimed to have been a cocaine pusher. He and Leigh Ann Zaepfel, 17, met in the spring of 1988 while both were incarcerated as incorrigibles at a juvenile home in Indiana. For the next three years, the couple's on-again, off-again courtship included a bizarre combination of spats, fights, and suicide attempts.

"All we ever did was argue," Carrion admitted. "It was a rocky relationship. We'd break up and get back together. Like that."

171

Carrion said he never actually beat Leigh Ann, although he did admit to striking her on occasion. He described one incident that occurred in a Louisville, Kentucky, motel room after the two juveniles ran away together. Leigh Ann was pregnant at the time.

Carrion said he got so mad that he strangled her until she passed out. Zaepfel was later picked up by police for being a runaway and her baby was given up for adoption.

Carrion attempted suicide several times in response to his girlfriend's having affairs with other men. Zaepfel's family remembered a time in March 1990 when Carrion telephoned saying he was about to kill himself. He called back six days later to report that he was in the hospital.

"I told Leigh Ann about it," one of Zaepfel's relatives would later testify. "It didn't seem to bother her. It was like common that he would do something like that."

Court transcripts further detailed how Leigh Ann's family met Christopher Carrion in August 1989, when he made a surprise visit to their home 140 miles from his own residence in Fort Wayne.

"He just wanted to come down and introduce himself," one of Leigh Ann's relatives would later testify. "He told us a little of his life. . . . He talked about hitting someone when they made a pass at Leigh Ann."

Carrion carried all his belongings in a duffel bag. He had no money and was sleeping in the streets. Leigh Ann was still away at the juvenile home. Zaepfel's family took Carrion to a mission, but he returned the next day. They bought him a one-way ticket back to Fort Wayne, but he came back a few weeks later.

"I think he's crazy," one of Leigh Ann's relatives

exclaimed. "I've seen him acting like he could be violent. We began to sleep with a gun because we were afraid of Chris Carrion."

Leigh Ann reportedly returned home from juvenile detention in the summer of 1990. She found a job and made plans to go to college. Carrion showed up again in September. Even a court restraining order could not prevent him from meeting his lover. On September 28, 1990, the young couple slipped off together like Romeo and Juliet.

Then began a strange odyssey that took the teenage boy and girl through Indiana and Missouri and into Oklahoma on their way to California.

On October 1st, in rural Caddo County, Oklahoma, 62-year-old Dolly Whiteside had gone to bed early, about 8:30 p.m., while her husband George stayed up to watch TV. Dolly heard a soft knocking at the door.

"I had to holler at George three times to answer the door," she would later remember.

A boy and a girl stood on Dolly's front porch. "They were two good-looking young people, clean-looking, and just as pretty as any you'd ever look at," Dolly Whiteside would later say.

Asking for directions, the teens followed George Whiteside into the house. Once inside, the girl whipped out a black snub-nosed revolver.

"This is a robbery!" they announced.

The girl gave the pistol to her companion who held the Whitesides at bay while she ransacked the house for cash.

"We're farm people," explained Dolly Whiteside later. "Some weeks we have cash, some weeks we pay for everything with checks. We didn't have any money here."

The teenagers escaped with a small green tin box

173

containing approximately 30 silver dollars.

Deputies responding to the robbery broadcast a BOLO for two young people—a white male of 17 or 18 wearing a black leather jacket, and a younger white female wearing cutoff jeans over pink leotards. The lawmen had no vehicle description. Officials throughout the county stationed themselves on all likely avenues of escape.

An hour after the robbery, police received their first tip when a young couple stopped at a convenience store in Binger and bought gas with five silver dollars. The clerk hadn't seen that many silver dollars together in years. People just did not spend silver dollars anymore. The clerk called the police, saying the couple was heading west in a small, sporty-looking two-door, like a Toyota or Nissan.

Deputies and Oklahoma Highway Patrol troopers sped toward Binger, converging along several different routes.

Off-duty Reserve Deputy Don Recker of Caddo County noted the alarm over the police radio he kept at home. Rural Oklahoma always had a shortage of lawmen; off-duty officers commonly responded to hot calls. Recker jumped into his car and sat down to wait and watch along State Highway 152, 17 miles west of Binger.

He didn't have long to wait. A small gray car zipped by, occupied by a male and female. Recker fell in behind it, followed it west a short distance until the suspects apparently grew suspicious and whipped a right onto Colony Road. Deputy Recker made a felony stop on the running car, flashing his emergency lights and pulling it over.

"Get out of the car, slowly, with your hands up," he ordered.

Christopher Alan Carrion and Leigh Ann Zaepfel

emerged from the silver-gray Ford Probe with their hands grabbing at the sky. Officers soon recovered a green tin box containing the remainder of the Whitesides' silver dollars. Underneath the driver's seat lay a fully loaded, blue-steel .38-caliber revolver.

"This gun has been recently fired," a detective noted shortly thereafter.

"No," Carrion allegedly replied. "No, it hasn't."

Zaepfel and Carrion were charged the next day in Caddo County District Court with armed robbery and held in lieu of $25,000 bond each. Although the young bandits unquestioningly accepted the charges, they nonetheless refused to discuss the crimes in which they may have been involved.

The standoff between the youngsters and the police continued silently from Sunday night until Thursday morning, October 4th. While the teen bandits nursed their silence, detectives successfully traced the Ford getaway car to Timothy McClellan in Indiana.

"How did you get the car? Where is McClellan?" police demanded of the jailed duo.

Chris Carrion reportedly gave a noncommittal shrug, while his girlfriend tittered and glanced away.

"They're hiding something," one detective surmised. "They're hiding a lot."

The silence finally broke on Thursday morning when Carrion promised authorities he would give them a statement about the car if they let him confer with Leigh Ann for 30 minutes. The teenagers quarreled during the visit. Police watched Leigh Ann jump up in a rage and leave the room when Carrion told her about the deal he made with detectives.

"They're going to burn you, you know," Carrion shot at her back.

Carrion kept his promise. Detectives were stunned

175

as the web of silence maintained by the Indiana bandits finally unraveled. Sergeant Joe King of Indiana's Allen County Sheriff's Office began calling the teens' bloody odyssey "a Bonnie-and-Clyde type of thing."

Late that afternoon, deputies in Ottawa County, Oklahoma, and in Allen County, Indiana, were busy retracing the Zaepfel and Carrion race across two states. In Anadarko, the teenage "Bonnie and Clyde" were busy giving details about it. OSBI Agent Ed Briggs videotaped the teenagers' confessions, later replaying them before a shocked jury. He recalled that Leigh Ann showed no emotion during her statements, other than "a few nervous giggles."

"The only reason we committed these [crimes]," Leigh Ann said during her taped interrogation, "is because we ran out of money. When we had money, we didn't do anything wrong."

That wasn't exactly true. The odyssey started with murder, Chris Carrion admitted. He described how he lured Timothy McClellan, a casual acquaintance, to a deserted side road near Churubasco where he shot the man in the back of the head, robbed the body of approximately $100, and stole the dead man's car.

"I knew he [Carrion] shot him . . . ," Zaepfel said on the tape, "because he told me. He asked if I loved him whatever he did."

Armed with the revolver Carrion had lifted from a relative's boyfriend, the young couple set out for Los Angeles in the stolen Ford. The first part of their trip through Indiana and Missouri proved uneventful. But then the teens ran out of money as they crossed the Oklahoma-Missouri border driving on the Will Rogers Turnpike.

They exited at Fairland, south of Miami. They

burglarized one farmhouse, but they found no money there. The next farm they came to was the Greningers'.

"I had the gun and I was planning on shooting them and taking the money," Zaepfel's unemotional voice droned from the tape.

Carrion said he waited in the car as getaway driver because Zaepfel did not know how to drive a stick shift. A light burned in the living room. Zaepfel went to the door, knocked, and requested permission to use the telephone. Moments later, Carrion heard a "muffled pop." He hurried into the house to find an old man lying face down in the hallway and a woman equally dead in the bedroom.

"I asked him [Greninger] for all his money and he went for my gun and I shot him," Zaepfel claimed. Her version of events failed to explain how, if this were true, both gunshots turned up in the man's back. But, she went on, "I know I shot him somewheres in the head. It happened so fast. I was shaking. . . . Then I shot his wife. I was scared—scared of getting caught."

The murderous lovers searched the Greningers' house quickly but superficially, finding only $19 in change. They then drove to nearby Miami, where they bought pizza before turning west again.

After spending the night of September 29th at a Tulsa motel, they drove on. The evening of September 30th found them lost in Caddo County in southwestern Oklahoma. The pair decided on another robbery after quarreling in a park.

"I guess we were planning on doing the same thing again, but both of us got scared and didn't want to," Zaepfel said.

George and Dolly Whiteside subsequently survived their encounter with the rampaging teens 300 miles

177

away.

"It sounds like the Lord was with us," sighed Dolly Whiteside after learning of the teens' arrest and their two-state murder spree.

Three months later, after having been charged jointly with Leigh Ann Zaepfel of two counts of first-degree murder in Oklahoma and an additional charge of murder in Indiana, Chris Carrion took the witness stand and testified against his former lover.

"Believe it or not," he quipped, "I don't condone the death penalty for anyone."

His testimony resulted in Leigh Ann Zaepfel's conviction on December 13, 1991, for murdering the Narcissa farm couple. In arguing for leniency in her sentencing, Zaepfel's attorney called the convicted murderess "an obviously troubled young girl. She was immature and in and out of institutions for behavior problems." Instead of the death penalty, she received two consecutive life terms.

On Tuesday, January 29, 1992, Christopher Alan Carrion pleaded guilty to the murders of Ira and Vivian Greninger. "It was just something that happened," argued his attorney. "He's just a young boy who got started out in life wrong." Carrion also received two consecutive life sentences and currently awaits trial in Indiana for the murder of Timothy McClellan.

"I did not know that I had looked into the face of the future," wrote a columnist in discussing teenage killers like Zaepfel and Carrion. "These youngsters gun down anyone who gets in their way. . . . They do not seem bothered by it at all. And that part is frightening as hell."

EDITOR'S NOTE:
George and Dolly Whiteside are not the real names

178

of the persons so named in the foregoing story. Fictitious names have been used because there is no reason for public interest in the identities of these persons.

"HOUSEWIFE WAS RAVAGED, THEN STRANGLED"

by Barbara Geehr

The Wednesday afternoon of October 23, 1991, was just melancholy enough to fit the reminiscent mood of Sergeant Jim Eckert of the Alachua County Sheriff's Office, in Gainesville, Florida. Only a few moments before, the sergeant had returned to headquarters from the courthouse where he attended the sentencing in a murder that had taken place a little more than two years before in nearby High Springs.

The case hadn't been sensational enough to attract the attention of the national news media, and the investigation that led to the killer had not been particularly action-packed. The killing was one of an ever-growing number of senseless crimes that take place nationwide every day and mean little to anyone except the people who knew and loved the victims.

Though Sergeant Eckert had not known the victim, a 27-year-old mother and homemaker, during her life, he had come to know her well in her death. As a result, he had come to hold her in the same high regard as did her family, friends, and neighbors.

A year after she graduated from Temple Christian

180

School in Jacksonville, Wendy Knowles sought a more meaningful life than she believed she could find in her native city. She moved to a small town in rural Alachua County where she met and married a local man and raised two children with him. Wendy sang in the choir of the local church, conducted services for children of parents attending Sunday worship and, only two days before her murder, had held a prayer meeting in her home for members of her church.

To Sergeant Eckert, who had been the lead investigator in the case, it was almost beyond belief that Wendy had died with the hands of a rapist clamped tightly around her throat.

At five o'clock on the Friday afternoon of September 29, 1989, a woman telephoned the Alachua County Sheriff's Office from a High Springs service station. She reported that she'd gone to a nearby mobile home to pick up her 15-month-old child, whom her friend, Wendy Knowles, was babysitting. To her horror, the woman had found Wendy dead.

In a later meeting with Sergeant Eckert and accompanying investigators outside the mobile home, the woman related that when she got there, she'd seen Wendy's own two children outside. "They're preschoolers and get dropped off every afternoon by a schoolbus," the woman explained. "I thought it odd that they were still wearing their school clothing because Wendy always made them change into other clothes before going outside to play.

"I asked them why they were playing in their school clothes, and they answered that the doors to the house were locked so they hadn't been able to get in. I didn't believe them until I tried the doors myself and found they really were locked. I called out for Wendy and got no answer.

181

"Then I noticed her car was gone, and I panicked. My first thought was that something had happened to my baby and Wendy had driven him to the hospital. Then I realized she would never have done that without calling me first. I knew I had to get into her mobile home somehow."

"So how did you do that?" Sergeant Eckert asked.

"I managed to pry a window open and push Wendy's little boy through," the woman answered. "He was able to open the front door from the inside. I went in and saw Wendy lying on the floor in the hallway. I didn't need to look twice to know she was dead. I found my baby safe, unharmed."

"What did you do then?"

"I quickly grabbed up all the children, piled them into my car and drove to the service station down the road to telephone the sheriff's office. The deputy who took my call asked me to return here to talk with investigators he would immediately dispatch to the scene. I dropped all the children at my home before coming back."

Sergeant Eckert wanted to know about Wendy's husband. "Where can he be reached?" he asked.

"He works at the big supermarket in Alachua."

The sergeant obtained the woman's address and telephone number before releasing her from the scene. He then telephoned Wendy's husband and asked him to come home. While awaiting the husband's arrival, Eckert and accompanying investigators began checking the crime scene for physical evidence. He also arranged for removal of Wendy Knowles' body to the medical examiner's office for autopsy.

Wendy's husband, upon arrival at his mobile home, was understandably shocked to learn his wife had been murdered and her car stolen. Under Sergeant Eckert's questioning, he gave information that Wendy usually kept her car keys in her purse—which she always kept on the kitchen counter near the back door, "in case she had to go somewhere in a hurry."

"The purse isn't there now," the sergeant commented. "It's likely the killer saw the purse, rummaged through it for the car keys and then just took the purse along with him for whatever money was in it. We'll get a BOLO out on the car right away. I need a description and a tag number."

Knowles described his wife's missing car as a 1980 four-door, dark-blue Pontiac Parisienne with whitewall tires and tag number EVJ47V. "We always kept a baby seat inside," he added sadly.

Asked by Eckert if he could think of anyone who would want to harm his wife, Knowles quickly answered, "Absolutely no one."

Investigators received the same response in questioning neighbors, friends, and other family members. Neighbors expressed the opinion that the killer had to be someone Wendy knew. "He couldn't very well be someone like a vagrant or a hitchhiker who just happened to wander into the neighborhood," they said. "The Knowleses' mobile home sits well back from the highway, and the whole front of it is hidden by trees. Not one of us observed any strangers walking around, and neither did we see anyone driving away in Wendy's Pontiac."

A former pastor at the Countryside Baptist Church said he had known both Wendy and her husband since they first met and started dating. "She's always been a solid person, and he is the same way. They've been devoted to their children. Several of the congregation members refer to Wendy as 'the perfect woman.' "

The pastor at the Community Evangelical Free

Church in Gainesville, where the couple regularly attended services and had become personal friends, said he was having a hard time dealing with the murder. "Wendy was an awfully sweet girl," he said. "She was always cheerful. She took a quiet delight in church activities; she had lots of friends. Outpourings of grief and support have been tremendous."

A check of the couple's respective family backgrounds gave no indication of anyone in either family having any enemies. Eckert and members of the investigating team had to conclude that both Wendy and her husband had come from fine families with strong Christian backgrounds. However, that did not help any of them in coming up with a motive for Wendy Knowles' murder or a clue to a person who may have wanted to kill her.

Their only hope of finding solutions to both problems seemed to lie in finding Wendy's 1980 Pontiac Parisienne. A BOLO had been put out on the vehicle earlier. They spent the night searching for it in neighboring areas.

The following morning—Saturday, September 30, 1989—crime scene technicians made a thorough search of the interior of the Knowleses' mobile home and the surrounding property for evidence, while investigators continued interviewing the couple's neighbors and friends and renewed their efforts to locate Wendy's missing Pontiac.

That same day, the medical examiner issued a preliminary report stating that the victim had been sexually assaulted and then strangled to death.

Meanwhile, funeral arrangements were being set for the following Tuesday, October 3rd, at 11:00 a.m. Preparations for a massive turnout got under way immediately. The pastor of the Countryside Baptist Church was invited to come to Gainesville to help conduct the service.

By sun down on September 30th, investigators had to admit that they were stumped. They had no suspect, no motive, and no clues. Little could they have foreseen at that point that a minor automobile accident on a highway hundreds of miles away would eventually lead to the apprehension of Wendy Knowles' murderer.

At precisely 8:52 that Saturday night, a vehicle occupied by two male teenagers struck another driven by a middle-aged man on an expressway outside Hampton, Virginia. The teenagers, instead of stopping to check on damage to the struck vehicle and possible injury to its driver, fled the scene. The driver of the struck vehicle raced after them but was unable to overtake them before they reached an exit, sped onto it and disappeared into the darkness. The man reported the incident to the authorities.

Meanwhile, the teenagers, trying to make a clean getaway, swung onto a side road and began traveling down it at a high rate of speed. Not knowing where they were or even if they were still being followed, they found themselves suddenly being flagged down at what they soon learned was the security gate outside the guard shack at the entrance to Langley Air Force Base. Base security officers wanted to know where the teenagers thought they were going.

"We seem to be lost," the young driver said. "We were traveling north on the expressway and pulled off to find a place to eat. We thought we might find a restaurant down the road."

"Well, you thought wrong," the security official said. "Let's see your license and registration."

The teenage driver was able to produce a license but not a registration.

"Maybe your friend has it," the officer suggested.

185

"No, he couldn't have it," the youth said. "And he's not my friend. In fact, he's someone I don't even know. He was hitchhiking, and I picked him up down the road a few hours ago."

"Well, I'll just have to detain both of you for a while until I run a check on the vehicle you're driving."

The Air Force Base security officer quickly learned there was a BOLO out on the 1980 four-door, dark-blue Pontiac Parisienne and that whoever was driving it was to be held for questioning by Alachua County, Florida, sheriff's investigators concerning the murder of Wendy Knowles.

The base security officer, having noted the address on the teenager's driver's license as High Springs, lost no time in contacting local police to pick up and hold the teenagers. He then notified the Alachua County Sheriff's Office that the 1980 Pontiac on which their investigators had issued a BOLO had been found and its two teenager occupants would be held at the Juvenile Detection Center in Newport News, Virginia.

Pending the arrival of Hampton police, Langley Air Force Base security officers first questioned the driver of the stolen Pontiac about the theft of the vehicle and, after that, about the murder of Wendy Knowles. The 17-year-old, now known to be Shawn David Jackson, told them he knew Wendy Knowles. She was a neighbor. He and his mother lived in a trailer about 100 yards away from the Knowleses' mobile home.

Jackson related that he'd gone to the Knowleses' mobile home the previous day to ask to use the telephone because the phone at his own home was out of order. He said he was upset about several things at the time, and after completing the phone call, he noticed Wendy's purse on the kitchen counter near the back door. He said he picked the purse up as he left. Once he was outside, he rummaged through it and found the keys to Wendy's Pontiac and some money. His finds somehow made him decide to "take off," the teen said.

Jackson reacted with surprise when asked what he knew about Wendy Knowles' murder. He said he did not know anything about it. "She was in the living room, playing with some little kid she was babysitting when I left," he said.

Under additional questioning, Jackson gave some answers which the base officers found incriminating. "The very fact that you were in the Knowles home on the day she was found murdered may incriminate you in the murder," one of the base security officers pointed out.

Asked what he did after leaving the Knowleses' mobile home, Jackson answered that he picked up his friend Wade Riley and "the two of us just headed north."

"Then Riley wasn't a hitchhiker you picked up along the highway, as you said earlier?" the officer asked rhetorically. "He was really your friend and was with you in the stolen Pontiac from the very start?"

"That's right," Jackson admitted.

Wade Riley, 18, verified that the account of events that Jackson had given base security officers was the same as the one Jackson had given him when Jackson came by and asked him to "hit the road" with him.

"Then you did know you were getting into a stolen vehicle when you hit the road with Jackson?"

Riley admitted he did. "But I don't know anything about what might or might not have happened before Shawn showed up at my house," he added. "All he said to me after telling me about the phone call and stealing Wendy's car was, 'Let's head north.' "

Hampton police officers picked up Shawn Jackson and Wade Riley at the security office at Langley Air Force Base and drove them to headquarters in Hampton, where the two repeated their previous statements almost verbatim. This time, however, Jackson signed a statement that police investigators believed implicated him in the Wendy Knowles murder. But they arrested him only on possession of a stolen car and charged Riley with helping to steal the vehicle. Following that, both youths were booked into the Juvenile Detention Center in Newport News, Virginia, to await extradition to Florida.

Sergeant Eckert, accompanied by two other Alachua County sheriff's investigators, drove to Newport News on Sunday, October 1st, and questioned both Shawn Jackson and Wade Riley the next day. Though they could not find a motive for either of the suspects in the murder of Wendy Knowles, they found some of Jackson's statements incriminating enough to charge him with first-degree murder, burglary of a dwelling with assault, sexual battery with the use of physical force, and grand theft auto. They also charged Wade Riley with auto theft.

The two were drive back to Gainesville on Tuesday and booked into the Alachua County Jail. At first appearance the following morning, they were ordered held without bond.

A check on 17-year-old Shawn David Jackson revealed that he had been arrested on burglary and criminal mischief charges and put on community control the previous year. He was still on community control when he was picked up for stealing Wendy Knowles' car. He had recently dropped out of Santa

Fe High School, giving as his reason his intention to attend night school. Coincidentally enough, a relative had reported him missing on the Friday evening after Wendy Knowles had been found murdered.

Wade Riley's police record showed he had been arrested on auto theft charges two years before. On the present auto-theft charge, he was placed in a community-control program under the supervision of the state attorney's office.

On Thursday, October 19, 1989, an Alachua County grand jury indicted Shawn David Jackson on all counts with which he had been charged: first-degree murder, burglary of a dwelling with assault, sexual battery with the use of physical force and grand theft auto. Despite Jackson being a minor, prosecutors said they would probably seek the death penalty. State Attorney Len Register explained that the law allowed prosecutors to seek the death penalty in this instance because Jackson's previous crimes had to be taken into consideration along with the present crimes on which he had been indicted.

Though a true bill had been returned at the indictment, a motive for the strangulation-murder of Wendy Knowles had yet to be established. Shawn Jackson's public defenders, deciding to pursue an insanity defense, asked the court for a psychiatric evaluation of the defendant. The court appointed a clinical psychologist to make the evaluation.

The psychologist made little headway with Jackson until the teen agreed to undergo hypnosis. Once he was induced into that state, however, he was able to recall a series of events that began with his going to the Knowles home to use the telephone to call a friend.

According to the psychologist's report, Jackson, for no reason he could remember, became very angry when he got no answer to the call to his friend. He got no answer in several more attempts, and with each no-answer, he became more and more angry. He finally got so angry that he wanted to kill someone. He saw a knife by the kitchen sink and thought about using it on Wendy, who happened to be sitting on the couch in the living room, "watching some little kid." The thought, however, was fleeting. He decided to go home.

As he walked into the living room to leave by the front door, Wendy smiled at him. He did not see the smile as friendly, but, rather, one that made him feel she was laughing at him. Something inside snapped. Before he knew what he was doing, Jackson found himself strangling her. It was unclear when he began to rape her.

The psychologist concluded that Shawn Jackson was "wracked with feelings that he was inadequate, that other people—especially females—were always ridiculing him or laughing at him." She described him as a loner who often resorted to fantasy to deal with his feelings. "He admitted he often played the fantasy game Dungeons and Dragons," she stated.

The psychologist, however, did not find the defendant a cold, calculating killer. "Rather," she reported, "he is a young man with emotional and psychological problems, who acted on impulse and misinterpretation. Though he was not legally insane when he committed this crime, he was suffering from an emotional disorder which caused him to step outside his personality and act on impulse. The rape was not committed out of sexual desire but, rather, was an act of anger and power."

Following additional sessions with Jackson, the psychologist related that the defendant often said he couldn't believe he was capable of killing someone with his own hands. "When he talked about this," she explained, "he would look at his hands as though they didn't belong to him, as though they had some kind of supernatural power. Shawn still has great difficulty associating this act with himself."

After two years of wrangling in the courts by prosecuting attorneys and public defenders, October 21, 1991, was finally set as the trial date for Shawn David Jackson, now 19, in the rape and strangulation-murder of High Springs homemaker Wendy Knowles.

In pretrial hearings, defense attorneys, contrary to expectations, presented no motions pertaining to the defendant's mental health. "We do not expect that to become an issue," they said. "There's a lot of mitigating evidence on the question of Shawn Jackson's mental health."

The public defenders did present a motion, however, to have the incriminating statements that Jackson had made to the security guards at Langley Air Force Base, to Hampton, Virginia, police officers, and to Alachua County sheriff's investigators thrown out as evidence at the trial. They argued that the statements had been coerced and that Jackson had not been read his rights before he made them.

Circuit Judge Stan Morris ruled that Jackson's statements had been made voluntarily and could be presented as evidence at trial.

Though that particular ruling would benefit the prosecution, lawyers in the state attorney's office began to have second thoughts about seeking the death penalty for Jackson. Several of those close to the case doubted a jury would recommend a death sentence for someone who looked "so young and unassuming."

In an effort to determine the strength of the death-penalty argument, the chief prosecutor on the case, together with the chief public defender, presented their evidence to Chief Circuit Judge Elzie S. Sanders for an opinion.

Judge Sanders advised, "Under the law, aggravating factors, such as the cruel nature of the crime and the defendant's prior criminal record, are weighed against mitigating factors, such as youth, mental health and prior record. I do not think a death sentence is warranted in this particular case."

Following the meeting with Judge Sanders, prosecutors entered into a plea bargain with Shawn David Jackson. They agreed to drop the burglary-with-an-assault and grand theft-auto charges and not to continue to seek the death penalty on the murder charge. In return, Jackson would plead guilty to the murder and rape of Wendy Knowles.

With first-degree murder carrying only two possible sentences in Florida—death in the electric chair or life in prison with no chance of parole for 25 years—that meant Jackson would have to serve a mandatory 25 years on the murder charge and, according to state sentencing guidelines, 10 to 17 years for the sexual battery charge. The judge would determine the two sentences would run consecutively or concurrently.

In the aftermath of the plea bargain, prosecuting attorneys stated that a great deal of thought and effort had been put into deciding what was the right thing to do for Shawn Jackson. Public defenders said, "Given the evidence in the case and the possibility of the death sentence, the plea bargain was the best choice Shawn had."

At a plea hearing on Monday, October 14, 1991, a teary-eyed Shawn Jackson, dressed in blue jail clothes and with his public defender at his side, answered Judge Stan Morris' questions in a quiet voice. He then pleaded guilty to the murder and rape of his former neighbor, Wendy Knowles. Judge Morris set sentencing for October 23rd.

At the sentencing, prosecutors argued that Judge Morris should go outside of the state guidelines and hand down a second life-in-prison sentence for the rape. They also asked that the second life sentence—or whatever sentence was given for the rape—run consecutively to the murder sentence. "That would assure Jackson [of] spending the rest of his life in prison," they said.

Jackson's public defenders argued that Jackson should be sentenced within the state guidelines on the rape and that the murder and rape sentences should run concurrently. "That would give Shawn the possibility of being released after twenty-five years," the public defenders calculated out loud.

Whereas members of both Wendy Knowles' and Jackson's families had declined comment after the plea hearing, they presented emotionally draining testimony at the sentencing. Wendy's husband, who is raising their two children, now aged seven and nine, said he had forgiven Jackson but wanted to see him sentenced to death. "I wish for justice to be done," he said, "but to be quite honest, I don't think it has. One of the things that has been most frustrating is the way the criminal justice system works in the state of Florida. We have the death penalty for heinous crimes, but by whose definition is a crime heinous?

"I wish my wife would have seen her children's report cards this year because she would have been very proud. For Wendy not to have been able to do that and for the children not to have had her here to do it is, to me, absolutely heinous."

A male relative of Wendy's said he could not forgive Shawn Jackson. "Wendy was five-foot-two and one hundred and three pounds," he said. "There was no way she could put up a defense against her attacker. I have mentally killed Shawn Jackson in every way possible. I do not feel sorry for him."

One of Jackson's relatives said, "The boy who committed the crime is gone. In his place now stands a young man who has much to give. He wants to get a college education during the time he is in prison, become a writer, and use his talents to help others."

Jackson, pale and shaken, cried openly as he listened to other family members and friends paint him as a human being capable of compassion and remorse. When he stood before Morris for his sentencing, he told the judge he had prepared a written statement but had now decided against reading it. "There's nothing I can say to make up for what I've done," he said. "I just want you to know I'm sorry. I never meant to hurt anyone. I would do anything to have Wendy's family forgive me, anything that I could."

Judge Morris sentenced Shawn Jackson to life in prison on the murder charge and to 15 years on the rape charge. Since he directed that the two sentences be served consecutively, Jackson will not be eligible for parole for at least 40 years. By that time, he will be 59 years old.

In bringing the sentencing hearing to a close, Judge Morris said, "Mr. Jackson, the bottom line is that there is a light at the end of your tunnel. From everything I have heard today, I believe you can be rehabilitated."

Sergeant Jim Eckert had left the sentencing with Judge Stan Morris' last words to 19-year-old Shawn David Jackson resounding in his ears. He heard them again now as he sat at his desk mentally trying, once again, to close the file on the Jackson/Knowles case. But he knew that he would probably never be able to close the door to the feelings that swept over him whenever he thought about it. The case had made no sense from beginning to end. There was neither rhyme nor reason for it to have happened at all. Had he read the story of it in a book or seen it on a movie screen, he would have considered it not worth the time spent in the reading or the viewing.

But the case was not a fictional one like Theodore Dreiser's *American Tragedy*. This was a real American tragedy. It was a slice of real life in a real small town and the killer and the victim were real people. And the saddest part of it all, Sergeant Eckert reminded himself, was that such tragedies were taking place across the country in such increasing numbers every day that people had to accept them as a regular part of the daily news.

EDITOR'S NOTE:
Wade Riley is not the real name of the person so named in the foregoing story. A fictitious name has been used because there is no reason for public interest in the identity of this person.

"MURDERING FOR SIX YEARS — AND WAS STILL A TEENAGER!"

by Michael Litchfield

Hull, England
April 27, 1977

It started with the sadistic murder of a six-year-old epileptic boy, Richard Ellerington, who was burned to death while he was lying helplessly in bed.

Six years and twenty-five murders later, the killer who had become known as the "Holocaust Man" was still at large, terrifying the people of northern Britain.

Like the Boston Strangler, the Yorkshire Ripper and the original Jack the Ripper, he was proving hard to catch because he was striking at random. There never seemed to be a connection between killer and victim. It was all mindless human destruction, with no apparent motive, other than a love of fire and a lust to burn up people. A deadly cocktail, indeed!

The beginning was June 23, 1973. It had been a warm, sunny day. Summer was settling in. A dry, mild night had been forecast. Little Richard Ellerington had attended the Jackson Memorial

School, for handicapped children, during the day, being taken and collected by his mother.

At 7:30 p.m., Richard's mother, aged 26, who was separated from her husband, put her only son to bed in their small, terraced house on Askew Avenue, Hull, a fishing port city in Yorkshire, Britain's largest county.

Half an hour later, the mother realized that she had run out of cigarettes. She called upstairs to her son, telling him that she was just popping out to the corner shop to buy some cigarettes and would be back "in 10 minutes — at the most."

When she turned the corner, on the way back, no more than eight or nine minutes later, smoke and flames were belching from her son's bedroom window.

She dashed to her house and started to race up the stairs, but was beaten back by flames that were already engulfing the staircase.

Stranded at the foot of the stairs, she could hear the pathetic wails of her physically handicapped son . . . "Mummy! Mummy! Help me! Save me! I'm burning!" Then a long, harrowing and withering scream . . . and he was dead.

The house burned so rapidly that it was reduced to a black shell by the time the Fire Brigade arrived. Richard was carried out in a black plastic bag: he had been reduced to cinders.

Over the next six years, the Holocaust Man's victims included two babies, an old woman of 82, a 72-year-old recluse and another epileptic. And in one fire alone, 11 elderly men were set afire in an old people's home.

In June, 1976, the fire raiser struck at a house in Hull where three children were asleep in one bedroom — a year-old baby named Andrew Edwards,

197

his five-year-old brother and their seven-year-old spastic sister. Babysitting downstairs was their 77-year-old grandmother.

It was a little after nine o'clock when the grandmother caught smoke coming from somewhere in the house. She went to investigate, following the scent which led her upstairs. When she opened the door of the children's bedroom, she was knocked backwards by the surge of flames.

The children were screaming and fighting to get out. The grandmother helped out the spastic girl, while the five-year-old boy made his own escape. But by the time the grandmother was able to get back to the bedroom, the baby was already dead.

Two hours later, despite a brave fight by firemen, the house had been completely gutted.

The grandmother was so distressed by the tragedy that she has spent the rest of her life in a mental hospital.

The breakthrough for the police eventually came after a fire on Selby Street in Hull, on December 19, 1979. Papers and rags had been stuffed through the mailbox of the Hastie family, soaked in paraffin, and then set alight. In that fire, three children — Charles, aged 15; Paul, 12, and Peter, 8 — all perished.

Since the very beginning, the investigation had been in the hands of Detective Superintendent Ronald Sagar, deputy head of Humberside Criminal Investigation Department, and for the first time he had a real clue, a piece of evidence that he believed would eventually lead him to The Holocaust Man.

In the fire at the Hastie house, not all the papers used to start the blaze had been destroyed. In a corner of one piece of paper was printed the words, William Booth House. This was the name of Hull's

Salvation Army hostel.

Sagar immediately went to the hostel and interviewed everyone, from the warden and his wife to the residents. As he was about to enter D15, the warden said, "It's no good going in there. That's Bruce Lee's room, but we haven't seen him for a couple of days. I think he's run out on us."

Detective Sagar became excited. More than ever he was now determined to enter that room. He had a feeling . . . a cop's instinct that the hounds were closing in on the fox.

Inside room D15 was a bed, a locker and a chair. It was all very spartan. Nothing more than the barest of essentials, but it provided a bed and a shelter for someone who otherwise would be sleeping rough.

Adorning the walls were color photographs of Bruce Lee, the Hollywood Kung Fu film star, Elvis Presley, and Jesus Christ, as portrayed by the actor Robert Powell.

Sagar looked puzzled. "Did you say this room was occupied by Bruce Lee?" he asked, screwing up his face, sensing that something was not quite right.

"That's what he calls himself," said the warden. "Bruce Lee he wants to be, so Bruce Lee he is as far as we're concerned."

Sagar snorted, then looked under the bed. That's when he found the empty can of paraffin . . .

An immediate investigation was launched into the background of the missing young man, believed to be aged about 19. Sagar suspected that Bruce Lee was a false name. But something else was worrying Sagar. If Lee was The Holocaust Man, and he really was only 19, that meant he first killed when a mere 13-year-old.

Could that possibly be? Could the most prolific and elusive killer in criminal history in the northeast be a mere kid? Sagar found it hard to believe . . . yet he could not ignore the evidence. It was there . . . he'd found it . . . it was inescapable.

As the picture of Bruce Lee began to unfold, though, more and more Sagar became convinced that this *was* The Holocaust Man.

Bruce Lee had been born Peter Dinsdale, the epileptic and slightly deformed son of a prostitute. Later in life, he changed his name by deed poll, making it official, to Bruce Lee, after the Kung Fu fighter who was one of his boyhood heroes.

He had never known his father. His mother had convictions for prostitution within weeks of her son's birth, and she speedily rejected the partly-paralyzed baby with the withered right arm.

Peter was taken into care and spent most of his childhood in a variety of Humberside council homes. Trial periods spent at home with his mother always ended in disaster. Always he was neglected and pushed aside while she entertained clients.

He was happiest when he was fostered to a woman whose efforts to help homeless children are legendary in Hull. After bringing up nine children of her own, she now fosters six boys at a time in her home on Beverly Road.

"Bruce was here for 16 months between the ages of 16 and 18," she told Sagar. "He was quiet, never brought anybody home and never raised anyone's suspicions that he'd ever done anything wrong. I've got a fairly recent photograph of him. Would you like it?"

Sagar couldn't believe his luck. Now he had not only a name and a background, but also a photograph, which immediately he had copied and circulated throughout the media.

Even after the newspapers carried front page pictures of Bruce Lee and television gave special time to Sagar to make an appeal, The Holocaust Man remained at large. Not one single person called the police to say that Lee had been seen. It was unnatural, uncanny.

"I even began to feel that I was hunting someone who was more than human," Sagar was to say later. "As if he was superhuman, or a ghost-like figure. I know it sounds crazy, but that's the way it gets to you in the end.

"I used to wander round the streets at night, fearing that he might strike again, just to torment me, because we were getting so close to him . . . and yet [he] still remained so far away.

"We had scrutinized every other area of crime to see if the arsonist could be linked with it, [but] without success. Then, without any firm reason, I wondered if our target was into the world of homosexuality."

In the next six weeks, 20 men who regularly frequented a public urinal in the city's downtown area for homosexual purposes were followed by the police. On June 6, 1980, the 40th anniversary of D-Day, Bruce Lee was spotted in the company of these men. Sagar was instantly informed of this over a walkie-talkie radio and he ordered that all the men should be rounded up.

"Bring 'em all in," he said. "No mistakes. I want the lot."

Lee made a run for it, but was busted ten minutes later in an amusement palace, which he tried to set afire by short-circuiting the wires leading to one of the machines.

Four sobering hours later, Sagar was convinced beyond all possible doubt that Bruce Lee was The Holocaust Man, and he charged him with the murder of the three Hastie children.

Lee, aged 20, replied, "I didn't mean it."

Two days later, Sagar visited Lee in jail. "Look," said Sagar, "I know all about your background. You have not just been dragged up, Bruce, you have been kicked from pillar to post since the day you were born."

Lee said nothing, but from that moment Sagar had become a sympathetic friend to whom Lee could talk. Some days later, Lee admitted starting a fire which injured two people. For the sake of keeping the conversation going, Sagar said, "You've killed before, haven't you?"

"I killed a baby once," Lee confessed. And with that, the floodgates opened, and all his crimes were blurted out.

Toward the end of his signed statement, he wrote: "Ever since I can remember it has been, 'Do this, Do that, Where are you going? Go to bed, I've got a man friend coming: I don't want him to know I've got a kid, especially a crippled one. Do This. Do That.' I just got sick.

"It's my mother's fault, all this. If she had given me a decent home in the beginning, there would not have been these fires. I know what I've been doing. I am telling you the truth.

"I'm The Holocaust Man, I've done well to become that famous, haven't I, considering my background? I've really got on well in life . . ."

At his trial at Leeds Crown Court on January 28, 1981, Mr. Gerald Coles, QC, the prosecuting counsel, said, "On one particularly gruesome occasion, Lee poured paraffin onto the clothing and body of a sleeping man and set fire to him.

"He would wander the streets of Hull with a bottle of paraffin under his coat, and he told the police after his capture, 'My fingers used to tingle when I was doing a fire.' "

The court heard that Lee had begun his obsession with fire by the time he was nine. It first resulted in death when he had just turned 13.

But he was able to get away with it for so long because fire, which Lee described as his "God and master," so often destroys its own evidence.

Lee remembered starting his first fire at the age of nine, which had no serious effect, at a Hull shopping precinct. "Ever since I could remember, I liked seeing bonfires," he told the police.

"Two of his crimes were especially merciless," one witness said. "David Brewer, 34, was a pigeon fancier who clipped Lee's ear when he found Bruce, then 13, interfering with the bird's loft. To avenge this 'insult,' Lee wrung the neck of every bird.

"Then, finding Brewer asleep, possibly from the effects of alcohol, he poured paraffin over him and set him on fire at 4 p.m. one autumn day. Brewer lived for seven awful days in a coma in a hospital before dying . . . never regaining consciousness sufficiently to give the police a statement or to name his assassin."

It was about this time, the court was told, that Lee became an active homosexual.

Charles Hastie came from a family of tearaways who lived on Selby Street in Hull. His father was in prison and he and his brothers were blamed by neighbors for mugging elderly people, demanding money from them with menaces and all kinds of vandalism.

It is not known whether Charles Hastie, 15, had a relationship with Lee, or was simply blackmailing him over his homosexuality. But Charles' financial demands became unbearable for Lee.

That's when Lee decided he would kill all the children of the Hastie family.

By the time Lee left his foster mother's care, he had killed 23 people in less than five years. Some died because of personal grudges; others because, unlike Lee, they were members of happy families. All died horribly, trapped by fire.

It was the development of an arsonist's expertise, mainly in laying paraffin trails, which enabled Lee to avoid detection for so long.

Time and again the police and Fire Brigade officers were misled as to the exact cause of the fires.

By the time Lee was arrested, 18,000 people had been interviewed. And in his chilling confession to the police, he revealed that he caused the catastrophic fire at the Wensley Lodge Old People's Home after going out with just matches and a bottle of paraffin under his coat.

"I stole a bicycle and off I went with my paraffin," he said. "I didn't really know where I was going. I was just out to do a big house, a really big house.

"When I found this place, I knew there were lots of people in there, and that excited me. I got that old tingle back in my hands and fingers. I knew I was going to have a good time.

"I'm only happy when I see houses burning and people roasting. The screams make me feel very powerful.

"It was fairly late at night when I did the job at the old people's home. I smashed a window and climbed in. I heard some old men talking, but they didn't know that I was in there with my paraffin and matches.

"It was a nasty fire, a really rotten fire I did, and I knew it was going to kill lots of people in there.

"As I made my getaway, I could hear the old men

204

screaming their heads off as they roasted. I didn't feel sorry. No one had ever felt sorry for me. Why should I feel sorry for other people? No one cares.

"All I bothered about was getting away from the place. As I got on the bicycle, I heard a man shouting: 'God help me!'"

That blaze killed 11 old men.

Of his next crime, Lee explained in his statement: "I was just wandering about. I didn't have anything planned. I called at a hardware store. I don't remember exactly where it was.

"You concentrate on your job, just the way I dedicate myself to mine. I saw this door and as quick as a flash poured paraffin into the doorway. I set it alight and fled.

"I didn't know who might be killed, but I knew if there was anybody in, the fire was going to be big enough to kill 20.

"Fire was in my head and I had to do one that morning. It was just hard luck on it being that house and people being in it."

In that fire at Brentwood Villas, Reynoldson Street in Hull on January 6, 1978, burned to death were Mrs. Christine Viola Dickson and her three children, Mark Christopher, aged 5, Steven Paul, 4, and Michael Ian, three months.

After another fire—on April 27, 1977 at Belgrave Terrace, Rosamond Street in Hull—Lee arrived at a friend's house, a fellow homosexual, where he asked, "I did another fire tonight. Have you heard anything on TV?"

When his friend replied, "No," Lee went on, "I haven't slept for nights. I've been dreaming of fires and people burning. I heard them screaming in my dreams because they couldn't get out."

In that fire, two children had perished—Mark Andrew Jordon, aged 7, and Deborah Pauline Hooper, 13.

At the outset of his trial, it took a full half an hour just to read out the charges. The indictment accused Lee of 26 murders and to each charge, when asked how he pleaded, he lowered his head and answered softly, "guilty."

One witness testified at the trial that Lee had made a big mistake at the home of the Hasties, by using too much paraffin.

Police collected spent matches and newspaper clues and some headed notepaper at the Hastie home, and this led them, in the end, to Lee.

Lee's confession ended up: "I've never had a real friend. I've kept myself to myself. Trust nobody, that's me. Do a fire by yourself, tell nobody, then only you know."

Just before sentencing him to life in Broadmoor—a prison for the criminally insane—the judge asked Lee if he wanted to tell the court why he had deliberately killed so many innocent people, mostly children, the elderly and the infirm.

Lee thought for a moment, rubbed his chin, then replied by quoting from the Bible, the book of St. Matthew, chapter six, verse 24. "No man can serve two masters," he said. "My master is fire. I had to give my life to fire. . ."

"FREAKED-OUT TEEN MURDERED, THEN RAPED A WOMAN OF 90!"

by Brian Malloy

Cabin fever, the psychological effect of being shut in by winter's foul weather, is little more than a joke in this modern age. At one time, though, cabin fever was an actual medical disorder. In the days of the pioneers, the long, cruel winters affected some people in bizarre ways. Whole families would sometimes go mad from the combination of poorly preserved food and interminable isolation.

Progress through the centuries has rendered this form of madness extinct. And yet, for all our modern convenience and medicines, occasionally a senseless, heinous crime reminds us of the days when winter was the season of madness.

Stockholm, Maine, is located in the far northern tip of the state. The town is remote from the ills that plague the cities. Three hundred fifty people call Stockholm their home. Many of the residents are descendants of the original settlers.

Crime is present in Stockholm, of course, just as it is wherever humans live. Yet in Stockholm, crime is self-regulated. During those rare times when a minor crime is committed, the people watch out for themselves without the aid of a police force.

This old-fashioned form of neighbor helping neighbor is usually concentrated on everyday problems. For instance, if someone's car breaks down on the side of the road or if someone's cat gets stuck up a tree, a friend might stop by to offer assistance.

So when 90-year-old Elvie Johnson became ill and house-bound, many of her neighbors took over the chores she was no longer able to do. Winter is hard on all residents of Stockholm, but it is the elderly who are in the greatest danger. A power outage or a furnace malfunction can be deadly. The residents kept a close eye on Elvie all through the winter of 1987 and 1988. By the time winter began to break in March, it appeared that Elvie would live to see another spring.

On the morning of Monday, March 14, 1988, a neighbor went to Elvie Johnson's house with her mail. It was a routine the neighbor had been following for three years. Upon entering the house, however, the neighbor saw a sight that was so unexpectedly grotesque, he dropped the mail and ran to a nearby house to call for help.

What the neighbor had seen was blood, a knife, and Elvie Johnson's lifeless body. The Maine State Police were called immediately.

Because of the town's remote location, however, a crowd of concerned friends and relatives were at the scene long before any troopers arrived. Unfortunately, the crime scene had not been secured, and by the time the first uniformed state trooper appeared, the body had been moved, out of respect for the victim, to a place near the sofa. The first officer on the scene was also informed that several blankets had been placed over the victim's body, as well.

The state trooper asked everyone to leave the house immediately. The well-meaning mourners had already tampered with the body's position, which was strictly taboo in a crime scene investigation. The trooper was well aware that their fingerprints and other tracks would only interfere with solving the murder. The house was roped off until detectives could arrive.

Detective Ronald Graves of the Maine State Police arrived soon after the uniformed officer. Graves began his investigation by removing the blanket from the body. His police training allowed him to view the grisly scene with a degree of detachment, but training can never completely eradicate emotions.

The kitchen knife protruding from the victim's stomach was the most disturbing sight, but Detective Graves became aware of other signs of murder. The detective observed that the victim's sweater and dress had been pulled up above her breasts. Her corset had been removed and lay on the floor beside her body. A bloody rag was stuffed into the victim's mouth. Her neck and shoulders were caked with dried blood, and the detective discovered a number of stab wounds to her throat.

Detective Graves then examined the area around the body. On the floor lay the crutch that Elvie Johnson needed to walk. And there were other signs of the victim's advanced age: a wig, a pair of eyeglasses, a hearing aid, some dentures, and a pair of slippers.

Once the detective had examined the body, he began searching for additional information in the house. Graves observed that the drawers of a desk in the dining room were pulled out. Graves also found the contents of Elvie Johnson's pocketbook scattered on the kitchen table. This indicated that the murder may have occurred during a robbery. By the side of the refrigerator, however, the detective came across a substantial bundle of cash. Without trying very hard, he had stumbled upon $1,100.

This discovery led Detective Graves to rule out robbery as a motive. Then again, even if the evidence suggested that the whole house had been burglarized, it would still hardly be a motive for such a ghastly murder.

After his preliminary search, Graves decided to leave the house to the lab technicians. The Maine State Police's mobile crime lab had been dispatched to the scene. The only problem was that the mobile unit was stationed in Augusta, which was at least a five-hour drive away. Detective Graves used the time lag to interview witnesses to determine if anyone had seen or heard anything suspicious.

The detective found some confusion among the witnesses. The person who had made the original discovery of the body was positive that he found the body sitting on the couch. This clashed with what other people told the sleuth. Every other witness stated that the victim was found lying on the dining-room floor near the hallway, and that she had been moved near the couch. Detective Graves concluded that shock was clouding the first witness' memory.

Aside from that discrepancy, the detective discovered that nothing unusual had been seen in the small town. A relative recalled seeing Elvie's living-room light on around 6:00 that Sunday evening. Another person said that Elvie was wearing the same clothes as the previous day. This information helped the sleuth determine that Elvie Johnson was probably killed sometime after six o'clock on Sunday night, but it still wasn't the kind of information that suggested a suspect, and that was what Graves desperately wanted.

More and more detectives and uniformed officers began to descend on the crime scene. After sharing his information with the new arrivals, Detective Graves decided that a comprehensive collection of fingerprints was needed. During the brief span of time since Graves began his work on the case, it became apparent to him that nearly everyone in Stockholm knew the victim and had stopped at her house at one time or another. The house was bound to be loaded with a confusing number of prints.

A house-by-house request for fingerprints got under way. The officers who were conducting the fingerprinting also took the opportunity to ask each person where they were on the evening of March 13th.

It was well into the evening of the 14th before the mobile crime lab arrived in Stockholm. No fingerprinting had been conducted in the victim's house up until that point. Detective Graves and the other law officers who were searching to find the killer were anxious to see what the lab technicians would discover.

The mobile crime lab was laden with a variety of sophisticated detection devices and chemicals. When the technicians heard that the house was probably overrun with misleading fingerprints, they decided to concentrate on whatever evidence the body had to offer.

When the equipment was set up, technicians fumed the body from head to toe with an iodine mist. The chemists and detectives waited as the mist settled over the body. The trace residue of a fingerprint was all they needed. The waiting proved fruitless, however, when nothing was uncovered by this technique. The iodine mist would have saved time, if successful, but now it looked as if the whole house would have to be dusted. Before any further tests could begin, though, the body had to be removed.

As the body was being bagged in preparation for transportation, Detective Graves discovered yet another example of how violently the victim had been attacked. The broken handle of a small paring knife, which the detective presumed had inflicted the wounds in the victim's throat, had been hidden from view under the body. The knife was bagged and marked for evidence and subsequent analysis.

Once the body was removed, the lab technicians went to the top of the stairs and sealed it with plastic. Then the entire downstairs area was fumed with cyanoacrylate, popularly known as "Super Glue." This particular chemical is used when a large area needs to be tested for fingerprints. Once the downstairs was completely fumed, the heat was turned up inside the house, activating the cyanoacrylate. When the air temperature became hot enough, the entire downstairs turned into a museum of latent fingerprints.

The lab technicians settled down to the task of lifting and cataloging the prints.

The body was transported to Augusta, where Dr.

Henry Ryan performed the autopsy. The doctor was experienced in murder investigations, and he knew that most clues are discovered only by following procedure. He began by examining the exterior of the body and recorded what he saw.

Dr. Ryan observed that the victim's face had fresh bruises. Further examination of the face revealed two stab wounds to the right temple. The medical examiner then counted a minimum of 12 stab wounds to the victim's throat. Two additional stab wounds to the chest were noted, as well as the stomach wound from which the kitchen knife had protruded. It also appeared that the vagina had been penetrated by some object, indicating that the victim may have been raped. Tests for the presence of semen would prove positive.

As the autopsy progressed, the examiner discovered a broken knife blade in the victim's throat. The blade matched the handle that had been found under the body. The stab wounds to the neck had been violent enough to nearly snap the spinal column, but apparently the knife had broken first. Dr. Ryan had evidence to suggest multiple causes of death. He let the evidence speak for itself and listed the cause of death as multiple stab wounds resulting in a loss of blood. The final report of the autopsy also confirmed that the victim had been raped.

The body was subjected to one last test before it left the medical examiner's office. Although the iodine test performed the previous night had produced a negative result, no one involved in the investigation believed that the body was completely clean of fingerprints. The iodine test would not have detected a fingerprint if it had been left on a blood surface. Ronald Kaufum, a chemist for the Maine State Police, was called in to determine if the killer had left any clues in the blood of his victim.

The chemical compound orthotolidine is so sensitive to the presence of blood, it can detect a single drop in 10 gallons of water. In this case, Kaufum hoped the chemical would reveal a transparent film of blood containing the killer's fingerprint.

Chemist Kaufum mixed up a batch of this compound and then sprayed a fine mist of it on the body. Blood was all over the body, of course, and the orthotolidine instantly turned it blue-green. Along with the already apparent areas of blood, multiple areas of undetected blood splotches began to show. On the inside of the victim's knees were two more previously undetected blood spots, and closer examination by the chemist led to the discovery of a clear fingerprint and palm print. There, in blue-green, was the evidence the police needed to nab the killer.

The elation of the discovery soon gave way to the drudgery of eliminating fingerprints. The task of compiling a database of fingerprints was not nearly so tedious as trying to make the correct match with the fingerprint found in blood. For two days, Detective John Otis, fingerprint expert for the Maine State Police, eliminated one set of prints after another. For two days, speculation and rumor ran through Stockholm as the residents waited for the killer to be apprehended. Doors which hadn't been locked for years were now suddenly bolted shut as the fear of the unknown killer spread.

As tedious as the task might have been, the police were getting closer to the killer with every print that was eliminated. Finally, on March 18th, Detective Otis made the critical match. The bloody fingerprint and palm print belonged to a 19-year-old neighbor of Elvie Johnson's, Robert Rossignol. The warrant to arrest Rossignol was ordered as soon as the match was made. In this particularly bizarre case, the arrest would have to take place at the local high school, for the suspect had not even graduated yet.

Detectives Graves and John Darryl Ouellette of the Maine State Police readied themselves for their interrogation of the suspect. The detectives looked for the story Rossignol gave police during a brief routine interview on the first day of the investigation when he wasn't yet a suspect. The experienced sleuths knew that nothing shakes up a suspect more than being confronted with his own lies. The detectives compiled a list of Rossignol's apparent lies. The biggest contradiction was Rossignol's statement that he hadn't seen the victim for at least three months. The detectives could use a statement like that. They planned to counter it with the question: Well, then, how did your fingerprints get on the inside of her knees?

There were other holes in Rossignol's story. The suspect had originally told the police that he had left his friend's house around 8:15 that Sunday night and went directly home. Based on the new evidence, however, a member of Rossignol's family admitted that Robert hadn't arrived home until approximately 9:25 p.m. The detectives wondered what excuse the suspect would have for that discrepancy.

When the teenager was finally brought into the

police station, he was read his rights. Rossignol declined to exercise his right to be represented by an attorney. The detectives turned on a videocamera to record the entire process and then settled down to business.

Rossignol was nervous, and the detectives turned up the heat by confronting him with the fingerprint evidence. Rossignol held to his original story, but not for long. After a mere 10 minutes of interrogation by the state police detectives, the teenager broke down and spilled his guts.

Rossignol confessed all the details of the murder. For a full 75 minutes, gory detail after gory detail poured out of the teenager killer-rapist's mouth. The detectives listened intently. They were after additional evidence that would link Rossignol to the crime. A motive would also have been nice, from the detectives' standpoint, but Rossignol said he had absolutely no idea why he had murdered and raped a 90-year-old woman. He explained to the police that he "just freaked."

The defendant did enhance the case against himself when he stated that he had stolen the victim's change purse. Rossignol admitted that he had removed eight dollars from the victim's purse, and then disposed of the handbag in a field while fleeing the crime scene.

After the interview, Rossignol got his first taste of jail while the detectives enlisted the help of Warden Frederick Jackson, who was given the task of finding the victim's change purse. The detectives informed the warden of Rossignol's directions. The game warden searched the area for about three minutes. The victim's change purse was exactly where Rossignol said it would be.

The investigation was wrapping up neatly, thanks to a bit of science and good police work. The detectives discovered a glitch when they reviewed the videotape of Rossignol's interrogation. Apparently, the camcorder had been placed too close to the ventilation system and background noises covered up virtually all of the conversation. This would not destroy the case against Rossignol. It was, however, an open door for the defense. The actual content of the tape could be "rewritten" by Rossignol's defense attorney.

When the case went to trial in March 1989, Assistant District Attorney Jeffrey Hjelm had every reason to believe that the flawed videotape would be exploited. To defuse any suspicion in the jury, the prosecutor called Detectives Graves and Ouellette to the stand. Although the videotape had partly failed to record the conversation, the detectives remembered Rossignol's words vividly. They would never forget the teen's disturbing statement, Graves said.

The jury listened as the prosecutor asked Detective Ouellette to reconstruct Rossignol's confession. The detective stated that Rossignol said he had gone to the victim's house to make a phone call.

"And what happened next?" the prosecutor asked.

"He indicated that the door was unlocked and that Mrs. Johnson had been watching TV," Ouellette replied. "She was standing there on a crutch and she seemed impatient. She seemed anxious to get back to her TV program."

"Then what happened according to the defendant?" Hjelm pressed.

"He said that Mrs. Johnson then turned to walk

back to the TV, and at that point, he grabbed her from behind."

"Then what did he say happened?"

"He decided to go to the kitchen and get a knife."

"Did he describe the knife that he got?" Hjelm asked.

"He described it as being a paring knife with a one to one-and-a-half-inch blade on it," Ouellette replied.

"What did he say happened next?"

"He said he returned to the living room and Mrs. Johnson was laying there on the floor, her eyes wide open. He didn't notice any movement except for her right leg. Her right leg was moving, twitching. He then went over and stabbed her in the throat."

"Did he say . . . how he was moving the knife around?" the prosecutor asked.

"He worked a knife around in her throat attempting to cut it off," Ouellette said. "He said he witnessed someone doing this to a cow, attempting to cut a cow's throat. He was attempting the same process. . . . After the first knife broke, he got a second knife . . ."

For several more minutes, the jury was subjected to Detective Ouellette's recollections of Rossignol's confession. The detective testified that after Rossignol stabbed the victim in the throat, the defendant admitted that he began to remove her clothing. It was at this point in the interview, according to the detective, that the question of motive was brought up.

"I asked him why—why he did this to Mrs. Johnson," Ouellette said. "He said he just freaked

218

out. When he was moving her clothes around, bringing her dress up [to stab her in the chest], when he was undoing her corset, he advised that he started getting an erection."

"Did you ask him further questions about any sexual contact he had with Mrs. Johnson?" Hjelm asked.

"Yes, I did," Ouellette testified. "I asked him if he placed his penis in her vagina. He initially indicated that he hadn't."

"He had not?" Hjelm pressed.

"He had not," Ouellette said. "When I questioned him — I believe Detective Graves questioned him about the presence of semen. Then he admitted that he had inserted his penis in her and that he ejaculated."

After Ouellette was through testifying, the prosecution then presented the jury with the hard physical evidence. There was really no doubt that the right man was being tried for the murder of Elvie Johnson. The bloody fingerprint and palm print proved that. The defendant's knowledge of the location of the victim's stolen purse strengthened the case all the more, as did the testimony of various people to the effect that Rossignol had disappeared for over an hour the night Elvie Johnson was murdered.

But for the flawed videotape, the defense didn't really seem to have a leg to stand on. The prosecution and the detectives waited with interest for Rossignol's rendition of his confession.

The defense called Robert Rossignol to the stand. The accused killer began his version of the story by claiming that the detectives had refused to grant him his constitutional right to an attorney, along with his right to make a phone call. This standard defense rhetoric was followed by Rossignol's statement that the police got him scared, and that he had only told the police what he thought they wanted to hear. In fact, according to Rossignol, they had the wrong man.

Rossignol testified that he did go to Elvie Johnson's house to make a phone call, but he maintained that she was already dead when he entered the house. He found her mutilated body, and he then touched her legs to see if she was still alive. Rossignol said he then fled the scene because he feared he would be arrested for the murder.

Rossignol's story failed to explain how he knew exactly where the victim's purse could be found. The prosecutor drove that point home to the jury during his closing arguments.

After a short deliberation, the jury returned to the courtroom with their verdict. They found Robert Rossignol guilty of the murder of Elvie Johnson.

At the sentencing hearing, Prosecutor Hjelm asked the court to impose a 90-year sentence on Rossignol. Judge Paul T. Pierson found the murder particularly disturbing, and while he did not fulfill the prosecutor's sentencing wish, the judge still ordered Rossignol to spend the next 75 years in prison. Rossignol is currently serving that term.

"DID THE TEEN TERROR TOAST THE SLAUGHTER OF THREE?"

by Elaine Baum

The air was crisp and cool in the gathering darkness. It was December 1st and Christmas would soon arrive. Tall pines in the woods rustled in the wind and there was a hint of snow in the air. Any day, any minute, there would be a strong snowfall blanketing the ground and trees.

How the kids loved the snow, he thought as he drove home from his law offices in the small rural town of Townsend, Massachusetts, a hamlet close to the New Hampshire border. The little ones, 5-year-old William and 7-year-old Abigail, often said it was their favorite time of year. They loved Thanksgiving and the festive family gathering they always had — and then there was Christmas, with the lights and the trees and most of all, the presents.

Christmas may have been meant for us all, he thought, but it was especially meant for the children. Nothing could match the excitement of little kids helping to trim the tree, then waking up on Christmas morning to open presents as they chattered and shrieked with delight.

Abigail had an extra bonus. Her birthday was next

week, and that meant an extra celebration, an extra set of presents. She was going to play hostess at a party, and she never seemed to stop talking about it.

He smiled as he drove up the wooded street. Many of the houses were already sparkling with Christmas lights. As he approached his house, he wondered why it was so dark. Normally, the lights shone at this hour because it was fully dark out. Maybe Priscilla Gustafson had gone out for some last-minute groceries she'd forgotten and taken the children with her. Still, she usually left some lights on.

He opened the front door and called out each of their names: "Priscilla . . . Abigail . . . William . . ." It didn't make sense, of course, because they couldn't be here in this darkened house.

In his bedroom, he saw the grisly, unbelievable sight—his 33-year-old wife Priscilla dead, with something like a gunshot wound in her head. It couldn't be real—it was a nightmare from which he would surely wake up. She was in the early stages of another pregnancy and in months ahead would be giving life again. How could she be dead? Why? How?

When he walked through the house, stumbling weakly, he found his children dead, drowned in the bathtubs. It had to be a nightmare—but his realistic, legal brain told him it was real, horribly real.

The tragic murders in the Gustafson house shook the town as nothing else ever had. Townsend had a population of about 8,000 and everybody knew everybpdy. They were 60 miles from Boston, but big-city crime seemed far away, something that could only happen in other places. Murdering women and children—that was unspeakable, unheard of.

He had found the bodies of his wife and children at 5:20 p.m. on December 1, 1987. One neighbor said, "This is not supposed to happen in this kind of town. Everyone's crushed, scared and trying hard to figure out a way to deal with it."

The authorities established that the murders had been committed between 3:30 p.m. and 5:20 p.m. when the husband and father found the bodies. Witnesses reported seeing Priscilla and William alive at 1:00 p.m. when the mother returned home from picking up her son at a babysitter's. Abigail was last seen alive about 3:30 p.m. when she walked home from a schoolbus that brought her from the Spaulding Memorial School, where she was in the second grade, to the end of Saunders Road. Priscilla, daughter of Congregational ministers, was the head teacher at the Townsend Cooperative Play School, a pre-school institution, and her son was a student there.

The autopsy revealed that Priscilla was sexually assaulted before being shot, and her children were strangled before being placed in the filled separate bathtubs in their Cape Cod-style home. From that day on, neighbors locked their doors, which they'd never thought of doing before.

Investigations were conducted by the local police, state police, the Middlesex district attorney's office and the FBI. Joseph Lawless was the chief investigator. A roadblock was set up by state police near the murder scene, and motorists were ordered to stop. They were asked if they had traveled along Route 119 during the time span when police believed the murders occurred.

Saunders Road is a dead-end street off Route 119 on the West Side of Townsend. Authorities were desperate for information and suggested that any information would be crucial.

They asked, "Can you recall something important — or anything at all that might have taken

223

place that Tuesday afternoon?"

People wanted to cooperate. They were just as eager as the investigators to solve this heinous crime. They were told that even a slightly suspicious event might be worthwhile. But nobody came up with anything that could help the investigation.

Initially, the police thought that the motive could be burglary. Townsend Police Chief William May said that the Gustafson house had been burglarized on November 16th, but nothing seemed to be missing from the home. Minor house burglaries had increased in Townsend in the last six months. Chief May said that 50 state troopers were brought in to bolster the 13-member force and increase security in the town.

Police dogs and helicopters searched the woods near the murder scene. About a dozen police cruisers were parked near the home, and the long dirt driveway leading to the house was completely blocked. State Police Detective Lieutenant Robert Long led a team of state troopers investigating the crime, along with others.

Five suspects emerged. Most of them were men who'd been in and out of town, and in a small hamlet like Townsend, strangers were suspected at a time like this.

They were questioned exhaustively. One man had served time in prison, but he seemed to have an alibi. He'd been seen in two stores at the time of the murders. In between, he'd talked to somebody in a parking lot; all told, that seemed to account for his time.

Another man was a drifter. Drifters drift—they go here and there and live in and out of places, never settling anywhere. They were not viewed as responsible people, but that didn't mean they would commit major crimes, or any real crimes at all.

The next suspect had been in prison for about three months as a juvenile. Now he was 28 and there was nothing to tie him to the ghastly murders on December 1st. He hadn't even been in the vicinity—he was moving from one bar to another, having a drink, looking for work, hanging out. You can't tie a man to murders just because he was hanging out.

Lawless was stumped. May was stumped. The easy suspects weren't easy at all. The other suspects were in the same situation. They had minor records, but no motives for the crime. Nothing had been stolen, and nobody could tie them to the scene of the crime. They couldn't leave town, but still they couldn't be considered serious suspects.

Neighbors were questioned, to no avail. The grieving widower was questioned, but nobody could ever believe he had anything to do with the crime. That was unthinkable. Besides, he had been working most of the time when the slayings could have occurred, and he was obviously a deeply broken, grief-stricken man.

But Joseph M. Lawless and other investigators were relentless. They had to be.

One suspect in town aroused more suspicion than the others. Daniel J. LaPlante, 17, lived on Elm Street, near the Gustafson home. He had been in trouble with the law, which was unusual for any residents in Townsend.

On December 11, 1986, LaPlante was charged with terrorizing a family with a hatchet inside their Lawrence Street home on Pepperell's west side. He'd worn a black ninja mask and, dressed as an Indian, he chased four people through the house. He smeared ketchup and mayonnaise on the walls and stuck knives into them, too. One of the girls in the house had been his girlfriend.

LaPlante was arrested and charged with breaking and entering a dwelling, kidnapping, armed assault and larceny over $100, as well as malicious destruction of property. His behavior was certainly considered bizarre, but the townspeople had mixed emotions about him.

"Strange," said one.

"Disturbed," said another.

But others felt he was a young man who just hadn't found himself yet, and while he probably needed help, he was incapable of the brutal murders in the Gustafson home.

"He grew up around here—and he couldn't have done this," declared one neighbor.

LaPlante had played football and run track, and he was an average student at St. Bernard's High School in town. Some of his classmates felt he wasn't the sociable type, but they didn't feel he could have killed the young mother and her two children.

Lawless, Long and May pressed for information about LaPlante. While some saw him as an ogre, others felt he was totally harmless. Lawless wondered whether this could be a dead end, just because one boy had performed all kinds of antics in a town where everybody else seemed to be cut from the same mold was no reason to suspect him. It was all too neat, too pat, too obvious.

But the investigation had to go on, and LaPlante was the leading suspect, or at least the leading one they had now.

LaPlante's family had lived in a simple wood frame house on Elm Street for approximately 15 years. Most townspeople felt he was a troublemaker. At a time like this, everybody suddenly remembered a lot of things about him.

A local variety store had been broken into five

226

years earlier, and Danny LaPlante and a friend were under suspicion. Way back when Danny was about six years old, a neighbor who had a greenhouse with her husband remembered they'd hired him, giving him small change for his work, to pick up stones from the fields where they grew such vegetables as squash and pumpkins. But one day, Danny smashed the pumpkins and squash in the field, earning himself the reputation of being a bad boy. That reputation stuck and it still seemed to be sticking today after the murders. Perhaps it was even escalating now that no real suspects had turned up except Danny LaPlante.

After the Pepperell incident when LaPlante masqueraded as an Indian and damaged a home, he was held in a state Department of Youth Services facility, a secured institution. When his case was moved from a juvenile court to Lowell Superior Court, he was held in lieu of $10,000 bail.

LaPlante's attorney, really his parents' attorney, pointed out, "These LaPlantes are the salt of the earth. Danny couldn't have come from a better family."

But the neighbors maintained that Danny was different from his family. One, in particular, said, "He was always by himself. That's not right for a young boy. Danny would walk by himself. You'd see him in the woods by himself."

It was these woods LaPlante might have passed through to reach the Gustafson home. But could he have done this—and why?

According to his brother-in-law, LaPlante could not have committed such atrocities. He was a loner, sometimes. A little unusual in his thinking and behavior, yes. But nothing more sinister than that.

"It's absolutely out of the question to link him

227

with these crimes. In fact, he can be warm and affectionate."

His brother-in-law stated quite clearly that on that terrible Tuesday, LaPlante came to his home in Fitchburg to help celebrate his daughter's—and Danny's niece's—birthday. He behaved like everybody else—he had cake with all the guests. Then he started playing with the birthday girl—a real family scene.

"You should have seen him," people at the party said. "He was playing with his niece on the couch, even tickling her while she laughed and giggled."

All agreed he thoroughly enjoyed the occasion. He loved playing with her and the other kids. His niece was six, in the same age range of the Gustafson children. He enjoyed being a good uncle.

"Now I ask you," the brother-in-law demanded, "could he go off the same day—within such a short time—and murder children so like his own niece and so full of life and fun? Impossible!"

Still the investigation plowed on. When the investigators first questioned LaPlante, they had to admit, "There just wasn't enough evidence to charge him."

But after the first interview, LaPlante ran into the woods surrounding his home—and the Gustafson home. This triggered a large-scale manhunt.

By the evening of that day, the search focused on a locale around a lumberyard in Ayer. LaPlante had also been traced through a Registry of Motor Vehicles check after police saw him driving a van reported stolen in the Pepperell incident. Officer Charles Nelson chased LaPlante and the van, but the youth abandoned it and ran into the woods.

In the massive search of the woods surrounding the Gustafson home, one investigator called out,

"Look at this!" He had found a sneaker print.

Just a little farther away, some of the others shouted, "There's something else here!" They came upon a torn pillow case and two spent .22-caliber casings. The pillow might have been used to muffle the sound of the gunshots.

State police officers followed dogs tracking a scent along a trail to a wooded area. "Whoa! Hold up!" one of the officers shouted at the dogs he was handling. The scent was overpowering that the police officers in charge were practically dragged by the dogs.

In those woods, they also found a blue plaid shirt, two wet gloves—one yellow, one white—and a name signpost from the Gustafson home. Police officers reported, "The dogs picked up the scent and they were off."

That led them to LaPlante's Elm Street home which they had a warrant to search. It also led to the discovery of both sneakers LaPlante wore.

"Look what we have here. This guy leaves evidence all over." In the LaPlante cellar, they found a spent .22-caliber casing, which had been fired from the same gun that killed Priscilla Gustafson. (District Attorney Reilly would use this later on.) They also discovered a yellow glove that was the mate to the one found near the home.

Their discoveries kept building. The manhunt was extended to a home in Pepperell where a woman had reported her home had been burglarized and a gun had been stolen. They found a brown leather jacket there, which was identified as LaPlante's.

Then the story became really complex. Police now picked up on a report that LaPlante had just broken into still another Pepperell home. There he was confronted by a woman. He kidnapped her in her orange Volkswagen van, but the woman managed to escape from the van. LaPlante kept driving until he was spotted in Ayer driving the stolen van at 5:04 p.m., leading to his capture.

LaPlante was arrested, but he pleaded innocent and told investigators he was "watching music videos" at the time he was supposed to have killed the victims. Telecast on MTV, the videos were studied by investigators to see if they matched his story. Actually, they were also being looked at for clues to the murder, which bore the mark of ritualistic killings.

"At one of the Pepperell houses he broke into, he opened a bottle of wine, set out two glasses, but never drank anything," one police officer pointed out.

"Almost like he was toasting his victory," another police officer mused wryly.

"Exactly. And at the Gustafson house, he opened a can of beer, but he didn't drink there, either."

"Another toast?" the officer asked.

"Another toast," his partner agreed.

Middlesex District Attorney Reilly filed a motion asking for permission for authorities to take samples of blood, saliva, head and pubic hair from LaPlante. Reilly believed the hair and blood samples were crucial to compare to hair, bloodstains and seminal fluid taken near the victims. While the mother had apparently been raped, the children had not been sexually abused. A condom, its end snipped off, had been recovered from the floor next to the bed where Priscilla Gustafson was found dead. Two condom wrappers and several unopened ones were found, too.

According to the police, Priscilla Gustafson was wearing a shirt and dark pants when her body was discovered. But a friend had seen her just before the murders, and reported that she'd been wearing a turquoise blouse. Police believed that LaPlante made the woman redress after the rape or redressed her himself before he shot her twice in the head. Police also believed that he tied or locked her up while he killed her son William before assaulting her. When Abigail came home, after her mother and brother had been killed, the same fate awaited her.

The trial of Danny LaPlante was the most sensational in the history of the rural community. In a 15-page affidavit filed with the original search-warrant request allowing authorities to search LaPlante's house, State Trooper Joseph Lawless detailed the use of the two dogs involved in the hunt. The German shepherds tracked the scent from the murder scene to the LaPlante house.

LaPlante was held at Bridgewater State Hospital after his arrest. In his trial in October 1988, he was charged with three murders—those of Priscilla Gustafson, her daughter Abigail and son William—as well as with breaking into their Townsend home.

LaPlante's defense team wanted a change of venue out of eastern Massachusetts. They felt the publicity surrounding the crime would limit the possibility of a fair trial. That was not granted, however. The prosecution had testimony from several witnesses, police, doctors involved in performing the autopsies. But the defense called no witnesses at all for Danny LaPlante.

In a crowded, emotional courtroom, Daniel J. LaPlante was convicted of murdering the three victims and was sentenced to three consecutive life terms with no chance of parole, commutation or furloughs. Many people cried out for the death penalty, but in Massachusetts, there is no death penalty. Judge Robert A. Barton, who presided over the packed Middlesex Superior Court, declared, "There are some who would say that you should receive the same sentence that you imposed on the Gustafson family—that is, death by ligature or hanging—but we have no death penalty in Massachusetts." He bellowed this at Danny LaPlante, now 18, who would never be free again, according to the sentence imposed on him.

An appeal is automatic in first-degree murder, and of course, there would be an appeal. LaPlante's lawyers were contesting the search and seizure of LaPlante's home, claiming the procedure was illegal, even though a search warrant had been issued. They also questioned Judge Barton's refusal to instruct the jurors to consider whether or not LaPlante was insane and therefore not guilty.

The convicted youth was formally sentenced to serve his terms in the Cedar Junction State Prison in Walpole, but courthouse sources disclosed that the Department of Correction changed that. The department wanted him confined to Concord State Prison because his safety could be better assured there.

LaPlante showed no remorse throughout the trial and at his sentencing. His mother still protested his innocence.

As a postscript to the trial, the judge released four letters supposedly written by Daniel J. LaPlante to an inmate in the Salem Jail. Barton had impounded the letters until after the verdict so that their release would not influence the jury.

The inmate, who had a heavy criminal record for theft and forgery, testified in pretrial hearings that he wrote to LaPlante to induce him to confide in him. He wanted to trade the information for reduced sentences and transfer to a jail that might be safer. He offered the help of his attorney.

In one of the letters, he said that he'd be happy to cooperate. "I'm worried about killing three people," he wrote. In another letter, he wrote, "I would be more than willing to cooperate with your lawyer, but I murder two kids and a lady. Can he help still?"

Assistant District Attorney Thomas Reilly pointed out that he decided against using the letters because the inmate would have had to testify and "it would have been a circus. This case would have become the trial of (the inmate), rather than the trial of Daniel J. LaPlante."

LaPlante's attorney did not believe the letters were genuine or the state would have used them. In any case, they were not part of the trial.

"I saw Daniel LaPlante grow up since he was a small boy," one neighbor said. "He was always troubled, but I never imagined this would be the grand finale of his life."

"THEY ROBBED, RAPED & SHOT PRETTY LOIS UNDER 'SUICIDE BRIDGE!' "

by Don Lasseter

Martial drumbeats. Piercing whistles. Thunderous cheering. These are the sounds you might hear if you could listen to the imagination of visitors who paused near the famous Rose Bowl Stadium in Pasadena, California. Each New Year's Day, the "Granddaddy" of all college football bowl games is played there, and seven Super Bowls, including the 1993 edition, have been slugged out on the immortal gridiron. The thrill of the game has attracted millions to the classic stadium for most of the 20th century.

The scene of so many pitched athletic battles became the site of a more elemental struggle on a cool autumn night in 1988. On October 18th, a real life drama, infinitely more violent than any sporting event, unfolded within a stone's throw of the Rose Bowl.

On that day, Lois Haro, 26, was at her Pasadena home a few miles from the stadium, and had started preparing dinner for her husband when she suddenly remembered an important chore she'd left unfinished. Her co-workers in the sales department of a local seismographic instrument firm had planned a baby shower for a friend the next day, and Lois had postponed buying a present until the last minute.

Setting aside dinner, the attractive young woman with sparkling brown eyes scribbled a note to her husband: *"I went to the store, probably J.C. Penney's. I'll be back at 8:00 p.m. Lois. 7:15 p.m."*

Lois brushed back her shoulder-length dark hair, changed into a beige, flower-print jumpsuit and high-heel shoes, then headed out the door. The fashionable clothing Lois wore enhanced her trim, 120-pound figure and made her look taller than her 5 feet, 2 inches.

After parking her 1983 Toyota Tercel in the subterranean garage of the Plaza Pasadena Mall, Lois Haro rode the escalator up to the array of stores. The enclosed shopping center was bordered on one side by Colorado Boulevard, the street millions of people worldwide know as the address of the Tournament of Roses Parade.

The mall presents the image of being a sanctuary from violent crime. Security guards patrol the promenade to assure the safety of shoppers. A closed-circuit television camera monitors the parking garage, and radio-equipped guards patrol among the cars.

Lois browsed through several of the major department stores, but she still hadn't found the right present. Shortly after 7:45 p.m., she walked out of J.C. Penney's, near the escalator to the parking garage.

One hour and 18 minutes later, at 9:03 p.m., Officer Michael Villalobos of the Pasadena Police Department was on routine patrol along Arroyo Drive near the Rose Bowl stadium when he and his partner spotted something on the median strip in the middle of the block between Holly Street and Arroyo Boulevard. They stopped immediately and leaped from their black-and-white car to investigate.

About eight feet from the curb, a dark-haired Caucasian woman, clad in a beige, flower-patterned jumpsuit, lay crumpled in the dirt on her side. Blood dripped slowly from her nose and ears and from a wound in her head, which appeared to the officers to have been made by a bullet.

Officer Villalobos kneeled quickly to see if the still form exhibited any signs of life. He was surprised when he put his ear next to the victim's mouth and heard faint gasps. Realizing that the victim was struggling to breathe, the officer told his partner to radio for medical help.

Within minutes, a paramedic's ambulance screeched to a halt next to the patrol unit, and an emergency medical technician wasted no time starting life-saving procedures. He saw the pool of blood soaking into the ground and knew that the woman would need replacement fluids. Checking her respiration, he noted that it was agonal (symptomatic of agony), which often indicates that death is near. Loosening the victim's clothing — normal procedure during emergency treatment — the paramedic was startled to notice that the victim was wearing no underwear.

Moments after the victim was loaded into the ambulance, her breathing stopped, and the paramedic began administration of cardiopulmonary re-

236

suscitation, including intubation, or the insertion of a tube into her throat to facilitate breathing.

The heroic efforts of the officers and the paramedics continued, but the woman's tenuous hold on life slowly ebbed away. She was pronounced dead shortly after arrival at nearby Huntington Memorial Hospital.

Because of the circumstances of the death, it became necessary for an officer to observe the examination of the body at the hospital, to preserve a trail of any potential evidence. Michael Villalobos performed that unpleasant duty. He jotted in his notebook a confirmation of what the paramedics had noticed, that no underclothing had been found on the deceased victim.

The bloody head wound noted by the patrol officers clearly demanded the involvement of the homicide team.

Detective Brian Schirka drew the duty as lead investigator. Schirka's 12th year with the Pasadena Police Department had been on the homicide squad, and in that 12 months, he had investigated 10 brutal murders. A native of Utah, the slim six-footer joined the Ogden Police Department after graduating from Weber State College, spent five years there, then migrated to California. Lawbreakers who had faced Schirka would never forget his penetrating blue eyes, which could enhance his friendly smile or turn cold when he questioned a murder suspect.

Called out from his home at 10:00 p.m., Schirka went directly to the hospital where the body had been taken. Other members of his investigative team met him there. One handed Schirka some jewelry that the victim had been wearing, a ring, a bracelet, and a pair of earrings. When the detective looked at the victim herself, he was appalled at the damage the bullet had inflicted to her head and face. He knew that it would be difficult to identify her from the facial features, and no purse or documents had been discovered at the crime scene to reveal who she was. At that point, she was just another Jane Doe.

Near midnight, a police assistant contacted Detective Schirka at the hospital. In Pasadena, a police assistant is a khaki-uniformed, unsworn officer who takes crime reports, issues parking citations, helps at crime scenes, and performs other collateral duties not requiring contact with suspects. The police assistant, who had heard about the terrible discovery of the unidentified victim, told Schirka that he had a frantic woman on hold who was calling to report a missing family member. The details, the assistant said, seemed to match what he had heard about the Jane Doe.

Thanks to the attentive police assistant, Schirka identified the body within three hours of the discovery. Relatives were able to confirm that the jewelry and clothing belonged to Lois Haro.

The absence of underwear on the victim and the bruises on her body prompted Detective Schirka to summon Heidi Wolbart, criminalist for the Los Angeles County Coroner's Office, to examine the body for evidence of rape. The technician used the standard sexual assault kit to take samples of fluid from body cavities and from the jumpsuit the woman had worn. Later, when criminalist Elizabeth Kornblum microscopically examined glass slides containing smears of the fluid samples, she found spermatozoa present in the victim's vagina and traces of seminal fluid on the jumpsuit.

The most difficult duty for homicide investigators is to interview relatives who have been waiting in vain for their missing loved ones to return home safely. Detective Schirka went to the Haro home to perform that painful duty. The shattered family members struggled through their grief to give the officer some information about Lois. "She was a friend to everybody, a friend to the world," one said. She was outgoing and tried to make the best of everything. "She really loved people," they said.

Lois' family had moved to Pasadena about seven years earlier from the Philippine Islands, where her American-born parents were involved in missionary work and where Lois graduated from high school. Lois herself had been born in Thailand. Recently, Lois had been working on a degree in anthropology at Cal State, Los Angeles.

"She was planning to make a pie for the [baby shower]," a relative sobbed, "but she never got to do it."

Detective Schirka read the note that Lois had left, and learned that she owned a blue 1983 Toyota Tercel. The car was missing, so it was reasonable to assume that she had driven it when she left to go to the mall. The investigator ordered an immediate search of the entire parking structure at the shopping center. The car, Schirka realized, was the only tangible lead they had to the savage killer, or killers, of the young woman.

Working through the night, officers scoured the basement parking area and all of the adjoining streets. The car was not located. Detective Schirka arranged for a description of the automobile, with the license number, and a BOLO (short for "be on the lookout") to be issued at morning roll call for all Pasadena Police Department patrol officers.

On the following morning, October 19th, Dr. Sarah Reddy of the L.A. County Coroner's Office performed the autopsy on Lois Haro while Detective Schirka observed. The cause of death, Reddy found, was a gunshot wound that had traversed from the top of the head to the base of the skull, where the lethal bullet was found. The absence of "stippling" around the entrance wound indicated that the shot had been fired from at least 18 inches away. The pathologist also found "numerous small bruises" on the victim's thighs, knees, and both legs, along with "small scratches" on her right hand and bruising on her left hand. There was little doubt in the minds of investigators that the woman had been raped before she was savagely executed.

Another contact with Lois Haro's family became necessary. It was the exceptionally difficult task of the detectives to ask a sensitive and personal question. Had Lois Haro had sexual intercourse within the last few days? They found out that she had not. No, she did not have any bruises on her body. Yes, she certainly was in the habit of always wearing underclothes. That information underlined the probability that she had, indeed, been raped.

Detective Schirka also learned that Lois Haro had been carrying several credit cards, including one from Wells Fargo bank. Her family had taken the precaution, hours after she was missing, of canceling the cards.

Homicide investigators often ponder the whims of fortune that influence a murder investigation and the little twists of fate, or more often the results of hard work, that cause the job to have speedy results or to stretch into weeks, months, or years. Such a twist accelerated the investigation into Lois Haro's death.

At 8:15 a.m. on October 19th, at the same time the pathologist prepared to conduct a postmortem on the victim's body, Lawrence Zimmerman was still thinking about the BOLO description of a 1983 Toyota Tercel he had heard at morning roll call. Zimmerman, another Pasadena police assistant, was driving a marked white vehicle one mile east of the Rose Bowl when he spotted a car going in the other direction that seemed to match the Toyota's description. Quickly making a U-turn, he followed the vehicle.

The Toyota turned right on Pepper Street, sped to the end of the block, and pulled into a parking lot behind some apartments. Zimmerman halted a half block back, exited the car, and casually strolled to a point behind a concrete block wall, where, by cautiously looking over the wall, he could catch a glimpse of the Toyota.

A young black man emerged from the car, walked to the rear, looked around, and began to fumble at the locked trunk with a ring of several keys. After a few unsuccessful attempts, the youth found the right key, opened the trunk, and rummaged around inside it.

Zimmerman did not want to be conspicuous, so he alternately watched the suspicious scene, then

241

concealed himself behind the wall. Just after he had dropped behind the wall again, he heard the trunk lid slam down. Peering over once more, he saw the youth disappear into one of the apartments. The rear license plate on the car, which Zimmerman had seen earlier, was now missing.

Back in his patrol unit, Zimmerman contacted to report his observations and then waited for the arrival of Detective Sergeant Monty Yancey and another investigator.

When the lawmen arrived, the trio knocked on the door of the apartment. A youth opened it. He precisely fit the description that Zimmerman had given the officers.

Following a brief introduction, Sergeant Yancey announced that they were conducting an investigation and asked the young man for identification. "I'm Ronald Jones," came the frosty reply. He told the men he was 19 years old.

We have a few questions, Mr. Jones," Yancey said. "Will you step out to the car with us?"

Jones sullenly complied. Outside, he didn't resist or object when Sergeant Yancey indicated he wanted to "pat him down" to check for any weapons.

A lump in Jones' right front pants pocket prompted Yancey to ask what it was. "Nothing," Ronald Jones snapped.

"Would you mind showing me?" Yancey requested.

Jones pulled a set of keys out of the pocket. "These are my house keys and the keys to my Audi." The lump, however, hadn't completely disappeared. Yancey wanted to know what else Jones

Billy Shane Willingham killed the man who stood in the way of his marrying his 16-year-old girlfriend—his father.

Store clerk
David Conley Scott.

Scott's body was found in
the aisle of the convenience
store where he was
stocking shelves.

For delivering the death blow
to Scott, gang leader Philip
Negrete took an extra 50
cents of the booty.

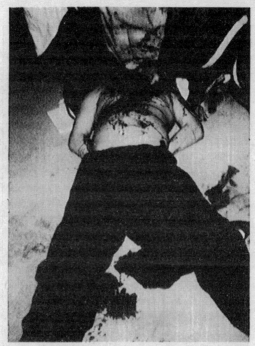

15-year-old
murder victim
Chang Seok Ean.

Ean's
17-year-old killer,
Yong Ho Han.

On the last night of their lives, Jason Brown and his girlfriend, Nanette Scott, attended a party with their killers.

Carl Purvis, 19,
Steve Anthony Pigg, 16,
and Curtis R. Burke, 17,
were convicted
of killing Scott
and Brown.

When 15-year-old
April Barber decided
to kill her grandparents,
her 32-year-old lover
Clinton Lawrence
Johnson provided her
with the means.

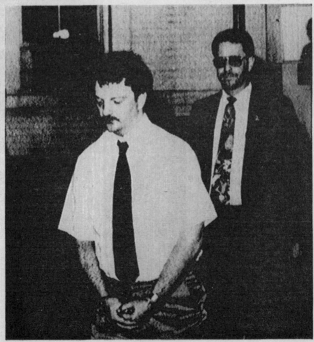

Allan David Terrell
was taking a
shortcut through
Coconut Grove
when three robbers
approached his car.

Taryn Lagrome, an
experienced armed
robber and Terrell's
killer, was only
15 years old.

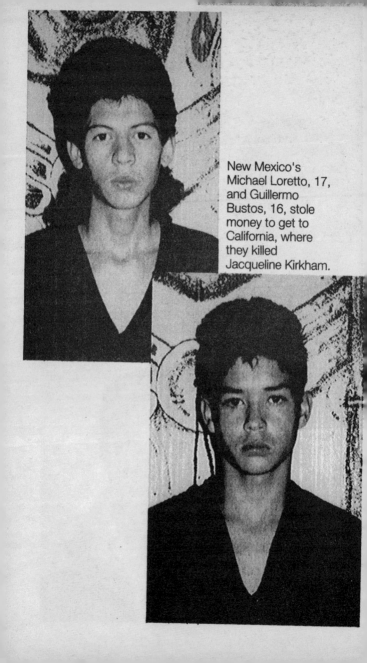

New Mexico's Michael Loretto, 17, and Guillermo Bustos, 16, stole money to get to California, where they killed Jacqueline Kirkham.

Housewife
and mother
Wendy Knowles.

Knowles's killer,
17-year-old
neighbor Shawn Jackson.

The Hoopes family—from left to right:
Dan, Doug, and their mother, Louise.

Eric Motis confessed
to killing the Hoopeses,
including his friend Doug.

Christopher Scot Weaver and
Daniel Geier snuck off to play where
they weren't supposed to—
and paid with their lives.

16-year-old child killer Shawn Novak.

had in his pocket. The youth insisted that he didn't have anything else, but he eventually pulled more keys from his jeans. The last set of keys had a metal tag inscribed with the word, "Toyota."

At Sergeant Yancey's request, Police Assistant Zimmerman tried the keys on the blue Toyota in the parking lot. They fit perfectly. Lying on the backseat of the car was a license plate that matched the numbers Lois Haro's family had given to the police.

Sergeant Yancey placed Ronald Anthony Jones under arrest on suspicion of murder.

Ronald Jones refused consent to a search of his apartment, but it didn't take Yancey long to obtain warrants authorizing investigators to examine the car and the interior of Jones' apartment. Sergeant Yancey found a wallet containing credit cards and other items with Lois Haro's name on them in a trash can.

Another member of the homicide team, Detective Donald L. Gallon, watched as Ronald Anthony Jones was booked on the morning of October 9th. Gallon had to hold back a laugh when he saw Jones twisting into some odd positions while removing his clothing. The teen's gyrations didn't work as he apparently intended them to. A small plastic wallet insert fell from his crotch. It contained more credit cards in the name of Lois Haro.

In the back pocket of Jones' blood-stained jeans, the detectives found an automatic teller machine receipt for a transaction involving a Wells Fargo bank card.

At ten o'clock that morning, Detectives Schirka and Gallon began questioning the suspect, Ronald

Jones. After being read his Miranda rights, Jones announced, "I'll talk to y'all, but I—when I . . . if I have to go to court. . . . I'll talk to y'all . . . ," and his voice trailed off.

"Well, Ronald, I'll be honest with you," Gallon said. "We have done some preliminary checking and some work with evidence we have. And all indications suggest that we are able to place you not only in the car where the victim of this crime was, but at a certain point in time, we are able to place you at another location . . ."

"We're not going to b.s. you. We have some evidence that suggests that you were involved in a very serious crime."

Gallon was a skilled interviewer, a master of the bluff and the use of words that sound very specific, but are really just vague suggestions carefully designed to lull a suspect into spilling his guts. That technique usually takes reiteration and time. Just as Gallon expected, Ronald Jones started by denying any involvement or participation in the crime. He'd been with a girlfriend, he said, and later at the home of a relative. Then, he asserted, he went to the park to meet a friend of his named George Trone. He didn't know how the credit cards belonging to Haro got in the trash can or in his jeans.

"Were you at the Plaza Pasadena Mall last night?" Gallon asked.

"Yeah, man," Jones admitted. "Me and George Trone's went there a little after eight. We went to a couple of stores, saw some people we knew, then left about nine. I went over to my [relative's] house till nearly ten. Then I went home on my bicycle and went to bed." His story conveniently put him and Trone still at the mall during the time that Lois Haro was found.

"Do you think cops are stupid?" Gallon snapped. "We have witnesses who saw you driving the victim's car."

Jones had a ready answer for that. He had received the car on that same morning, he said, from another friend of his, and had just taken it for a short drive. Then the police showed up and arrested him. Maybe he had picked up the credit cards inside the car.

"Look, Ronald," the detective said. "I've been conducting interviews like this for eighteen years, almost as long as you've been living. I've been looking at your eyes and I've been watching your motions and listening to you talk, and everything you've told me is a basic lie."

Now, the sleuth thought to himself, it was time to escalate the bluff. Keeping a straight face, Gallon explained to the young suspect, "We've got something that you may not have heard about. It's called a mass spectrometer. It's a scientific instrument we can use to place people at certain locations."

Detective Schirka turned away, struggling to keep from laughing out loud. Gallon paused to watch the effect on the suspect.

Squirming in his seat, looking confused, Jones began to deny that he ever had a gun. Gallon shook his head and countered, "I didn't say anything about a gun." The trap was starting to work.

The detective pursued the subject of guns. "Do you know what a gun residue test is?" He explained to Jones that such a test would show whether someone had fired a gun in the last three days. "Just how do you explain the fact that the test [on you] would come back positive?" he demanded.

Jones lamely replied that he had fired a BB gun.

While Gallon and Schirka were interviewing Jones, Sergeant Yancey and his partner were following the trail of the friend Jones had named, George Marvin Trone. They located a woman who knew the young man quite well and told the officers that she had seen him at about 9:30 on the evening of the killing. Trone, who was 18, had shown her a watch and ring and told her that he had bought them "from a girl up the street."

"Do you know any of his friends?" the investigators asked. The woman readily gave them names of people who would be able to tell them about Trone. One acquaintance was particularly helpful.

"I've known George for years," the friend admitted. The two pals had talked on the morning of the 19th. Trone had told him, "We killed somebody last night," and described how "they" had taken her from the mall and killed her at the Rose Ball. "Anthony was with me," Trone had told his buddy.

The friend added more. "George handed me a gun, one that he had all the time. And he had two rings."

Detective Yancey suspected that the youth had more to say and prompted him to do so.

"Yeah, okay," Trone's friend went on. "I saw George just a little while ago. He came and got the gun. Said he was going to get rid of it up in the mountains."

With the help of the informant, the detectives located Trone's girlfriend. They learned from her that Trone had brought two rings to her house the night of the Haro murder and had tried them on the girlfriend's fingers. The rings were too small, so she gave them back to Trone. She confided that Trone had seemed "kind of distracted" and "mean" that evening.

Meanwhile, in the interview room at police headquarters, Detective Gallon continued to work on gaining the confidence of Ronald Jones. "You're in a real complicated situation," he told the suspect, "and the only way you get out of situations like this is to be completely truthful. And you're looking at me now like, 'Why should I trust you?' . . . . What I'm saying to you is, we have evidence that's going to link you directly with this crime and that's why I want to give you the opportunity to help us."

Jones was perspiring and squirming, but he still insisted that he was innocent. "How can I be on my bike and in a car at the same time?" he asked.

Trying another tack, Gallon asked Jones about some rolled-up, wet underwear found in his apartment. He pointed out that the crime lab could still do "blood work" on underwear, even if it had been washed. Jones claimed he knew nothing about the wet underwear.

"Have you had sex in the last two days?" Gallon wanted to know. "We can tell if you have."

"I guess y'all are capable of doing anything," Jones whined.

Without making any promises, Gallon cajoled, persuaded, talked, suggested, and pleaded with the suspect to come clean with the truth.

Finally, after a short rest period, Ronald Jones began to cave in. He gradually revealed how he and George Trone had seen the victim at the mall, followed her down the escalator, and forced her to let them in her car. He was driving, he said, when Trone pulled out a gun, which "surprised" Jones. On the 210 Freeway, he continued, Trone made him pull over to a side street, then forced the woman to get in the backseat and take her clothes off.

"I saw George had his pants pulled down and was pushing her head down. I couldn't actually see what they were doing, but I heard her choke. I told George to cut that out." Trone then ordered the woman to "lay down" and had sexual intercourse with her, Jones claimed.

After that, they drove to the Colorado Street Bridge, popularly known as "Suicide Bridge," near the Rose Bowl. There, Jones said, Trone had sex with the victim again. The victim was then allowed to get dressed, without her underwear, and get out of the car. She started to walk away.

According to Jones, Trone yelled, "Bitch, what are you doing?" The woman stopped. Trone stood outside, in the dirt alongside the car, and talked to her.

"I heard a shot," Jones muttered, "and saw her curled up on the ground. George came back and said, 'Cool man, let's go.' I asked him why he had killed her. He said, 'Why do I let her live when she could report both of us?' "

Complimented by the detectives for his "honesty," Ronald Jones finally admitted that he, too, had sex with the victim. He had "only touched her on the breast," he confessed. Detective Gallon adroitly coaxed some more, and slowly Jones admitted that he had sexually penetrated her, but "just a little bit." He denied that he had ever engaged in oral copulation.

A member of the investigative team was sent to Wells Fargo bank with the ATM receipt recovered from Jones' pocket. The detective was disappointed to find out that it was not associated in any way with Lois Haro's account.

At 9:30 that same evening, Officer Alejandro Peinado went to Brenner Park, a few blocks east of the Rose Bowl, where he found and arrested George Marvin Trone.

Two hours later, having worked nonstop for 24 hours, Detectives Schirka and Gallon, the master interviewer, confronted George Trone in a police station cubicle. Just as Jones had done, Trone started with denials. Yes, he had been at the mall on the night of the killing. It wasn't with Jones, he claimed, but with another friend. They met Jones, later, after the mall had closed, in a park, when he drove up in a Toyota. He'd "bought it from a woman for eight hundred dollars."

"Did you touch the car anywhere?" Gallon wanted to know. Yes, he had touched it in several places, he said.

"Do you know much about police work, I mean do you ever watch television, things like *Miami Vice?*"

Yes, he had.

"Do you know what a mass spectrometer is or do you know anything about the scientific evidence that police can use?" Both detectives kept a straight

249

face.

"I just know a little about it," Trone replied.

After laying some more groundwork, Gallon looked directly at the suspect. "We know that you were in the car with Ronald Jones and that you were with the lady."

Trone shot back, "Well, there wasn't no lady in the car when I was there, and the only female I was with was my girlfriend."

Gradually, though, just as they had with Ronald Jones, the detectives convinced George Trone to start admitting details. They told him that Jones had confessed, on tape, and named Trone as the shooter. That opened the floodgates, and Trone stated that it was Jones who had actually been the triggerman.

"Did he [Jones] shoot her?" Gallon asked.

"Yes," Trone answered.

The suspect pieced together his story, confessing that he and Jones had taken the victim down the escalator at the mall, and Jones had driven the car while he rode in the backseat. The plan was just to rob her. She gave them her money.

"How much money, do you remember?"

"It seems like twelve . . . eighteen dollars." The victim's life hadn't been worth much to these two. In addition, Trone said, they had found a Wells Fargo ATM card on the victim, and Jones had demanded that she give him the personal identification number necessary to use the card.

"She asked him to let her go," Trone mumbled, "and she said he could keep the car. Then he told her to get out of the car by a bridge. All I heard was the gunshot, and he just ran to the car and drove off."

Now, both men had blamed each other for the murder. And Trone, just as Jones had, denied complicity in the rape. "I didn't have sex with her, [Jones] did. He got in the backseat with her, and made her take off all her clothes. I just sat there and watched." Little by little, though, Trone admitted that he had "touched" the victim, then he acknowledged that he had sex with her, including oral copulation.

At last, Trone agreed to write a confession.

"Me and Ronald Jones was hanging out at the park, drinking and smoking pot," Trone's statement began. "He said, 'Let's go to the mall.' We were walking around the mall. Ronald never mentioned anything about robbing anybody. I didn't even know he had a gun with him.

"We seen this lady. . . . We started to go down the escalator with her [to] the parking lot. Ronald was ahead of me by about seven feet talking to the lady. He followed her to the car and they both got in and he told me to get in the backseat. I thought he knew her, so I got in.

"We drove off. That's when I heard him tell her to give him the money and when I seen the gun. He told her to give the money to me, so she handed it to me, and the rings and watch. I just stuck them in my pocket of my jacket.

"She was asking him to let her go and he could keep the [car]. That's when I cut in and told him to let her go. He act [sic] like he didn't hear me.

"We got off the freeway and went down to Brookside Park [which surrounds the Rose Bowl]. We stop, and I got out, and Ronald and she got

251

out. He told her to get in the backseat, and he got in with her. He told her to take off her clothes. She did, and he pulled down his pants and had sex with her. He finished and told me to go back there and get me some. I thought about it . . . and went back there with her and had sex with her.

"She got dressed, and Ronald told her to get back in front, and we drive off. We went to this little field, and she got out and was walking in the field. He got out, and then I hear [sic] a shot."

Part of Trone's confession included information that some jewelry taken from the victim had been given to a mutual friend of the two suspects. Detective Schirka tracked down the man and learned that he had sold two rings to a local jeweler. At the jewelry store, the sleuth was able to recover both items, which were subsequently identified by Lois Haro's family as her wedding rings.

The rings were the ones Trone had tried to give his girlfriend, but they wouldn't fit her fingers. When Detective Schirka reinterviewed her, she divulged that Trone had, within the last few hours, called her from the jail and told her about the killing, saying that Ronald "pulled a gun and forced the lady to drive them around. Then over at the Rose Bowl, Ronald ordered her out of the car, pulled a gun, and shot her in the head."

When Detective Schirka presented the evidence to Deputy District Attorney Walt Lewis of the Los Angeles County D.A.'s Office, Lewis was sure he could convict both Trone and Jones. But he was still curious about the Wells Fargo automatic teller receipt found in Jones' back pocket. It had not matched Lois Haro's account number, so why did

Jones have it? Schirka agreed to find out.

Tracing the owner of the account number, the detectives found out that the man had simply left the receipt at the Wells Fargo ATM after withdrawing some cash. The time of the transaction was printed on the form.

With a subpoena, Detective Schirka obtained a printout of all transactions related to Lois Haro's account after she disappeared. Even though the card had been canceled by the worried family, attempts to access the balance were still recorded. Sure enough, the computer record revealed no less than six attempts to access her funds, within minutes after the time listed on the receipt found in Jones' pocket. He had gone to the ATM, found the unrelated receipt, jammed it into his pocket, and started trying to use Lois Haro's card to steal the money in her account.

The evidence against both suspects was substantial. The murder weapon would have been a nice complement, but it was never found.

D.A. Walt Lewis prosecuted both defendants at separate trials. In May 1991, Jones testified in his own behalf. He told the jury that after the killing, he went home, fixed himself a hamburger, and laughed while watching *The Honeymooners* on television.

The jury found Ronald Anthony Jones guilty of first-degree murder, kidnapping, robbery, rape, and forced oral copulation. After a short penalty phase of the trial, they recommended that he be sentenced to death.

In December 1991, another jury found George Trone guilty of the same charges.

Superior Court Judge Charles C. Lee looked sternly at Ronald Jones on June 6, 1991, and ordered him to be taken to San Quentin Prison to be held pending execution. Eight months later, the same judge sentenced George Trone to serve the rest of his life in prison without the possibility of parole.

The California legislature passed a new law, effective at the beginning of 1993, to allow condemned inmates to choose between the gas chamber and lethal injection. Ronald Jones will have several years to ponder that choice.

On the grassy strip along Arroyo Drive, near the Rose Bowl, there is a circle of white stones, placed there by the family of Lois Haro to mark the spot where she was found, robbed of her possessions, her dignity, and her life. It is a small memorial, to express the hope that she will never be forgotten.

"TEENAGE SERIAL KILLER WHO CLAIMED FIVE!"

by Bob Spurlin

Athens, Ga.
May 12, 1988

Donna Brown left her home in Winterville, Georgia, on Wednesday, April 27, 1987, at approximately 9 a.m. She carried a small potted plant with her to the car and drove about 10 miles north to visit her friends, William and Rachel Sutton in Athens, Georgia. William was 82 years old and had been having a lot of trouble with his back over the past few weeks. Donna knew that Rachel, 78, did her best to care for William, but she wanted to be sure that the couple was okay. She knew that the family member who lived near the couple and checked on them regularly was out of town.

Donna arrived at the Sutton home at about 9:30 and visited until about noon. Once assured that everything was in order, she left the plant with them and returned home.

At approximately nine o'clock on Saturday, April 25th, a neighbor of the Suttons received a phone call from a family member who lived in Nevada.

He told the neighbor that he had been trying to call William and Rachel since the previous evening and had gotten no answer. He asked if the neighbor would go and check on the elderly couple. The neighbor agreed to do so and told the relative that he would call him back.

After dressing, the neighbor walked the short distance to the Sutton home and knocked on the door. After receiving no answer at the front door, the neighbor tried the door and found it locked. He went to the back of the house and tried again with the same result: No answer and a locked door. The back screen door, however, was not locked.

The neighbor started to go back home and then decided to check the garage door. It too was locked but the neighbor could see through the glass panes of the doors that both of the Suttons' cars were inside. This caused the neighbor concern and he immediately went home and called the family member in Nevada. After a very short conversation, it was decided that the police should be called.

At 10:33 a.m., Officer John A. Davis, a wiry, sandy-haired veteran of the Athens Police Department, arrived on the scene. Davis first repeated the actions that the neighbor had taken with the same results. Davis then contacted the Sutton family member in Nevada and received permission to forcibly enter the residence.

By the time this permission had been received, Davis had been joined by Sergeant Loyd Nash. The two officers examined the house and decided to gain access to the home through one of the larger upstairs windows. Davis would later write in his report that this was done to deter any burglary of the home during the time it would take to repair the window.

Davis broke the window and he and Nash entered the Sutton home. Both lawmen would later report that they had immediately been confronted with a strong, foul odor as they entered the house. The two veterans systematically searched the rooms of the upper floors and after finding nothing, they moved their search downstairs. The living room and den were empty. Officer Davis noticed that the stale odor he had noticed upon his entry seemed stronger as he and his partner approached the dining room. He pushed open the door and immediately saw the fully-clothed, bloodstained body of William Sutton on the floor.

The body lay in a small pantry between the dining room and kitchen. Rachel Sutton's body was not visible until the officers moved closer. Her body had been stuffed into a laundry bag and was forced underneath her husband's legs.

A large carpet had been pulled over the bodies, partially covering them; two brooms were placed on top of the carpet. A bloodstained dustpan was on a nearby shelf. The officers could see several cut and stab wounds on the neck and shoulders of William Sutton.

The officers were very careful not to touch anything and to watch where they stepped. There was no chance of either of the victims being alive and the probers wanted to be sure that they did not disturb or contaminate any possible evidence.

By the time the officers had finished their search, Lieutenant Linda Evans had arrived on the scene. She immediately summoned the detective units after receiving the initial reports by the officers. While awaiting their arrival, the trio proceeded to rope off the scene with the bright yellow crime scene tape.

Once the scene was secure, Evans dispatched the officers to start questioning neighbors, while she and Detectives Tim Smith, W. J. Smith and Sergeant Jeff Ingram entered the home. What they found was the most bizarre crime scene the officers had ever seen.

The officers noticed bloodstains on several areas of the floor, not only in the dining room but throughout the rooms on the first floor. It was also quite obvious that some attempt had been made to wash up some of the blood. The officers noticed that a rug had been removed from underneath the dining room table and that all of the items on the table had been neatly replaced.

The dining room floor had been mopped up with a sponge mop. This was determined from an examination of the water stains on the hardwood floors and officers found the mop in the kitchen. Members of the investigation team checked every door and window of the house and found them all locked. This led investigators to conclude that the killer had either entered through an unlocked door or had been invited by the victims into the house. There was no evidence that anything had been taken from the house. Police found William Sutton's wallet undisturbed and when the search moved upstairs, his reading glasses were found on a small table in the bedroom.

Once the search moved outside the house, the sleuths discovered a broken window in the garage.

Both of the couple's vehicles, a Chevrolet and a Buick, were in the garage. Probers decided to open the trunk of the brown Chevrolet and if they had not been confused and puzzled before, they certainly were now. In the trunk they found several throw rugs, some women's clothing, and a dishpan containing a bottle of Ivory dishwashing liquid. All of the items found were bloodstained.

Police moved on to the Buick, but before opening the trunk of this vehicle, they noticed what appeared to be a fresh dent and several fresh scratches. When they opened the trunk, the investigators found 14 more rugs, all bloodstained. After the rugs were removed, probers found more women's clothing, some old purses, a potted plant and another cleaning pan. After removing all of these items, sleuths found a large, kitchen butcher knife, which would later prove to be the murder weapon.

Apparently, the killer had entered the home unarmed, sleuths deduced.

Another officer noticed that a cedar tree near the garage had been recently scratched. It appeared that scratches on the Buick and the tree were a match, leading probers to wonder whether or not the killer had driven the Suttons' car.

Detectives found an unidentified set of fingerprints in several locations within the house. These were forwarded to the Federal Bureau of Investigation in the hope that the killer's identity could be determined. This of course would only happen if the killer had been fingerprinted before. Any seasoned police officer knows that this is not always the case.

The autopsy report showed that Rachel Sutton

had died from a fatal wound to the back. She had sustained six stab and slash wounds, plus several "defensive cuts" on her hands. The medical examiner found 13 wounds on William Sutton's body. The fatal one was a stab wound to his throat. Pathologists determined that 11 of these wounds had been made by the butcher knife found in the trunk of the Buick. Two other wounds, one each in William's chest and neck, had been made by a double-edged weapon. Police had recovered a decorative African spear from the Suttons' dining room and this proved to be the cause of the additional wounds.

The sleuths began their investigation, away from the scene, by questioning as many of the Suttons' neighbors as possible. They found that both of the Suttons had been employed as professors at the University of Georgia. William had also worked for 18 years in Washington for the U.S. Tariff Commission. Even though they had lived in the community for years, not many people knew much about them.

However, it did not take long for the news of the gruesome killings to reach the community. Police asked citizens to come forward with any information they may have and the community began responding almost immediately. As always, most of the tips that the lawmen received were worthless, but they did receive an important call from a young woman. She told them that she had seen a slim, white male, possibly Hispanic, with dark skin, frizzy hair and a clean-shaven face, running toward a car from the Suttons' property at approximately 8 p.m. on April 22nd.

The witness explained to police that she had been jogging on Sunset Drive when she had glanced into the backyard of the Sutton home. She said the man she had seen appeared to be in a big hurry. Since she did not know the Suttons, or whoever lived in the house, she didn't think there was anything strange about the incident at the time.

The witness did come to police headquarters and assisted the officers in preparing a composite drawing of the man she had seen. Police might have released this drawing at once but they also received two more leads on Monday, April 27th. The first of these leads came from another resident of the neighborhood who told police that she had seen a white van parked in the Suttons' driveway on the day in question. Another couple from the neighborhood confirmed that they had seen a similar white van in the area of the Sutton home but they could not place it on the property. Based on this information, police decided not to release the composite drawing.

On Tuesday, the funeral home, which was preparing a service for the Sutton couple, received a phone call from someone who stated that the Sutton funeral would be "an unforgettable funeral." Police immediately staked out the funeral home and cemetery. The license number of every vehicle in attendance was recorded, but the funeral went on without incident.

For more than two weeks, investigators continued to follow up on the leads which continued to come in from the community. On May 11, 1988, an elderly woman, who lived on Oglethorpe Avenue, just blocks from the Sutton home, received a phone call. The caller told the terrified woman, "I'm going to do the same thing to your family that I did to the Suttons."

The woman immediately called the police and the officers arranged for a tap on the woman's phone. Four days later, another threatening call was received. The police were able to trace the call to a house in the nearby community of Bogart, Georgia, some eight miles from Athens. Investigators drove by the house and noticed that a white van was parked in the driveway. They decided to obtain a warrant.

When investigators returned to the Bogart home with the warrant, they learned that the calls had been placed by a 16-year-old boy. After several hours of investigation, it was determined that the youth was in no way involved with the Sutton slayings, and had simply been playing a "very bad joke."

Approximately a week before this event occurred, the police had asked the Federal Bureau of Investigation for assistance, and Special Agent Joe Hardy was dispatched to the Sutton home to examine the scene and to try to develop a psychological profile of the killer. Hardy's report concluded that the killer had apparently left the scene in a state of panic. The killer was probably a male based on the fact that most female killers have an aversion to the amount of blood found at the scene. It was also evident that the killer had a compulsion for cleanliness. Hardy stated it was possible that the Suttons' killer was involved in some type of cleaning work. The killer was probably very controlled on the outside but "inside" he was very much out of control. Also, said Hardy's report, there was probably a history of jail time in the killer's past.

During their investigation, the police found that the Suttons had owned 12 rental properties in the city and surrounding areas. Investigators spoke to all of the present and some of the former tenants, but again without results.

Meanwhile, police received a call from a woman who told them that she had seen a car near the Sutton home on the night in question and that a black man had left the car and run into the woods near the Sutton home. She gave the police the vehicle's license number and the police traced the vehicle's owner. The young man confirmed that he had been in the area on the evening in question and explained that his friend had indeed run from the car and into the woods, but only because he had to urinate.

Much of police work involves plodding along, doing tedious tasks and remaining constantly aware of things that are out of the ordinary. On the morning of June 2, 1988, Officer Ray Chinn was on routine traffic patrol when he stopped a white van for a traffic violation. During the course of his conversation with the offender, the man asked Chinn if they had caught the Suttons' killer yet. Chinn reported his conversation to the detective division and they paid the man a visit. While this ordinary traffic incident report did not produce the killer, another traffic report later would.

On Thursday, July 9th, the police released the composite drawing that they had prepared on April 22nd. The police had determined that normal investigative techniques were not working and therefore they had no reason to hold on to the drawing any longer. From the moment the composite appeared in the media, the police were deluged with calls.

Police received reports from citizens who claimed to have seen the man in locations from Atlanta, Georgia, to Jacksonville, Florida. He was reported as being enrolled in college courses and had apparently been spotted driving around Athens in a light blue Mercedes. All of the reports proved to be groundless.

Throughout the months of July and August, the police kept working and the community kept talking but absolutely no progress was made in solving the gruesome double murder.

At approximately 10:30 p.m. on August 15, 1988, Athens police received a call from a relative of Ann Orr Morris. The man stated that Mrs. Morris had left home at approximately 9 a.m. to visit her friend, Sally Nathanson, and had not returned. The relative had called the friend's house several times and had received no answer. The desk sergeant told the man that a car would be sent to the Nathanson address to see if everything was all right.

Officer Roger Huff received the call to go to the residence of Mrs. Sally Nathanson on Carr's Hill Road at approximately 10:45 p.m. and arrived at the house shortly before 11 o'clock. As Huff pulled into the driveway of the large 19th century antebellum estate, he was joined by Sergeant Michael Turner. Both officers noted that while the house was situated in a fairly populous area, it was protected from view by several large trees and an enormous amount of shrubbery.

The two officers, flashlights in hand, walked down the darkened driveway toward the darkened home. Their flashlight beams cut through the darkness. As they approached the front porch of the home, Huff's light trailed slightly off of the concrete walkway and into the grass. As if it had been guided by an unseen hand, it stopped on the brutally beaten and twisted body of 63-year-old Ann Orr Morris.

The two officers immediately called for backup and within moments, Officers Royce Carter and Glen Green arrived and were dispatched immediately to the back door of the house. As the officers entered the house with their weapons at the ready, the only light they could see was apparently the glow of a television set. As the officers proceeded, they were confronted by another woman's body lying in a pool of blood on a small bed. All four officers entered the living room from two different directions and found still another body, this one too was female, but it was obvious that she was much younger than the other two women. Police continued to search the house until they were sure that the perpetrator was not on the premises and then they called in the crime lab team and set about securing the crime scene.

Agents from the Georgia Bureau of Investigation (GBI) and technicians from the state crime lab were on the scene within the hour. Even the most seasoned of the investigators stated that the crime scene was too horrible for words.

As investigators worked through the early morning hours, they tried to piece together two things.

First, what kind of weapon had been used to cause the destruction and mayhem they were witnessing? And second, in what order did the victims meet their gruesome fate? It did not take long to answer the question of whether this case was related to the Sutton murders. The speculation early on was split. Many of the agents did not believe the two cases were connected, because no elaborate attempt to clean up the blood had been made at the Nathanson home. Another thing that led police to think the two crimes might not be related was the fact that neither of the two cars they found at the Nathanson home appeared to have been tampered with.

After several hours of examination, the order in which the victims had been attacked was established. Sally Nathanson had been slain first. The phone line beside her bed had been severed, apparently by the killer's weapon. The police concluded that the killer had entered the back door of the home, just as Sergeant Turner and Officer Carter had a few hours earlier.

"She was just the first person the killer encountered," said one seasoned officer. "In cases like this there usually isn't a specific motive in the killer's mind. He may have simply been a burglar who was surprised 'in the act,' but that isn't likely."

The reason for the unlikeliness of the burglar theory was the fact that in most cases, when a burglar is confronted he will flee instead of fight. In this case, not only did the intruder fight, but he continued his intrusion and next encountered the younger woman who it turned out was Sally's daughter, Helen Nathanson.

Apparently Helen Nathanson had been in the process of eating breakfast when the killer attacked. Her body was found partially underneath a small dining table in the den. On the table police found a plate containing two waffles and a glass of milk. Only one bite had been taken from the food.

The final victim, Ann Morris, had probably been attacked as the killer was trying to make his exit, detectives theorized.

"She apparently arrived after everything was over and scared the killer on his way out," said one crime lab official.

This was the only logical explanation for Morris being attacked outside the home.

While in the Sutton case, police had reason to believe the killer was a male, this case left no doubt. Technicians found evidence that both of the Nathanson women had been sexually assaulted, and found specimens of the killer's hair on both women's bodies.

In another room of the house, police found a pair of men's jockey shorts and a white pair of women's panties. On the jockey shorts, officers found hairs from both of the Nathanson women and the killer. In an upstairs bedroom, police found that several items on the dresser had been disturbed. Also, a substance, talcum powder, had been spilled on the floor and police found a footprint in the powder.

Sleuths still had not located the murder weapon. The medical examiner told them that the weapon was probably a large meat cleaver or a small ax. This was based on his findings that each of the victims showed signs of bludgeoning and not just cuts.

"The killer seemed to become more agitated with each victim," said one officer. "Each victim was hacked up worse than the one before."

While most of the blows to all three victims were to the head and neck area, the medical examiner found several "contused wounds" on the victims' shoulders and torso. Two of the victims had "defensive cuts" on their hands from trying to ward off the assault.

While the crime lab was sorting through the physical evidence at the scene, Detectives Tim Smith and W.J. Smith interviewed the family member, who had first alerted them. Based on his information, the probers determined that there should have been three automobiles present at the Nathanson home, instead of the two that were found. The missing vehicle belonged to Sally Nathanson and was described as a gray 1984 Dodge Diplomat. By searching through the papers in the Nathanson home, police were able to find the vehicle's license number. Police immediately issued a lookout for the vehicle.

Officer Kirk Graham arrived at the Athens Police Station at 6:45 a.m. as usual for roll call prior to his seven-to-three traffic watch. During roll call, he and the other officers of the watch were informed about the Nathanson killings and given a complete description of the vehicle which was missing.

Just 26 minutes after coming on duty, Officer Graham spotted a gray Dodge that matched the description of the missing vehicle parked at a home on Moreland Avenue in East Athens. Graham noticed two men in the yard of a neighboring home and asked them if they knew anything about the vehicle or its possible owner. Both men answered no, and Graham proceeded to check the license number of the car against the one on his sheet. Once he determined that this was the Nathanson vehicle, and after notifying the detective division, he approached the house and rapped on the door.

The door was answered by a young black man, who identified himself to Graham as Clinton Bankston, age 16. Graham noticed immediately that the young man had a set of Dodge keys looped through his belt. When Graham asked the youth about them, Bankston said they were his. Graham immediately took the youth into custody and read him his Miranda rights.

Officer Graham had just finished reading the suspect his rights when the detectives arrived on the scene. Detective W.J. Smith asked the youth where he had gotten the vehicle. Bankston told him he got it from a friend about two days before. When Smith asked the youth the name of the friend, Bankston gave him the name Chris Ward. Smith asked if Chris was black or white and Bankston answered "white."

Detective Smith later wrote in his report, "The suspect seemed very nervous. It was obvious he was not telling the truth from the manner in which he answered our questions."

Smith told Bankston that some "really bad things" had happened and told him that "the truth was very important." At this point, Bankston became visibly shaken and said that he had found the car. Then he volunteered that he had seen some "dead people" while he had been looking for work.

At this point, Smith noticed another set of keys in Bankston's shirt pocket. He removed the keys and found that they were to the Nathanson residence. Smith was ready to discontinue the interview, but as a last statement he told Bankston, "We need to talk about something that happened in April involving some more people and you know what I'm talking about."

Bankston nodded his head yes, and as Detective Smith placed the youth in the police car for transport to the station, he knew that five, not three murders, were about to be solved immediately.

Once at police headquarters, Clarke County District Attorney Investigator Scott Berry set up a video camera and joined in the interview.

Bankston told police that he had gone into the Nathanson home with his friend Chris. Bankston laid all the blame on Chris, denying any part in any of the violence.

In response to one question about the murder of Helen Nathanson, Bankston responded with details about both the Nathanson slayings and details of the Sutton killings.

Bankston told investigators initially that Chris had used a sword-ax to kill the three women and that he had taken the weapon with him when the two of them parted company. Later, however, Bankston told investigators that Chris had dumped the weapon. Detective Smith and Investigator Berry went to the location that Bankston gave and found a bloodstained hatchet, a pair of bloody gloves, a blood-spattered men's dress shirt and a pair of women's slippers.

Bankston continued to give flawed information that appeared to be laced with the truth. In response to one question about the murder motive, Bankston replied, "Then I asked what Chris was doing and he said he was getting back at her for what she done to him. He acted like he already know her and I said I'm fixing to go. He, ah, the first house we did I went along with him as getting the money, but I ain't did, I didn't kill nobody. . . ."

For several days after the arrest of Clinton Bankston, police searched for the man named Chris Ward. On four occasions, Bankston identified houses where Ward supposedly lived. No one named Ward lived at any of the residences identified.

Discussions with friends and relatives of Bankston revealed that Clinton had made up the imaginary Chris Ward so he wouldn't feel so lonesome. The friends told probers that on several occasions they had asked Clinton if they could meet Chris, but Chris always seemed to have just left before they arrived.

After more than a week of searching for the elusive Chris Ward, Bankston finally told officers and the police psychiatrist that Chris was not real and that he had made him up. Bankston still refused to admit that he committed the murders, however.

Based upon the fact that only Clinton Bankston's fingerprints had been found at both the Sutton and Nathanson crime scenes, the hair samples taken from the bodies of the Nathansons matched Bankston's and the fact that he had been in possession of the Dodge, the district attorney was prepared to seek the death penalty in the case.

After more than six months of legal maneuvering, it was ruled that state law prohibited the execution of anyone under 18 years of age. Bankston was only 16.

On May 12, 1988, Clinton Bankston, on the advice of his attorneys, pleaded guilty to five counts of murder and was sentenced to five consecutive life sentences, thus bringing to an end one of the most bizarre and brutal cases ever faced by the city of Athens, Georgia.

EDITOR'S NOTE:
Donna Brown is not the real name of the person so named in the foregoing story. A fictitious name has been used because there is no reason for public interest in the identity of this person.

"THROAT-SLASHED VIRGINS TOOK 15 MINUTES TO DIE!"

by Maryann Eidemiller

It was an evening that had started out as a lighthearted adventure, but it had turned into a nightmare. The girl was only 12 years old and had just been raped. Now she lay in the bathtub with a 10-inch slash across her throat.

If the young man with the knife thought that murdering someone was as easy as it looked in movies, he was wrong. There was blood everywhere, but his victim was still alive.

"Why won't you die?" he asked the helpless, petrified girl.

"Why are you doing this?" she responded.

He had no good answer. He knew what he was doing, but, he would later claim, he didn't know why. A Catholic priest would later try to prove that this young man had dissociated himself from reality, that it was as though someone else had taken over his body. The priest would try to convince a jury that it was Satan, not the young man, who had control of the knife that night.

Whoever or whatever was to blame, the reality was that it happened. On that pleasant summer evening, on the eve of a high holiday among followers of Satan, the girl was taking too long to die. So the young man plunged the knife into her heart to ensure her death.

The brutal tragedy began on Tuesday, August 2, 1988, in North Huntingdon, a sprawling, constantly developing township located about 30 miles east of Pittsburgh, Pennsylvania. U.S. Route 30, which cuts through the municipality, is a heavily commercialized strip. Condos, shopping centers, fast-food places, car dealerships, and countless other businesses compete for the driver's attention for miles and miles on both sides of the highway.

It was at one of these shopping centers that 13-year-old Penny Lee Ansell and 12-year-old Melissa Marie Baker were dropped off by a relative of Penny's with whom they were staying over night. It was a carefree summer evening for the vacationing schoolgirls. They were planning to go to the Irwin Community Day Picnic the next day. But this evening the girls were going to hang around the video gameroom at the shopping center. The relative was supposed to return to pick them up at 10 o'clock.

Penny lived in North Versailles and Melissa was from East McKeesport, both towns just a few miles west down the highway. They were students at East Allegheny Junior High School, and they were known to be good kids, just typical girls starting to grow up.

Both girls had been warned repeatedly about talking to strangers, as children are routinely warned. That evening, though, whatever admonitions they'd heard were put aside. Perhaps the two handsome young strangers seemed harmless. Perhaps at ages 12 and 13, the girls felt wise enough to take a risk. Or maybe they were tempted by the lure of adventure and the opportunity to act grown up. Maybe the girls thought they could leave for a while, be back by 10:00, and no one would be the wiser. Unfortunately, no one will ever know what the two girls were thinking and why they got into the red pickup truck and rode away.

Later that evening, the relative returned to the shopping center to pick up Penny and Melissa. When the appointed time passed, the girls had still not shown up. No one the relative questioned had seen them either. With irritation giving way to alarm, the relative called the North Huntingdon Police Department to file missing-person reports.

The police did all they could do at that early point in the case. The information was sent out over the radio, so neighboring departments were made aware that the girls were missing, and officers on patrol were alerted to watch for them.

The relative went home and enlisted the aid of family members. They did what any family would do in that situation, checking with the girls' friends and other relatives and keeping an all-night vigil. None of their efforts mattered,

though, not even their prayers. By the time anyone realized that Penny and Melissa were even
missing, something wicked had already happened
to them.

Very few people would have reason to know
that August 3rd was the eve of a devil worshipper's holiday known as the Satanic Revels. "Celebrations" called for having sex with young
virgins. Very few people knew, either, that the
driver of the red truck the girls had climbed into
had a satanic bible in his bedroom.

Sometime after midnight, a young man in
nearby Monroeville, shaking and confused, was
in his bedroom wondering what to do. The night
had turned sour. His good friend had done
something despicable, the worst thing one human being could do to another. Finally, 20-year-
old Jimmy Murphy woke up his mother. "I went
out with Steven and these two girls were with
us," he told her, then added, "and the two girls
never came back."

They woke up his father. Then all three of
them headed for the Monroeville Police Station,
where Jimmy Murphy told Sergeant David Jones
about "two murders."

He then directed Patrolman Jeffrey Herbst and
another officer to a remote illegal dump off
Johnson Road. There, along the pavement, they
found a plastic trash bag covered with masking
tape and what appeared to be spots of blood.
They continued to search the area for about half
an hour. At 3:30 a.m., when they were coming
up an embankment, something that was partially

hidden under evergreen branches caught Herbst's attention. He shined his light toward the trees and saw a leg sticking out.

Herbst had found the girls the North Huntingdon police were looking for. The bodies of Penny Ansell and Melissa Baker were wrapped in plastic trash bags and dumped together with their heads uphill and their feet downhill.

The officers radioed the station for assistance from their department and from Allegheny County investigators, including the coroner's office. They spent most of the night searching the floodlit scene, but found nothing relevant. The victims had obviously been killed elsewhere, then just dropped off here.

The dump area was secluded enough so that the bodies might have remained undiscovered for at least a short time if Jimmy Murphy hadn't directed lawmen to the site. Back at the station, he was telling the police how it had happened, how the girls, whom he didn't know, had come to such a tragic fate.

The perpetrator, he said, was his good friend Steven Patrick Mignogna, an 18-year-old high school dropout from nearby Trafford. Because the murder had taken place in another jurisdiction, the Monroeville police contacted the Trafford police and Westmoreland County detectives, who staked out Mignogna's home and the vicinity around it.

County Detective Roger Eckels pulled in to the lot of a convenience store to meet another officer, but quickly took off in pursuit when he spotted a truck and driver fitting the suspect's description. The truck zipped through town at high speed, sometimes exceeding 75 mph, with the police right behind. It screeched to a stop in front of Mignogna's home.

Detective Eckels twice ordered Mignogna out of the truck. When Mignogna failed to comply, Eckels finally pulled him out, threw him down on the lawn, and handcuffed him. A half-dozen other officers, three of them with their guns drawn, surrounded them.

"You have the right to remain silent," Eckels began. After he finished reading Mignogna his rights, he asked, "Do you wish to talk to us?"

"Where's my cigarettes?" Mignogna replied.

Once in the holding cell at the Trafford Police Station, Mignogna asked to see Acting Chief Charles Noll. Further advised of his rights, Mignogna related how he and Jimmy Murphy had picked up the victims at the shopping center, then went to his house in Trafford.

"What happened then?" Chief Noll asked.

"I don't want to talk about that right now," Mignogna replied. "Maybe we'll talk about that later."

At around 7:00 a.m., Westmoreland County Detective William Manning began interrogating the suspect. Mignogna admitted that he took Melissa Baker (whose name he did not know) to his mother's bedroom where he had sexual intercourse with her.

"Did she agree to have sex?" Detective Manning asked.

"I sort of talked her into that," Mignogna replied.

"How and why did you kill Melissa Baker?" Manning asked.

"I don't want to talk about that," the suspect answered.

He had a similar reply when questioned about Penny Ansell. But he did describe how he took the bodies down two flights of stairs to the basement, covered them with garbage bags, and loaded them into the back of his pickup truck. He appeared to be cool and calm, and he told the investigators, "Whatever Jimmy said is the truth. Jimmy had nothing to do with it, but Jimmy said he wouldn't say anything."

Mignogna wasn't saying much more, but he didn't have to. When the lawmen began processing the murder scene, the physical evidence filled in many of the gruesome, bloody details.

Westmoreland County Detective Michael Paden noted that the bed of the pickup truck had traces of water from the truck having apparently been freshly washed and that it looked "particularly clean." But fortunately for investigators, criminals almost always miss something. In this case, Detective Paden found three bloodstained areas of the truck that were overlooked. Paden also found drag marks on a concrete sidewalk, blood in nearby weeds, and bloodstains on an aluminum loading ramp. All of those areas were also wet and there was a hose, with water still in it, on the other side of the house.

Inside the suspect's two-story home, investigators removed a section of plastic carpet runner and carpet fibers that appeared to be blood-stained and confiscated a bloody maroon rug. The bathroom upstairs appeared to have just been cleaned, but Paden still found traces of blood behind a towel rack and samples from the wall that would later be found to be consistent with the victims' blood types.

Paden also confiscated a sheathed hunting knife from one desk in Mignogna's bedroom, a scalpel-type knife from another desk, and two other knives from a dresser drawer. In the master bedroom, he seized a bloodstained sheet and bed pad. He also found white trash bags similar to the one found near the dump and a box of brownish-green trash bags similar to those wrapped around Penny Ansell's feet.

The stairs to the basement were very clean, but upon meticulous examination, Detective Paden discovered two blood spots beneath the lips of two steps. He also found a fifth knife in the basement, as well as a sponge mop, a scrub brush, and a piece of paper towel, all containing blood. Criminologists from the state police crime lab at Troop A would later match the stains to the murdered girls' blood types.

In his statement to the press, Westmoreland County District Attorney John Driscoll said that Steven Mignogna had given no motive for the double homicide, although neither drugs nor alcohol appeared to play a role in the crime. In fact, friends of the suspect told reporters that the family was virulently anti-drug because of drug problems a family member had had. At that time, no one knew anything about Mignogna's alleged interest in the devil.

Steven Mignogna himself had nothing to say to reporters, either. Led from the arraignment in handcuffs, he commented, "What's fair is fair."

The bodies of the murder victims were transported to Pittsburgh, where Allegheny County Coroner Dr. Joshua Perper performed the autopsies. Pretty Melissa Baker had been slashed on the neck three times and had sustained fatal stab wounds in the chest and through the heart. The coroner also found defensive slashes on her hand, bruises "consistent with blows" on her face, and vaginal injuries, including "a recent laceration to the hymen."

In short, the postmortem examination showed the young virgin had struggled while she was apparently raped. Penny, her friend, had not been sexually assaulted, but her throat was slashed and she had been stabbed in the chest. She, too, had defensive wounds on her right hand.

Because of the autopsy findings, Detective Manning was later able to file additional charges of rape and statutory rape against the suspect.

On August 6th, Mignogna was transferred to Mayview State Hospital because he expressed suicidal tendencies while in custody at the county jail. While he was being transported, he asked the two guards accompanying him about the procedures at the mental hospital.

"What possesses a boy like you to do something like this?" one guard asked him. It was not a custodial interrogation, as the defense attorney would later try to claim, but a casual conversation.

"Well, I know I did it," he replied, "but I don't know why."

The "why" of the whole senseless double murder would become the big issue at Mignogna's trial. Right from the start there were rumors that Mignogna was a Satan worshipper, but those allegations were officially denied by both the defense and prosecution while the trial was being prepared.

However, in Mignogna's bedroom, sleuths had found a satanic bible and numerous heavy metal rock music albums with violent lyrics. It was a lifestyle that the defense attorneys would later try to turn around to their advantage.

Later that year, Mignogna became so dissatisfied with his court-appointed counsel that on Christmas day he signed a poorly written brief and subsequently filed it in the U.S. District Court. In it, he sought to have Public Defender Dante Bertani and Assistant Public Defender Debra Pezze removed from the case because he claimed "there [sic] neglect and there eneffective practices are going to get me the death sentence." He also sought $10,000 in damages from each of them.

Pretrial hearings were held on February 3, 1989, at which time Westmoreland County Common Pleas Judge Donetta Ambrose ruled that Assistant District Attorney John Peck presented enough evidence to proceed with the trial.

Mignogna's defense counsel did change, but not because he had successfully ousted Bertani and Pezze. A new attorney came aboard, one who would lend a carnival aura to the proceedings, one who would shock spectators, bedevil the judge, and enrage the victims' families. He was Father Orlando Prosperi, a Catholic priest who was also an attorney for the Vatican, and he offered his services to Mignogna for free. He was back in Westmoreland County, his home area, because of poor health.

Prosperi prepared a bizarre defense in his intention to prove that the real perpetrator in the murders of Penny Ansell and Melissa Baker was not Steven Mignogna, but heavy metal music, pornography, and Satan himself.

News reporters revealed a further irony: A.D.A. Peck, assigned to represent the Commonwealth, had once been in the seminary but did not become a priest. These two lawyers with backgrounds in theology would be pitted against each other in the courtroom where the defendant's religious beliefs — or lack of them — would become a central issue.

Peck filed official notice of the circumstances that he would seek first-degree murder convictions and the death penalty. He claimed that the aggravating circumstances included raping Melissa, killing her to prevent her from testifying against him about the rape, and killing Penny because she was a possible witness. Peck also stated that he would attempt to prove that Melissa Baker was killed by means of torture, as legally defined, with Mignogna inflicting pain on her before the slaying. That is, there was evidence that she had lived for some time after he slashed her throat.

On March 3rd, Judge Ambrose refused to ban a possible death penalty and ruled against separate trials for each of the slayings, as had been requested by the defense attorneys.

Mignogna's trial began on Monday, March 6th, with the arduous task of selecting jury members who hadn't already formed opinions about the well-publicized slayings. One by one, candidates were excused because of personal hardship, aversion to the grisly details, or refusal "to play God" with someone's life and death. One woman was excused because she said she had already thought about "what to do with him."

It took five days to seat the first 10 jurors. After the last two and four alternates were finally selected, the trial began on March 14th, in front of Common Pleas Judge Joseph Hudock.

Steven Mignogna showed up with shoulder-length dark hair, wearing jeans and a blue T-shirt. His right arm was tattooed with a death's head skull. A rose and crosses tattoo bedecked the other arm.

In his opening statement to the jury, Peck said the prosecution would prove that Mignogna "forcibly and at knifepoint had intercourse with a twelve-year-old girl . . . cut [her] throat . . . and stabbed her in the heart." Furthermore, he "called Penny Lee Ansell upstairs and cut her throat, causing her death."

Detective Manning, one of the first prosecution witnesses, related details of his interrogation of Mignogna.

"He had realized what he had done," Manning said. "He indicated to me that he was wondering what kind of sentence he would get and if they would try him as a juvenile or as an adult." (That was not a moot point since at the time of the murders, Mignogna, at 18, was no longer a juvenile.)

Dr. Perper testified about his autopsy findings showing that both of the victims had inhaled blood into their lungs. It was his opinion that Penny and Melissa had continued to live from 5 to 15 minutes, "possibly more," after their throats were cut.

The hunting knife that Detective Paden found in Mignogna's bedroom was entered into evidence. It was believed to have been the murder weapon.

Jimmy Murphy was one of the prosecution's chief witnesses. Choking back tears, he told the jury about the evening of August 2, 1988.

He and Mignogna had been friends for years and shared an interest in some music, Murphy said. They both liked the Beatles and Elton John, but in more recent times, Mignogna had been listening to a lot of heavy metal music.

Early on the evening of August 2nd, Murphy said, he and Mignogna drank "one or two" beers, then cruised around the Monroeville Mall before heading for North Huntingdon. There they met the two girls, who they thought were "about fifteen." Murphy felt uneasy about the girls, he testified. He wanted to shoot pool, but Mignogna soon convinced him that everything was cool, and the girls agreed to go with them. They drove around for a while, stopped briefly at one of the girls' homes for cigarettes, and then headed for Mignogna's home in nearby Trafford. His parents were away.

The foursome listened to music for a while; then Mignogna kissed Melissa, "the dark-haired girl." Everyone then went upstairs and listened to the radio and looked at some cassettes. Jimmy and Penny returned to the living room downstairs. It was getting late, so Jimmy yelled up to Mignogna that the girls had to be back at the shopping center.

"Let's get going!" Murphy remembered hollering up the steps. When there was no reply, he called up several more times.

Mignogna finally emerged and came halfway down the steps, Murphy testified. "Your girlfriend wants to see you in the bathroom," Mignogna told Penny. "She wants to talk to you." Penny went up the steps. A moment later, she was screaming.

"I jumped up and went upstairs," Murphy testified.

Upon hearing this, the victims' families started crying. Mignogna appeared to be emotionless, as he had through the rest of his friend's testimony.

Upstairs, Jimmy Murphy continued, he found Melissa in the bathtub with her head toward the

286

drain and her feet hanging over the top.

"There was blood . . . blood everywhere," the witness said. "Her arm was moving . . . like she was trying to breathe."

Murphy said he didn't remember anything else. He blacked out and regained consciousness downstairs in a chaise lounge.

"I need your help," Murphy quoted Mignogna as saying, but Jimmy said he was sorry, that he "couldn't handle all that blood," and he ran off to a nearby convenience store to call his parents.

Nobody answered at the Murphy home. Murphy said he then tried offering money to people to give him a ride home, but it was dark and late, and in his emotional condition, he didn't look like someone anyone would want for a passenger. Terrified, Murphy started walking home toward Monroeville. When he was nearly across the bridge over Turtle Creek, Mignogna pulled up alongside in the pickup truck. "Get in," he ordered.

"I'm not going with you," Murphy told him. "I don't want to see you anymore. I'm just going home."

According to Murphy's testimony, Mignogna started crying, then said, "Get in the truck."

Murphy feared that his friend had a gun and a knife. He thought he would be stabbed or shot. In his rattled state of mind, he felt that his only choices were to jump off the bridge, try to run again, or get into the truck. So he got in. He told the jury that he felt he had "no choice."

"I can't believe what I've done," Mignogna

said to Murphy.

Neither could Murphy, who was mostly silent while Mignogna drove to the dump along Johnson Road in Monroeville. He stopped and got out, and Jimmy looked back into the bed of the truck.

"I saw them there," his testimony continued. He was referring to the bodies, which were in plastic trash bags. "I saw him drag them off."

Murphy waited alone in the truck; then Mignogna came back and slid into the driver's seat. While they headed toward Murphy's home, Mignogna made plans for them to meet the following day. He asked Murphy not to say anything, and his parting words were "I love you."

Murphy went to his room to think for a while. He resolved to tell his parents about the lurid events.

Under cross-examination, the witness admitted that he shared some of Mignogna's taste in rock and roll music with violent lyrics, and that the two of them had gone to pornography shops together.

As the trial shifted into its next phase, rumors persisted that the defense would claim satanic influences as a mitigating circumstance in Mignogna's alleged crimes.

"Would it be correct that the defense will inject satanism in its defense?" a reporter asked Defense Attorney Prosperi.

"I cannot say anything," the latter replied.

But Prosperi did criticize the prosecution's investigation because none of the lawmen "went to the Murphy home." It was a hint of what was to come, that the defense would eventually make a last-ditch effort to blame it on the prosecution's chief witness, Jimmy Murphy.

On March 16th, the rumors of satanism officially surfaced at the trial. After Detective Paden, called by the prosecution, recounted how he found blood and bloody evidence in the Mignogna home, Defense Attorney Debra Pezze disclosed that the deaths took place on the eve of Satanic Revels. Quoting from a state police bulletin entitled "Satanism: The Law Enforcement Response," she revealed that the holiday is observed by male adherents with sexual acts with females between 7 and 17 years of age. She further quoted the bulletin as saying, "Many rituals have violent sexual overtones and violent criminal acts have come to the attention of investigators as a result of these satanic coven rituals."

Detective Paden said his investigation failed to substantiate the rumored link between Mignogna and devil worship. However, Pezze pointed out that the defendant indeed had been exposed to satanic influences. There was a satanic bible in his bedroom, which belonged to another relative, as well as record albums by heavy metal groups that had references to violence and the occult.

At the time Paden processed the murder scene, he did not confiscate those items. Under cross-examination, he admitted that he was now aware that August 3rd was a satanic holiday. Asked by Pezze whether or not that prior knowledge would have influenced how he examined the

Mignogna home, he replied, "I'm not sure I can answer that. It may have."

Defense Attorney Pezze displayed one of her client's T-shirts that advertised the heavy metal group Black Sabbath and was emblazoned with a skull and the number "666," the number of the beast or Anti-Christ.

"On the night of this crime, they listened over and over to this Guns 'n Roses stuff," Pezze said about the period immediately preceding the murders. The album "Appetite For Destruction" includes two songs with violent lyrics. Furthermore, she said, an Ozzy Osbourne album that Mignogna frequently listened to included "Live Mr. Crowley." That song refers to Aleister Crowley, who was a leading advocate of satanism during the early 1900s.

When Defense Attorney Prosperi questioned Jimmy Murphy under cross-examination, Prosperi asked the witness if he indulged in kinky sexual practices with young girls. Murphy calmly replied that he did not.

The young man was in sharp contrast with the defendant. While Mignogna was long-haired and tattooed, Murphy was neatly groomed and wearing a suit and tie. But Prosperi tried to use that to argue against Murphy's credibility. "Steve's appearance is genuine," he said. "It has not been changed, so he is not masquerading."

There was also a marked contrast between the styles of the prosecutor and the defense counsel. Prosecutor Peck presented his case in a logical, subdued manner while Defense Attorney Prosperi repeatedly clashed with the bench. Prosperi was flamboyant. He made long speeches and was often warned by Judge Hudock to stick to questioning witnesses.

The defense relied heavily on reports and testimony from people who had delved into Mignogna's state of mind and claimed that he had problems at home, felt unloved, and was heavily influenced by rock music and by satanic cults.

A school psychologist testified that Mignogna had problems at age 14. A clinical psychologist from Pittsburgh told the court that the murders were not "intentional, conscious, or deliberate" but rather had been committed as if each was an "automatic act." Mignogna, he said, was incapable of deliberating; he exhibited significant hostility and was not certain about what was real and what was not.

"For years this has been an angry, confused young man," the psychologist said, adding that the young man's anger had been directed toward women, including his mother. Although Peck pointed out that Mignogna was in control of himself because he made a series of decisions to clean up the blood and dispose of the bodies, the clinical psychologist said that such attempts to conceal evidence did not necessarily show premeditation.

The defense also called a social psychologist from Reno, Nevada. The witness, an expert in subliminal communications, had spent 90 minutes talking to Mignogna. He testified that the music and videos of such groups as Mötley Crüe, Judas Priest, Billy Idol and others Mignogna listened to contained subliminal messages that "legitimize" violence toward women and authority figures.

"It's powerful stuff," he said.

Although Mignogna denied an interest in satanism, this witness told the jury that "there is a great deal more there than we could get at." Mignogna was, he said, "a time bomb" waiting to explode, and the "trigger" was when he had a sexual encounter with the victim on his mother's bed.

The defense presented another psychologist from Topeka, Kansas, who never personally spoke with Mignogna, basing his $150-an-hour testimony on the other reports. In his opinion, the defendant had lashed out against his mother and his girlfriend when he raped and murdered Melissa Baker.

The psychologist claimed that Mignogna went into a dissociative state when he had his first sexual experience with the young victim. "It was like somebody else had taken over his mind," the witness said.

The psychologist apparently assumed the defendant was a virgin prior to the double homicide, but he was wrong. It was already established that Mignogna had sexual experiences before the slayings.

The witness further stated that Mignogna did not receive love, care, or respect from his family, and that he was influenced by subliminal messages of violence from heavy metal music and pornography.

The psychologist read from the report made by the Pittsburgh psychologist. It stated that Mignogna had made the decision to kill Melissa Baker while he was raping her in his parents' bedroom, that he went to his room to get the hunting knife, then forced her into the bathtub where he slit her throat.

"Sometime after he cut Melissa's throat, he asked her, 'Why won't you die?' " the witness said, citing the statement Steven Mignogna had given to the school psychologist. In that statement, Mignogna mistakenly told the psychologist that Melissa Baker replied, "Penny never dies. Jimmy, why are you doing this?" In the psychologist's opinion, Mignogna's confusion about the girl's name and his own name indicated his weak grip on reality.

The girls' families became visibly upset by evidence that Mignogna talked to at least one of the victims while she was dying. They became further agitated when the psychologist testified that he assumed Mignogna had consensual sex with Melissa, that he erupted at the sight of her being undressed, and that he was disappointed that the encounter did not live up to his undisclosed sexual fantasies, which had been fueled by pornography.

At that point, the girls' parents and other relatives angrily stormed out of the courtroom. In another emotional incident, a family member had to be physically restrained when he attempted to confront Defense Attorney Prosperi in the hallway.

That day, the jurors had a surprise in store for them when they returned from lunch. Mignogna was no longer shaggy-haired and sloppily dressed. He now had a haircut and sported a suit and a tie.

"In light of the aspects of our defense, we thought it would be a scam to clean him up before the trial," Defense Attorney Pezze explained. "We wanted them to see him as he was then, and not all cleaned up. We wanted them to see, just as a transformation is possible in physical appearance, transformation is possible internally."

Steven Mignogna might have looked different, but he still had a hostile attitude. When a photographer from the local daily newspaper took his picture as he was being returned to the county detention center, Mignogna made an obscene gesture. That photo of the "transformed" defendant and his extended middle finger appeared on the front page of the following morning's edition. But the jurors missed it because they were prohibited from seeing anything from the news media during the trial.

The defense called another member of Mignogna's family. He told the jury that the defendant grew up in a "cold" home without love. The witness also related that he and Mignogna had discussed the witness' interest in satanism. But the witness had since given it up.

"Satanism practices the belief you should have no guilt to practice your instincts, which is killing," he testified. "Seeing how the devil's going to work in my life, he isn't helping out. He's corrupting me and Steven." The witness also said that in the past year, Mignogna's taste in music changed from Elton John to heavy metal.

"I believe it got into his subconscious," the relative said. "Music can be an addiction, too."

When asked if he believed that Mignogna was "evil," he replied, "no." He went on to tell about an incident in which he tormented a stray cat and Mignogna cried.

The defense also called the manager of a Pittsburgh pornography shop that Mignogna had frequented. He and Jimmy Murphy were there just three days before the slaying. However, the judge ruled that the defense could not show the jury sexually explicit and violent magazines and videos from the store because that particular merchandise presented in the courtroom had not been in stock when Mignogna was in the store.

This futile attempt by the defense cost Westmoreland County taxpayers $1,379, which included the fee charged by a private investigator to "research" the porno shops and purchase $150 worth of pornographic films and magazines.

During the sidebar conference when Judge Hudock disallowed pornographic materials to be admitted as evidence, Defense Attorney Prosperi caused so much disruption that Judge Hudock charged him with contempt of court after repeatedly warning him not to interrupt. It was only one of many confrontations between the judge and the priest/attorney. Time and again, Judge

Hudock had to warn Prosperi to cease his ti-
rades and histrionics. Hudock, who in his 11
years on the bench didn't even keep a gavel, had
to borrow another judge's gavel to restore order.
When Judge Hudock later left Westmoreland
County to take a seat on the Pennsylvania Superior Court, he told a reporter that he "still
shakes" when he thinks about this trial.

A.D.A. Peck later told the press that Prosperi's behavior was "a classic case in judge bait-
ing." In his opinion, the obstructionist tactics
were designed to time the jury's penalty deliberation closer to Good Friday. The trial was coming
to an end during the middle of Holy Week. At
this most solemn Christian observation, both
God and the devil were highlighted at the nine-
day trial.

For the prosecution's final witness, Prosecutor
Peck chose someone to rebut the defense's con-
tention that their client was influenced by satanism. A teenager who had been Mignogna's
girlfriend for two years said that in their daily
contact, she never heard him discuss satanism.

"At certain times he told me he wanted God
to make his life better because he wanted to finish school and he wanted to be married in a
church," she said.

The defense had also said that Mignogna's tattoo of a rose and crosses was emblematic of satanism. However, the pretty blonde read a letter
that he had written to her from jail, dated September 21st. "About my tattoo and the rose," he
wrote. "I did get the rose because of you. Be-

cause I felt you were the rose of my life and the rose slowly died and I'm slowly dying."

In another letter, he wrote to his girlfriend, "Maybe I'm the devil and now it's time for me to go to hell. . . . I think if I did kill myself, which I'm this close to doing, nobody would miss me."

Concerning the homemade cross tattoos, the witness said they were chosen because they were simple to do with a needle and India ink.

In his 45-minute summation, A.D.A. Peck told the jury to disregard the psychological assessments of Steven Mignogna, which he said were inconsistent with each other and with the defendant's own statements. He asked the jury for convictions on all charges and to mete out the death penalty.

Defense Attorney Prosperi took one hour and 45 minutes to try to convince the jury that Mignogna lacked the mental capacity to form the premeditation necessary to sustain a first-degree murder conviction. His summation was marked by repeated objections from the prosecution when he kept trying to refer to items ruled inadmissible as evidence. Prosperi suggested that Mignogna was guilty of nothing more than aggravated assault for admitting that he cut Melissa's throat, which according to the autopsy was not a fatal wound. Rather, Prosperi suggested that Jimmy Murphy was more involved in the slayings than he admitted. "He was a possible and probable accomplice, and he was there when the bodies were disposed of, making him an accessory after the fact," Prosperi said.

Prosperi contended that the Commonwealth had failed to provide direct evidence that Mignogna had slain both the girls, and that this was "unfair to the parents and families of these two young girls."

The jury thought otherwise. It took them just two and a half hours to return with a verdict of guilty of first-degree murder on both counts and statutory rape. Now they had to listen to both the prosecution and defense argue over whether Steven Mignogna deserved the death penalty or a life sentence.

During that proceeding, the prosecution introduced a witness who said that Mignogna had told her and some friends the previous summer that he wanted "to rape a girl and then kill her." She said this statement was made to a group of friends on June 19th, when they were sitting around a picnic table discussing their futures.

"Steve said he wanted the ultimate power," the girl testified. "He wanted to kill a superior being. He said he wanted to rape a girl and then kill her. I said 'You're a sick pup,' because I thought he was joking."

The witness also said that on the night of the murders, she saw Mignogna at the same shopping center where he picked up the victims. She was going to ask him for a ride home, but her mother arrived to get her.

Mignogna's girlfriend was present when that remark was allegedly made around the picnic table, but when questioned by Defense Attorney

Pezze, she had a different version. The girlfriend said, "I remember Steve saying something about Jimmy, that Jimmy had a dream [that] he always wanted to rape and kill a girl."

Prosperi took advantage of the day—Holy Thursday—to present even more drama in his sometimes rambling defense. In his closing remarks, he quoted Jesus Christ's dying words on the cross.

"Forgive them, for they know not what they do," Prosperi said. "Look at Steve. Look at him. For he did not know what he was doing."

The defense attorneys also wanted Mignogna kept alive so that he could be studied in relation to the harmful effects of pornography. But A.D.A. Peck asked the jury why Steven Mignogna should be spared when "everybody on death row would make an excellent study."

When the testimony ended, the same jury went behind closed doors to decide if Mignogna's life should be spared. They considered five mitigating circumstances, including his poor family life, his exposure to heavy metal music and satanism, and his exposure to pornography. Four hours later, just before midnight, they returned with their decision. For murdering the two girls, Mignogna would be spared the death penalty and instead spend the rest of his life in jail.

Mignogna and his defense attorneys embraced and kissed. The families of the victims left the courtroom heartbroken. One relative told a reporter, "I think he should have had the death penalty because he took two innocent lives."

Formal sentencing was scheduled for Friday, April 14th, at which time Melissa's mother testified before Judge Hudock. "We have lost our only child," she said. "We have lost thousands of moments with Melissa. Good times and bad, we wanted to share them all with her. Over and over, I imagine the intense fear and pain these two innocent girls endured before their deaths."

Mignogna, who was usually emotionless during the trial, got tears in his eyes as the woman spoke. She further claimed that the families suffered "beyond necessity" at the hands of Mignogna's attorneys.

"The unprofessional and disrespectful manner in which the defense, particularly the Reverend Orlando Prosperi, have presented their case and themselves was inexcusable. We were provoked numerous times in and out of the courtroom. We did not deserve to be treated so."

The mother asked the judge to act on behalf of the memory of the two young victims and sentence their killer to two consecutive life terms, with additional maximum sentences for the convictions of rape and statutory rape.

And that's exactly what Judge Hudock did. He further made it clear that he would do everything in his power to ensure that Mignogna will never be released. When he imposed the formal sentence of two consecutive life terms, he told Mignogna, "To put it in plain language, you, sir, are a cold-blooded killer who is fully responsible for your atrocities."

EDITOR'S NOTE:
Jimmy Murphy is not the real name of the person so named in the foregoing story. A fictitious name has been used because there is no reason for public interest in the identity of this person.

"ALL-AMERICAN KID SLIT LISA'S THROAT WITH A BOY SCOUT KNIFE!"

by Gary C. King

Wilsonville, Oregon
August 13, 1991

Pretty Lisa Jenell Flormoe was talking on the telephone with her fiancé, David Lesh, when the doorbell rang again at a few minutes past 1:00 p.m. on Tuesday, August 13, 1991. Currently staying at the home of friends in the exclusive, affluent Charbonneau district of Wilsonville, Oregon, a Portland suburb, Lisa had by now become annoyed. It was the third time someone had come to the front door while she was on the phone. David had called long-distance from Lisa's hometown of Eugene, some 100 miles south of Wilsonville. Lisa excused herself again and laid the phone down, with David still on the other end, to answer the door.

As David patiently waited with his ear to the receiver for his wife-to-be to come back to the phone, he could hear someone else talking to her. It was a male voice trying to describe someone—a girl—who apparently lived in the neighborhood. David could tell by Lisa's responses that she didn't know the girl being described to her, and by her tone that she'd become even more impatient with the stranger's persistent questioning. Instants later, what David heard made him realize that the questions had been only a ruse to get the door open. Lisa was in serious trouble and nobody was there to help her.

"Turn around and shut up!" David heard the male voice order Lisa. "Put your hands on the wall!"

"Please don't hurt me!" Lisa cried. "Please, don't!" Terror in her voice, she pleaded again and again. David was horrified as he heard Lisa's cries and violent thumping noises. He could only imagine what was going on, and shudder.

Fearing for Lisa's life, David hung up and immediately called 911. He was quickly put through to the Portland Police Bureau's emergency communications center. Precious minutes were being lost as he was told that Wilsonville was not within Portland's jurisdiction. Nonetheless, the concerned Portland officer managed to get Lesh connected to the Clackamas County Sheriff's Department, which did have jurisdiction. David Lesh, his voice quavering with fear and a sense of helplessness, explained what he had just heard happening over the telephone.

It was about 1:30 p.m. when the team of deputies reached the address where Lisa was staying. It was a newer home located in the 32000 block of Southwest Lake Drive, next to a large golf course. They saw a black, two-door BMW parked in the drive, and they noted its license-plate number. The deputies approached the house cautiously and listened at the front door to determine if an altercation was in progress. Hearing nothing but deadly silence, they rang the bell. There was no answer. A turn of the handle revealed that the door was locked.

303

The lawmen walked warily around the house, peering into the windows. It wasn't until they reached the window of the family room that they realized they had something far more serious than a suspected assault to investigate.

Through the family-room window, the deputies were able to see beyond, into another room, possibly a bedroom, in which they observed what appeared to be the body of a naked young woman. The deputies promptly called headquarters to report their discovery and to ask for backup and paramedics. Then they broke down the front door and entered the house.

When the deputies reached the bedroom, they saw that the nude woman was lying in a massive pool of her own blood. They checked for signs of life, but found none. Although she was dead, her flesh was still slightly warm to the touch. The deputies, not wishing to inadvertently contaminate what was now obviously a crime scene, retraced their steps back out of the house and radioed for a homicide unit.

Detectives Candace Dufur and Larry Beckwith arrived at the scene less than half an hour later. When they viewed the body, they could see that the victim's throat had been stabbed and slit. The wounds, they observed, were not "clean," easily made ones. It looked more as though someone had hacked away haphazardly with something sharp and pointed. The victim also had slashes to her hands and arms, which the sleuths believed were defensive wounds sustained while she was trying to fight off her assailant. The fact that she was naked left little doubt in the detectives' minds that this was a sex crime.

Deputy Judy Gage, a spokeswoman for the Clackamas County Sheriff's Department, confirmed that the victim was positively identified as 22-year-old Lisa

Flormoe. Gage said that the detectives did not know what type of weapon was used. Because of the slicing and stabbing nature of Lisa's wounds, however, they knew it had to be a sharp instrument, likely a knife or pair of scissors. Unfortunately, a thorough search of the house failed to turn up the murder weapon.

The detectives felt that everything in the house appeared to be in order. The house had not been ransacked, as would be expected in a burglary, and aside from Lisa's naked body and all the blood, they found surprisingly few signs that any struggle had occurred there. The probers guessed that the perpetrator had very quickly and easily gotten Lisa under his control by wielding a weapon and threatening her with bodily injury or death. Because it appeared that nothing had been taken, Detectives Dufur and Beckwith virtually ruled out robbery as a motive.

The two sleuths soon learned that the house in which Lisa was killed was owned by a Californian who had rented it to a family—a couple and their teenage daughter—whom Lisa had come to visit. When Detectives Dufur and Beckwith contacted the neighbors, they learned that the renters had kept to themselves.

"I had never seen them before, ever," one neighbor said. "I didn't even know the place was rented."

"This is really kind of jolting," another neighbor declared. "I kind of hope it was a crime of passion. We're kind of shocked, but we're not as worried as if it had been a break-in or something from off the street."

Of the neighbors who were home all day, none had heard or seen anything suspicious or unusual. By the time the sleuths had canvassed both sides of the street a block in either direction, they still knew little more about the murder than they had learned at the outset of their probe.

"We do not have a focal suspect at this point," Detective Beckwith told a group of hungry newshounds who showed up at the crime scene.

The detectives knew from the report given by Lisa's fiancé that she had been killed shortly after 1:00 p.m., and that she had gone to the door at least three times to answer questions from someone who'd said he was trying to learn the whereabouts of a teenage girl. Although the details were sketchy, Detective Beckwith learned that the first time the person had come to the door had been shortly after 11:00 a.m. It had been the same person in each instance, but unfortunately, Lisa had not provided her fiancé with that person's description. Apparently, Lisa had thought that the inquiries from the stranger were innocent enough, so she had not been alarmed on the first two visits, and therefore had no reason to describe him.

Beckwith told reporters that no one had been ruled in or out as a suspect. He pleaded for information from anyone who might have seen or heard something suspicious in the vicinity of the crime scene between 11:00 a.m. and 2:00 p.m.

The detectives soon learned that the black BMW parked in the driveway was registered to Lisa's fiancé, 30-year-old David Lesh. Motor Vehicles Division records indicated that Lesh and Lisa had lived at the same address in Eugene. Lesh, who arrived at the crime scene at 3:00 p.m., after driving frantically from Eugene, told the sleuths that he had loaned the car to Lisa for her trip to Wilsonville. He said that he and Lisa had lived together for five years and had planned to be married in December. Lisa, he said, left Eugene the day before — on Monday, August 12th — to visit her friends in Wilsonville, whom she had known for about five years. She had planned to return the same day, but for some reason, she'd changed her mind and decided to stay overnight.

"Something came up," Lesh explained. "She wanted to talk longer with her friends."

He said that Lisa had been happy and excited the last time they'd talked. They had even made plans to build their dream house after their marriage. "I had just sold my house and we were very excited. I bought property, and we were going to build a house together. She was in very good spirits."

Lisa had not given David any indication that she'd been facing any kinds of problems on the day of her death or on the night before. "We shared everything," Lesh said. "If something weird was going on, she would have said something. I just have a feeling somebody knows something. I think she was an innocent bystander to something."

Lesh then told the sleuths about how he had been talking to Lisa over the telephone from Eugene when she heard someone ring the front doorbell and put the phone down. "I heard what happened," he said, explaining that he heard a male voice when Lisa opened the door. "He came to the door trying to describe somebody. Lisa was getting annoyed about it because she was on the phone with me."

Lesh said that he could hear the person describing a younger woman to Lisa. After a few moments, it sounded as though the stranger had forced his way into the house.

"He told her to turn around and shut up and to put her hands on the wall. Lisa begged, 'Please don't hurt me!' over and over." That was when Lesh hung up and called the police.

"Lisa was a very classy and a very beautiful woman," Lesh said. "She was the world to me. I loved her. I always will. For Lisa's sake, I'm telling all my friends to pray that the person who did it is found. Somebody murdered her, but they'll catch him. They have to. . . . He took Lisa's life and he took a big part of everybody else's life, as well."

Detectives Dufur and Beckwith learned that Lisa Flormoe was not employed at the time of her death, but she had plans to start a career in finance or real estate. Background information showed that Lisa was very bright. She attended North Eugene High School until midway through her junior year, then she entered Lane Community College and earned her high school diploma by the time she turned 15.

"She was always really quiet and shy and always wanted to grow up real fast—get out, make money, have nice things," recalled one of her friends from high school. "She always dated older boys. She didn't even go to the prom."

After finishing her high school studies, Lisa got work as assistant buyer at a women's clothing store in Eugene and was later promoted to buyer. Later, she managed a store for a while, and then managed a tanning salon for approximately two years.

The detectives learned that there was nothing in Lisa's background that could provide any clues to her killer's identity. She was well liked by everyone who knew her, and the sleuths failed to turn up anyone who might have wanted to harm her. Thus, it looked as though she had been killed by a stranger.

The autopsy on Lisa's body, performed by Dr. Karen Gunson, deputy state medical examiner, showed that Lisa had died from blood loss and deprivation of blood to the brain because of the "incised" wounds to her neck. Gunson told the investigators that the multiple wounds were made by cutting and stabbing with a sharp instrument. Gunson's opinion concurred with the detectives' that cuts to Lisa's fingertips were defensive wounds caused by a knife blade closing on her fingers.

When Detectives Dufur and Beckwith recalled Lesh's statement that Lisa might have been an innocent bystander, they began to wonder about the identity of the teenage girl the killer said he'd been looking for. Did she truly exist? When they began asking more questions, it didn't take them long to determine that the renters of the house where Lisa was killed had a female teenage relative who hadn't lived there for quite some time but was, in fact, due to move back into the house the day that Lisa was murdered! One of the relatives suggested that the teen had been the killer's intended target, and that Lisa's presence there had made her a victim of opportunity.

However, when the detectives located and questioned the teenage girl about such a possibility, she told them that she could think of no one who might want to target her as a murder victim. Like Lisa, the girl had no known enemies, nor did she have any recently soured relationships with any boys. Nonetheless, the lawmen cautioned her to be careful in her dealing with others until Lisa's killer was apprehended.

Several days passed with no new clues or leads to the killer's identity being developed. The few calls that came in the first few days after the slaying ultimately failed to offer anything that might help the sleuths find Lisa's killer. It wasn't until Saturday, August 24th, that any substantial information surfaced. And when it did, it turned the community upside down.

According to the sheriff's detectives, a Charbonneau resident provided them with information about a young boy who had received a minor cut on the day of Lisa Flormoe's murder. Tracking down the source of that information led the sleuths to a teenage girl who'd told her family that a boy she knew, 16-year-old Todd Daniel Davilla, told her he'd been chased by someone with a knife on the golf course next to the crime scene. The person who chased him, Davilla purportedly told the girl, had cut him. Exactly which part of his anatomy was cut, he had not disclosed.

Pondering all that they had been told, the investigators had to wonder why Davilla, or someone on his behalf, hadn't contacted the authorities to report the alleged attack. After all, Lisa's murder had made headline news. Anyone else who had been similarly attacked or had information about another attack would surely have reported such an incident, sleuths reasoned. So why hadn't Davilla?

The detectives arrived at Davilla's home, which was located about two blocks from the house where Lisa was killed, at 5:30 the next morning, a Sunday. They figured that if Davilla was the killer and they roused him out of bed and questioned him while he was still sleepy and bleary-eyed, it would be more difficult for him to fabricate a story without falling into inconsistencies.

The sleuths soon found out that their speculation was on the money. Before long, Davilla told Detectives Dufur and Beckwith that he'd pushed his way into the house where Lisa Flormoe was staying, shoved her into a bedroom and, wielding a Boy Scout knife, forced her to remove her clothes. Weeping, Davilla told the sleuths that it became necessary for him to kill Lisa. He just couldn't leave behind a witness to identify him, he said.

The two detectives arrested Davilla without incident

as his shocked relatives looked on in stunned disbelief. Davilla was charged with intentional murder, four counts of first-degree burglary, and two counts of first-degree attempted rape. Because he was a juvenile, the suspect was lodged in the Donald E. Long home in Portland, a "jail" of sorts for juvenile delinquents. Meanwhile, a check of police records established that Davilla had no prior criminal history.

"He has absolutely no criminal history at all," remarked Robert Hussey, a Clackamas, County community service officer. "He's a real clean-cut, all-American kid."

The investigators learned that Davilla was a junior at Canby Union High School. Interviews with his friends and teachers portrayed him as an honor student—many described him as "trustworthy," and school records showed that he was on the honor roll most of the time. No one could believe that he was capable of the brutal crime he was charged with.

"He was really good in math," said one of Davilla's classmates. "He never had to do any homework."

"There is absolutely nothing I ever observed that would prove other than that he is a perfectly normal kid," commented a relative of one of Davilla's friend's.

A football coach at Canby High told one of the investigators that Davilla had played on the freshman football team and went on to play part of the season the next year. "Whether he finished the season or not, I don't know," the coach said. "He did play as a freshman sometimes—he was there sometimes and gone sometimes. He had some attendance problems. He was real quiet and very polite," the coach summed up.

"If someone had said my own son had done this, I couldn't have been more shocked," remarked one of Davilla's former teachers. "The word I always used with Todd was 'squeaky clean.' This was a kid who was never late with an assignment, always got straight A's, and was never late for class. I could probably count on one hand the times he was absent."

A school official described Davilla as the type of kid who went out of his way to please his parents and those in positions of authority. "If there was a problem in the classroom," said the official, "he would be the one to whom you'd go to get a straight story."

A school counselor told the detectives that Davilla, in addition to playing football, had been on the track team during his freshman and sophomore years, played on the basketball team as a freshman, and went on to become a team manager the next year. He was a member of the Future Business Leaders of America program, was taking college-prep course work — and he was a Boy Scout.

"If I had heard that Todd had been arrested for shoplifting, I would have been shocked," said the counselor. It was ironic, the probers agreed, that someone as bright and intelligent as Lisa Flormoe would be slain by someone with similar academic traits and high degree of intelligence.

It was midway through his freshman year, the detectives learned, that Davilla joined the Boy Scouts. In practically no time at all, he obtained the rank of First Class. Shortly thereafter, he became an Eagle Scout.

"The whole troop is in shock about this!" a scoutmaster declared.

"Everybody liked him," a troop member said. "It's not like him at all. I'm confused."

A short time later, after executing a search warrant at Davilla's home, the investigators seized a Boy Scout knife which they believed was used to inflict the wounds on Lisa Flormoe. Although preliminary tests

312

at the Oregon State Police Crime Laboratory in Portland were inconclusive, technicians told the probers that it looked as though the knife had recently been thoroughly cleaned.

After conferring with the detectives and reviewing the evidence, Clackamas County Deputy District Attorney Terry M. Gustafson filed a petition of charges in Clackamas County Juvenile Court. The petition charged Davilla with four counts each of aggravated murder and first-degree burglary, one count of intentional murder, and two counts of first-degree attempted rape.

"This was a premeditated crime, well thought-out and well concealed," D.A. Gustafson declared. She indicated that she could seek to have Davilla remanded to adult court where, if convicted, he would receive the maximum sentence of life in prison. Because he was only 16 when the crimes were committed, David was not eligible under state law to be sentenced to death. The deputy D.A. made it clear that if the case was prosecuted through the juvenile system and Davilla was convicted, he would be released on his 21st birthday.

"It's a very complex case," said William T. Lyons, an Oregon City attorney hired by Davilla's relatives. "The allegations are so serious, and it's a sixteen-year-old kid with no criminal history."

During hearings in mid-January 1992 before Judge Robert J. Morgan, Deputy D.A. Gustafson presented strong arguments for having Todd Davilla remanded to adult court. She explained how Davilla had admitted to detectives that he had gone three times to the house where Lisa Flormoe was staying on the day of the killing, supposedly to visit a girl related to the renters who lived there. After the first visit, when he found

313

Lisa alone, he returned two more times.

When Lisa opened the door on the third visit, Gustafson said, Davilla "slammed it open, stepped inside, pulled out the opened knife, and held it to her throat." Then he pushed his way into the house, prodded Lisa into a nearby bedroom and, wielding the knife, forced her to remove her clothing.

"He momentarily set his knife down while he was trying to rape her," Gustafson said. "Lisa grabbed the knife, and, as they struggled for control of it, they fell off the bed. Todd jumped on top of her and tried to get the knife away but was unable to until he threatened to cut off her fingers by folding the knife down on them and slicing into them. Todd then used the knife to kill her by slashing her throat again and again. . . . Lisa fought with Todd for control of the knife. When she lost that battle, she lost her life."

According to the investigative reports presented in court, the detectives had learned from witnesses that Davilla went to the Clackamas County Fair later on the day Lisa was slain. The statements of those interviewed indicated that he did not appear upset and was apparently enjoying himself. "At the fair," Prosecutor Gustafson went on, "Todd saw many of his friends, who said he was in a good mood and was joking around and having a good time there."

On Wednesday, January 15, 1992, following two days of hearings during which Davilla's attorney said he would not oppose Davilla's being remanded to adult court, the unexpected occurred. After working out an arrangement with the district attorney, Davilla waived his right to a trial and pleaded guilty to murder, first-degree burglary, and first-degree attempted rape.

To make certain that Todd Davilla fully understood what he was doing in making the plea-bargain arrangement, Judge Morgan told him, "There is certainly a strong possibility that you will never be out of confinement." After Davilla affirmed that he knew what he was doing, the judge ordered a presentencing investigation.

A relative of the victim's expressed relief that Davilla had pled guilty. "I didn't want my family to have to sit there and hear the details of what he did to Lisa," said the relative, who was also upset that Davilla was sent back to the juvenile detention home instead of directly to jail pending the sentencing hearing. "What he did was so horrendous — why should he be able to go back to a boys' camp?"

In the meantime, it was revealed that in 1989 Davilla allegedly had attempted to rape two teenage girls. Many people, especially relatives of Lisa Flormoe's, were dismayed that those girls had not come forward sooner. As a result, one of Flormoe's relatives pointed out, "Todd Davilla was not prevented from committing similar acts of violence."

"Very few sex crimes are reported," Detective Candace Dufor explained, "especially in cases in which the victims are juveniles. They are embarrassed and they don't think anyone will believe them."

At the sentencing hearing, Deputy D.A. Gustafson argued, "Davilla's sentence must be life confinement in order to be proportional to his heinous crime." She recommended a 100-year sentence. Even with time off for good behavior, she said, "Todd Davilla would remain in the penitentiary until he was ninety-six years old. He would be released when his body would be so decrepit and arthritic that it would be physically impossible for him to ever repeat the crime he committed against Lisa Flormoe."

Judge Morgan, referring to "the dastardly nature"

of Lisa Flormoe's murder, agreed with the prosecutor. Ruling that Davilla was a tenacious and determined sexual predator with a strong inclination for violence and cruelty, Morgan declared "It is my thinking, based on what I've heard, that there should be no parole." The judge said he believed that Davilla suffered from a personality disorder for which there may be no cure.

"Bit by bit," Judge Morgan said of Davilla, "I saw an individual—the defendant—who apparently has the heart and empty soul of an assassin." Morgan added that he could never be convinced that Davilla would not kill again if he were ever allowed back on the streets.

On Friday, March 6, 1992, Judge Morgan sentenced Todd Davilla to life in prison without the possibility of parole. In addition to the life sentence, Morgan also imposed 16 months for the first-degree attempted rape and three years for the first-degree burglary associated with the case.

One of Lisa Flormoe's relatives said that she "was really pleased with how it turned out. I'm just grateful that Todd is not going to get out to hurt any more people like he hurt Lisa."

"We want him to never have a chance to do something like this again," said David Lesh, the victim's fiancé.

"Todd had two lives," said Detective Candace Dufur. "One he showed to only three people—the two girls [whom he allegedly tried to rape] and Lisa Flormoe."

Todd Davilla's attorney said he would appeal the sentence to the Oregon Supreme Court on the grounds that the law prohibits minimum sentences for remanded juveniles. "I think the sentence is clearly in error and contrary to statutes," Defense Attorney Lyons declared. "But I can understand why the judge did what he did."

Todd Daniel Davilla is spending the first part of his sentence at the MacLaren School for Boys, a reform school. When he turns 18, he will be transferred to a prison in the Oregon Correctional System in which, unless his sentence is overturned on appeal, he will likely spend the rest of his life.

EDITOR'S NOTE:
David Lesh is not the real name of the person so named in the foregoing story. A fictitious name has been used because there is no reason for public interest in the identity of this person.

"WAS THE COED KILLED BY A GHOULISH TEEN?"

by Bruce Gibney

Greenfield, MA
November 29, 1988

Mischief and excitement sparkled in the wide eyes of Greenfield, Massachusetts children. It was late October 1988; Halloween was just around the corner.

As in years past, the children marked off the days until they could slip into their costumes and comb the neighborhoods of this old New England town in search of candy and treats.

It was a special time for the children—and parents, too, who remembered when they, too, were young and scampered from house-to-house, giddy as only young, excitable children can be, hands grasping brown bags bulging with forbidden sweets.

But 1988 was different than years past. Just one week short of Halloween, a shocking crime stunned this small community, as the imaginary suddenly became all too real.

The horror began a few minutes past noon on Tuesday, October 24, 1988, when a woman called Greenfield Police to report the possible suicide of a relative.

The victim was Sharon Gregory, 19, of South Shelburne Street.

A patrol car sped to the quiet, tree-shaded neighborhood and stopped in front of a two-story home. One of the officers stepped out of the cruiser and went into the house.

Sharon Gregory lay on the upstairs bathroom floor. Her fully-clothed body was covered with blood as was a good portion of the floor. Blood was also spattered onto the walls and trailed out the door.

The radio message indicated suicide. The patrol officer accepted this as he stood in the doorway looking at the still body in the huge blood pool. But crouching beside the young coed, he noticed things that did not fit the suicide scenario.

For one thing, the blood welling on the floor had not come from slash wounds on the wrist or neck but from wounds in the chest, neck, face and back. Also, the suicide weapon was conspicuously missing.

Suspicious, the officers tramped back to the cruiser and radioed headquarters. Detectives under the direction of Captain Joseph LaChance arrived.

To their trained eyes, the patrol officer's suspicion that this was something other than a suicide was absolutely correct.

Sharon Gregory had not committed suicide; she had been murdered.

The murder was Greenfield's third that year and by far the most shocking. Searching the house from top to bottom, investigators concluded that the stabbing began on the first floor, where searchers discovered a huge blood pool, and continued up the steps into the bathroom where it tragically ended.

Medical Examiner Dr. Thomas Smith determined the 19-year-old coed had been dead less than an hour when her body was discovered.

The relative who made the shocking discovery was questioned. She said that she had come home at noon and had gone up to her bedroom to change clothes. As she passed the bathroom, she glanced in and that's when she saw Sharon on the floor.

She immediately called police.

Neighbors gathered in front of the two-story home, their faces tight with shock and disbelief. Sharon Gregory was one of the best liked persons in the neighborhood. No one could think of a single reason why anyone would want to kill her.

The same could be said for anyone who came in contact with the pretty brunette. A popular student at Greenfield High School, Sharon had enrolled at Greenfield Community College where she was taking classes in art and art history.

Although she had talent, Sharon did not have plans to begin a career in art. In fact, the lovely teen, who got good grades while in high school and worked on the school paper, didn't know what she wanted to do with her life.

One possibility was a career in nursing. Sharon was the type who liked caring for people and had volunteered her time as a nurse's aide at a nursing home.

She had also given some thought to taking business courses and starting her own business.

It probably didn't matter what she chose because, as one student sadly remarked, "Sharon was the type who would probably succeed at anything she did. She was always so positive and happy."

Happy described the cheerful coed to a "T." She never seemed sad or subject to mood swings.

Why then had she been attacked? The answer confounded detectives.

Sharon was fully clothed, which seemed to eliminate sex as a motive. Robbery or burglary was also unlikely because the house had not been ransacked.

Another clue that puzzled police was the fact that the house showed no signs of forced entry, suggesting that the coed had let the killer into the house.

Detective Peter Clarke asked Sharon's relative if she knew of anyone who wished Sharon harm or could think of any reason why someone would want to hurt her.

She replied that, to the best of her knowledge, Sharon didn't have any enemies and that she had never said anything about being in trouble or fearful about her life.

Pressed for information, the grieving relative said Sharon had been acting upset lately about a boy she had met named Mark.

The relative didn't know Mark's last name or much about him. He hung out with a bunch of kids on Maple Street and went away to school. That's really all the relatives could tell sleuths.

She added that Sharon had complained about Mark because he made crude remarks and stared at her oddly.

Police knew the youngsters who hung out on Maple Street. One of the boys was Mark Branch, 18, who lived on Meadow Lane. Two detectives went to his house, but no one was home.

Later that afternoon, police returned to the house. A woman answered the door.

"Is Mark home?" one of the detectives asked.

The woman shook her head. She said she hadn't seen Mark since 10:30 that morning when he left the house with his friend, Arthur Lowens, 19. She suggested that probers try a store in town where Mark worked.

Police went to the market. The manager said Mark had stopped at the market that morning to pick up his check, then left. He was due to work that evening. Strangely, he had missed his shift.

"Mark is very reliable," the manager told police.

He described Branch as a good employee who got along with just about everyone. He promised to have him call police when he got in.

A crime check supported the claim that Branch was a good kid. Other than a few speeding tickets, the 18-year-old had a clean record. A motor vehicle mugshot showed Branch to be a handsome man with blond hair and just a hint of a smile.

Unable to reach Branch, lawmen contacted his buddy Arthur Lowens and asked him to please come down to the stationhouse.

Lowens arrived at 5:30 p.m., accompanied by a relative. Seated in an interrogation room, he told the following story:

Lowens said he went to Branch's home at 8:15 that morning to give Branch a ride to a medical appointment. After the appointment, they returned to the house where they moved an air conditioner from Branch's truck. The two continued on to Lowens' house to watch television and record segments of MTV.

While watching television, Lowens got a call from Sharon Gregory. "She was crying and asked if I had a car," the teenager recalled.

"She said she wanted to visit her boyfriend at high school, only she could not get her car started.

Gregory said, according to Lowens, that she had tried to reach her boyfriend at high school, only he was not allowed to take the call.

She wanted to visit him but couldn't start her car.

"I told her how to start the car and to call me back if it wouldn't start," Lowens told police. "She said she would, only she never did."

The witness said he told Branch about the call and Branch had asked him why Sharon didn't use her parents' car. "I told him that her parents were working and weren't at home."

Fifteen minutes later, Branch went into the bedroom to make a telephone call. When he came out of the bedroom, Lowens said he asked what was up and Branch told him he wanted to go home and get his car.

Lowens said he drove Branch to his home and then went back to his house where he fell asleep. He slept till noon when a friend stopped by for a visit. The friend stayed about five minutes and left. Lowens' girlfriend stopped by at 12:30 p.m.

After she left, he said he received a phone call from his mother who told him that Sharon Gregory had committed suicide. He said he went to the high school and told Sharon's boyfriend the tragic news.

Lowens said he didn't know who Branch called when he went into the bedroom. He also didn't know why his friend would suddenly want to go home and get his car.

He said it was possible that Branch had called Sharon Gregory from the bedroom, then left to give her a lift to the high school to see her boyfriend.

If so, that put Branch at the home with the victim at the approximate time she was murdered.

Shortly after the interview, police received a phone call from a neighbor who lived west of the Gregory home. He told police that at noon he had just begun to watch television when he heard the sound of a car door closing. He looked out the window and saw a dark blue Chevette, possibly a two-door, parked facing into the driveway of the Gregory home.

A man got out of the car. The neighbor described him as a white male, 6 feet tall and approximately 180

323

pounds, wearing pants and a jacket of stonewashed denim, with dark hair in a long military cut.

"The guy was clean-cut. He had his hands in his pockets and walked up to the house," the witness recalled.

Five minutes later, the neighbor heard the sound of a car door closing and saw the man seated in the Chevette back out the driveway and head west.

About 40 minutes later, the neighbor heard another car in the same driveway. He said he looked out the window and this time he saw one of the Gregory cars pull into the driveway. About 20 minutes later, police began to arrive.

The neighbor said he was too far away to get a good look at the driver, but police figured they knew who it was after a check revealed that Mark Branch drove a two-door Chevette identical to the one the neighbor had seen pulling into the driveway.

Investigators notified the district attorney's office. Within the hour, they returned to the Branch home on Meadow Lane to conduct a search of Mark's room—and were stunned by what they saw.

The neat-as-a-pin room was filled floor-to-ceiling with "slasher" videotapes, books, magazines and paraphernalia, including knives and a machete.

"It was a shocker," one detective remarked later. "It was like walking into a Hollywood museum."

A horror museum, he might have said.

Carted away were such classics of Grande Guignol as *Texas Chainsaw Massacre, Part Two, Night of the Living Dead, Bloodsucking Freaks, Nightmare on Elm Street, Part Three, Psycho II and III, Demons I and II, The New York Ripper, The Howling, I Spit on Your Grave, The Boogeyman, The Evil Dead, Faces of Death I and II, The Gates of Hell, The Grim Reaper, Christine,* and *Zombie.*

324

On top of a table-model television was an unmarked videotape. Inside a nearby VCR was a videotape titled "Friday the 13th, Part VI."

Obviously, Mark Branch read about gore as well as watched it. A bookcase near his desk was jammed with Stephen King novels and other horror classics by best-selling writers. The juicy parts were underlined in yellow marker. There were also stacks of horror comics including "Fangoria Magazine," the quick-read Bible of horror aficionados.

"It is just amazing how much of this stuff is available to the general public," the detective commented later.

The surprises weren't over. In a search of the closet, shocked police officers discovered costumes worn by actors in the horror films Branch so dearly loved. They also found combat boots, plaid shirts and four hockey masks worn by "Jason" in the *Friday the 13th* movies, one of Branch's favorite films.

According to friends, Branch was fascinated with horror films and had joined several horror fan clubs. One chum said Branch had molded his life around the characters like "Freddie" from *Nightmare on Elm Street* and "Jason" of *Friday the 13th* and once wondered aloud what it would be like to be a horror hero and actually murder someone.

Because most of the kids who hung around Maple Street liked the same horror films, no one took Branch seriously.

Police, however, were taking him very seriously. Captain LaChance was no psychiatrist, but after viewing the body in the bathroom, it appeared that Branch had just flipped out and decided to act on his fascination with death and horror. And Sharon Gregory was the unfortunate victim.

On October 26th, police issued a photograph of

Mark Branch, warning that the teen store clerk was wanted for the murder of Sharon Gregory and was to be considered armed and dangerous. Anyone with information was asked to contact the Greenfield Police Department or the state police.

Hours later, police got a hot lead when Branch's Chevette was spotted abandoned off Avery Road near Buckland, about three miles east of Greenfield. The vehicle was towed to police headquarters where it was meticulously searched by lab technicians. This proved to be very useful.

Any doubt that the ghoul-fascinated teenager was responsible for the slashing murder of Sharon Gregory went out the window when technicians discovered bloodstains on the accelerator and brake pedals, steering wheel, automatic shift lever and the outside and inside door handles. The blood matched the slain girl's.

Heavily armed state police and volunteers convened on Avery Road where the car was recovered. Led by tracking dogs, they searched the thick woods that unfolded on both sides of the road.

They returned that evening empty-handed. If Branch had escaped into the woods, they had missed him.

Meanwhile, more information on Mark Branch was beginning to surface. Authorities learned that Branch had dropped out of Greenfield Junior High School, for disciplinary reasons, and attended a nearby academy where he got into trouble after sending notes in which he requested sex from a coed.

Trouble worsened after he was reported for pulling a knife on one of the coeds and threatening to slash her to pieces because she told him to go away.

That incident got Branch committed to a state-run school for emotionally disturbed children in Boston and later to a psychiatric school in Northampton.

That institution, a 328-bed, private, non-profit hospital affiliated with Harvard Medical School and Massachusetts General Hospital, was considered one of the best in the nation for treatment of patients with severe psychiatric disorders.

Branch reportedly was doing well and was no longer considered a threat to society or himself.

In the wake of the coed murder, hardly anyone believed that now.

With Halloween fast approaching, Greenfield was rife with wild rumors. One teenager told authorities that Branch said he planned to go trick-or-treating this year dressed as his favorite movie character Jason, the hockey-masked hero of *Friday the 13th.*

Worried that Branch might do just that, city fathers in Greenfield and nearby towns met to decide what to do. Several towns discussed the possibility of canceling Halloween parades, always a big event in western Massachusetts. Later, they decided to let the parades go on as scheduled, but only with a heavy police presence.

Greenfield selectmen also decided to let planned festivities go on, but did request that children trick-or-treat during daylight hours.

Some of the kids took the advice; others went trick-or-treating at night as they always had, and a few worked both the daylight and evening shifts. Fortunately, there were no incidents.

Police breathed a thankful sigh of relief. But their job wouldn't be over until they had located the disturbed young man in the city's most notorious murder case.

On October 28th, searchers returned to the woods off Avery Road where Branch's car was abandoned, this time led by dogs trained in locating corpses.

The search went deep into the woods on both sides of the road. But it was no more successful than the first. It was the first of many searches.

On November 2nd, investigators received notice of a break-in at a summer house in Buckland. The owner said he was returning from work a iittle before six o'clock Tuesday evening and found the front door kicked open.

Officers from the Buckland Police Department sped to the home located in thick woods on Bray Road, about four miles from the spot where Branch's car was found.

Though break-ins of summer houses are not uncommon, this one was significant, as much for what wasn't taken as for what was.

The burglar had passed up such items as money, jewelry, a VCR and 12-gauge shotgun, all in plain sight, and instead had taken a hunting knife, a can of soup, some leftover roast beef, a bag of Fig Newtons, a red and blue hunting vest and a red ski jacket.

The items stolen suggested that the thief was more interested in filling his belly and warding off the cold than in money or easily fenced goods. This led police to believe that Branch might still be in the area.

State police again brought tracking dogs to the area to search the woods. They did a sweep of houses, shacks and barns and other outbuildings within a half-mile radius of the Bray Road house. They also questioned neighbors for anything they might have seen or heard.

But again, all their efforts met with futility.

State Police Staff Sergeant Norman Roberts told reporters that there wasn't enough evidence to prove that Mark Branch was the one who had broken into the house. "We might be dealing with a bunch of goofball kids out having fun," he said.

No one along Bray Road reported seeing strangers lurking about or in fact anything suspicious. This was not unusual, since homes were well-spaced apart and separated by dense woods and undergrowth.

"Two days later, searchers returned to the area after a homeowner reported seeing Branch in his backyard. The man told searchers that he heard his dog barking and looked out the window, expecting to see his girlfriend who was due back from town. Instead, he saw a stranger walking out of the woodshed carrying an ax. He described the man as six feet tall, 180 pounds with blond hair and wearing blue jeans, boots and a thick, dark coat.

The man had read news stories about the Greenfield murder and was certain the man he saw was Mark Branch. Armed searchers scented their dogs and combed the woods around the house. The search turned up nothing.

The search for Mark Branch became a massive media attention, and searchers and investigators who once worked in quiet obscurity were now thrust into the media limelight.

In addition to reporters and TV news cameras, also present were national tabloid shows, like "America's Most Wanted" and "A Current Affair."

Greenfield Police Chief David McCarthy had had his fill of talking to reporters but welcomed the media anyway, since he knew that the national exposure added to his chances of finding Mark Branch.

The chief described search efforts to find the young man who was the only suspect in a crime that had turned his little town upside down. He said investigators would follow up on every lead and would not rest until Mark Branch was found.

Media coverage had already produced numerous sightings: Branch had been spotted in a donut shop in

Gardner, Massachusetts. He was also seen buying a soft drink at an Enfield, Connecticut, store, hitchhiking along the Massachusetts interstate, and on his way to North Carolina.

More ominous for local residents were rumors that Branch was camped out in the woods and was waiting for things to die down before making his escape.

Police, however, placed little credibility in this last theory. According to their information, Branch knew almost nothing about camping and except for an occasional hike, he rarely went into the woods. He would have stood little chance in the harsh November weather when morning rains turned to ice and temperatures dropped into the teens.

This judgment still did not answer the question about what had happened to Mark Branch and why had he abandoned his car where he did.

An answer was soon provided.

On November 29th, a deer hunter kissed his wife goodbye and headed up Hog Mountain Road to hunt his favorite game.

At about 8:00 a.m., he flushed two deer from the brush, then followed them illegally onto an off-limits preserve. Searching the terrain for sight of the frightened deer, he spotted what looked like someone sitting on the hillside. He waved to the figure who refused to respond. Curious, the hunter stepped closer and saw why the person had been so unfriendly.

The stranger was not sitting—he was hanging. A rawhide cord was wrapped around his neck and secured to a pine tree. He was dangling about five feet off the ground.

The eyes of the hunter widened in horror as he stared at the blackened face and swollen tongue protruding from the corpse's distorted mouth.

"If he had shown any signs of life I would have shot him," the hunter later told reporters.

But there had been no life in the body for a very long time.

Ignoring the two deer, the hunter eased the safety onto the trigger and bounded down Hog Mountain Road to his parents' home. He waited until officers arrived, then led them and a medical examiner to the pine tree where he had spotted the hanging man.

Officers took one look at the hanging man and knew they could close the book on the search that had occupied them for over a month. There was no doubt the hanging man was Mark Branch. Identification in his wallet and fingerprints confirmed eyewitness observation.

Branch had been precise and methodical in his own execution. He had fashioned a noose from a boot lace and tied it to his belt, looping the leather strap around the tree limb. He had then hiked up the collar of his blue cotton shirt so that the lace would not cut into his neck, leaned forward and asphyxiated himself.

Branch was clothed in jeans, a light-blue cotton shirt with no bloodstains that could be seen and black, army-style boots. The lace used in the hanging had come from the right boot, still on the foot.

A medical examiner cut down the limb from the tree and placed the corpse in a black body bag. Five police officers carried the hefty bundle for the 15-minute trek down the hill.

According to the postmortem examination, Branch had been dead for several weeks and had likely hanged himself shortly after abandoning his Chevette.

Buckland Police Chief James Basile told reporters that searchers may have been within about 100 yards of Branch's body during the late October search that was led by cadaver-trained dogs and helicopters. He said he didn't know why the dogs had missed the body; it had been raining and perhaps that had something to do with it.

The news that Mark Branch had been found hanging swept through the county like a brisk autumn wind. District Attorney Judd Carhart said that Branch had been the only suspect in the Gregory slaying and the discovery of his body officially closed the murder investigation.

Although reactions to Branch's suicide were mixed — some wished he had been caught to stand trial, while others said it was best he went the way he did instead of facing a possible life sentence behind bars or in an insane asylum — just about everyone was glad that it was finally over.

"This finishes it, I hope," one resident said. "Now we can get back to normal."

EDITOR'S NOTE:
Arthur Lowens is not the real name of the person so named in the foregoing story. A fictitious name has been used because there is no reason for public interest in the identity of this person.

"DEMENTED TEEN VIRGIN RAPED/MURDERED A GIRL OF 7"

by Philip Westwood

Detective-Superintendent (DS) Peter Bottomley was speaking to a crowd of newsmen gathered on the grassy slopes of Kilner Bank at Rawthorpe, a suburb of the northern English industrial town of Huddersfield. "This was a particularly horrendous and brutal attack on a normal, happy seven-year-old, and I shall not rest until the man who did this dreadful thing has been caught and convicted," he said.

There were no doubts in the reporters' minds that Bottomley meant every word. He was visibly upset when he spoke to them on that bright, sunny afternoon of Sunday, August 11, 1991. But that was understandable. A few yards away from where they stood, screened from open view by a densely wooded thicket and a hastily rigged police tarpaulin, was a sight that would have upset anyone, even a hardened and experienced crime investigator such as Bottomley.

The search for Angela "Angie" Flaherty—known to her family, friends, and neighbors as "Little Angel" because of her lovable and trusting nature—

had begun 18 hours earlier. On Saturday afternoon, Angie had gone out to play. She had taken her bicycle, a gift for her seventh birthday the previous October. When she did not return home at 6:00 p.m. for her tea, her parents became worried. By 8:00 p.m., they were frantic. They reported her missing to the local police and an immediate hunt for the little girl was launched. It went on throughout the night. Officers were told to look out for Angie's bicycle. Painted a bright pink, and with the trade name "Jenny" in large black letters on the frame, it was a very distinctive bike. But the night passed without any trace of Angie or her pink bike.

With the onset of dawn, the hunt was intensified. Two police helicopters scanned the area from the skies above, while, on the ground, 100 officers, some on horseback, embarked in a detailed search of the area. They were joined by friends and neighbors of Angie's now distraught family.

It was late morning when a police horseman spotted Angie's bike lying in undergrowth on the edge of the thicket. Twenty minutes later came the discovery that everyone had been dreading. Angie's body was found on a small patch of open ground on the far side of the thicket. She was just 500 yards from her home.

Though he would have to wait for the autopsy report to give him the full story of how the little girl had met her death, Detective Bottomley could see enough at the murder scene for himself to know that Angie had fallen victim to a particularly ruthless and depraved killer. Angie was practically naked. Her clothing lay in a neat pile a few feet from her body. The trickle of blood that had caked and congealed on the insides of her thighs showed that Angie had been subjected to a vicious sexual assault. The marks on her throat indicated how the killer had tried to ensure that she would never talk about what had taken place. And her smashed-in skull was a clear manifestation of how that objective had finally been achieved.

"This is the work of a real sicko," Bottomley remarked to his boss, Detective-Chief Superintendent (DCS) Stuart Clough, as they conferred shortly after the body's discovery. "We've got to catch him quickly."

Chief Clough agreed. "Do you think it's the work of a local man?" he asked Bottomley.

"I hope so," replied the detective. "If not, we've got a real problem. If the killing is the work of a drifter just passing through, then he could be miles away by now. And there is very little chance that we would be able to get an identification, or even a good description, of him. Nobody that we've talked to so far has spoken of seeing a stranger hanging around over the past few days."

There was some indication that a stranger to the area could have been responsible for the heinous deed. Rawthorpe had not been the scene of any assaults on children. This was a one-time incident. And no known child molesters lived in the vicinity. So it seemed possible that the killing was the work of a stranger. But Bottomley did not think so. And, as the investigation progressed, he became convinced that the perpetrator lived locally.

"It's the place where Angie was killed," Bottomley explained to Chief Clough. "Only someone with an intimate knowledge of the locality would have known about it."

To an outsider, the thicket appeared to be just another area of dense vegetation like dozens of others on Kilner Bank. But this one was different. This one had a small grassy area at its center. Local children had found a way in through the bushes and used the grassy center as a den. They had outfitted it with some old boxes that they used as chairs, and an old mattress that served as a couch or bed.

"A stranger would have no way of knowing about the den," said Bottomley. "Even to simply find the place would require a great deal of local knowledge. It is very well hidden. It is not the sort of place that anyone would just come across."

There was also evidence that Angie knew her killer and went with him willingly to the den. Tire tracks showed that the victim had ridden her bicycle to the place where she was killed. She had not been dragged kicking and screaming to the place. "The simple fact that she took the bike with her all the way to the thicket would seem to indicate that she was lured, not forced, to the scene," concluded Bottomley.

In the first few days following the murder, Rawthorpe was besieged by newsmen eager for a story. They wanted to learn everything that there was to know about Angie Flaherty and her family. It was only natural. The killing had shocked the entire nation and the entire nation wanted, in a way, to share in the family's grief. There was genuine feeling for their plight.

But Angie's family was far too upset to talk to

newsmen. And that was where Emily Forbes and Anthony Craven came in. They were neighbors of the Flaherty family and were also looked upon as friends. Emily had two children of her own, so she could well appreciate what Angie's family must be feeling.

Seventeen-year-old Tony Craven was in a slightly different position. He had been friendly with Angie and was still friends with her three older sisters.

"Words cannot express how they feel," Craven, speaking about Angie's family, told newsmen at one of several impromptu news conferences, which he held in the street outside the victim's home. "How can they believe it when they last saw her safe and sound, playing just a few yards from safety?"

"Strange kid," Detective Bottomley remarked to a colleague as they watched Craven, straddling his bicycle and with the headphones of his Walkman slung around his neck, dealing in a strangely professional manner with the gentlemen of the press.

"How do you mean?" Bottomley's colleague wanted to know.

"Well," Bottomley answered, "he's seventeen or eighteen . . ."

"Seventeen," Bottomley's colleague cut in.

"Seventeen," Bottomley corrected himself. "Yet he spends his time hanging around with kids less than half his age. I would have thought that he preferred spending time with girls his own age rather than playing kids' games with little children. It just doesn't seem natural."

"Perhaps he doesn't feel ready for girls just yet," suggested the colleague. "Not all boys of that age feel the overwhelming desire to prove their manhood."

"Maybe you're right," said Bottomley. But the sleuth wasn't convinced. Bottomley made a mental note to take a closer look at the activities of Anthony Craven. There was something that didn't seem quite right. It was just a gut feeling. But it was beginning to gnaw away at him.

The autopsy report on Angie confirmed what Bottomley had suspected. The little girl had been crudely and viciously raped before an attempt had been made to strangle her. But her death had been the result of the massive brain hemorrhaging that had occurred as a result of her being repeatedly battered about the head with a large rock.

Bottomley called for reports from his investigating team on the activities of Tony Craven. What had they learned about him during their routine inquiries? What impressions had they formed of the youth as they went about their various tasks? The responses Bottomley received only served to deepen his doubts about the strange young man.

Though 17 years of age, Craven looked much younger. Several officers initially thought him to be only around 13 or 14. Craven worked at a local food-processing factory, though all of his free time was devoted to following the Flaherty murder inquiry. He took an interest in the inquiries that went far beyond mere curiosity. There was, of course, the role that he had taken upon himself of dealing with the press on behalf of Angie's family. But there were also other matters.

Investigators reported that they had noticed that Craven was always hanging around as they went about their work. Sometimes he would approach them directly and ask how they were getting on and what progress they were making. Sometimes he would try to look over their shoulders as they filled in the forms on their clipboards or made entries in their notebooks.

The DS pondered this information. "Bring him in! I want to have a talk with him," Bottomley told his team. "Nothing formal. Just a little chat. I want to see what makes him tick."

Bottomley was pretty good at seeing what made people tick. It was a technique that stemmed partly from his police training and partly from a genuine interest in his fellow human beings.

It didn't take the detective long to get the measure of Tony Craven. He found him to be an immature youth, far too immature for his years. Perhaps that was why Craven preferred the company of young children to that of people his own age. Bottomley also found that Craven possessed a genuine interest in the activities of the investigating team. It was as if he wanted to be a part of it. He saw the members of the team as important people doing an important job. And he, too, longed to be important. But he wasn't.

"I have something to tell you," Craven said suddenly after 15 minutes of general chitchat about nothing in particular with the detective.

"What's that, Tony?" Bottomley responded as casually as he could. Was this going to be a confession? The detective was half expecting it. There was something about the youth that Bottomley found deeply disturbing. Bottomley couldn't put his finger on exactly what it was. It was simply another of those gnawing feelings, churning away at his insides. But the detective's expectations were to be dashed. Tony Craven was not about to confess.

"I saw him," said Craven quietly.

"Saw who, Tony?" Bottomley asked calmly, and equally quietly.

Craven looked at the detective. On his face was an expression of wide-eyed surprise, as if the detective should know exactly what he meant. "Why, the bloke who did it!" Craven replied. "The bloke who killed Angie!"

Craven went on to describe a balding middle-aged man, whom he claimed to have seen in the area near the thicket on the afternoon that Angie disappeared. He didn't know the man. He had never seen him before.

"He was walking down the field and he climbed through a hedge at the bottom of the road," Craven told the detective. "And then I saw Angie riding her bike through the fields." A wistful, faraway look came into Craven's eyes as he continued to speak. "She was such a nice little girl. I used to ride around with her and the other children on my bike."

"Yes," said Bottomley in an expressionless tone. "I know you did."

There wasn't much else that Craven could tell the detective. He had never seen the man before and he hadn't seen him since. But he felt sure that he was the one. Something told him that he was the one who killed Angie.

"Well, thanks for coming in," Bottomley said politely at the conclusion of their "little chat."

"Have I been helpful?" Craven asked with an eagerness that betrayed his overwillingness to please.

"Oh yes, Tony," Bottomley replied truthfully. "You've been extremely helpful."

"I want him watched," Bottomley told his team after the youth left the station. "And I want you to find out everything that you can about him. Talk to his neighbors. Talk to the people he works with. Talk to anybody who might have the slightest knowledge of him. But do it discreetly. I don't want to give anyone the idea that Craven might be the man we're looking for."

Bottomley thought for a moment. "And check out his story about seeing a stranger in the vicinity at the time of the killing," he added. "Frankly, I don't believe it. But you never know."

The investigative carried out their chief's instructions. Talks with neighbors turned up nothing to confirm Bottomley's growing concerns over Tony Craven. Everyone whom the investigating team spoke to saw nothing suspicious about the youth. He was a most pleasant boy. A bit odd, some thought, in his choice of companions and activities. But nothing untoward, and certainly not dangerous. If anything, he had a naive, almost childlike, innocence. In fact, most people found Craven's politeness, civility, and helpfulness very refreshing at a time when young people come in for so much criticism concerning their behavior and attitudes.

But investigators who visited Craven's place of work were given a totally different impression of the youth. There, Craven was regarded as something of a weakling by his colleagues. There, his preference for the company of young children

rather than people his own age served only to rein-
force just how different he was from other adolescents. And the simple fact that he was so different
meant that he was singled out for special treatment. Anyone who doesn't conform to normal be-
havioral patterns it looked upon with suspicion and
even fear. That suspicion and fear leads some
people to turn on the nonconforming individual
and try to subjugate, and even to destroy, him. The
destruction tends to be mental rather than physical
since mental torture is more subtle, but just as
deadly.

Anthony Craven suffered the torture that comes
from being different. His colleagues discovered that
he had never been with a woman. He had never
even had a girlfriend. They discovered that he was
a virgin. And, day after day, he was taunted and
teased over his total inexperience with the opposite
sex. He was shown magazines packed with pornographic pictures. "What do you think of that?" he
would be asked, as he gazed at some woman bar-
ing her all for the camera, and for the gratification
of the magazines' "readers."

But sexually, Craven didn't think anything of the
pictures. Sexually, they did nothing for him. There
was no feeling of lust for the women pouting allur-
ingly at him from the glossy pages. All of the
women in Tony Craven's life were "decent."

But the women in the pictures did elicit some
kind of response from the youth. They were an
abhorrnce to him. They represented to his immature mind everything that was evil and wicked in
women. "I hate them!" Craven would scream when
the taunting and the teasing became so bad that he

could take it no longer. Some of his colleagues thought that such an outburst represented his views on the women in the pictures. Others took it as an expression of his opinion on women in general.

Detective Bottomley was very interested in the findings of his team. Whatever else he was, Tony Craven was certainly a young man in a state of turmoil. He was constantly singled out at his place of work because of his lack of sexual experience. He didn't fit in. He was an outsider. But, as Bottomley knew from the fact that Craven followed his investigators around, taking a great interest in their work and trying to be helpful, and from the way in which he attempted to shield Angie's family from the attention of the press, the youth didn't like being an outsider. He wanted to fit in, to be accepted.

Maybe he wanted so badly to fit in and be accepted that he had decided to correct his deficiency in the sphere of sexual activity. Perhaps he had thought that losing his virginity would increase his standing in the eyes of his colleagues and put a stop to their taunts. But he couldn't lose his virginity to a woman like those in the magazines. He couldn't go with someone like that. He certainly couldn't do it with any of the women who were part of his everyday life. He had far too much respect for them. Anyhow, he was sure that they wouldn't let him.

That left only one alternative. It would have to be with one of his friends, one of the little children with whom he spent most of his free time innocently riding around on his bike. Perhaps one of them would let him.

"We're going to do some tests on all of the young men and boys in the area," Bottomley told Craven when the youth was called back for another interview.

"What kind of tests?" the youth wanted to know.

"Blood tests," replied the detective. "We take a small sample of blood and compare it with certain evidence that we found at the scene of the crime."

"And what will that tell you?" Craven inquired with an interest that Bottomley did not doubt was genuine.

"It will tell us who couldn't possibly have killed Angie," Bottomley replied.

Craven's interest grew. Bottomley looked him straight in the eyes. "And it will tell us who did kill her," he said sternly.

If the detective had been hoping that this last remark would worry Craven, he was in for a disappointment. Not even the remotest flicker of concern registered itself on the youth's face.

"Will it tell you that for sure?" was all that Craven asked.

"For certain sure," Bottomley replied. Still there was no hint of worry on the young man's face.

"That's clever," Craven replied. "How does it work?"

Ignoring the last question, Bottomley asked Craven if he would have any objection to taking part in such a test.

"No objection at all," the youth replied.

The arrangements for the blood testing of all the young males in the area were already well in hand by the time that Bottomley spoke to Craven. It had been agreed between Bottomley and his superiors

344

that the tests would involve boys and young men between the ages of 10 and 26. The tests were voluntary; nobody could be forced to take part. But anyone who refused would, simply by his refusal, automatically bring suspicion upon himself.

In all, there were 9,000 individuals whose ages fell between those specified. As things turned out, no one refused to take the test. All 9,000 individuals came forward. Tony Craven was one of the first to volunteer. He was, in fact, the third person to provide a blood sample.

In arranging the blood tests, Bottomley faced something of a dilemma. He could have saved a great deal of time and trouble by simply testing his suspect. But the detective had no real evidence against Craven. All he had was a gut feeling and the statements of a few people from Craven's workplace. And that did not count. He needed something tangible against the youth if he was to single him out for testing.

But Bottomley didn't have anything tangible against Craven. And to have singled him out for testing under those circumstances could have been very dangerous. It went against police procedures. And if the test had proved negative, both the investigating team and Bottomley himself could have found themselves in the kind of trouble that went far beyond the mere damaging of a reputation. As enforcers of the law, the police had to abide by the laws they were pledged to uphold.

So the testing procedure was played strictly by the book. When the tests were completed, they were sent away for analysis. Tony Craven's test was one of the first to be processed. And it proved positive. His DNA pattern matched that of a semen sample taken from Angie Flaherty's body.

But still Bottomley couldn't act. Even though the test result on Craven meant that the chances of the killer being someone other than the youth were around one in 90 million, the detective had to wait until all of the tests had been processed. And that took time. In all, it took 18 weeks.

Christmas came. Tony Craven sent Angie's family a Christmas card. He signed it, "Love from Tony C."

Christmas went. The results of all the blood tests were in. Anthony Craven was arrested and charged with Angie's murder.

At the police station, he was still anxious to be accepted and to fit in. He was still only too willing to be helpful. He confessed to raping and killing the little girl.

Detective Bottomley was puzzled. Something had been gnawing away at him for the past 18 weeks. He just had to know the answer. "Tell me, Tony," he said to the youth. "Why did you so readily agree to the blood test?" I told you that it was certain to identify the killer. And yet you still agreed to it. Why?"

"Because I thought I was safe from the test," he replied. "I didn't leave any blood at the scene." Craven's immaturity and naivete had finally caught up with him. He had totally failed to understand that the DNA pattern of his blood could be matched with the pattern of the DNA present in all of his bodily fluids, including his semen.

Tony Craven's story was that he had grown so tired of the constant taunts of his colleagues over his virginity that he decided to lose it. He lured Angie to the den that they both knew. There, she removed some of her clothes after being dared to do so by Craven. He helped her to remove the rest. Then he removed his own clothes and raped the little girl. When it was over, Angie started crying. Then the pain came and she started to scream.

"She just wouldn't be quiet," Craven said. "She just kept on screaming and screaming. Louder and louder. She said that she was going to tell what I had done to her. I asked her not to. But she went on saying she was going to tell."

Craven as not so naive that he did not realize the consequences of Angie talking about the rape. He had wanted to be accepted, to be "one of the boys." But if Angie talked, then he would never be accepted. He would spend his entire life as an outcast, shunned by society. So he had to make sure that she didn't talk.

At first, he tried to strangle her. But that was no good. So he picked up a large rock. There were several of them scattered around the den. With his left hand around her throat, he pinned Angie to the ground. With the rock in his right hand, he smashed in her head. He didn't know how many times he hit her, but it couldn't have been too many. It was all over in a matter of seconds.

After that, Craven hid her bike in the undergrowth, cleaned himself up a bit, and went home. He tried to carry on as if nothing had happened in the hope that no one would suspect him. And, for a time, it worked. Certainly none of his neighbors thought that the helpful youth who handled the press so well on behalf of Angie's family was anything other than he appeared to be—friendly, polite, and wishing to help.

The day after being formally charged with Angie Flaherty's murder, Craven appeared before the local magistrates. They remanded him to prison to await trial at Leeds Crown Court.

During the weeks that he was held on remand in the gloomy and forbidding confines of the city of Leeds' Armley Road Jail, Tony Craven reflected on the deed that had brought him to such a sorry state. He was filled with remorse over the past and consumed with fear over the future. Prison is a notoriously difficult place for any young man. But for someone as immature and naive as Tony Craven, it can be sheer hell. To make matters worse, he was in prison for a crime that most "ordinary" criminals find totally repugnant. Anyone serving time for the sexual molestation of a small child is regarded as the lowest form of life. And the time that they serve will be filled with the constant danger of violent retribution from the other inmates. For Tony Craven, facing a lifetime of such danger was too much.

A few days after his arrival at the jail, Craven tried to hang himself. But prison officers discovered him in time, cut him down, and sent him to the prison hospital. After recuperating for a few days, Craven was sent back to his cell, where, once more, he tried to end it by knotting his bedsheets together and constructing a makeshift noose. Again, prison officers found him in time and cut him down.

The next time, he tried slashing his wrists with a knife. But, again, quick-acting prison staff foiled

Craven's suicide bid. Just how the youth managed to get a knife into his cell still remains a mystery.

Following his three suicide attempts, Craven was kept under constant surveillance by prison staff. As a result, the remainder of his time on remand passed without incident.

Early in May 1992, Craven appeared before Mr. Justice Connell at Leeds Crown Court, where he pleaded guilty to the murder of Angela Flaherty. Prosecutor Malcolm Swift, Q.C., detailed the crime to the court. "Craven killed Angie so that she wouldn't tell anyone about the rape," the prosecutor said. "He took a rock, or maybe more than one, and hit her repeatedly over the head with considerable force, holding her by the neck as he did so in order to deliver the blows."

There was little that Defense Counsel James Steward, Q.C., could say in rebuttal, but he tried. "The killing came about because of panic," Mr. Stewart said. "Craven feared that Angela would tell her family what he had done."

Mr. Stewart went on to say that neither the rape nor the killing had been planned. "Craven and Angela started playing dares," he told the court. "And one thing led to another." He claimed that the youth was grossly immature and had been influenced by the constant taunting of some of his work colleagues, and by the pornographic material that he had been shown.

But whether or not the rape and murder had been planned, and whatever the influences were that led Craven to perpetrate such a dreadful crime, the result was that a little girl had been brutally defiled and viciously killed. The outcome of the trial was never in doubt.

"This was an appalling crime in which your victim was a defenseless young girl on whom you satisfied your lust, and whom you then murdered," Judge Connell told Craven before sentencing him to life imprisonment. Craven must serve at least 17 years before parole can be considered.

The children still play on the streets of Rawthorpe and ride their bikes on the hills about the town. But they don't use the former den anymore. After Angie Flaherty's death, the items that they used in their play were removed and destroyed. The little space in the center of the thicket is now inhabited only by birds and small animals. A thick mat of vegetation covers the place where the boxes and the mattress lay. Nature has wiped out all traces of the awful crime that was perpetrated on that sunny afternoon on Kilner Bank.

EDITOR'S NOTE:
Emily Forbes is not the real name of the person so named in the foregoing story. A fictitious name has been used because there is no reason for public interest in the identity of this person.

350

"MASSACRED A FAMILY OF 3 WITH A SLEDGEHAMMER!"

by Barry Bowe

Jack-o-lanterns leered from the windows of homes on Key Drive, and white sheets in the shape of ghosts were draped around the lampposts. Despite the diminishing value of human life in nearby Philadelphia— 525 homicides in 1990—the Hoopes family never dreamed of becoming murder statistics in their quiet suburb. Yet before the sun rose on Monday morning, October 15, 1990, the Halloween ghosts and goblins on the Hoopeses' quiet street would provide an appropriately spooky backdrop to a gruesome tale.

It was sunny and mild on Sunday, October 14th, in Hilltown Township, some 30 miles north of Philadelphia in rural Bucks County, Pennsylvania. Around noon, 14-year-old Dan Hoopes felt the sun's warmth as he stepped outside the family's four-bedroom colonial home, one of only 13 houses on Key Drive. The street was a short cul-de-sac and each home sat on a one-acre lot.

Pushing the lawn mower, Dan hurried back and forth across the grass, eager to finish his chores and spend the rest of the day goofing off and playing Nintendo. Later that afternoon, his 16-year-old brother

Doug washed his 1978 Buick Regal in the driveway, as he so often did. A neighbor described Dan and Doug as "typical boys, always making jokes."

The Hoopes family moved into the house when Key Drive was developed in the 1970s. There were four Hoopes in those days—Howard, Louise, and the two boys. But Howard had died from cancer three years before, and Louise was now an attractive 42-year-old widow. "The thing I remember about Louise was her smile," one neighbor recalled. "She was like a little cherub."

"They were very nice people," another neighbor said. "They kept to themselves, but a lot of people keep to themselves here because the homes are so far apart. But they were very pleasant to talk to, and she had lots of friends."

One of Louise's friends was a boyfriend. "He was seen with her late Sunday afternoon," Bucks County District Attorney Alan M. Rubenstein would say later. "She was a churchgoer, a member of the Episcopal Church, a hard worker, and they were law-abiding people."

Louise worked as a part-time secretary in the public relations office at Grand View Hospital in Sellersville. When Louise failed to report for work on Monday morning, her boss tried calling her at home. She got no answer, so she decided to call one of Louise's neighbors to see if she knew where Louise was. The neighbor didn't, but she agreed to check the Hoopes residence.

At 9:45, the neighbor walked across to Louise's house. She found the garage door open, Louise's car gone, and the kitchen door unlocked. The neighbor stepped inside and called, "Louise!" There was no answer, but something stirred deeper inside the house . . .

Officer John Thomas received a dispatch from headquarters at 9:58 to respond to a report of dead bodies. He raced to Key Drive and found Louise Hoopes' neighbor standing outside. The neighbor said that she had heard a noise upstairs. In the hobby room, she found the fan running, nothing more, and she shut it off. But the rest of the upstairs was a blood-drenched nightmare.

"I went to the master bedroom first," Officer Thomas wrote on his official report. "I saw a white female lying on a bed. She was covered with blankets. Her face was exposed. There was a bloodstained pillow on her chest." The neighbor had removed the pillow from Louise's face when she discovered the bodies. The victim's face "was covered with blood," Thomas reported. "There were lacerations on her neck. A pair of black panties were on the floor. She showed no signs of life."

Officer Thomas moved to the next bedroom. Inside, the empty mattress was drenched with blood and what appeared to be brain matter. When Officer Thomas stepped into the bedroom, he saw the form of a young white male lying on the floor in a zippered sleeping bag. It was Dan Hoopes. A bloodstained pillow partially covered the boy's crushed skull. In the next bedroom, a blue quilt covered the third bed. When Thomas pulled back the quilt, he found Doug Hoopes' dead body.

At 10:03, Officer Thomas called the station to request that detectives be dispatched, then he started sealing the crime scene with barrier tape. Officer Dave Mahaffey finished fingerprinting a petty criminal at the station and rushed out to Key Drive. Detectives Bill Leyden and Kerry Traugher followed right behind.

While Detective Leyden was snapping pictures of the victims, Officers Mahaffey and Thomas searched the house. Aside from the bloody horror on the second floor, the rest of the house was tidy, except for a small table in the living room. Heavy dust had formed a rectangular pattern around the table's perimeter, and the loose end of the cable hookup was lying on the floor, next to the table.

As the two partners searched the rest of the downstairs and the basement, they found no signs of a forced entry and nothing else seemed to be missing. Meanwhile, Detective Traugher called Chief Paul Gourley, who, in turn, called the Bucks County District Attorney's Office to request assistance. Traugher tried then to call for a county evidence collection team, but since none was available, he called the Pennsylvania State Police.

Soon, a state police helicopter was chopping overhead, and the shocking news was spreading throughout the traumatized neighborhood. Before noon, additional investigators from the Hilltown Township Police Department, the state police, the Bucks County detective squad, and an evidence team borrowed from Montgomery County had converged upon the scene. Detective Traugher, Detective John Wagner from the D.A.'s office, and Trooper Edward Donorovich teamed up to head the three-pronged force assembled from the different jurisdictions.

Trooper James Sulfare took charge of evidence collection, with Officer Thomas assigned to log each clue. While Detectives John Durante and Cedric McKeever from Montgomery County scanned the entire home with laser fingerprint equipment, District Attorney Alan Rubenstein moved from bedroom to bedroom. Rubenstein wondered aloud who could have inflicted such a heinous assault on these three helpless victims.

"It appeared as if they didn't know what hit them,"

the D.A. told the press Monday afternoon. "We have no idea why anyone would kill these people. We have no suspects and no one with an apparent motive. No one readily meets the description of having great animosity toward her or her kids." Rubenstein said there was no sign of forced entry, no signs of a struggle, none of the neighbors reported any strange noises, and only one item—the family car—was certainly missing from the home.

"We believe the assailant or assailants took the car and may have it now," Rubenstein said, describing the vehicle as a 1990 silver Chevrolet Lumina. The state police broadcast an APB for the missing vehicle with Pennsylvania tag WUW-647.

"Initially," Detective Traugher would say later, "judging from the massive destruction of the victims' skulls, we thought the [perp] had used a large-caliber handgun at close range. When we saw the scene, we wrongly thought Eric Motis, the boy across the street, had used the gun to kill his neighbors. Eric had stolen two handguns from a family member in August and one of them, a .357-Magnum, was still missing. Later the coroner arrived and said no."

"It appears all three victims suffered multiple blows and wounds from a sharp instrument," Coroner Thomas J. Rosko said. When the coroner pulled the blanket away from Louise Hoopes, he saw that her nightgown was pulled up over her abdomen, and her legs were slightly akimbo. She was naked below the waist and a secretion other than blood appeared on the sheets between her legs. It appeared as if sex had been part of the killer's diabolical scheme.

The evidence team sent the pillows, pillowcases, sheets, bed clothes, Louise's panties, doorknobs, dozens of blood samples, and assorted hairs to Barbara Rowley, a forensic scientist at the state police crime lab in Bethlehem.

Before noon, Corporal Michael Ryan and Detective Wagner were talking to students and teachers at the local schools, while a dozen investigators canvassed the neighborhood. At the same time, Detective William Kling had tracked down Louise's boyfriend.

The boyfriend said that he had been dating Louise for nearly a year. He got along well with Louise—the boys, too. He said he saw Louise six or seven days a week and had spent Sunday afternoon at the house, watching TV with the boys. He went home around 5:30, then called Louise later that night, around 10 o'clock. She was already in bed.

Detective Kling asked the boyfriend about the last time he had sex with Louise.

"Sunday," the boyfriend answered.

"Where?" the detectives asked.

"My apartment," the boyfriend answered.

"When was the last time you were in bed with Louise in her own bedroom?" the investigator wanted to know.

"Month ago," the boyfriend answered, "probably more like two months."

At the same time, police officers were checking the boyfriend's place of work, an engineering service in the town of Dublin. There, they learned that the boyfriend had arrived for work at eight o'clock that morning, as usual. From friends of the victim, policemen verified that the relationship between Louise and her boyfriend exhibited no signs of turbulence. At the end of the interview, the boyfriend submitted to blood, semen, and hair testing and agreed to survey the victims' house to help the investigators catalogue possible missing items.

With the loss of their primary suspect, the sleuths turned their entire focus onto Eric Motis, the neighbor boy. But Trooper Greg Langston learned that Eric had driven a stolen car to Florida near the end of September or the beginning of October with Heather Goodman and Luke McCabe.

Heather lived with an aunt in northeast Philadelphia. She was 5 feet 8, thin and pretty, wore braces, and was described as a thrill-seeker. Luke was from the Lancaster area. He was described as 5 feet 8, blond, and "not too bright." In addition, he was described as a "skinhead," had a Metallica tattoo on his shoulder, and often greeted people with a Hitler salute.

"I was driving my Barracuda up to Penn-Jersey Auto Parts in Richboro, buying some parts," an informant told Trooper Langston. "I saw Eric driving a newer model blue Pontiac station wagon. Heather and Luke came over and we all talked until around four-thirty. They talked about going to Miami.

"The reason I gave Luke three-hundred dollars," the informant explained, "was that I had some feelings for Heather. I thought that if I gave Luke the three-hundred dollars, he and Eric could go down to Florida and they would leave Heather here, and I could take her into my house and maybe have her as my girlfriend." But the informant's plan went awry when Eric, Luke, and Heather piled into the blue station-wagon and left for Miami, all of which placed Eric Motis 1,300 miles south of the murder scene.

"The police told me that Eric is a suspect, but [Eric] didn't have anything to do with it," one of Eric's relatives told reporters on Tuesday. "[Eric] wouldn't do anything like that. He's not a murderer. He's just a rebellious teenager, mixed up and confused. He was friends with [the Hoopeses], but the police are after him like hot water now. Eric had some trouble, but it's domestic and I don't want to go into detail. The last six months have been pure hell."

357

Eric, 19, had once been an A-student at Pennridge High School. Eric's friends described the 5-foot-9, 135-pound teenager as intelligent. They said he had always shunned drugs and dressed meticulously. Doug Hoopes was Eric's friend because they both loved cars. Teachers said that Eric had planned to attend college and become a chemical engineer. In a high school English essay, Eric described himself. "People who know me know I am creative and smart," Eric wrote. "I like to have a good time and take control of the situation. . . . I am so calm even in the toughest situations."

During his senior year, Eric joined a new peer group. He began arguing often and loudly with his family. At school, he became withdrawn and passive. His dress deteriorated and he cut classes so often that the assistant principal called him into his office three weeks before graduation to discipline him. "I was dumbfounded when he told me he was going to quit school rather than serve his detentions," the assistant principal said.

Late Tuesday, Dr. Isidore Mahalakis performed the autopsies at Grand View Hospital with Coroner Tom Rosko assisting. The forensic pathologist determined, "All three victims suffered head and facial fractures caused by multiple blows made with a large, heavy, sharp object." The pathologist placed the time of deaths as somewhere between 2:00 and 8:00 a.m. on Monday.

Coroner Rosko said that Louise Hoopes received 10 to 12 stab and slash wounds to her head and neck. One of the wounds had been delivered with such force that it penetrated the victim's neck all the way through to her spine. Rosko added that Dan Hoopes suffered similar stab wounds, along with bruises on his left thigh and left shoulder.

"Apart from these bruises," Rosko told the gathered press corps, "there is nothing else to indicate a struggle. The blows were vicious and repeated. They were definitely an attempt to kill." The absence of defense-type wounds led Rosko to theorize that all three victims had been attacked while they slept, one after the next.

Vaginal swabbings and smears indicated the presence of semen in Louise Hoopes' body. That evidence, along with a blood sample and samples obtained from the sheets on Louise's bed, was sent to Cellmark Diagnostics Laboratory in Germantown, Maryland, for DNA testing and comparisons.

"A motive doesn't jump out at you," D.A. Rubenstein said. "These people seemingly had no enemies. They were an upper middle-class family that was not involved in any controversy or offbeat activities. It was a classic suburban household, absent a father.

"It appears the person who did it took great pains to be undetected and knew exactly where he was going. He went into a dark home at night and nothing was damaged, nothing overturned, nothing was disturbed, and there was no noise. Police believe whoever did it was familiar with the family and the area."

Detectives from Hilltown Township Police Department remained convinced of Eric Motis' guilt. An arrest warrant already existed because Eric had failed to appear at a preliminary hearing on October 1st. The charges stemmed from an August 24th complaint filed by a family member of his. At that time, Eric was accused of stealing the family's GMC truck, along with a .25-caliber automatic and a .357 magnum.

Two weeks later, around 2:30 a.m. on September 4th, a Key Drive resident heard strange noises and phoned the Hilltown Township police. The resident said she had seen Eric running away from a car parked in front of her house. It looked to her as though Eric had been trying to siphon gasoline from the car's gas tank.

When Officers Mahaffey and Thomas responded, they spotted a four-by-four parked way back in the woods. When Mahaffey approached the vehicle, Eric fled into the woods. Mahaffey found an empty box for the .25 inside the cab. He broadcast a local police alert for Eric Motis.

Three hours later, Montgomery Township policemen observed Eric Motis walking along County Line Road, near its intersection with Route 202, and made the arrest. The .25-caliber gun was tucked into Eric's pants.

Eric spent eight days in the Montgomery County Prison — September 4th through 12th — before being turned over to Bucks County officials. He was charged with the theft of the two weapons, unauthorized use of a vehicle, and attempted theft of gasoline. He was arraigned on the 12th, then released when a family member posted 10 percent of Eric's $5,000 bond. From then on, Eric had been missing.

A check of stolen vehicle records uncovered a 1982 Pontiac T2000 blue station wagon that had been reported stolen from in front of an auto parts store on Route 309 on September 24th. Mysteriously, the blue station wagon had reappeared near Key Drive on the day of the murders. Was this the car that Eric had stolen? Had the station wagon been returned because Eric was now driving the Lumina?

On Thursday, October 18th, Detective Kling and Trooper Lee Walesyn led Louise's boyfriend and a neighbor on a tour of the Hoopes residence. Between them, Louise's two friends identified several missing items: a house key marked "H-3," a 19-inch Sylvania television set, Doug's set of Lumina keys which he kept on a Buick Regal key chain, a red plastic flashlight, the Nintendo game, a stackable stereo system and speakers, Louise's American Express card, a large Tootsie Roll bank full of quarters, a portable white and gray telephone, a maroon leather shoulder bag, a jewelry box, and a gold heart-shaped diamond necklace that Louise had recently purchased.

The next day, Trooper Langston and Detective Kling interviewed a teenager at Philadelphia police headquarters at 8th and Race Streets. The teenager said that Eric had arrived at her house shortly after noon the previous Sunday, the day before the homicides. Better yet, Eric had taken her and two other teenagers for a ride in a blue station wagon.

"Eric does not do drugs," she told the detectives. "He has extremely long fingernails for a guy, but he's extremely straight. He's a very bright guy."

During the ride, Eric whined about how badly his life was turning out, and he constantly complained about his parents. When the three girls told Eric that he was annoying them with his nagging, he freaked out. He started driving fast, scaring them, and acting like a maniac. At one point, he punched the windshield.

Later, Eric told the girls he had made a deal with a friend from his old neighborhood to buy a Chevy Lumina. Eric planned to finance the purchase with between $700 and $2,000 of birthday money he was anticipating. After that, he planned on returning to Florida, where he was renting an apartment in South Miami Beach.

With all the clues pointing south, a three-man arrest team flew to Miami. On Friday, October 19th, Officer Thomas, Trooper Langston, and Detective Richard Batezel were driving a rental car on Collins Avenue, between 15th and 16th Streets in South Miami Beach, when they spotted Heather Goodman and Luke McCabe walking along the street. The officers screeched to a stop, identified themselves, and transported the subjects to the Miami Beach Police Station at 1100 Washington Avenue. Along the way, the sleuths overheard snippets of conversation from the two subjects in the back of the car. "I know what they want to talk to us about," one whispered to the other. "I knew they would be coming after Eric. The police aren't stupid."

The arrest team met with Sergeant J.I. Yero at the Police Administration Building. Heather and Luke were placed in separate interview rooms on the third floor, while the Pennsylvania lawmen updated Sergeant Yero on the case and supplied Eric's photograph for duplication and distribution. The out-of-town lawmen identified the silver Lumina and gave Yero the location of the apartment where Eric Motis was supposedly holed up. Sergeant Yero immediately disseminated the information to the Miami Beach Patrol Division.

At 10:15 p.m., while the arrest team was conducting preliminary conversations with Heather and Luke, the Miami Beach Patrol Division stopped a silver Lumina that was driving down Collins Avenue. Minutes later, Eric Motis was in custody and Detective Batezel was reading the Miranda warning from the Bucks County D.A.'s Office "yellow card." Batezel asked the suspect if he wanted to have a lawyer present during the conversation.

"I don't know," Eric answered, "but you can ask the questions and, if I want a lawyer, I'll tell you and not answer any questions I don't want to."

"We can put you in Bucks County [at the time] when the Hoopes murders occurred," Detective Batezel advised the suspect.

Eric never responded. He sat in his chair and stared

straight ahead at his inquisitors, his face expressionless.

"Are you afraid?" Detective Batezel asked.

"I fear nothing or no one," Eric replied.

"How did you happen to be driving Louise Hoopes' car?" the detective pressed. At this point, Eric requested an attorney and the interview ended.

Next, the arrest team interviewed Heather Goodman. Without any prompting from the investigators about the crime or the facts surrounding the homicides, Heather wove an incredible narrative. From the minute they arrived in Florida, Heather said that Eric complained about his parents, threatening to return to Bucks County to kill both his parents and his grandparents. At Eric's urging, Heather pawned some of her jewelry on October 11th to raise gas money. The next day, around 3:00 p.m., Eric said that he was leaving for a few days.

"Are you going back home?" Heather asked.

"I'm going back around that area," Eric answered, telling Heather he'd bring back a Chevy Lumina and a lot of cash.

"From where?" Heather asked.

"The less you know, the better," Eric told her.

Heather next saw Eric the following Tuesday, October 16th. She and Luke were approaching the corner of 11th and Collins on foot, when Eric walked up and hugged her. He led them back to the apartment and showed them a silver Chevy Lumina parked in the lot. A stereo sitting on the backseat caught Heather's eye.

When Eric flipped open the trunk, he showed her a television set and a Nintendo game. Then he showed her a pair of bloodstained brown gloves, a small sledgehammer, and a knife. Eric told her that these were the murder weapons that he had used to kill an entire family. That was when Heather noticed the crusted blood underneath Eric's long fingernails and the rusty-looking spatters on his sneakers and socks.

"Don't tell me it's the Hoopeses," Heather said.

"What if it is the Hoopeses?" Eric answered.

After they carried the loot inside the apartment, Eric flashed a roll of cash—he said it was $500—a diamond necklace, a pearl necklace, Louise Hoopes' American Express card, and an audio tape with Doug Hoopes' voice recorded on it.

"Do you want me tell you detail for detail?" Eric asked.

"Why not?" Heather replied. She would later recount Eric's grisly murder saga to the police.

Knowing that the family usually left the garage door ajar to allow the cat to come and go, Eric slipped into the garage. He knew that Doug kept his house key under a nail can in the garage. Eric removed the key and entered the house. The clock read 3:30 a.m. when he reached Louise's bedroom. Eric tiptoed across the room and covered Louise's face with a pillow, pressing down hard.

"It isn't easy to suffocate someone," Eric had told Heather. When he lifted the pillow, Louise screamed, "Help me!" To silence his first victim, Eric smashed her head with the sledgehammer—seven times. Incredibly, Louise was still breathing after the attack. When Eric slit Louise's throat, blood shot all over the place. According to Eric, air was still coming out of her severed windpipe when he crept down the dark hallway like a vampire in search of his next victim.

Eric told Heather that Dan "was sound asleep" when he entered the 14-year-old's bedroom, but Eric couldn't remember whether or not he had slashed Dan's throat. "Danny was hard to kill," Eric said, saying that Dan started screaming, "Mommy, help me!" To silence his second victim, Eric pounded the teenager's head until "blood and stuff" flew all over the place.

Only Doug remained. But when Eric reached Doug's bedroom and peered inside, his third victim had awakened. Eric hid behind the wall and watched, as Doug sat up in bed. When Doug turned off his radio and laid back down, Eric got down on his hands and knees and crawled into the bedroom, lying flat on the floor, waiting for his friend to fall back asleep. Suddenly, Doug grabbed Eric's wrist. Eric jumped to his feet and started hammering his buddy's head with the sledgehammer until Doug surrendered his grip on Eric's wrist.

On his way back down the hallway, Eric glanced into Dan's bedroom. Unbelievably, Dan had crawled out of bed and was now lying on the floor, next to the bed, but he was definitely dead. In Louise's bedroom, Eric found another surprise: air was still coming out of Louise's windpipe. Eric pulled back the covers and yanked off Louise's panties. Tossing the panties onto the floor, Eric mounted the dying woman and raped her.

"Why did you have to kill them?" Heather asked Eric.

"How would I be able to come back and forth, in and out of the house, taking the things I took without killing them?" Eric answered.

"How did you feel?" Heather asked.

"I looked at it and just smiled and laughed," Eric confided to Heather. "I enjoyed every minute of it."

On Sunday, Detective Batezel phoned Bucks County officials to request that an evidence collection team be sent to Florida. Batezel told his colleague that Eric Motis was in custody, the Lumina had been impounded, and Heather Goodman had made an incriminating statement that tied the whole case together.

At 6:00 p.m. on Monday, Trooper Sulfare, Detective Durante, and Officer Frank Dilworth searched the Lumina and found a red plastic flashlight. Shortly after midnight, they executed a search warrant on Eric's apartment. In less than two hours, the evidence team uncovered a stereo unit and speakers, a bloodstained pair of brown gloves, a small sledgehammer, a wooden-handled butcher knife, a filet knife, four keys on a Buick Regal key chain, a maroon leather shoulder purse, a gray and white telephone, a heart-shaped diamond necklace, a pearl necklace, a Tootsie Roll bank containing a large quantity of quarters, and a Nintendo game.

In the bedroom, Detective Batezel found a handwritten list of the stolen property in a bureau drawer. On one side of the paper was written: "I want to die." On the other side were the words, "Suicide is the solution to the end."

The next day, Eric Motis waived extradition at a 10-minute hearing in Miami Beach and returned to Bucks County. D.A. Alan Rubenstein was already buttoning down the state's case. On November 1st, evidence technicians collected blood, hair, and sputum samples from Eric at the Bucks County Prison. Four days later, the state police crime lab confirmed that Louise's bedsheet contained "spermatozoa, acid phosphatase and choline, enzymes found in seminal fluid."

On January 15, 1991, Cellmark Lab concluded that "two (2) DNA banding patterns were found on the bedsheet stain, one of which was similar to the DNA banding pattern found in Louise Hoopes and the other matched Eric Motis' banding pattern." Two weeks later, Cellmark estimated that Eric's particular banding pattern existed in the Caucasian population at a frequency of no more than one in 1.9 million.

On March 11, 1991, a curious crowd packed Judge Isaac Garb's courtroom in Doylestown for the first day of Eric Motis' murder trial. The defendant stood before the court in gray slacks and a charcoal-colored pullover sweater. He folded his hands in front of himself.

"How do you plead?" Judge Garb asked.

"Guilty, your honor," the defendant replied.

"Are you sure you want to enter this plea?" the startled judge asked the defendant.

"Yes," Eric replied in a meek voice, then admitted to murdering Louise, Dan, and Doug Hoopes. He also admitted to raping Louise Hoopes and to taking several valuable objects from the Key Drive home.

Judge Garb accepted Eric's plea the next day, but frustration filled the judge's brain. None of the detectives, lawyers, psychiatrists, or witnesses had succeeded in discovering why a quiet, intelligent young man from such a fine middle-class environment could commit a crime like something out of *Lord of the Flies* or *A Clockwork Orange*.

"You can almost always find some explanation," Judge Garb said, as he stared into the murderer's eyes. "This is one of those rare, rare instances where there is no explanation, there is no reason, there is no motive.

"I have no doubt that something is going on in there. This just doesn't happen. . . . We can go to the moon, we can circle Mars, but we don't know what goes on in someone's mind, someone who would commit crimes such as these.

"Do you have anything to say?"

"No, your honor," Eric responded.

Moments later, Judge Garb sentenced Eric Motis to three consecutive life sentences with no chance for parole. Because Eric was young, because he had no criminal record, and because the judge believed that Eric must have been mentally disturbed when he killed his three neighbors, the judge spared the triple-killer's life.

EDITOR'S NOTE:
Heather Goodman and Luke McCabe are not the real names of the persons so named in the foregoing story. Fictitious names have been used because there is no reason for public interest in the identities of these persons.

"RAPED, SHOT, DOUSED WITH GAS & TORCHED IN THE STREET!"

by Charles W. Sasser

Tulsa, Oklahoma
July 27, 1990

"Self-destructive behavior is common among runaway girls," says Tulsa's director of clinical services for the Shadow Mountain Institute, a private counseling and substance-abuse treatment center for children and teens. "Real or perceived abuse at home causes many girls to identify themselves as victims, and they often invite abusive situations. They buy tickets to disaster."

One such ticket to disaster was apparently bought on the early morning of Friday, July 27, 1990, in Tulsa, Oklahoma. A Northside woman reported to police that her daughter had run away from home following an argument. The girl was only one of about 100 persons under the age of 18 reported missing in Tulsa that month.

"I tried to chase her, but she got away," the mother declared.

The runaway was described as a 12-year-old white female, 5 feet 2 inches in height, weighing 95 pounds, with long blonde hair and hazel eyes. She was last seen wearing blue denim trousers and a pink top.

Disaster came mere minutes before midnight that same Friday. A teenager watching TV in the living room of her home on 49th Street North suddenly noticed a fiery glow through her window. She darted to the door.

"All I saw were the flames," she later told investigators. "I thought it was a grass fire, at first." The teenager telephoned her sleeping neighbors, who got up and dashed into the street. They recoiled in horror at what they saw there. It was no grass fire. The flames were consuming the bound corpse of a young girl.

When Patrol Officer Bill Yelton and Homicide Detective Johnny Uhles arrived at the 2000 block of East 49th Street North, responding with sirens and lights to a "burning body in the street" call, they found what seemed like the entire neighborhood crowding around the human pyre. Detective Uhles quickly blasted the flaming body with a fire extinguisher.

The smoldering corpse lay grotesque near the street's center line. It was charred and stank of cooked flesh and gasoline. Shreds of the plastic trash sacks in which the victim was wrapped and of the thin rope that encircled the grisly package had melted into the blackened flesh.

The victim's facial features, however, remained recognizable. Tufts of blonde hair hung from her scalp. The victim was barefoot, but scraps of blue denims and a pink top still clung to her charred flesh. The body bore no identification.

Detective Uhles, a 25-year police veteran, has often expressed the common police viewpoint that people will do anything they can to irreparably harm other people. But this crime, he later remarked, went far beyond that. This, he declared, was one of the vilest deeds he had ever witnessed during all his years as a cop.

"I have to hope she was dead before she caught on fire!" he said.

Casting personal emotion aside, Officer Yelton and Detective Uhles cordoned off the crime scene, culled possible witnesses from the crowd, and began questioning them. Because of the dead girl's burned condition, it was not possible, initially, for Uhles to check for other direct signs of violence. Soon, however, after the state medical examiners checked the body, they were to report that someone had pumped at least four .22-caliber bullets into the victim's face and chest.

"It looks like she was killed elsewhere and dumped here in the street," Uhles speculated. "They burned the body to destroy the evidence."

From what the medical experts determined, the victim had also, apparently, been raped prior to death.

Assistant Fire Marshall Curtis Ozment brought his fire-investigator dog, Hydro, who sniffed out the residue of a flammable substance that had leaked into a crack of the pavement near the body. Probably gasoline, the fire official announced, taking samples for analysis.

Detective Uhles directed the forensic experts in photographing, measuring, and collecting evidence. He also launched a door-by-door canvass of the working-class neighborhood—an undertaking that extended into the next day.

Most of the neighborhood residents had been sleeping at the time the flaming corpse was discovered. Only one woman who lived four houses down from the scene had anything to report. "I guess it was about eleven-fifteen tonight," she said. "I heard several boys or young men down the street, arguing and going on."

"Did you see them? Do you know who they were?" Uhles asked.

"No, sir! They waked me," the woman replied. "But in this neighborhood, you learn to mind your own business."

Using the victim's description, the detective soon turned up a police missing-person report that generally fit the dead girl. The report had been filed that Friday morning. It led Uhles to a rundown bungalow two miles southeast of the crime scene in the 2800 block of East 41st Place North. By daybreak that Saturday, the pitiful human torch had been positively identified as 12-year-old Kimberly Dawn Allison, a Monroe Middle School student.

Police said that Kimberly's at-home relative drew a portrait of the missing girl, now deceased, as a precocious preteen who tried to appear and behave much older than she was. Kimberly, the relative said, would often sneak out her bedroom window late at night to carouse about the Tulsa streets with older individuals. She had taken to drinking and sleeping with boys, sometimes grown men, the relative said.

"She hung out in a bad crowd," the relative told newsmen. "Maybe I was a little strict, but I wanted her to die of old age, not be murdered at twelve . . . I tried to tell her, 'You'll go out and get raped and beaten and murdered.' It scared her, but I guess it didn't scare her enough."

The woman added sadly that Kimberly must have had a premonition of violent death just the week before. "She wanted to know what it would be like to be cremated," she said of the girl.

In front of the bungalow was a little flower garden. Kimberly had planted it with flowers from her grandfather's grave. She had put up a little hand-printed sign that read: "GRANDPA'S FLOWER GARDEN."

372

Detective Uhles completed his preliminary investigation and turned over his reports to Sergeant Wayne Allen, the officer in charge of the homicide investigation detail. As Saturday, July 28th, dawned bright and hot, Allen assigned the case to Detectives Fred Parke and Colleen Hogan. It was Tulsa's 28th homicide of the year, with five months still to go. Like most cities in the nation, Tulsa was setting new records for violence.

Detective Colleen Hogan, young, attractive, and skilled, was an investigator with about 15 years' experience as a police officer. Fred Parke had served nearly 30 years, the last 20 as the city's most accomplished homicide detective. Grizzled, gray-haired, and soft-spoken, Parke had tracked down more killers than any other cop in the department.

Since Saturday was Parke's day off, Hogan decided to let him sleep for a while that morning. She called him at home around noon. "Fred, we have a little problem here," she said when she finally did call her colleague.

The two sleuths were to remain on duty almost constantly for the next four days.

Together, they picked up a trail so faint that it might not have been a trail at all. Through systematically questioning residents in the vicinity of the previous night's human burning, they found an elderly woman who recalled a single incident that caught her eye either Friday or Friday night.

It was around 11:00 a.m., Friday, the woman said, when she saw a young man, about 17 or 18 years old, run out of a house so fast down the street that he didn't even bother to stop and pick up his hat when it blew off. She pointed out the house to sleuths. The address was on East 49th Street North. It faced the street where Kimberly's body had burned.

373

"I know this kid, but I don't know his name," the woman continued. "He used to live around here, but he moved away or something. I guess he must have been visiting that Simpson boy down there."

Nothing really suspicious here, the sleuths thought. Kids were always running, jumping, and yelling for no apparent purpose. After making notes on the incident, Detectives Hogan and Parke returned to Kimberly Allison's own house in an attempt to pick up a trail there. This time, they questioned the victim's female relative in depth, asking for every detail about the girl's activities within recent days, asking about family backgrounds and attitudes. The probers knew that clues sometimes came from the most obscure or unexpected angle.

According to her relative, Kimberly had lived a short but rough life. One male relative was in prison, and another was hospitalized for drug addiction. Still a third teen relative had run away from home several years earlier and was still missing.

"We live in a bad area . . . I think she was killed by some crazy person who wanted to watch her suffer. She was a little girl trying to be an adult, and that's what killed her," the woman declared.

On Thursday night, the woman explained tearfully, Kimberly sneaked out of the house and stayed out until 5:00 a.m. on Friday morning, when the relative found her asleep outside on the porch. She and Kimberly had a terrific argument, which climaxed with the young girl fleeing the house. Shortly afterwards, the relative called the police and filed a missing-person and runaway report.

"That's the last I seen or heard of her until . . ."

Until Detective Uhles had driven up on Saturday morning bearing the bad news.

Another young girl who lived next door to the Allison residence reportedly informed the detectives that she saw Kimberly return home around 2:00 a.m. on Friday. She said a dark-colored car stopped in front of the house. Kimberly staggered from the car, obviously intoxicated or high on drugs. Then Kimberly fell on the lawn near her front door and apparently passed out. She slept there on the grass or on the porch until her relative discovered her at about 5:00 a.m.

"Can you describe the people inside the car?" Detective Parke asked the young witness.

"It was dark. All I could see was, they were two black guys," the girl said. "They looked a whole lot older than Kimberly. They just dropped her off there and drove off."

The autopsy results confirmed that the victim had indeed had sexual intercourse prior to death. Although sex with a 12-year-old was definitely rape, according to law, the autopsy reportedly revealed that there probably had been little or no physical compulsion used. In other words, it was technically and legally rape, but it had not likely been forced.

Had Kimberly voluntarily consented to sexual intercourse with her killer? Was the killer someone she knew?

As the abominable crime swept across the front pages and TV news broadcasts, police dispatchers were swamped with calls reporting sightings or providing tips on possible suspects. Each call had to be checked out.

One of the most credible tips came from a middle-aged man who'd been on his way to work an hour or so after sunrise on Friday, when he stopped for gas at a convenience store near North Lewis Avenue and 41st Street. That was only a few blocks from Kimberly's house. He said that a young girl there asked him for a ride. He was able to identify Kimberly Dawn Allison from her photograph.

"I drove her to Monroe Middle School and let her out in front of the school," the man said. The Monroe School was located on 48th Street North, one block from where the victim's body went up in flames 16 hours later.

On Saturday evening, Detectives Parke and Hogan received more information from a young friend of Kimberly's. The friend said that she had been telephoned that afternoon by one of Kimberly's classmates, a 15-year-old boy named Adriel Simpson. Adriel reportedly announced to Kimberly's friend that he knew who had been with Kimberly on Friday before her death.

"Kimberly had been seeing Adriel a lot," the young friend told police. "That's all she talked about. Everything was Adriel, Adriel, Adriel."

Adriel Simpson's house on East 49th Street faced the exact spot where Kimberly's burning body had awakened the neighborhood. Both Detectives Uhles and Hogan had questioned the youth and his relative during their routine canvassing. Simpson and his relative reportedly told the sleuths they knew Kimberly, but they had not seen her that day.

Upon being questioned again, however, Adriel Simpson changed his story. Under the gaze of his relative, the boy told Parke and Hogan that Kimberly had telephoned him before noon on Friday.

"She wouldn't tell me where she was at," Simpson said, according to the sleuths' accounts of the session, "but I hear a voice in the background that I recognize. It was B.G. Walls."

That night, near midnight, Adriel Simpson continued, he looked out his window and spotted B.G. Walls and two other local teens driving up and stopping in the street in front of his house. Their headlights were doused.

"They pull something out of the car in trash bags and pour gas or something on it," Simpson told the detectives. "Then they lit it up and drove off. I find out later it was Kimberly."

"Why didn't you tell the police then about it?" demanded one of the sleuths.

"He was scared," Adriel's relative put in.

"Who were the other boys with Walls?" one of the detectives asked.

"They were Akil Jones and that dude, Prince Harolds."

Simpson described the murder suspects as black males, all about 16 years old. All were slender and about the same height. Jones was dark-skinned, while the other two were lighter, about Simpson's complexion. They left speeding in a dark-colored sedan.

Were these the same males who had dropped Kimberly off drunk in front of her house at 2:00 a.m.? Had Kimberly rejoined them only to meet her fate?

The detectives immediately issued an APB (all-points bulletin) on the trio, requesting that they be picked up and held for questioning in Kimberly Allison's slaying. At the same time, Parke and Hogan personally spearheaded the manhunt. Their search took them to adjacent cities and beyond.

By 5:00 a.m. on Sunday, the hunt had led the weary detectives to B.G. Walls' residence in nearby Bixby, Oklahoma. They raided the house with a search warrant. Walls was not present.

"We found nothing that could be construed as evidence," Parke later reported. "Nothing at all."

Undaunted, though sleepless now for over 24 hours, the investigators continued their relentless pursuit of the three suspected murderers. It led them to

377

some puzzling, unexpected ends.

Akil Jones, they learned, was being held in the juvenile detention center on a previous unrelated crime. He had been there for several days. Could he have escaped, committed murder, and then returned? No, came the reply.

As for Prince Harolds, he was staying in Oklahoma City, 100 miles to the southwest. He, too, had been gone from Tulsa for several days.

Both suspects had airtight alibis.

Somewhat confounded by this turn of events, Detectives Parke and Hogan charged back to 49th Street North to confront Adriel Simpson and his relative.

"You've lied or something," Parke admonished the youth. "We've found two of the three boys you said you saw setting fire to Kimberly. They could *not* have been involved. One of them was even in jail."

"Well, uh, maybe I was mistaken about Akil and Prince," Simpson responded. "But I ain't mistaken about B.G. Walls. I seen him set the fire."

Parke let the APB stand on Walls, but he subtly shifted the direction of the probe.

"Where were *you* on Friday?" he asked Simpson.

"I was with Pops," Simpson replied quickly.

Adriel's relative jumped in swiftly. "He stay all day with Pops," she said, according to official accounts. "When I get off work Friday night, I pick him up from Pops'. We went shopping, then came home—and that's where we stay. We were asleep when the fire woke us."

Pops, who was about 80 years old and slightly senile, lived more than a mile away, near Mohawk Boulevard and North Lewis. He reportedly corroborated Adriel's alibi.

"That boy was with me all day," he insisted to the sleuths.

The state medical examiner had said that Kimberly died sometime between ten o'clock Friday morning and five o'clock Friday afternoon.

So Adriel Simpson's alibi appeared to be as airtight as Akil Jones' or Prince Harolds'. Still, Detective Parke had worked enough convoluted cases to know that sometimes an alibi could simply be too good.

"Something was beginning to smell as fishy as Moby Dick," he later growled softly.

On a hunch, the sleuths sought permission to search the Simpson residence. Permission was granted, reluctantly. The detective later described the house as "trashed." Old boxes of clothing, used TVs, broken furniture, and other debris filled the rooms virtually from floors to ceilings. It would have taken days, Parke said, to adequately search the house with any hope of finding evidence.

As the investigator went through the home in a cursory, superficial inspection, the lady of the house followed him, talking nonstop. Parke said she appeared to be nervous.

"You say somebody seen a boy run from my house on Friday?" she allegedly chattered on. "Adriel and me have been talking. It must have been that no-good Coke here while we were gone."

Coke's complete name, Parke soon established, was Damon Dubois, and he was 16 years old.

"He is a no-good boy," Adriel's relative stated flatly, according to official reports. "I don't want Adriel hanging with him. He's always trying to get Adriel into trouble."

Into the attached garage, on the dirty floor next to a broken meat freezer, Detective Parke spotted a dried stain of what appeared to be blood.

"That's blood, all right," the woman agreed. "We had a puppy die on us there this week. That's its

379

blood."

Parke summoned forensic experts to take samples of the blood for analysis. Then, temporarily stopped cold by a wall of apparently solid alibis, he left Simpson's residence to pursue one of the only other leads remaining. For the rest of that summer weekend, he and Colleen Hogan tracked Damon Dubois from one end of Tulsa to the other. Apparently, Dubois moved frequently. No one seemed to know where he lived currently.

Exhausted, Fred Parke went home on Sunday night for his first real sleep since Friday night.

The case hung cold, bogged down, until Monday evening, July 30th, when Parke's phone rang at the homicide office. Parke listened for a moment, then said, "I'll meet you at the detective division in a half-hour."

Shortly, a boy with large, frightened eyes and a man who said he was the boy's uncle arrived. Parke led them into an interrogation cubicle. For the next hour, the seasoned detective listened in silent horror as Damon Dubois laid out a tale so foul that it could only have sprung from the bloody depths of a sociopath's imagination.

It was a tale about youth—those whom Criminologist James Fox has called "the young and the ruthless."

Like most homicide cops, Parke was familiar with the rising brutality among the nation's young. Violent crime among teenagers had soared by 121 percent since 1985. Homicide rates for those of ages 13 to 16 had nearly doubled. Cities were experiencing a 40 percent increase in homicides—and the perpetrators were getting younger every time.

"You have a dangerous mix of guns and violence in our cities at the same time you see a tremendous reduction in society's investment in children," one sociologist explained. But sociologists saw only the bare statistics and worked with the *theory* of juvenile crime. Cops like Fred Parke worked with the cold reality.

Subsequent testimony disclosed what was contained in 16-year-old Damon Dubois' initial confession. In it, he said that Adriel Simpson telephoned him early on Friday morning, July 27th. Adriel's relative had already gone to work by then. Adriel skipped school, as did Damon.

"Coke, get on over here," Adriel said. (The conversation here is paraphrased to correspond with Dubois' testimony.) " I got a white girl here wants to [have sexual intercourse with] both of us."

"No, man! Did she say that?"

Adriel put Kimberly on the telephone. "Yeah. I'll [have sexual intercourse with] you," she said.

Damon hurried over to Simpson's house on 49th Street. But Kimberly apparently changed her mind after he arrived. She had sexual relations with Adriel Simpson, but she refused to take Damon Dubois into the bedroom.

"You can't dis [show disrespect to] my homie like that!" Simpson shouted at her. In his rage, he snatched a .22-caliber nine-shot revolver from hiding and began shooting up the house to frighten Kimberly into doing his bidding. He fired two bullets into the cluttered floor of the living room, then he chased Kimberly into the bedroom.

"You gonna give my homie some [sex], bitch?" he yelled, firing three more bullets into the bedroom floor.

Kimberly, sitting on the bed, folded her arms across her chest and refused.

Then, coldly, deliberately, Adriel Simpson, age 15,

turned the gun on Kimberly Allison, age 12, and began shooting her. He blasted her in the face and chest four times. He blasted her until the gun clicked empty.

So that was it? Detective Parke sat back in his chair, looking at Dubois. A 12-year-old girl died because she refused to give sex to her 15-year-old boyfriend's pal?

Life could be that cheap.

After the shooting, Damon reportedly continued, he and Adriel wrapped the corpse in garbage bags, tied the large bundle with rope, and stored it in the garage next to the broken freezer. That wasn't puppy blood on the floor, after all. And the forensic experts soon determined that it was human blood matching Kimberly Allison's.

Damon continued his grisly narrative: After some thought, young Adriel produced a bottle containing gasoline and said he was going to burn the body. Damon ran out of the house so fast he lost his hat.

Damon Dubois' confession proved to be the key that broke the case. What remained was the cleanup.

On Tuesday morning, July 31st, Detectives Park and Hogan arrested Adriel Simpson at his residence and served him and his relative with a search warrant. This time, the sleuths found the bullet holes just as Damon had described them. They also detected smears of blood on Adriel's bed.

At first, Parke later said, Adriel's relative staunchly defended the youth, insisting that he had been either with her or with Pops at the time the murder was committed. Soon, however, she relented in the face of overwhelming evidence and reportedly admitted that she and Pops had both lied to provide Adriel an alibi. Later, as the probe continued, she also turned over to the police a .22-caliber handgun, which ballistics tests eventually proved to be the murder weapon. The gun belonged to Pops, but it had been taken from his garage several weeks earlier without his knowledge.

Up until now, neighbors had refused to talk about Adriel Simpson and his relative, claiming they were afraid of retaliation if they said anything.

"Adriel's been a threat to us for a long time," declared a neighbor, who appeared to be relieved at seeing the youth handcuffed and taken to jail. "Everybody around here is afraid of him and his [female relative]. They're always threatening people with guns."

Police reports revealed that the teenager had been arrested on March 6th, four months earlier, for allegedly shooting at other students on the Monroe Middle School playground.

On the same day that Adriel Simpson joined Damon Dubois in the county jail, Kimberly Dawn Allison was buried, dressed in her favorite jeans skirt, new shoes, and a "New Kids On The Block" T-shirt. Her favorite doll was placed in the casket with her.

On Friday, August 3, 1990, District Attorney David Morse charged Adriel Simpson with first-degree murder and Damon Dubois with accessory to murder. He said he would strive to have both defendants certified to stand trial as adults.

The certification process took nearly two years to work its way through the court system. Reportedly unrepentant over the brutal crime of which he was accused, and showing no remorse, Simpson and his relative complained bitterly that he was being mistreated in jail. Lawsuits filed by him in U.S. District Court alleged numerous civil rights violations, including the following:

• Denial of his Bible and a no-pork diet necessary for his religion;

- Denial of proper medical treatment;
- Deprivation of clean clothing;
- Discovery of hair and cigarette ashes in his food;
- Fondling of his genitals during searches;
- Denial of visitation rights;
- Confiscation of edibles he bought from the jail commissary.

Tulsa County Sheriff Stanley Glanz recalled one occasion when Simpson and other "troublemakers" threw feces at jail guards.

Finally, in early 1992, Adriel Simpson, then 17, was certified to stand trial as an adult. Damon Dubois testified against him in a trial that ended on Friday, June 5, 1992. Simpson was found guilty of first-degree murder and sentenced to serve life in prison without parole. Damon Dubois received probation until his 18th birthday.

Adriel Simpson is currently serving his sentence in maximum security at the Oklahoma State Penitentiary. GRANDPA'S FLOWER GARDEN, which Kimberly Dawn Allison planted, has since died.

EDITOR'S NOTE:
B.G. Walls, Akil Jones, Prince Harolds, Pops and Damon "Coke" Dubois are not the real names of the persons so named in the foregoing story. Fictitious names have been used because there is no reason for public interest in the identities of these persons.

" 'CHRISTIE CHROME' BLASTED 'SMILEY' IN THE GUT!"

by Bill Kelly

Lake Forest, California
December 29, 1991

Five shadowy figures bundled up in heavy clothing, their collars pulled up against the bitter cold of that early winter morning, were outlined in the moonlight as they approached the two vehicles and started climbing in. It was about 1:00 a.m. on Sunday, December 29, 1991, in the community of Lake Forest, California, and the temperature was dipping fast as the doors of the two cars slammed shut.

The driver of one of the vehicles, a white Toyota pickup, nodded to the driver of the other car, a red souped-up Chevrolet Camaro, and both switched on the ignitions almost simultaneously. Both vehicles lurched forward at the same time, wheels screaming, with the Toyota's muffler sputtering loudly. With the Camaro trailing the Toyota, the two vehicles roared down El Torro Road, which is bounded by Rockfield and Los Alisos Boulevards and the I-5 Freeway.

In the Toyota, a man on the passenger side pulled out a gun and checked to see if it was fully loaded. It was a .38-caliber six-shot revolver, and he referred to it as "Christie Chrome." On this night, "Christie Chrome" had some deadly business to attend to . . .

Half an hour later, the Toyota and the Camaro pulled up to a flat-fronted house on the 24000 block of slumbering Palmek Circle. At that hour, it was the only house on the block with any lights on. The two cars circled the block once, then twice, to see if the coast was clear.

A man who was out walking his dog in the area spotted the cars. He smelled trouble brewing, so he turned and hurried away, tugging at his dog's leash to make it move faster.

In the Toyota, the larger of the three men—the one with the gun—kissed the chrome-plated revolver and whispered to it, "Time to go to work, Christie Chrome." His companions chuckled. A few seconds later, the vehicles were slowly moving on the street at the side of the house, and the riders were peering through the blinds of a small bedroom window. Inside the dimly-lit room, three figures could be seen talking away in the early-morning hours.

One resident of Palmek Circle thought he heard an abrupt burst of drilling that came in several short spurts. Another neighbor thought it was an automobile backfiring three times in succession. A neighborhood woman, suddenly awakened by the staccato reports, peeked out her window and saw two dissimilar vehicles with silhouetted figures inside pass by and then speed away. Later, the woman told the police she thought it was just another late-night party breaking up.

Meanwhile, some seconds after the noise, an annoyed neighbor lifted his window and yelled out, "Shut up that damned noise!" There was some confusion in the later recollections of other witnesses. Some

386

said they heard three loud reports that sounded like firecrackers. Others said they heard four bangs in quick succession. One thing the witnesses all agreed on. They all heard a panic-stricken voice yell, "Help! Help! They've shot my boy!"

As best as anyone inside the house could remember, after hearing the series of rapid-fire blasts, the family members and their out-of-town guests rushed into the back bedroom and found 17-year-old Bylan Hanna sprawled on the floor. He was bleeding profusely from a gunshot wound to his abdomen.

"Help me," Hanna moaned. "I'm dying."

The police were immediately notified and officers arrived on the scene within minutes. Some officers canvassed the neighborhood homes and found a woman who said she saw two vehicles racing towards El Torro Road. That road borders the freeway, which runs southbound towards San Diego and northbound to Los Angeles—a possible escape route in either direction.

Patrol cars came streaming out of nowhere to block off the exits to the freeway. But they were precious seconds too late.

Meanwhile, a family member purportedly told the paramedics who arrived with the police contingents, "I held a compress to his side, but it was too late." She was referring to Bylan Hanna, the youth who had been shot.

Blood was spattered everywhere—on the floor, the bedspread, and across the walls. Two of Bylan's young relatives, who had been sitting next to him, were also sprayed by the victim's blood. The scene was so shocking that those present would never be able to completely erase it from their memories.

Outside, officers lined up as human barriers at both ends of the block to keep out curious onlookers.

Lieutenant Richard J. Olson and a contingent of investigators from the sheriff's department substation in Laguna Niguel searched for clues around the house and questioned the victim's family members in hopes that they could shed some light on the mysterious shooting.

Outside, neighbors from across the street looked on as paramedics loaded Bylan's body into an ambulance for transport to Saddleback Memorial Medical Center in Laguna Hills. There, a short while later, a doctor officially pronounced the 17-year-old dead.

Sheriff's Lieutenant Lawrence Richey subsequently ordered every available prober into the operation. He also alerted the California Highway Patrol (CHP), officers of which immediately went into action by combing every thoroughfare leading to and from Lake Forest. But the drive-by killers had apparently gotten clean away.

The autopsy was performed on Monday, December 30th. An official of the Orange County Coroner's Office told police investigators that Bylan Hanna had died from a single gunshot wound to the stomach. The lethal slug had come from a .38-caliber pistol.

The following morning, the local newspapers provided Orange County dwellers with the known details of the shocking murder. One journalist who interviewed the residents along Palmek Circle found several neighbors who had noticed a white Toyota pickup cruising the area the day before the murder. Those witnesses could not provide any definite descriptions, but they were able to recall that the three men in the pickup were dark-complexioned.

From the witnesses, investigators figured that the white truck was the same Toyota pickup seen fleeing the scene of the crime. They concluded that the men seen in the suspect vehicle were apparently casing the

Hanna residence. Those persons who had noticed the truck rushed into their houses and shut their doors. They didn't want to get involved—they knew that the area was full of troublemakers on the prowl.

The shocking slaying of the teenager in the sanctuary of his own bedroom sparked tensions and outright fear in the seashore community. From what was known so far, the slaying of Bylan Hanna, Mission Viejo High School's star athlete, was not a random shooting or the act of a deranged person running amuck, the police stressed in their public announcements.

"Citizens should not be concerned that there's some crazed lunatic running loose in Lake Forest, killing people at random," Lieutenant Olson said. "We believe the victim knew the killer. This certainly doesn't appear to be an outsider-on-outsider crime."

"We need help from the public," said a spokesman for the Mission Viejo substation. "If anyone has seen the Toyota or the red Camaro—or anything else that might help—we want them to come forward. Anonymity is assured."

The murder led to an all-points bulletin being issued for the bunch who'd slain Bylan Hanna. A description of the white pickup with the loud muffler, as well as the souped-up Chevy Camaro, went out over the police frequencies. Soon, every law enforcement officer in the vicinity was on the lookout for the white Toyota and the red Camaro.

On the Monday evening following the murder, a Mission Viejo patrol-car officer spotted a white Toyota with a loud muffler barreling down Interstate 15 toward San Diego—and the Mexican border. The Border Patrol was alerted and the highway was sealed off. An observation helicopter kept track of the suspect vehicle from the air.

Law enforcement teams from connected cities boxed the Toyota in, and the rest was easy. The two Hispanic occupants of the vehicle surrendered without resistance and were immediately transported to police headquarters in Lake Forest. After being advised of their constitutional rights through an interpreter, they were questioned at length.

Following several hours of what seemed like a verbal cat-and-mouse game, the police realized that the only thing the two men were guilty of was driving while inebriated—and without an updated registration. Their families paid their bail, and the two men were released—and ordered to appear in court to answer those charges at a later date.

In the meantime, pressure on the homicide sleuths to get Bylan Hanna's killers came from as high an authority as Mayor Helen Wilson. The mayor kept pressing the police chief for results, and the chief was passing orders down to Lieutenant Olson and the others in the homicide bureau to get cracking harder.

"We're just a week old as a city and already have our very first homicide," Councilwoman Marcia Rudolph told reporters. "All I know is that if there ever was any question that we need to secure our city, I think this proves it." Rudolph said she would bring up the issue of supplying more sheriff's deputies at the next meeting.

Meanwhile, one Laguna Beach detective was quoted in the newspapers as saying, "This is a typical gang-related instance. Everywhere, the officers believe, people are refusing information about the killer, protecting him and his companions with tips as to the officers' movements."

Nevertheless, detectives and officers fanned out and gathered a great deal of information from civic-minded people who were interested in making their neighborhood safe. This information was sorted out and filed into the memory bank of the police computers. It was no easy task. No one could properly identify any of the suspects because it had been too dark to get a look at them. No one had gotten the license number of either getaway vehicle because everything had happened so fast.

So the main tactic was to go after the killers on the theory that at least one of them would confide to a family member or a friend about the killing—a person who, in turn, would find the crime so cruel and senseless that he or she would be compelled to notify the police.

"All we need is one," said a detective working close to the case. "He'll eventually tell on the others. The more people involved in a crime, the better chance we have of catching the ambush team."

While the story of the murder was unfolding, 300 family members and friends of Bylan Hanna attended funeral services at Fairhaven Memorial Park in Santa Ana to say goodbye to the boy they affectionately called "Smiley."

After the graveside services, the family members filed past the robin's-egg-blue casket and each placed a red rose on the lid. The immediate family declined to be interviewed, but friends of the family spoke well of the victim.

"He was a good boy," one friend said. "We called him 'Smiley' because he was always smiling. I don't think I ever saw him without a smile on his face. He was happy-go-lucky. We'll miss him."

One relative who was visiting the family and had been present at the time of the shooting said, "It's like a nightmare. I'm angry. I'm damn angry at whoever killed Bylan. To come up to our yard and put three or four rounds in our house and shoot that boy—it's a violation of the highest order!"

"I was never for the death penalty," another relative put in, "but if anyone deserves it, it's Bylan's killer."

A teacher at Mission Viejo High School, where Hanna was a straight-A student, told reporters, "Bylan was looking forward to playing football next year at Saddleback College. He wanted his father to be proud of him."

Several other teachers recalled Bylan as the All-American optimist making his way, fulfilling everybody's dream of overcoming the odds and triumphing.

Asked if Bylan was involved in any of the gangs that plagued the city recently, one teacher said, "Bylan had friends that were gang members, sure—it's hard to avoid that around here. But was he a gang member himself? No!"

Even as the victim's body was being interred, the news media were asked to play down the reports of his death. Lieutenant Olson had no idea where the killer and his accomplices might be, and he didn't want to frighten them off with excessive publicity.

With the hunt for Hanna's killers going full tilt, probers were also looking for a motive. Combining old-time savvy with investigative techniques, they started by discreetly questioning everyone who was even remotely connected to the victim. The sleuths took more than 100 statements from relatives, neighbors, and friends. Meanwhile, the probers also had to attend to other cases that required their time and effort.

As the probe continued, the sleuths found reason to believe that Bylan Hanna might have been killed because he had danced with the "wrong" girl at a recent party. At first, the police had ignored the testimony of several witnesses who had expressed this belief, because Hanna's relatives completely opposed it. But the closer police looked at the explanation, the more it began to make sense.

"The shooting appears to have resulted from a Friday-night party," Lieutenant Olson told newshawks. "It stemmed from a fight over a young woman at a party where Hanna was dancing, and another partygoer, who probably had too much to drink, got mad at him. As Hanna and a relative were leaving, they were accosted and threatened by a group of boys."

When investigators questioned him about the incident, the relative who was with Bylan at the party said he did not know why the other teenagers got mad at Bylan.

"In this day and age, kids seem to settle things differently," Lieutenant Olson said. "Unfortunately, there are a lot of weapons out there, and kids choose to deal with their problems in a more violent manner. The prisons are full of them."

The police began backtracking, questioning everyone who was at the party. Several persons broke down and identified two of the boys who had threatened Bylan because he had danced with the girl.

One girl who had attended the party and had witnessed the fracas, told the detectives that the shooting was in retaliation because Bylan had danced with someone else's girlfriend. Unclear about the particulars of the altercation or its outcome, she would only say that it involved a "hassle" over dance partners.

The very patient sifting of clues and information by the Mission Viejo probers was a shining example of police work at its best. On Wednesday, January 1, 1992, they finally had some names and enough evidence to obtain arrest warrants. The first suspects they sought were 19-year-old Christopher Michael

Womack, of Mission Viejo, and Carl E. Stewart, also 19, of Laguna Niguel. The arrest warrants were for the investigation of capital murder. The warrants and a comprehensive description of the wanted men were circulated to all law enforcement agencies in the counties of Orange, Los Angeles, San Diego, Riverside, San Bernardino, and Kern.

The case detectives methodically worked their way through the known haunts of the suspects until one day they spotted the pair entering a house in Santa Ana. The youths were arrested there without incident.

"It is mostly legwork and alert patrol officers in cruiser cars who were responsible for the quick apprehension of the suspects," Lieutenant Olson announced to the press. "We spent a lot of time on the streets where these two were known to hang out. It paid off."

The interrogation of the two suspects finally told the investigators what they wanted to know. One of the youths broke down and told the interrogators where the murder weapon was hidden. Sleuths drove the informant to a remote section of Laguna Hills and started digging. Soon, a gun was unearthed from the dry wash. It was a .38-caliber, six-shot revolver. Engraved on the handle was the name "Christie Chrome."

The police also found the 1983 red Camaro used by the killers. It had been abandoned in the southern section of Orange County. The sleuths canvassed the vicinity, hoping to find witnesses who had seen someone abandoning the vehicle. They came up with no leads there, however.

Further investigation concerning the Camaro fell into an all-too-familiar pattern. The car did not belong to either of the suspects. Apparently, it was a stolen out-of-state vehicle.

On Thursday, January 2nd, the two suspects were arraigned in the South Orange County Municipal Courthouse. The defendants pleaded innocent. At that proceeding, Carl Stewart asked Judge Ronald P. Kreber to prohibit his photographs from being published in the newspapers. The judge denied his request. Turning to photographers, Kreber said, "Gentlemen, take your pictures."

The immediate clamor in court had no sooner died away when the two defendants vehemently denied having fired the shot that killed Bylan Hanna. They admitted to being at the scene at the time of the murder—but only as spectators. Judge Kreber ordered both defendants bound over for trial on charges of conspiring to shoot at an inhabited dwelling. Stewart, the owner of the murder weapon, was additionally charged with assault with a deadly weapon.

Meanwhile, the other three suspects remained at large. For a while, they seemed to be beyond the grasp of the police.

Then, following up a lead from a tipster who requested anonymity, detectives named 19-year-old Matthew Lloyd Conant, of Mission Viejo, as a member of the murder team. Sheriff's Lieutenant Richey said that Conant had surrendered to the authorities on Friday, January 3rd, at the urging of a family minister. After a comprehensive interrogation, he was booked into the Orange County Jail and held in lieu of $250,000 bond.

At his arraignment, charges of murder and conspiracy were filed against Conant. In the meantime, a search was under way for the remaining suspects.

Of the hundreds of criminals who flee the United States for Canada each year, one person emerged as Orange County's "Most Wanted" fugitive. A picture and description of 19-year-old Jason Paul Legare was published in Canadian tabloids and on television as being wanted for questioning for a murder in the United States. When he surrendered to Toronto police on Saturday, January 11, 1992, he said he was tired of living life on the lam.

Prosecutors immediately began extradition proceedings, and Orange County sheriff's deputies flew to Toronto. The suspect arrived the following week at John Wayne Airport, handcuffed and sandwiched between two detectives. Legare was promptly hustled into an unmarked police car and whisked away from a curious crowd of onlookers that had gathered.

Following a lengthy videotaped interrogation—in which Legare flatly denied that he was the actual shooter—he was booked on suspicion of murder. His bail was set at $250,000.

By morning, the police had learned who the fifth suspect was. He was 17 years old and would remain unidentified throughout the trials because of his age. He was regarded not as a killer, but just a young hood, and he was arrested the next day.

On Thursday, January 23rd, the Orange County grand jury handed down an indictment against the five prisoners on charges of murder and conspiracy to commit murder in connection with the December 29th slaying of Bylan Hanna.

The district attorney's office announced that four of the youths would be tried as adults. The fifth suspect, the 17-year-old, would be tried as a juvenile. Since the five were indicted, a prosecutor said, there would be no preliminary hearings in the case. Instead, the defendants would go directly to trial.

Caught up as he was in the web of the law, Christopher Womack's gamin-like demeanor quickly evaporated when the district attorney's office speedily tried and convicted him of an unrelated charge of defrauding an innkeeper and resisting a police officer who was called to quell a disturbance in Mission Viejo. Found guilty, Womack was facing another stretch in prison for this incident. Appearing before the bar of justice was nothing new to Womack. He had served prison time in 1991 for burglary.

The first of the five suspects went on trial on Thursday, July 2, 1992, in Santa Ana's Orange County Courthouse on Civic Center Drive. In her opening statement, Deputy District Attorney Carolyn Kirkwood said that Bylan Hanna was the "victim of a senseless slaying" and that Matthew Conant murdered him because of a dispute at a party near Trabuco High School. She said that the argument had escalated into a fistfight which broke up with the exchange of threats.

"We know where you live," co-defendant Carl Stewart had shouted as they left the altercation, according to the testimony of a witness.

Conant sat with his head bowed as the prosecutor asked the jury to convict him of first-degree murder, a conviction that could net him 25 years to life behind bars in a state penitentiary.

Defense Attorney Tom Wolfsen told the panel that the shooting was a "tragedy for the victim as well as Mr. Conant.

"What you have is all these kids down in South County who were partygoers," Wolfsen said. "They went to a party and an outsider group came to this party—and there had been bad blood with this outsider group—and there was an immediate reaction."

The jury returned with a verdict on Monday, July 13th. After one and a half days of deliberations, they apparently rejected D.A. Kirkwood's demand for a first-degree murder conviction. Instead, they found Matthew Conant guilty of second-degree murder.

The decision astounded the prosecutor. She told an interviewer that she was surprised and puzzled that the jury could agree that Conant shot at a specific target—the silhouette in the window—and yet they could find that he did not shoot to kill.

"The only one reasonable interpretation of the conduct of a person—that he pointed a gun at somebody and fired it three times—the only reasonable explanation for that is shooting with the intent to kill," the disappointed prosecutor told members of the news media.

"We tried to go with the allegation that Conant tried to kill someone at the window, and the argument for that broke down every time," said one of the jurors. "There were too many other possibilities as to what was in his mind, and we had doubts that he was trying to kill somebody."

In September, a judge sentenced Conant to 20 years to life. Then Carl Stewart's trial followed. He pleaded guilty and was sentenced to 15 years to life.

On Friday, November 6, 1992, Jason Paul Legare's attorney, Robert K. Weinberg, argued that his client should serve his term in his native Canada. If imprisoned in Canada, Legare would be eligible for parole in 7 years rather than the 8 years and 10 months as provided in California.

Prosecutor Carolyn Kirkwood asked the court to impose the maximum sentence on Legare, to send a message that anyone who assists in a murder of this sort will be held as equally responsible as the shooter.

"My client apologizes to the Hanna family for their grief and hopes that the bloodshed will stop," Defense Attorney Weinberg pleaded.

"I don't share any hope that the bloodshed will stop," Superior Court Judge Robert Fitzgerald remarked. "I believe it will just go the other way." He then sentenced the Canadian national to a term of 15 years to life.

The fourth defendant, a juvenile, pleaded guilty to firing a gun into an inhabited dwelling and was sentenced to seven years in the California Youth Authority.

Christopher Womack was convicted of second-degree murder, conspiracy to commit murder, and the use of a firearm. On Friday, December 11, 1992, he was sentenced to a 7-year prison term.

"SHAWN NOVAK: LURED TWO INNOCENTS TO THEIR GRISLY DEATH!"

by John Railey

Two small boys were still out as the sun began to set on Monday, March 4, 1991, and their parents were worried.

Daniel Geier, 9, and Christopher Scot Weaver, 7, lived across a courtyard from each other in Wadsworth Homes, a middle-class cluster of townhouses in Virginia Beach, Virginia. The beach city is part of a five-city sprawl that also includes Newport News and Hampton. Although the boys' neighborhood was relatively crime-free, that wasn't true of the surrounding beach areas.

Daniel had left home on his bike about 4:25 p.m., after arguing about his homework. Across the courtyard, Christopher, who had been grounded, had pleaded his way into being allowed to take a ride on his bike about the same time.

By 5:30 p.m., the families of both boys were beginning to get anxious. One of Daniel's family members hollered for him but to no avail. Uneasily, they sat down to dinner without him. Their worry only increased when they had finished eating 25 minutes later and Daniel still wasn't back.

Christopher's family was getting nervous as well. Members of both families joined forces outside calling for the boys. The two families compared notes and decided the boys must have sneaked off to a nearby lake.

One of Daniel's relatives walked down to the lake to investigate. A woman walking her dog there told the relative that she hadn't seen any sign of the two young missing boys.

Now panicking, the relative ran home. She and other family members walked up and down the streets of the townhouse complex and through some nearby woods, shouting the boys' names.

At 6:50 p.m., Daniel's relatives called 911.

The dispatcher routed the call to the Virginia Beach Police Department. An officer there took down the report of the two missing boys, and officers responded to the townhouse area within minutes.

Meanwhile, both families continued to hunt for Daniel and Christopher. They walked around three lakes at a nearby subdivision, vainly calling out the boys' names.

The boys' family members tried not to think about the countless bad scenarios every family conjures up when a child is missing. Maybe, they told themselves, the boys were just at somebody's house and didn't realize how late it was.

When Daniel's family returned home, they found a squad car parked in the townhouse courtyard. The police radio blared that investigators had found two bikes in the lake. The families, taken down to identify the bikes, now knew something was terribly wrong.

Virginia Beach police officers set up a command post. Divers went into the chilly lake where the bikes had been found. Daniel's family nervously hung out at the command post until 4:00 a.m., when an investigator persuaded them to go home and get some rest.

At 2:00 p.m. on Tuesday, the next day, detectives called the Geiers to tell them that divers had found nothing in the lake. The family then told officers that the boys liked to play in a dense patch of woods near their home.

Police launched a massive search, trying to cover every inch of the woods on foot. Sailors from the U.S. Navy stationed in the area joined the hunt along with civilian volunteers.

About 3:00 p.m. on Tuesday, two residents at the townhouse complex, a man and a woman, were trudging through the thick, muddy brush. The exhausted couple had been hunting the boys for three hours. Coming across a 30-foot-long log, the man started to climb over. As he stood on top of the log and looked down, he suddenly caught a glimpse of a patch of blue beneath three large cut pine branches. The man jumped down and peered into the branches, realizing that the patch of blue he saw was Christopher Weaver's blue sweatshirt and that it was still on the boy's apparently lifeless body.

The man yelled for the police. Thirty seconds later, two officers ran up. The officers found Daniel Geier's body lying beside his friend's underneath the branches. Both corpses bore apparent stab wounds.

Officers quickly cordoned off the crime scene, which was a half-mile from the nearest house. After videotaping and shooting still photos of the scene, they carefully removed the three large pine branches that had been covering the boys. The tearful families positively identified the bodies as those of their missing children. The remains were sent to an office of the state medical examiner in nearby Norfolk.

By now, supervisors had assigned Shawn W. Hoffman, a husky detective with longish brown hair, to be lead investigator on the case. Hoffman, young but streetwise, was already one of Virginia Beach Police Department's sharpest investigators.

Hoffman and other officers scoured the damp soil for the first clues as to how and why the boys had met their deaths. Rigor mortis had already set in on the bodies. They were relatively cool, indicating that the boys had probably been killed soon after they left their homes the day before.

So Detective Hoffman was left not only with a clueless crime scene but with a cold trail and a killer still walking the streets. To make matters worse, darkness was falling fast, making the inspection of the crime scene impossible. Officers guarded the scene overnight to prevent citizens from inadvertently contaminating it.

The next morning, Wednesday, pathologists called Detective Hoffman with the preliminary autopsy reports. The reports suggested that the boys were victims of a deliberate killing. The pathologists had found that the bodies' gaping wounds were made by repeated cutting and not by any single deep slash. The cuts had severed Daniel Geier's windpipe and had partially decapitated Christopher Weaver.

Fingertip bruises found along Daniel's jawline indicated that someone had held the boy's jaw, apparently to stretch his neck while it was being slashed.

The detectives had one sick killer, or killers, to find. And they knew they had to find him fast.

At the crime scene on Wednesday, Giselle Ruff, a veteran evidence technician with the Virginia Beach police, decided to try a revolutionary evidentiary technique she'd learned about. Ruff had heard that forensic scientists could match a cut in any medium, such as a tree branch, with the blade that had made them. Although the probers didn't yet have the knife used in the murders or any prospect of finding it, Ruff wanted to be ready when — or if — the weapon was found.

Forensic scientists at the state crime lab in Norfolk had the pine branches found covering the bodies. Now Ruff wanted to give the scientists more. From the crime scene, she worked her way out through the dense woods — 50 feet in one direction and 30 feet in another — painstakingly examining hundreds of trees until at last she found the ones from which the killer had apparently cut the branches used to cover the boys. She sawed off the branch stubs, placed them in plastic bags, and took them to the lab.

Meanwhile, Hoffman and his fellow detectives interviewed the boys' families, looking for pieces of the puzzle. Christopher friendly and outgoing, had been a star player in his soccer league. He had been chosen by classmates at his elementary school as emissary to show new students around.

Daniel, more boisterous, had loved to ride his bike on the dirt trails near his home. He was generous, helpful, always looking to meet new friends.

In short, the emerging profiles Detective Hoffman was sketching in revealed two All-American boys. Who, the sleuth wondered, would want them dead?

Hoffman and his fellow detectives set up a hotline, appealing through the media for people to call in with information on the case. The killings had sparked widespread community interest and outrage. Several investigators spent Thursday and Friday tracking down hundreds of frustrating dead-end leads that developed from the calls and other sources.

There was however, one lead that held promise. One 16-year-old neighborhood boy seemed obsessed with the killings, neighbors said. He was constantly talking about them. More to the point, what he was saying seemed to reveal knowledge only someone who had seen the bodies would know; and by all accounts, the boy hadn't been on the scene when the bodies were discovered.

Neighbors told sleuths the boy bragged that it was he who found the bodies, but that he left the scene after he called the rest of the searchers over.

Hoffman interviewed the youth three times, getting nowhere. The boy's record was clean; he had no priors of any kind, Nevertheless, the teen's behavior was suspicious, and he did know the boys and had once baby-sat Danny Geier.

Detective Hoffman persuaded the youth, Shawn Paul Novak, to come down to headquarters for one more chat on Saturday morning. Hoffman knew it would be a tough interview. He'd found out that Novak was an honors student with a high IQ.

Novak, a slender, dark-eyed boy with shaggy blond hair, was wearing blue jeans and a purple tank top when he walked into the small interview room. Speaking calmly and quietly, Detective Hoffman assured Novak that he wasn't a suspect. Hoffman warmed the boy up for about 40 minutes with idle chatter before starting a deadly serious game of wits.

The detective, knowing the boy smoked, offered him a cigarette. Novak lit it and puffed, blowing out the smoke without inhaling it. Hoffman asked the teenager about his role in the hunt for the boys. Novak said he was right behind the man and woman who had found the bodies.

Hoffman had already interviewed the man and woman. They'd told him that Novak was nowhere around when they found the bodies.

Hoffman suggested to Novak that they take a short break. When they filed back into the interview room a few minutes later, the detective sat down facing the boy, still speaking softly but moving closer. Novak instinctively edged his chair backward against a wall. He nervously rubbed an elbow, then a shoulder. The investigator said he just needed to clarify a few points in the stories of people he had interviewed.

"You're a smart guy," Detective Hoffman assured Novak. "Don't think I'm going to sit here and try to trick you or something like that."

But the sleuth did, in fact, have a number of tricks up his sleeve. Hoffman told the teen that a special "laser fingerprinting technique" had lifted Novak's prints from Danny Geier's leather jacket. It was a bluff. Novak looked puzzled.

The detective continued, poker-faced. If Novak had touched the bodies when he found them, Hoffman said, that would explain everything. But if Novak did not recall touching them, Hoffman said "I would have a problem."

Now that he thought of it, Novak said, he may have touched the bodies. "I probably definitely did," he said.

"O.K.," Hoffman said. "All right."

The youth seemed relieved.

Though he didn't show it, Hoffman was shocked by Novak's answer. He'd been expecting the teenager to deny being anywhere near the bodies. The sleuth continued, playing a second bluff.

There was another problem, Hoffman said: A witness had seen Novak walking with the boys by a lake near the woods on the afternoon of the slaying.

The youth, slumped motionless in his chair, said he didn't remember doing that. Hoffman held out his hands, palms up, a foot away from Novak.

"You've got to recall something, O.K.?" Detective Hoffman said beseechingly. "We've got a problem if you don't."

Hoffman emphasized that nobody had said Novak was in the woods, just at the lake near them.

406

"I'm not saying you're a suspect, O.K.?" Hoffman said. "Let's get that out of the way. . . . I'm not trying to trick you, son. You know I'm not."

Novak acknowledged that he probably was with the boys by the lake — but not with them in the woods. The youth didn't know it, but he was getting in deep. Hoffman got up, saying he had to catch a phone call.

"Are you O.K.?" the sleuth asked Novak as he walked toward the door.

"Yeah, man," the boy replied.

A few minutes later, Hoffman walked back in. He decided to question the teenager about some curious statements searchers had quoted him as saying, such as his prediction that the bodies would be found near a hole covered with branches.

"Did you know those guys were dead?" the detective asked.

Novak said there was no way he could have known.

The detective suggested that Novak had found the bodies before anyone else and hidden them to avoid being wrongly blamed for the killings.

The youth leaned his head back, apparently pondering that idea.

Hoffman said softly, "I'm here for you, Shawn, I'm here to help you."

Neither said a word for an agonizingly long five minutes. Finally, Novak fished a smoke from the pack Hoffman had left on the table between them. He lit the cigarette and began to speak in a slow, dull voice. Things happened just as the sleuth suggested, Novak said.

Hoffman, thinking about the samples Ruff had taken, asked if Novak had cut the branches he used to cover the boys. Novak said, no, he had just found the branches on the ground.

"Shawn," the detective said softly, "you can talk to

me. Don't be afraid. Get it out. Don't be afraid. Something happened and you just went too far. Is this something that just happened?"

Novak answered, "Yeah."

"You killed them, didn't you?" the sleuth asked.

The youth hesitated, obviously deliberating. Then he slowly nodded his head.

Novak closed his eyes, and his features contorted into an expression of pain. He buried his head in his skinny hands and began to weep. He cried for several minutes, his elbows on his knees, his slender body quivering, his fingers snarled in his shaggy hair.

Another detective who now joined Hoffman in the interview room read Shawn Novak his Miranda rights. The suspect signed a paper waiving them. Still crying, he gave Detective Hoffman a full statement.

The day of the killing had been just another boring Monday at First Colonial High School, Novak said. When classes let out, Novak did what he often did on warm, sunny afternoons. He hurried home, picked up his bone-handled buck knife, stopped at the 7-Eleven for a pack of cigarettes, and headed for the nearby woods. He liked to spend hours alone in those woods near his home, target-practicing on trees with his knife. On his way to the woods, he ran into the two boys. He knew and liked Daniel Geier, who was good friends with his little brother. He'd never met Christopher Weaver.

The boys asked Novak to show them the way to a makeshift fort that some other boys had built in the woods, and Novak agreed to lead them. As they walked, Danny kept pestering Novak, saying he wanted to see the older boy's knife.

Near the fort, Novak and his young companions began wrestling playfully on the ground. Novak removed the knife from its sheath on his belt and set it against a tree so that no one would get accidentally stuck, he said. The next thing he knew, Danny was examining the knife.

"I looked up and Daniel had the knife and I freaked out," Novak said. He admitted to stabbing both boys to death and then covering their bodies with the branches he cut. He never said why he killed them.

Detective Hoffman ended the two-and-a-half-hour interview, which had been videotaped. He charged Shawn Novak with two counts of first-degree murder. The teen was placed in the Virginia Beach Jail without bond.

Moment after Hoffman completed the interview, Detective Jimmy Price, working with Hoffman, secured a warrant to search Novak's bedroom for the murder weapon. Novak's room was on the top floor of his parents' townhouse. In the room, Detective Price found a large poster of a Ninja warrior hanging above a wooden dresser. Jigsaw puzzle boxes were stacked on one side of the top of the dresser. On the other side was a bone-handled hunting knife with a six-inch blade.

There was no blood on the knife. Price had the weapon bagged and tagged and sent off for analysis, hoping Ruff's revolutionary test would pay off. Novak might try to deny his confession come trial time, and the knife was the only physical evidence linking the youth to the crime scene.

Fortunately, the forensic scientists at the state lab in Norfolk would find that the knife was the one that had cut the three pine tree branches found covering the bodies. The lab technicians studied the unique contours and indentations left by the knife blade on the stub and the branches. Their work marked the first time the test had been used in a local murder case. The forensic scientists also found that a bloodstain on Christopher Weaver's jeans matched the shape of the knife.

Detective Price had found other intriguing items in Shawn Novak's room as well: newspaper clippings headlined, "Texas killer's final plea" and "Police say man's death suspicious" and a book titled *Serial Killers*.

A neighbor of Novak's told police that the defendant had told her a few months before that he idolized Charles Manson. Apparently, the youth was a cold-blooded killer obsessed with violent criminals and their grisly crimes. The slain boys had just been in the wrong place at the wrong time.

Hoffman's work wasn't over after he charged Novak. While he'd been bluffing when he told the suspect that he had a witness who could place him with the boys shortly before their deaths, he later did find such a witness.

Shawn Novak's trial began in Virginia Beach Circuit Court on March 4, 1992 — one year to the day after the victims had disappeared. Robert J. "Bob" Humphreys, Virginia Beach commonwealth's attorney, would be leading the prosecution.

Humphreys, 41, has been a prosecutor for 18 years and won election to the top job in 1989. He was going for the death penalty against Novak, who had remained in jail pending trial. It would be one of the most challenging cases of Humphreys' career.

Judge John K. Moore had ruled that, given the defendant's age, the sentence would be handed down by him — not the jury — if a guilty verdict was returned.

Richard Brydges, one of Hampton Roads' top defense attorneys, was representing Novak. Humphreys and Brydges had battled it out in murder cases numerous times. Up to now, the defense attorney hadn't beaten the prosecutor. The pressure would be heavy in the Novak case as Humphreys fought to ensure that

Brydges didn't score one on him. The defense attorney was seeking a verdict of not guilty by reason of insanity.

Brydges admitted in his opening statement that Novak killed the boys. But his client lived in a fantasy world, the lawyer argued, and demons made him do it.

"The person or thing in the body of Shawn Novak was not Shawn Novak at the time of the horrible deaths of these children," Brydges told the eight women and four men on the jury. "He envisioned those killings from above, looking down upon these murders as they were being committed, disassociated, if you will, from what was going on."

After opening statements, the prosecution began its case with testimony about the discovery of the bodies and about techniques matching Novak's knife to branches at the murder scene.

On Thursday, the second day of the trial, Detective Hoffman told the jury about Novak's confession. Brydges battered away at Hoffman on cross-examination, but the detective kept his cool.

Prosecutor Humphreys then played the videotape of Novak's confession for the jury. By the end of the tape, the jurors were staring, transfixed, at the real-life drama on the TV screen.

Typed transcripts of the interview lay unnoticed in the jurors' laps. Novak, who couldn't see the tape from his seat at the defense table, looked straight ahead and twirled an ink pen. As he would throughout the trial, he showed no emotion.

Defense Attorney Brydges had fought in vain to keep the confession from being entered as evidence, arguing that Hoffman had bluffed Novak to get the admission. But the trial judge, John K. Moore, concluded after watching the tape that Hoffman had done nothing wrong. The U.S. Supreme Court has upheld the use of ruses and bluffs in interrogations, the judge noted.

Prosecutor Humphreys presented the testimony of a psychiatrist who had examined Novak a month after the slayings. The doctor said he had seen no mental disorders in the boy.

"He [Novak] was out of touch with his feelings, but aware of what was taking place," the psychiatrist testified.

But on cross-examination by Brydges, the doctor acknowledged that Novak was in an "altered state at the time of the murders and that limits existed on how well he could have restrained his behavior."

Brydges began his case on Friday. He presented the testimony of another psychiatrist who had also examined Novak since his arrest. The doctor read into evidence a statement Novak had given him describing how he felt as he committed the murders.

"It was like a TV with the sound turned off, no birds, no wind in the trees," Novak said in the statement. "I first heard wind when I stood up."

The psychiatrist told the jury that Novak suffered from a schizo-typal personality disorder. He was unable to handle interpersonal relationships, was paranoid, and often withdrew into dark depression, the doctor said. He testified that Novak lived in a world where the role-playing game "Dungeons & Dragons" ruled. In that game, participants pretend they are strange creatures in constant, violent struggle with other creatures.

A person called "Kender," a pony-tailed, Hobbit-like creature pictured in a drawing police found in Novak's room, was Novak's imaginary friend and became his alter ego, the doctor testified.

The day of the killing, "Kender" and Novak fused, the psychiatrist said.

"He did not, as Shawn Novak, understand what he was doing or understand at that moment the nature and consequences of his act," the doctor testified. "He was controlled, literally, by an alternate force. The person of Shawn held the blade. The driving force was Kender."

Humphreys attacked the psychiatrist on cross-examination.

"If Kender was the character who killed the two boys, who covered the bodies?" the prosecutor wanted to know. "At no point did Mister Novak excuse his behavior by saying Kender did it, did he?"

The doctor replied, "No, that is correct."

Brydges put Novak's high school art teacher on the stand. She told the jury that the teen, a happy-go-lucky type who often told his classmates stories to satisfy a chronic need for attention, had been acting strangely in the months before the killings.

Once, she said, she'd found him standing in the trash can in a dark corner of the art room. Another day, he sat on the floor in front of the classroom door.

The month before the murders, she said, he'd withdrawn from his classmates. His eyes danced, she testified, and he seemed "not to be there."

Through the doctor and the art teacher, Defense Attorney Brydges was trying to convince jurors that Novak had entered his own fantasy world. He presented as further evidence a file of newspaper clippings Novak kept beside his bed. Included was a headline that said, "Strange but true: Psychic animals that save human lives," and a photograph of a tarantula inside a man's mouth.

The following Monday, attorneys made their closing arguments. Humphreys maintained that Novak, fascinated by homicide and desperate for attention, lured the boys into the woods to murder them.

Brydges argued that his client had been insane at the time of the killings.

The jury got the case that afternoon. After 90 minutes, they returned with their verdict. Humphreys' string of wins against Brydges was secure. Novak was found guilty of two counts of first-degree murder.

Judge Moore set sentencing for May 4, 1992. On that day Novak sat silent and wooden, still showing no emotion, as he waited to hear whether he would die or receive a long prison term.

Novak's family testified that Shawn had never admitted to them that he killed the boys, and they still didn't think he had done it.

Humphreys asked the judge to sentence the defendant to death. Virginia law allows the death penalty if the killing is brutal and the killer seems likely to strike again.

Judge Moore agreed that the defendant qualified on both counts. Without knowing why Novak killed, Judge Moore said it was impossible to rule out future murders. Nevertheless, the judge gave the defendant life in prison instead of a death sentence.

"The case is primarily the product of a very young, very immature, and very disturbed young man," Judge Moore said.

Shawn Novak will be eligible for parole in 20 to 25 years.

Even though the case was over, a troubling question remained. Why did Novak kill the boys? He never told Detective Hoffman or the psychiatrists.

Defense Attorney Brydges told a reporter that Novak was an enigma to him as well.

"Shawn never fully communicated with us," the lawyer said. "He'd talk about TV, juggling, and what books he was reading in jail. But when we changed the subject to the case, he would just stop talking and shrug."

When his client did address the case, the lawyer said, he sometimes confused things further.

"He'd say, 'Some days I think I did it, some days I think I didn't,' " Brydges said.

In one statement to doctors, Novak had said he felt sorry for the victims and the families because "they will not be able to do things now." He told psychiatrists that he often cried himself to sleep in his jail cell at night. Whether or not he feels remorse for taking two young lives is anybody's guess.

wwwwww. condominiums replaced most of the farm
iiiiii. discrimi. did muntu. the range, shother
wwwww. sowldhns conduct nung. forther
ner base. Bone diys t mink t ight it some esys i

"HE STABBED KIM 95 TIMES . . .
THEN HE LEFT THE BLADE
IN HER SKULL!"
by Barry Bowe

Like most school kids, Kim Marie Anderson followed a daily routine to prepare for school. Since her classes at Lake Tract School in Deptford Township, New Jersey, didn't begin until nine o'clock, 12-year-old Kim was the last family member out of bed, shortly after seven o'clock. By then, everyone else was gone and Kim enjoyed having the house to herself. She would shower in solitude, dress at her leisure, then grab her books and scoot across the street to classmate Ruthie Spano's house for breakfast. But a sadistic intruder interrupted the blonde seventh-grader's routine one April morning in 1988 when Kim experienced a "close encounter of the very worst kind."

Around eight o'clock on Tuesday morning, April 19th, Sarah Riley, another classmate of Kim's knocked on the door of the Andersons' ranch-style home on Arline Avenue in the spread-out South Jersey community that lay within the shadow of the Walt Whitman Bridge on the other side of the Delaware River from Philadelphia.

Deptford Township used to be farmland, its residents raised tomatoes, lettuce, corn, beans, and — your nose told you when the wind blew the wrong way — hogs. In later years, housing subdivisions and yuppie condominiums replaced most of the farms, but the community retained a rural feel, safe if you forgot to lock the door one night. Crime — at least violent crime — was a problem in Philadelphia and Camden, not in Deptford.

When Kim failed to answer the knock at the door, Sarah figured her pal was already across the street at the Spanos'. But when Sarah checked there, Kim had not arrived.

Sarah and Ruthie phoned across the street. They got no answer. Maybe Kim was still sleeping, the girls speculated, or maybe she fell in the shower and hit her head on something. Ruthie grabbed the key her parents held for the Anderson house, and the two girls crossed the street.

Ruthie unlocked the door and shouted, "Kim!"

She got no answer.

"The sink was overflowing," Sarah would later recall. "We went over to turn it off, and Ruthie started to clean it up." Then 12-year-old Sarah walked down the hallway toward Kim's bedroom.

"I looked in and saw her," Sarah would recall. "I said, 'Kim's hurt.' I didn't go in. I just stood there in the doorway. I saw her lying on the floor. I saw the blood and just turned away."

In the kitchen, dishes were floating in the flooded sink. Water puddled on the floor. And 16-year-old Ruthie Spano turned off the water and looked in the utility room for clean-up gear. When Sarah Riley screamed, Ruthie raced down the hallway.

"Kimmy — hurt — bleeding — somebody — " Sarah stammered.

"She was really upset," Ruthie later said about Sarah. "She was using choppy words and I couldn't understand her. I tried to get to Kim's room, but Sarah was screaming. I saw Kim and immediately turned around." Ruthie ran back to the kitchen and phoned 911.

But the police dispatcher couldn't understand the hysterical girl. Frustrated, Ruthie hung up and the two girls ran screaming to the Spano house for help. Ruthie's father, Arthur, and her 25-year-old sister Lisa got the message at once. They sped to the Anderson house and into Kim's bedroom.

"I felt like my head exploded," Arthur Spano would recall. "I saw blood all over the floor. On [Kim] and on the bedspread. I started screaming her name and screaming to God."

"Kim! Kim!" shouted Lisa. But Kim didn't answer. Kim was lying on the floor, next to her bed, on her right side, a towel wrapped around her upper body, nude from the waist down. Her French-style telephone and a television lay in disarray next to her.

While her father ran through the house looking for an intruder, Lisa tried to help Kim.

"There was a lot of blood," Lisa would recall. "I started to panic. I had socks on, and I could feel the puddles of blood. It just started to soak in. The floor was saturated." Lisa grabbed Kim's wrist and felt for a pulse.

"I didn't feel anything," Lisa would later tell police. "I turned her over by her arm and felt her neck. I didn't feel anything. I called her name and she just laid there."

Lisa ran into the bathroom and returned with a towel.

"There was blood caked around her nose and nostrils," Lisa said. "I wiped her head off a little bit and tried to clean up her face." Then Lisa rolled Kim onto her back and tried CPR until the paramedics arrived. But they were too late. Kim Marie Anderson was dead, the apparent victim of a savage, overkill stabbing attack. None of the paramedics or Gloucester County detectives, who soon started arriving, had ever seen a homicide like this one—no one had.

Quickly, Investigator Angelo Alvardo photographed the brutalized body lying in the pool of blood on the bedroom floor, while other detectives dusted for fingerprints, testing the door, a motorcycle helmet, the bed, the telephone, the television, and anything in the room that might hold a latent print. Other than the home's entry doors, Investigator John Robinson said, the identification unit concentrated on "Kim's bedroom because that's apparently where the struggle took place."

In Woodbury, Dr. Claus Speth, the county medical examiner, began an 11-hour autopsy, finding an incredible 95 stab wounds. He determined that the first 76 wounds had entered the victim's hands, head, chest, and back, three of those wounds puncturing her lungs. At that point, the M.E. concluded the victim "was unable to move or respond" because her lungs had collapsed. But she was still alive. So her attacker flipped her body over, at least once, and continued stabbing her.

During the autopsy, Dr. Speth pulled back the victim's skin to check for facial bruises, then opened her skull, looking for stab wounds. In one wound, embedded near the back of the victim's skull, Dr. Speth found the tip of a serrated knife. Further examination revealed a series of wounds only three-eighths of an inch deep, which led Speth to believe that the attacker broke his or her knife a second time.

To Dr. Speth, the 19 wounds on the victim's hands were "consistent with defensive-type wounds, as if she were trying to defend herself or block [the attacker]." Speth also matched blood and hair from the French-style telephone at the murder scene with the victim's hair and blood type and determined that the bruises on her head were consistent with blows from the phone's heavy receiver. Speth said Kim Anderson "was conscious throughout the time the blunt injuries were inflicted."

Despite finding the victim nude from the waist down, the M.E. found no signs of sexual activity or abuse. That bit of information caused head-scratching among the detectives when they found a pair of woman's panties on the lawn outside the Anderson home — containing traces of body fluids, feces, and sperm. The detectives speculated that the attacker might have ejaculated from excitement while he was stabbing his victim. Or, he may have masturbated over her dead body after the attack.

With Sergeant Nadine Reese heading the investigation for the Gloucester County Prosecutor's Office, detectives swarmed the neighborhood, looking for additional clues. They fanned away from the home on Arline Avenue, questioning neighbors, looking for strangers, and contacting the victim's family members, trying to determine the last person to have seen Kim alive.

At Monongahela Junior High, sleuths tracked down an older relative who woke Kim around seven o'clock, adding that Kim was alone in the house, and alive, when he walked out the door.

Shortly after noon in the same school, Detective Jeffrey Wright interviewed a 14-year-old student who had arrived two hours late for school that morning. This teenager lived three blocks from the Andersons, around the corner on Kohler Avenue. He had played video games at Kim's house just five days before her brutal murder.

"He seemed extremely nervous," the detective said, describing the 6-foot-tall, 200-pound youth. "He rolled a white piece of paper in his hands, and his voice seemed to have little continuity." When Detective Wright noticed cuts on the teenager's hands, he questioned the school nurse, who remembered treating the wounds earlier that morning.

Surprisingly, the next day, Detective Wright was standing in the parking lot of a local fast-food restaurant with Detective-Sergeant David Wentz when the teenager with the sliced hands approached him.

"He apparently recognized me," Wright recalled, "and said, 'So you're watching me.' " The youngster asked Wright why the cops were putting pressure on Mario Pinto, a 20-year-old friend to whom he owed $50. Then he turned to Sergeant Wentz and said the kids at school were giving him heat because he'd arrived late at school on the morning of the murder.

"You're going to find my fingerprints all over that house," the teenager told Wentz, "even in Kimmy's room. I liked to listen to music in her room and stand in front of her mirror. And you'll find my fingerprints on Kimmy's bed because I liked to look out her window."

If 14-year-old Kenny Houseknecht's name wasn't on the list of suspects the day before, it was from that moment on. The detectives returned to their headquarters in the one-story, red-brick building on Glover Street in Woodbury and passed along the information. They decided to obtain a search warrant for the Houseknecht home on Kohler Avenue.

Earlier that day, Mario Pinto had walked into the detective bureau, saying, "I'm scared things will happen to me. Neighbors are stabbing me in the back by making it look like I had something to do with it."

When the detectives asked him what "it" was, Pinto explained that a story was going around the neighborhood that maybe Kenny Houseknecht was involved in

Kim Anderson's death. And since he was House-knecht's close friend, he, too, might be implicated.

"I want to tell you guys the truth," Pinto said, "so I don't have to worry about it being on my back all the time."

In his first statement, Pinto said Houseknecht owed him $20 for a gambling debt. Later, in his second statement, Pinto upped the ante to $50, claiming the teenager owed the debt to cover hard-core pornography magazines that Pinto had consigned to Houseknecht to sell at school.

On the day before the murder, Pinto said he had asked the suspect when he could expect the $50. Houseknecht told him he would have the money Tuesday morning and told him to meet him at the creek behind the Anderson house at 7:20. Pinto said he waited, but Houseknecht never showed. He figured Kenny took the bus or caught a ride to school, so he left. Later that afternoon, Pinto talked to the suspect after school. He remembered seeing a large cut on Houseknecht's hand and said "he was acting a little bit strange."

"[Kenny] said, 'Did you know [Kim Anderson] was killed today?' " Pinto told the sleuths. But Pinto thought his friend was trying to change the subject, so he pressed him for the money. "I just wanted him to tell me a day when he'd give me the money." The detectives asked Pinto why he thought Houseknecht was involved in Kim Anderson's murder. "I just know that a simple burglary to pay off a debt ended up in chaos," Pinto responded.

The detectives taped Pinto's third statement, in which Pinto said, "He owed me money. He knew I was growing upset about it, and he picked a way to do it. I don't know why he would do it that way. But it's obvious he clicked. Kenny was going to one of the neighbors' houses to rob it." Pinto surmised that his friend meant the Andersons' house because Kenny mentioned "there was always a lot of money around" their house. "He said they would never miss fifty bucks."

Around 4:00 p.m., Detective Alex Illas drove to Kohler Avenue. After advising Kenny Houseknecht to keep silent until he talked to an attorney, Illas transported him to the county M.E. to extract hair, blood, and saliva samples and to take his fingerprints.

During the exam, Dr. Speth also found five cuts on the suspect's right hand and several more on his left — all produced by a knife with a serrated edge. In the M.E.'s opinion, it looked as if the suspect was swinging the knife downward when he hit something hard — like bone — and his hand slipped off the handle onto the blade.

While Dr. Speth was testing the suspect, Sergeant Nadine Reese walked into the Houseknecht home on Kohler Avenue to executive a search warrant. When she entered the suspect's bedroom, a note sitting on the unmade bed caught her eyes.

"I walked over the bed area," the detective would later recall, "and the language immediately jumped out at me." Three "fairly large drawings" highlighted the notebook paper facing her. One drawing looked like a frontal female nude, the second was an enlarged vagina, and the third depicted a man and woman having anal intercourse.

"I immediately picked the letter up to turn it over," Detective Reese said. "It appeared [that] the letter was addressed to the Andersons." The note, handwritten in blue ink, read:

"Andersems [sic]: This is [Kim's] killer. I hope you know I used gloves. I found other fingerprints and put them on tape and put fingerprints all over. It can be your friend, 'the [expletive],' the one that's big and always wearing blue sweatpants. The one who lives across the street. I've been walking by your house all the time. I've been observing. Don't even think about looking for fingerprints on this."

While Detective Reese phoned headquarters requesting a photographer to shoot her find, the detectives scoured the bedroom and the rest of the house, looking for pornographic magazines, the clothing the suspect had worn on the day of the murder, and a piggy bank reported missing from the Anderson home. Their hunt for the magazines was fruitless, but in the closet, they found a jacket with a small bloodstain and, in a corner of the basement, they uncovered the rest of the clothes Kenny Houseknecht had worn the previous day. The clothing had been soaked with bleach.

Meanwhile, Detective Illas was driving the suspect back to the Glover Street headquarters, where the suspect's family members were waiting for him. Inside, a family member walked up to the teenager and slapped his face.

"Why did you murder that young girl?" the angry relative yelled.

"See there," the suspect replied, "you always blame me for everything."

Detective Illas, fearing trouble, stepped between the two family members. Seeing the suspect's hateful eyes and his clenched fists, Illas separated the pair, fearing the enraged boy was ready to hit his relative. Later, when things calmed down, Illas was prepared to release the suspect when he got the word that charges were going to be filed against him. Detective Illas then showed the suspect a copy of the statement Mario Pinto had made earlier in the day, incriminating Houseknecht in Kim Anderson's murder. The lumbering teenager jumped to his feet, clenched his fists, and pointed a finger at Detective Illas.

"I hate you!" he shouted. "I don't care if you're a cop, I'm going to kill you!" But the rage passed quickly. Once again, calm returned and the detective drove the suspect to the juvenile detention center in Clarksboro, a few miles way.

During the ride, Kenny Houseknecht started talking.

"Until I'm eighteen, do I get the chair?" Houseknecht asked, but Detective Illas told him he had a lawyer and he didn't have to say anything. "That's what scares me," Houseknecht continued. "Even if I told you I killed her and was sorry, I'd still get twenty years," he said, and he snapped his fingers, "like that."

Again, Illas reminded Houseknecht that he didn't have to talk. Instead, he advised, he should speak to his lawyer.

"I'm going to fight this all the way," Houseknecht said, this time his voice calm and confident. "And I'm going to win."

But Kenny Houseknecht lost the first round in a three-year fight to determine his fate.

After listening to more than 60 hours of testimony from law enforcement officials, the boy's family, and psychologists, Superior Court Judge John J. Lindsay ruled that Kenny Houseknecht would be tried as an adult, basing his decision on the fact that the accused showed no remorse for his act.

"For whatever psychological reasons he did it," Judge Lindsay said, "it was a deliberate, sadistic, depraved, and heinous attack." And Houseknecht lost the second round.

Superior Court Judge John E. Wallace ruled that probable cause existed when detectives searched the Houseknecht home the day after the crime and found a note on the suspect's bed. The defense called the note "the most damaging piece of evidence" against House-knecht and tried to squash it.

In November 1990, Public Defender Wayne Natale won a change of venue for the murder trial, saying, "I don't believe the boy can possibly get a fair trial in this county" and calling the affair "the most publicized case in the eighteen years I have been in this county."

The trial moved to Salem County Courthouse in Salem, a tiny town on the southern tip of New Jersey. It began on June 3, 1991. In that arena, Natale, assisted by Cesar Alvarez-Moreno, verbally wrestled with Assistant County Prosecutor Keith Johnson for the better part of two months in an emotion-ridden battle as heated as the 90-plus weather outside.

With the jury out of the courtroom, both sides argued to Judge Norman Telsey about the admissibility of enlarged photographs of Kim Anderson in a ballet costume in front of a Christmas tree with a group of friends.

"The jury will be continually confronted with the horrors of the attack," Defense Attorney Natale suggested, "and these pictures will only serve to intensify the emotional impact on the jury."

The prosecutor claimed the pictures provided the jury with a look at the victim. Since the defendant swore the 12-year-old attacked him twice during the altercation, the prosecution needed the pictures to paint a different story.

"Was she an Amazon?" Prosecutor Johnson asked. "A professional football player? No, she was a twelve-year-old girl."

Defense Attorney Natale objected, saying the pictures were too old.

"If I knew Kim Marie Anderson was going to be murdered on the nineteenth," Johnson retorted, "I would have done my best to get a picture of her on the eighteenth."

After Judge Telsey reserved his decision on the matter, the jury entered the courtroom and the opening remarks began. Prosecutor Johnson told the jury of 13 men and three women, including four alternates, that the defendant entered the Anderson home to commit a robbery. But, when young Kim stepped out of the bathroom and found the defendant in the hall, "a scene straight out of hell" transpired.

"He attacked her with such ferociousness that the tip of the blade broke off in her skull," the prosecutor said. Even after she was dead, Johnson said, Houseknecht continued to attack her. If that wasn't enough, he beat her with a blunt object.

"Sometime during the attack, Kim mercifully died. But for the majority of the attack, she was alive and suffering," Johnson said.

While the victim's family members sobbed in the crowded courtroom, Prosecutor Johnson told the court that the defendant stole a piggy bank, attempted to clean up, then sanitized the crime scene.

"No fingerprints of Kenny Houseknecht were found in Kimmy's bedroom," Johnson said, "because he took a can of Right Guard and sprayed the room to cover his scent."

"You're not here to cure the ills of the world," Defense Attorney Natale began his one-hour opening statement, "and you certainly can't bring Kim Anderson back to life." Then he outlined his case, based on three overlapping defenses of insanity, mental illness, and duress.

Natale pointed to the defendant's "inability to cope" in certain situations. His "mind just shut down." Natale claimed that the defendant's problems began in childhood, as a toddler who wasn't hugged enough, a youngster who was ashamed of his half-Asian heritage, and a teenager who was teased about being over-weight. Adding to those pressures was a 20-year-old neighbor who became a surrogate parental figure, someone who was able to "make him feel like a human being" while he introduced the defendant to mari-juana, pornography, and crime.

"Mario Pinto had developed a type of control over Ken," Natale said, pressuring the troubled teenager into burglarizing the Anderson home "to pay Mr. Pinto for the debt he owed."

After the opening statements, the attorneys locked horns again. After excusing the jury, Judge Telsey listened to the two men bicker. The prosecution wanted to introduce the underwear found on the lawn outside the Anderson home shortly after the murder. The defense objected. Prosecutor Johnson wanted the under-wear as evidence because it contained traces of body fluids, sperm, and fecal matter.

"I had no reason to believe these pants were damag-ing," Natale said, explaining that he was never in-formed they contained fecal matter. "This is a major trial. Mr. Johnson's case is not going to fall apart if the panties don't get in."

But Johnson countered, arguing that the sperm could show that the defendant had either ejaculated during the stabbing or masturbated afterward, which made the defendant, who kept cradling his head in his hands and chewing his fingernails for most of the seven weeks, shake his head violently. In any case, Judge Telsey allowed the panties to be introduced as evidence.

The prosecution then paraded the witnesses across the stand: Kim's neighbors who had discovered the body, the investigators, the medical examiner, and sev-eral psychiatrists.

On the trial's fifth day, Prosecutor Johnson called a

forensic scientist to the stand to discuss the blood found on the defendant's jacket. The expert witness said the blood on the jacket was consistent with a sample taken from the victim's body after her slaying. Defense Attorney Natale, interjecting an objection, asked if it was possible that the blood found on the jacket could have come from anyone else. The forensic scientist replied, "Yes, it was possible."

"And it's also possible it could be, let's say, some other innocent victim's blood?" Prosecutor Johnson countered. "Isn't that correct?"

"I can't imagine a more insidious comment coming from a senior trial attorney," Defense Attorney Natale yelled, on his feet, approaching the bench and demanding that the remark be stricken from the record. "That's an outrageous comment, and there's no excuse for it. He knew what he was doing, and it's outrageous. We spent weeks trying to find a jury that would be unaffected, and he was smirking before the jury and waving his arms."

"Let's not get to be silly about this," Prosecutor Johnson said.

"This was a planned and calculated statement to inflame the jury," Natale charged. "To really ensure a fair trial for Ken Houseknecht, a mistrial should be granted."

"I'm not here to do Ken Houseknecht any favors," Prosecutor Johnson shot back at his adversary.

"I don't feel a mistrial is necessary," Judge Telsey said the following day, giving the jury special instructions to "allay any improper inferences the jury may have gotten from the prosecutor's remarks."

When the trial resumed, Detective Illas related the self-incriminating comments the defendant had made to him on the day after the murder. Sergeant Reese read the letter she had found on the defendant's bed to the court. And Dr. Speth described the wounds the victim had sustained.

With no film to show the extent of the victim's injuries to the jury, the medical examiner produced a plastic mannequin to graphically locate, number, and describe the motion that produced each wound, detailing the exact depth and width of each thrust. The M.E. said the attacker broke his knife twice and beat the victim with a telephone.

On Tuesday, July 2nd, all hell broke loose in the courtroom. As one of the defendant's relatives was leaving the witness stand, one of the victim's relatives stood up in the second row.

"You're a liar!" he yelled.

Another relative of the victim joined the first, and they rushed forward. With the defense attorney yelling for order, sheriff's deputies surrounded the two men.

"It's the first time I've ever seen anything like this," said Deputy John McKibbin. Three deputies sustained injuries. To no one's surprise, Defense Attorney Natale once again moved for a mistrial.

"There was incredible anger and pain expressed by the Anderson family and friends that can't be set aside fairly," Natale said. "The sympathy will affect the jury's decision." But the prosecutor disagreed.

"Ken Houseknecht is on trial for murdering [Kim Anderson] and now his [relative] is hinting and accusing their [relative] of drug use and involvement," Prosecutor Johnson countered. "I don't know how anyone is supposed to act calmly and not react."

Judge Telsey sent the jury home to "pull themselves together and give their dispassionate attention" a chance to recover. But he denied Natale's motion for a mistrial, saying this was "not an ordinary jury." These 16 people were selected because they could decide the case fairly, based "entirely on the evidence." They were warned from the beginning that the trial would be "fraught with emotion."

"Kenny was very reactive," said a social worker who was called to testify by the defense when the trial resumed the next day. "In the incident, he unleashed a lot of anger . . . because he had no other way of displaying that anger," she said. "He didn't know how to express his anger, and he just flipped out, which he does about every two years."

On cross-examination, Johnson asked the social worker why her report concentrated on the defendant's inability to be breastfed, on his potty training and on his bed-wetting, yet had "nothing to do with the homicide."

"On a scale of one to ten," Prosecutor Johnson said, "bed-wetting is a one and the homicide is a ten."

"You just don't understand the purpose of my report," the social worker responded. "It's to identify problems in the boy's development."

"I just don't understand the purpose of your testimony," Johnson said.

On that note, the trial broke for a Fourth of July recess.

"We tried Maryland, New Jersey, and Pennsylvania," said Defense Attorney Alvarez-Moreno when the trial resumed on July 6th, but Mario Pinto had disappeared. Now the defense strategy to plead insanity, duress, and mental disorder had to fly on medical testimony alone.

"He turned to a person who taught him to use drugs, use and distribute pornography, and commit burglary," said a New Jersey psychologist, describing the defendant's attraction for Mario Pinto. "Houseknecht knew he was entering a danger zone when he broke into the Anderson home," the psychologist said, "but he was under duress."

Next, Defense Attorney Natale called a psychiatrist who said Mario Pinto was pressuring the defendant for money and the boy decided to steal it. The psychiatrist then described Kenny Houseknecht's version of the story.

Houseknecht had told the doctor that he waited outside the Anderson home in the bushes. After Kim's older relative left at 7:00 a.m., Kenny went around the back of the house. "I walked into the room and grabbed the bank," Kenny told the psychiatrist. "At that moment, Kim came out. She screamed and grabbed me. We started wrestling. I had the knife. She might have thought I was going to rape her. It didn't look good.

"She grabbed the knife," the teenager's story went on. "I started to give her little jabs so she'd get off me. I just couldn't knock her out. I didn't want to hurt her. Then, I blacked out. The next thing I know, she's under me."

"Why didn't he kill Mario Pinto?" the prosecutor asked the witness during cross-examination. "That's what I would have done."

"Maybe if he was cornered by Pinto and put in a similar situation, who knows what would have happened?" the doctor replied.

"It was Ken Houseknecht who wanted marijuana," Prosecutor Johnson said. "It was Ken Houseknecht who wanted liquor. It was Ken Houseknecht who wanted to drive around in Pinto's car. Have you ever thought about that?" Then the prosecutor asked the psychiatrist if it were possible that the defendant could have "been torturing her, saying 'Where is the money, where is the money?' " as he stabbed her over and over.

"That's ludicrous," the psychiatrist answered. "He knew the girl. He's not that type of person. He didn't want to hurt her."

432

"He did a damn good job," Johnson shot back.

"I object," shouted Natale.

"Are you objecting to 'damn' or 'good job'?" Johnson asked.

"Save those remarks for your closing," Judge Telsey instructed.

"In 1989," said a psychologist testifying for the state, "he [the defendant] was in worse shape than he is now. Kenneth Houseknecht is a very sick boy, but he is not insane."

"There's no kind of mental impairment at all," said a psychiatrist testifying for the prosecution. "The pressure from Pinto does not rise to the level of duress or coercion. This doesn't appear to be a life-threatening situation. Guys get angry at each other and yell."

"Ken Houseknecht has a problem," said Prosecutor Keith Johnson in his closing remarks. "The state readily admits he has a problem—he is a killer. Normal people don't kill. We call that person a criminal. We don't call him mentally ill.

"Was this an act of a magician casting a spell? Who has been able to influence his life? His teachers? No. His child study team? No. His parents? No. Mario Pinto? No."

Keeping in mind legal definitions of insanity, diminished capacity, and duress, the jury deliberated for two days.

"It was a very difficult decision," one juror would later say.

"It was emotional," said a second juror. "I'm sorry the whole thing happened, but he got a fair trial."

On July 17, 1991, with news crews from all the Philadelphia television stations awaiting the verdict, the jury found Kenny Houseknecht guilty of murder, felony murder, robbery, burglary, and weapons offenses.

Under New Jersey state law, because the defendant

was a juvenile when he committed the crime, the death penalty was never a factor in Houseknecht's sentencing. But Kenny Houseknecht will be spending the rest of his life in prison.

EDITOR'S NOTE:
Ruthie, Arthur and Lisa Spano, Sarah Riley, and Mario Pinto are not the real names of the persons so named in the foregoing story. Fictitious names have been used because there is no reason for public interest in the identities of these persons.

434

TEEN MURDERS AT SCHOOLS

by

Don Lasseter

There is no hopelessness so sad as that of early youth. . . .

George Eliot (Marian Evans Cross)
The Mill on The Floss

As the Twentieth Century fades to a close and doors to the next millennium swing open, violent crime rates in the United States appear to be on an encouraging downtrend, with a recent exception that is both startling and tragic.

In the first eighty years of this century, school-children's disputes usually started with the exchange of insults, escalated to loud arguments, and were often settled by fistfights. A dust-raising scuffle might take place behind the baseball backstop out of teachers' sight, with the grunting combatants encircled by noisy, shouting classmates. Torn clothing, a bloody nose, or a black eye was usually the most serious result.

In the mid-nineties, though, escalating violence at schools has developed into a horrifying pattern. Off campus, proliferating gangs have caused school-children to fear for their personal safety, especially while commuting, forcing some of them to carry weapons for defensive purposes. Gradually, gang warfare infiltrated urban classrooms. Cheap handguns called "Saturday night specials" began showing up in students' backpacks.

With the growing specter of juvenile homicide among gangs, education officials struggled to keep it away from schools. But somehow, fresh-faced adolescents had been inculcated with the idea that guns were the solution to problems. They seemed to think that verbal threats, real or imagined slights, and broken romances could be dealt with by unleashing a hail of deadly gunfire. In late 1997 and early 1998, three such incidents in the southern U.S. garnered massive, widespread news media coverage, and escalated all the way to Washington, D.C., into the halls of Congress and even to the White House. After one bloody massacre of four girls and a teacher by two schoolboys, President Bill Clinton was reportedly awakened during the middle of the night. He couldn't get back to sleep, and expressed his grief the next morning, calling for new preventative measures to be taken. Congress began considering legislation to limit ammunition supplies for certain firearms.

Considering the locale of these three notorious incidents, it might be easy to fall into a trap of thinking that schoolyard murder is endemic to southern states. When television reporters descended on Pearl, Mississippi, Paducah, Kentucky, and Jonesboro, Arkansas, viewers across the nation saw residents who spoke with drawls, drove pickups, and were accustomed to owning guns. But similar murders of students and teachers, in schools far less publicized, took place earlier in the opposite corner of the nation, in Washington and in Alaska. It is a national problem, not a regional one. The following six cases are worth studying and analyzing for the purpose of seeking answers to what causes these tragic outbursts of bloody murder.

February 2, 1996,
Moses Lake, Washington

Chilly winter winds sweeping across Moses Lake in the dry flatlands of central Washington often force the 12,000 residents who live in the small town of the same name to stay indoors. On February 2, 1996, the coldest day of the year, teenagers at Frontier Junior High School avoided the crisp breeze at lunchtime by gathering in protected areas to eat. When they resumed classes that Friday afternoon, looking forward to the weekend, two of the kids and one teacher had no idea that their lives would end within the hour.

At 2 P.M., fourteen-year-old honor student Barry Loukaitis, dressed all in black like an old west gunfighter, complete with cowboy hat and boots, an ammunition belt, and a long duster coat, strode into the algebra classroom. He moved stiffly, with one hand thrust through a slit he'd made in the ankle-length coat to clutch a concealed high-powered rifle. Loukaitis carried two handguns and seventy-eight rounds of ammunition also hidden by the bulky garment. Teacher Leona Caires, forty-nine, holding a chalkboard eraser and a Magic Marker, had been printing an algebra problem on the board. She glanced up at the youth just before he raised the rifle and pulled the trigger.

One slug, fired at close range, ripped into the body of Manuel Vela, age fourteen, just below the neck. He crumpled in a heap, mortally wounded. The acrid odor of gunsmoke filled the air as fright-

437

ened students shrieked, yelled, ran, or scrambled for cover. More ear-shattering shots sounded like thunderclaps. Arnold Fritz, also fourteen, clutched his midsection, staggered slowly to the back of the classroom, and dropped to the floor with a gaping hole in his chest. Bones had been shattered by the piercing metal, which also damaged his heart and lungs. At another eruption of gunfire the teacher, Leona Caires, fell near the chalkboard, her back pierced by a bullet that tore all the way through her body and exited from her chest. One more round slammed into the arm of a thirteen-year-old girl, shredded the flesh, and ripped into her body. Critically wounded, she screamed, "I can't feel my arm! I can't feel my arm!" The child would later recall seeing the stunned, horrified expressions of her classmates, some of them frozen in terror.

As cool as the mythical gunfighters he apparently tried to imitate, Loukaitis herded the remaining students to the back of the room. One sixteen-year-old girl would recall that he seemed quite composed while he directed her to sit down. According to her, Loukaitis calmly asked where she was originally from. When she managed to stammer out that she hailed from Dallas, Texas, he reportedly answered, as if engaging her in a casual conversation, "Dallas is a very pretty city."

Another girl remembered that Loukaitis wanted to take a hostage to protect himself. She reported that he said, "I imagine there is going to be snipers and cops."

Physical education teacher Jon Lane, nearby, also heard the explosive racket. He dashed into classroom fifteen. When he saw fallen bodies, heard young people screaming, and caught a whiff of the gunsmoke, he understood the severe danger. Lane

438

would later say, "The students were in sheer terror. They had a look of death on their faces." Recognizing Loukaitis as the shooter, the teacher dove for cover. "I tried to collect myself. I knew gunshots had been fired. I lay there and felt my heart beating." From his position behind a desk he could see the body of Leona Caires, her hands still gripping the eraser and marker pen. "There was no doubt in my mind she was dead. . . . she obviously had no time to react."

As Lane recalled it, Loukaitis ordered him to stand up, and threatened to kill more classmates if the teacher failed to respond. Rising carefully, Lane hoped to defuse the situation by asking Loukaitis if he could take the wounded girl for medical help.

Assistant Principal Steve Caires, husband of the fallen teacher, was on the phone in his office down the hall. A terrified student ran in and said he'd heard firecrackers or gunshots in classroom fifteen. "I got up and ran down the hall," said Caires.

Sprinting into the pandemonium of the classroom, Caires grimaced at the horror. The stench of gunpowder assaulted his nostrils. "I looked down and saw my wife. She was lying on the floor on her back. I saw the cartridges on the floor and knew they were from a high-powered rifle." Caires also realized at that moment his wife was dead. "My stomach was jumping up and down."

Jon Lane, determined to try to save some lives, at last got consent from Barry Loukaitis to take the wounded girl for aid. He also asked if he could take the damaged body of Arnold Fritz outside. According to the stunned teacher, Loukaitis replied in a matter-of-fact voice, "Just let him die." Persistent, Lane continued to press Loukaitis until the gun-toting boy finally granted permission. Because the flow of so much blood had made the floor slippery, Lane recruited help from a couple of the boys to drag Fritz's body out. According to Lane, Loukaitis, still exercising control, demanded that Lane return to the room. When he did, Loukaitis attempted to take him hostage by ordering Lane to put the rifle barrel in his mouth.

Pretending to submit, Lane moved closer, then lunged forward. With one hand, he pushed the threatening rifle aside, and with the other, pinned Loukaitis to a wall. "Get out!" Lane yelled to the students still in the room.

Within moments after the shooting, Moses Lake police had arrived at Frontier Junior High. To avoid a potentially disastrous slaughter, they remained outside the classroom while Jon Lane negotiated with Loukaitis. When they heard the teacher shout for the other children to escape, the police rushed in and subdued the young killer.

In a squad car, an officer read Loukaitis his Miranda rights, to which the youth reportedly looked up, cracked a smile, and said, "I know my rights, man."

Among the tangle of emergency and rescue vehicles flashing red lights, a helicopter landed. Medical technicians carefully loaded a stretcher on which the severely wounded girl lay. It lifted up into the gray, wintery sky, and whisked her a hundred and forty miles westward to a Seattle hospital for emergency treatment. She would require extensive surgery, grafts, and long-term rehabilitation.

Inside the police station, officers strip-searched Loukaitis before putting him in a cell. One of them said that the suspect was very sarcastic and acted calm and cold-blooded. Loukaitis reportedly crawled onto a bunk, pulled a blanket over his head, and fell asleep.

A few hours later, while a tape recorder ran, Barry Loukaitis confessed to killing the two boys and the teacher. In his statement, he explained that Manuel Vela was the only person he had intended to kill. Supposedly, Vela had once called Loukaitis a "faggot."

Flippantly, the suspect said about the other two deaths, "That was kinda crazy." Asked if he had felt any anger toward the victims, Loukaitis simply uttered, "No." That comment would eventually be disputed by an acquaintance of the young killer, with the statement that Loukaitis once been furious at the algebra teacher for marking an incorrect answer on a test. According to the informant, Loukaitis had threatened to kill Mrs. Caires.

Over the next few weeks investigators learned a great deal about the background of Barry Loukaitis. According to people who knew him well he had been a happy, outgoing child during his first ten years of life. Then he seemed to retreat into depression and solitude. Strife in the family home apparently contributed to his sullenness. He seemed deeply affected by a close relative's threat to commit suicide. Relationships with his peers also deteriorated. A classmate at Frontier Junior High said, "He was always mean to me. When I asked him to help me with answers in the math class, he would give me wrong answers."

Another acquaintance reported that Loukaitis became deeply interested in the motion picture, *Natural Born Killers,* and sat through it several times. "It was the only movie he ever talked about. He would quote from it, saying, 'Murder is pure. People make it unpure.' "

441

Loukaitis also reportedly loved to read books by author Stephen King, and he enjoyed writing dark poetry that frightened his friends. One of his favorite music videos was by the band Pearl Jam.

It didn't take defense lawyers long to announce they would offer a plea of insanity when Loukaitis came to trial. Washington is one of the many states that allow a juvenile as young as fourteen to be tried as an adult under certain circumstances.

Because of intense publicity in Moses Lake, hoping to find an impartial jury, a judge decided to move the trial to Seattle. With the usual motions, hearings, and delays, eighteen months passed before Loukaitis at last faced a judge and jury. His attorney announced plans to present evidence showing that Loukaitis suffered intense mood swings connected to bipolar personality disorder, the mental illness previously called manic-depression.

Lawyers for the state pointed out that the defendant knew right from wrong when he killed three people, and that he deserved to spend the rest of his life in prison. In opening statements the prosecutor argued that Loukaitis had taken four guns from his parents' home, dressed as a cowboy gunman, and refused a ride to school so he could surreptitiously carry his weapons with him. In chilling language, the prosecutor accused Loukaitis of cold-bloodedly carrying out the well-planned executions. When the attorney described the gory wounds inflicted on one of the victims in vivid detail, and how the child had tried to inhale air into his punctured lung, a middle-aged juror turned pale and passed out in his chair.

Among the prosecution witnesses, the injured girl showed her scarred arm to jurors, and told of the horror she'd experienced in the classroom massacre. "The only way I can describe it is pure terror and confusion." She said there was so much pain that she hadn't really grasped what was going on. Yet, she professed sympathy for the defendant, and wondered if he might have truly been mentally ill at the time.

A classmate testified that Loukaitis had boasted of thinking it would be fun to go on a killing spree, murder a lot of people, and get away with it.

An assistant principal recalled watching Loukaitis walk by his window that morning. "I said to the secretary, 'I think I just saw a tin soldier.' " He explained that his description referred to the stiff-legged manner in which Loukaitis had walked, with his arms held straight down at his sides. He didn't know that the boy carried a concealed rifle under his duster coat.

Heavy emotion filled the courtroom when gory photos of the victims were introduced into evidence. Anguished family members rushed out through exit doors. One juror asked for a break to compose herself.

Observers watched and listened in riveted silence when the prosecutor played the Pearl Jam music video reportedly loved by the defendant, and wondered if it had put ideas in the boy's head. It portrayed a miserable teenage boy, starved for affection, who sees his parents fight. He is a loner at school and is teased by classmates. The next segment caused goosebumps to rise on the skin of everyone in the courtroom. On the television screen, the lonely boy walks into a classroom in mid-afternoon. Students' faces turn toward him with horrified expressions, and make motions to protect themselves. The video closes with a picture of one of the students, blood-stained near his neck!

As is usual in a case involving a plea of insanity,

443

psychiatrists from both sides dueled in complex language about bipolar disorder, psychotic behavior, overdependence, emotional incest, delusional catatonic states, and disassociation.

Finally, the jury took the case into deliberations. When they returned their verdict found Barry Loukaitis guilty of two counts of aggravated murder, and pronounced him legally sane. Inexplicably, the jury found him guilty of second degree murder for shooting the teacher to death.

At a hearing to determine his sentence, the convicted killer sat with his head bowed while families of the victims testified. A relative of Manuel Vela read a letter aloud. It was from the dead boy's younger brother. In it, he wrote, "Hi. I was 9 years old when my brother was murdered. . . . I'm still sleeping in my parents' room at night." The message was clear. . . . the child still suffered anxiety and fear.

In October, 1997, a judge sentenced Loukaitis to two consecutive terms of life in prison, plus two hundred and five years. He will be confined at a recently built youth offender facility in Shelton, Washington, until he reaches adulthood, at which time the Department of Corrections will decide where he will continue his lifelong incarceration.

Feb 19, 1997,
Bethel, Alaska

Exactly one year and eighteen days after Barry Loukaitis unleashed a deadly hail of rifle fire against classmates and a teacher, another young man chose the same month, February, also in a cold climate, to take a gun to school and commit murder. Other strange similarities echoed all the way from Moses Lake, Washington, to the frozen tundra where Bethel, Alaska lies.

Located four hundred miles west of Anchorage and forty miles from the Bering Sea, in vast, level, treeless plains dotted by lakes and sloughs, Bethel is a hub town of 5,100 citizens, and is the core of commerce for dozens of surrounding villages. Frigid winters produce an average snowfall of fifty inches, and the temperature hovers from zero to less than twenty degrees. More than half of the residents are natives, many of them still communicating in Yup'ik, the Eskimo language. It's not unusual for the people to greet a stranger with the word "Camai!" which has been defined as a verbal handshake to welcome new faces. In recent years the population has grown and diversified with Korean, Greek, and Lebanese immigrants.

Bethel Regional High School serves a student body of a little over four hundred and fifty young people in grades seven through twelve. Two of those pupils, in February of 1997, were the children of school principal Ron Edwards. His wife also taught there. Another student, Evan Ramsey, age sixteen, along with his younger brother, lived in a foster home with Edwards's boss, the superintendent of the Lower Kuskokwin School District.

Just as children had tried to escape the cold in Moses Lake a year earlier, students at Bethel, arriving before the first morning classes, gathered in a main lounge area at 8:40 A.M. Evan Ramsey, a junior, reportedly marched into the warm room carrying a shotgun in one hand and a brown paper bag full of ammunition in the other. He wore a jacket and his usual black T-shirt, along with dark baggy pants he'd borrowed allegedly to conceal the weapon as he smuggled it on campus. His head had been shaved, and he sported a peach fuzz mustache.

One fifteen-year-old student's eyes grew large as he focused on the shotgun. He later said, "He had it in his hand and he was looking around." That boy's buddy, Joshua Palacious, sixteen, sat close by. Palacious, the witness recalled, initially retreated toward an exit, but apparently thought Ramsey meant no harm and returned to the chair where he'd been sitting.

Another classmate reportedly said later, "The kid came in with a shotgun. . . . but we have an ROTC program here, and lots of the kids thought it was probably [related to] that, so there was a delayed action."

According to reports, Josh Palacious, who had fought with Ramsey months earlier, started to rise again and yelled, "Hey, that's a shotgun. Why do you have that gun here?" When Ramsey allegedly raised the barrel in the direction of Palacious from several paces away, Josh gasped, "I'm going to get out of here." Just as he stood to his full height, five-foot four inches, an ear-splitting blast filled the room. Palacious reeled in pain, struck by a wide pattern of shotgun pellets that had pierced his shoulder and stomach.

Pellets that missed Josh struck a fourteen-year-old bystander in the shoulder. The second wounded boy recalled seeing ". . . a whole lot of people running and jumping out of windows. I found the nearest exit, went out, and tried to get some help." He didn't even realize he'd been shot until he reached a nearby diesel repair shop.

A female teacher ran to help Palacious, knelt by him, then stood to face Ramsey, who had started pacing back and forth, wildly pointing the shotgun in all directions. "Put the gun down," she pleaded. "You don't have to do this." But Ramsey ignored her, and the teacher dropped to her knees again to help the grievously wounded boy. As she did her best to apply first aid, Ramsey careened out of the lounge area into a corridor. He discharged the weapon repeatedly, usually toward the ceiling, and frequently stopped to reload it. A few times, according to a witness, he aimed the weapon at his own head without firing it. He did fire toward a third victim, age fifteen, who caught a dozen pellets in his torso. Wounded, the lad tried to recall the details of his experience, but could only say, "I dropped down and tried to crawl away." He survived the injuries.

One observer claimed that the gun-wielding teenager wore a grin, and often laughed as he roamed up and down the halls.

In the office of principal Ron Edwards, a teacher dodged as she saw Ramsey barge in from a corridor. Instantly, Ramsey leveled the gun again, and pulled the trigger. The teacher watched in horror as the impact of the twelve-gauge shotgun blast slammed Ron Edwards against a door.

A senior, eighteen, standing in an adjacent area, heard a piercing scream and turned to look through a window. He observed the sickening scene in the principal's office a split second after the shot, seeing Edwards collapse to the floor, face down. He later reported that he thought the principal had been shot in the back.

As Ramsey wheeled and strode away, the terror-stricken teacher, hoping the shooter wouldn't return, tried to pull her bleeding boss back into the office. She noted that his shoulder was a mess, but thought the wound didn't seem life-threatening since the victim could still speak. The teacher had no way of knowing that the blast had sent metal fragments into Edward's heart and lungs. "I'm going to die," Edwards groaned, then repeated his dire prediction.

"No, you're not," the teacher said. "We're going to make it through this."

In another eerie reflection of the Lake Moses tragedy, where a husband had seen his wife die, Edward's wife, who was trapped on the other side of an accordion room divider, and couldn't move it, heard her husband dying.

After Ramsey left the room he could be heard firing more shots at random. Then, he stopped. The entire attack, which seemed to the witnesses and victims to consume hours, had lasted only a few minutes.

A trio of city police officers arrived on the scene at 8:45, sent by a dispatcher who'd received frantic calls from the school. As the cops sprinted into the building they could still hear random shots being fired by Ramsey. Inside the commons area, where it all began, pandemonium reigned. Some students moaned in terror, while others, along with teachers, tried to help bleeding youngsters who had been hit. At that moment Ramsey allegedly walked again into the lounge, still holding the shotgun. Two more officers arrived, and the five men took cover. Reportedly the chief of police later described it as, "We went in. He saw us coming. He ran across the lobby and up one flight of stairs onto a landing. We hollered, 'Drop the weapon! Drop it right now!'"

At first, Ramsey ignored the order. A lieutenant stepped from behind a shielding door into Ramsey's view, and the youth discharged his shotgun again, but missed. A sergeant aimed his handgun high and fired two warning shots.

Alarmed at being a possible target instead of a shooter, Ramsey allegedly froze as the officers repeated demands for him to throw down his weapon. The now frightened youth reportedly began pleading, "I don't want to die for this. I don't want to die!" Ramsey tossed the shotgun down the stairs, and tentatively started to descend toward the sergeant. The officer rushed up the remaining steps, struggled briefly with Ramsey, wrestled him to the floor, and subdued him.

Moments later, medical personnel loaded Joshua Palacious aboard a small plane for transport to a hospital in Anchorage. There, doctors spent three hours in the ER trying without success to save the boy's life.

The second victim, Principal Ronald Edwards, would never reach his fifty-first birthday. He died at the scene of the shootings. Two other wounded teenage boys were taken to a local hospital and treated. They would survive.

The violence had ended, and now the investigation could begin.

As the pieces of the puzzle came into view, it became apparent that Evan Ramsey had not lived an ideal life. According to local newspaper accounts, twelve years earlier, his father had been involved in a bizarre incident that sent him to prison. It began with a claim that his Anchorage apartment was infested with vermin and full of asbestos. Apparently frustrated with city officials for inaction about his complaint, the father had tried to organize a drive to oust the mayor. Using unorthodox procedures, he reportedly tried to enlist the help of local politicians, and took out a full page ad in a city newspaper. When the ad was pulled after a short run, the father stormed into the newspaper offices armed with a rifle and smoke bombs. He allegedly tossed the bombs around, and tried to take the eighty-year-old editor and his daughter as hostages. The elderly man resisted, and with his daughter's help he wrestled the assailant to the floor. During the struggle the intruder reportedly fired several shots. In a 1988 trial for attempted murder, arson, kidnapping, and assault, the defendant said, "I ain't no arsonist or murderer." But the jury convicted him, and the judge sentenced him to fifteen years in prison. He served part of the time, and was released just one month before his son killed two people.

Following his father's conviction Evan Ramsey's mother reportedly sank into a life of "welfare and drinking," so he and his kid brother were placed in foster homes. They wound up in Bethel, living with the school district superintendent.

Now out of prison, the father told investigators that he'd kept in contact with his sons by telephone. Evan had been a gentle boy, he said, but admitted, "He's like me in one respect. He's slow to anger, but when he angers, he blows up."

Evan Ramsey's peers agreed with the charge that he was easily angered. They also characterized him as a rebellious loner, a misfit, who often got in fights. At school, kids called him retarded and taunted him as a "brain-dead spaz."

Gradually, more disturbing information surfaced. Some of the students told investigators that Ramsey had informed them on the night before the tragic attack that he planned to take a gun to school, kill the principal, and shoot Josh Palacious. He had stated that he wanted to make his victims suffer. As the evidence mounted, it appeared that two of Ramsey's young confidantes had previously discussed the assault plans with him. The police

450

arrested the pair, both fourteen, and charged them as accomplices. Officials at first announced that the duo would be tried as adults, but by April charges against them were reduced to "complicity" and their cases were handled by juvenile authorities.

According to local newspaper accounts, in the foster home where Ramsey lived, the police found two notes in his handwriting, written in the past tense, apparently intended to be made public after his planned suicide. In one he wrote that he wanted to kill someone, and mentioned the principal, Ron Edwards. He also expressed hope that a single 12-gauge shotgun shell might wound multiple victims. The second note reportedly contained a passage that declared, "I'm dead, you guys are living. You should be happy. I wanted to live to see the tomorrow world but time travels too slow ... I felt like taking someone down with me, but I couldn't kill anyone other than [a female acquaintance] but she wasn't around." Why he wished to kill the girl remained a mystery.

Alaska law, like Washington's, allowed a sixteen-year-old to be tried as an adult. One year after the killings, Evan Ramsey sat in a courtroom charged with two counts of first-degree murder.

The prosecutor told jurors that Ramsey had deliberately targeted Josh Palacious for several reasons. The defendant had been in a fistfight with Josh a year prior to the murders. Also, said the lawyer, Ramsey had been envious of Josh's status as one of the basketball "jocks", and had been angry because Josh had taunted him.

Ramsey's defense attorney openly acknowledged that his client had killed Palacious and Edwards, but claimed there had never been any intent to do so. Instead, he argued, Ramsey had taken the gun to school simply to act like a tough "cowboy," and to kill himself in the presence of people who made his life miserable. The reference to a cowboy image also mirrored the tragedy at Moses Lake, Washington.

Testimony revealed a childhood in which the defendant had felt rejected, unloved, mistreated, and abandoned, and was forced to fend for himself. Reportedly, he had once wandered from house to house asking for a warm bed and some food.

Without contradicting the problems experienced by Ramsey, the prosecutor pointed out that the defendant's younger brother had undergone the same hardships, but turned out all right.

The jury deliberated less than five hours. They found Ramsey guilty on both counts of first-degree murder, one count of attempted murder, and fifteen counts of assault.

Evan Ramsey still faces formal sentencing. The charges for which he was convicted made him eligible for a sentence of three hundred years in prison. It is likely that he will never be freed.

October 1, 1997,
Pearl, Mississippi

At age sixteen, Luke Woodham searched for self-esteem on two levels.

First, when he fell in love with Christina Menefee, he couldn't believe his own good fortune. Because of his appearance—chubby and spectacled—Luke's confidence in his ability to attract girls had been low. But Christina, also sixteen, accepted dates with him, boosting his ego and opening up a whole new world.

On the other level, Woodham allegedly thought he'd found strength by associating with a small group of boys who explored the dark side of power. Reportedly the prosecutor asserted they alternately called themselves, "The Group" and "The Kroth" —which they defined as a reference to satanic beliefs. The boys supposedly liked to think they were able to exercise mind control over others. Allegedly led by an eighteen-year-old college freshman, the boys professed a belief in the doctrines of Nineteenth Century philosopher Friedrich Nietzsche, who denounced religion and suggested that certain men could achieve perfection through forcible self-assertion. It was whispered among locals that the leader dabbled in satanism, obsessively hero-worshiped Adolph Hitler, and believed in the theory of *Ubermensch*, or supermen.

Woodham, often ridiculed by classmates at Pearl High School about his weight, his shoulder-length brown hair, his wire-rimmed glasses, and his "shabby" clothing, turned into a quiet introvert. He maintained reasonably good grades, but socially he seemed inhibited and clumsy. "He was picked on for as long as I can remember," said one girl. "Most people who aren't popular get picked on." In her recollection, Woodham didn't seem to react to the derision. "I never heard him say a cuss word." Other peers also noted that Luke never fought back when boys called him names or pushed him around.

According to people who knew Woodham, he particularly resented the worship heaped on athletes, and complained about the world ignoring intellectual achievement. One member of his group later said, "He was tired of society dealing the thinkers [and] the learners a bad hand." The acquaintance added that "Johnny Football Player" gets all the glory.

Pearl, Mississippi, the community in which Woodham grew up, sits close to the Pearl River in the state's midsection, just east of the capital, Jackson. The 22,000 residents regarded it as a comfortable, relatively crime-free region where teenagers could feel safe. A small town camaraderie existed, and young people often gathered at pizza restaurants, sometimes being served at one eatery by a chubby, part-time employee named Luke Woodham.

Luke lived with his mother Mary Woodham, fifty, who had been divorced for five years. She held a white-collar job as a receptionist, and provided a comfortable living for her only son. Her boss described Mary as a fine employee and said that she was, "a good friend to everyone." Most people regarded her as a typical mother, who kept her small, white home clean and faithfully tended the perennials in her flower garden. Mary usually drove Luke to school, even though they lived only a mile from Pearl High.

Although life in the Woodham home appeared normal, one of the high school students contradicted the illusion. The informant said, "He told me he hated his mother." Luke would one day write about Mary Woodham that she changed drastically after divorcing his father. "My mother started going out partying all the time. She was never there."

If Woodham suffered over his mother's behavior, the pain paled in comparison to the hurt he reportedly experienced when his relationship with Christina Menefee crashed. An average-looking girl, Christina garnered admiration for the compassion she gave to unfortunate people. Her father would say, "Christy is always for the underdog." And her mother observed that Christina might have decided to accept a date with Woodham because other girls shunned him. But Christina's sympathy could only extend so far, and when she reportedly realized that Luke had emotionally attached himself to her she gently informed him she wasn't ready for any commitment and that she wished to date other boys.

On Wednesday, October 1, 1997, Luke Woodham climbed out of bed unusually early. It is alleged that he entered his mother's bedroom and used a butcher knife to end her life by repeatedly stabbing and slashing her, then cutting her throat. Afterward, wearing a long overcoat, he allegedly loaded a .30-30 hunting rifle into his mother's car and backed out of the driveway. En route to school, he reportedly rammed into and uprooted a small tree, then left tire tracks across a neighbor's lawn.

After parking, Woodham entered the double doors and went into a common area where early arrivals gathered, close to eight o'clock that morning. Woodham reportedly pulled the rifle from under his baggy coat. With his face expressionless, he spotted Christina Menefee, the girl he'd loved and lost, and walked directly to her. Witnesses heard no conversation, but recoiled in horror when the explosion of a rifle echoed through the halls and Christina toppled over, mortally wounded in the neck. Still wearing an impassive expression, according to witnesses, Woodham strolled through the commons. Petrified students, screaming and panicky, sought cover or dropped down frozen in fear. The rifle thundered again and again. Several shots drilled into the flesh of young victims, inflicting multiple bloody wounds. Said a freshman who saw the whole thing, "He was shooting anybody he could find. He shot at me and hit the staircase."

Another boy said, "People were laying everywhere, bleeding. I didn't hear cries. Everybody looked dead." Most of the wounded suffered painful but superficial injuries. One volatile slug, though, slammed into the back of Lydia Kaye Dew, seventeen, who died within minutes.

Assistant Principal Joel Myrick, thirty-six, an army reservist and local National Guard Commander with movie star good looks, rushed into the commons area and couldn't believe what he saw. He momentarily locked eyes with Luke Woodham. Then he spun around and ran full speed to his pickup truck, where he grabbed his .45 caliber pistol. As he started to return, he caught sight of Woodham heading for his mother's car. "Stop!" Myrick shouted, but Woodham allegedly ignored the order, lunged into the car, and started it. Unsteadily, he headed up a tree-lined road, away from the school. An inexperienced driver, he didn't get very far, and the vehicle lurched to a halt.

According to newspaper accounts, Myrick sprinted to the stalled car to confront Woodham. "I could see him sitting there, holding on to the steering wheel," Myrick would recall. "His knuckles were white, those glasses on him." With adrenalin coursing through his system, Myrick jammed the pistol against Woodham's neck and shouted, "Why? Why? Why did you do this?"

Woodham reportedly uttered, "Mister Myrick, I'm the guy who gave you a discount on your pizza the other night."

Hardly hearing the strangely inappropriate reply, Myrick reportedly again asked, "Why? You killed my kids!"

"Well, Mister Myrick," Woodham allegedly answered, "The world has wronged me, and I couldn't take it anymore."

His emotions still jumbled, trying to suppress fiery anger, Myrick couldn't resist a bitter response. "You think the world has wronged you now! Wait till you get to Parchman!" He referred to the tough state prison in northern Mississippi.

Moments later the police arrived and arrested Woodham, taking him to Rankin County jail, where the youth would be charged with murder. The state's laws provide for a sixteen-year-old to be tried as an adult.

Inside the high school, emergency medics attended to seven wounded teenagers, one of whom was in critical condition. Christina Menefee and Lydia Kaye Dew were beyond any earthly help.

After police had taken Woodham into custody they went to his home, and made the grisly discovery of his brutally murdered mother.

As investigators began looking into the background of the accused killer, a member of "The Group" gave them a handwritten document that appeared to be the words of Luke Woodham. Evidently prepared a short time before his rampage and written in the past tense, the statement contained no signature or name. It set forth a chilling "manifesto" of a teenager's anger and plans to seek retribution. The author wrote, "I am not insane. I am not spoiled or lazy, for murder is not weak and slow-witted. Murder is gutsy and daring. I killed because people like me are mistreated every day. I do this to show society – 'Push us and we will push back.' I suffered all my life. No one ever truly loved me. No one ever truly cared about me. I only loved one thing in my life and she was Christina Menefee but she has gone away from me. All throughout my life I was ridiculed,

457

always beaten, always hated. Can you, society, truly blame me for what I do? Yes, you will. The ratings wouldn't be high enough if you didn't, and it would not make good gossip for all the old ladies."

Perhaps the most horrifying segment of the rambling document gave a hideous description of how the author and another boy killed a family pet. At the preliminary hearing for Woodham, an investigator read some of the repulsive passages aloud: "On Saturday last week, I made my first kill. The victim was a loved one, my dear dog Sparkle." In graphic detail, the writer explained how he and the accomplice had attacked the pet with clubs, beat her mercilessly, then encased the dog in layered, plastic garbage bags. "I will never forget the howl she made. It sounded almost human. We laughed and hit her more." The officer, his face betraying his own fury and pain, read on as stunned officials listened. According to the cruel account, the boys poured cigarette lighter fluid on the plastic bags, set them aflame, then tossed the gruesome bundle into a pond. As they watched it sink, the writer noted, the sight was "true beauty."

Social scientists have noted that cruelty to small animals is often the precursor to murdering humans, and is a common trait in serial killers.

Investigators wondered why, if Woodham had been seeking retribution for real or imagined abuse heaped on him, he allegedly shot and killed Lydia Dew. She, too, had been shy, introspective, had few friends, had been verbally abused and picked on by classmates, and had never done anything to offend Woodham. Assistant Principal Joel Myrick, who stopped Woodham, had spent weeks personally trying to help the girl. When her heartbroken parents later buried their beloved daughter, the mother made a touching gesture of appreciation to Myrick. She gave him Lydia's favorite ring.

The deepening investigation revealed that the alleged killer might not have acted alone. Interviews with scores of Pearl High students gave police information that six boys, Woodham's fellow members of "The Group," had possibly helped him plan the carnage. They reportedly told of plans for traveling as a team to Louisiana, crossing the border into Mexico, then chartering a boat to Cuba. According to some of the informants, the whole plot was "masterminded" by the college freshman leader who espoused Nietzsche and adored Hitler.

The Nietzsche connection as a motivator to murder certainly was not original. It had been used by a pair of teenagers decades earlier. In what was called "The Crime of the Century" in 1924, wealthy heirs Nathan Leopold and Richard Loeb, both nineteen, killed a young boy to prove they were "supermen" capable of the perfect murder.

One week after the Pearl killings, armed with the new information about Woodham's alleged cohorts in crime, the police arrested six boys and charged them with conspiracy to commit murder. Eventually they released four of them who agreed to cooperate and provide information. The remaining two, including the so-called leader, would face trial.

Luke Woodham was interviewed in jail, on the ABC television show *Prime Time Live* in early November. He apologized and claimed that he'd been influenced by "The Group". Woodham said, "Everything I did was influenced by [the leader]. . . . I tried so hard to get his acceptance, you know, 'cause he was the only one who accepted me. . . . he just put a lot of bad things in my head and it built up after time, the pressure of everything on top of that I just couldn't take it anymore.'' He added, ''My whole life . . . I just felt outcasted, alone. Finally, I found some people who wanted to be my friends. I was just trying to find hope in a hopeless world, man.'' In his apology to the parents of the dead girls, Woodham said, ''I know it's not going to bring their daughters back, but I'm sorry. . . . I mean, you know, if I could turn back time, everything would go differently. But you know, you can't.''

Luke Woodham has entered an innocent plea to the crimes. The trial for allegedly killing his mother is scheduled to be conducted in Philadelphia, Mississippi. A separate trial is scheduled in Hattiesburg for the murders of the two schoolgirls. If convicted, Woodham will not be a candidate for the death penalty, according to Mississippi law.

December 1, 1997,
Paducah, Kentucky

Christmas decorations had made early appearances in Paducah, Kentucky, by the end of November of 1997. Traditional carols filled the air for downtown pedestrians, and put smiles on the faces of crowds at Kentucky Oaks Mall, where many of the 27,000 residents had already started their holiday shopping. Nativity scenes decorated lawns at many of the county's churches, which represent nearly every religion. One of the largest meetinghouses is the Bible Baptist Heartland Worship Center.

Ten miles west of town, on the first Monday morning of December, students walked and drove along Metropolis Road making their way to Heath High School. They entered through an impressive portico supported by four massive, white, two-story pillars. Early arrivals filed into the building and assembled in a main lobby before the first bell rang to signal opening of classes. As was their custom, about thirty of the teenagers clasped hands in a circle to offer a morning prayer.

Religion is an important element of life in the scenic old town of Paducah in western Kentucky, named for Chickasaw Indian Chief Paduke. It stands in McCracken County, at the confluence of the Ohio and Tennessee rivers, which made the town an important shipping center for tobacco, timber, and livestock. Factories now dot the landscape. The county operates three high schools, the smallest of which is Heath, an attractive, Greek-style, red brick and white stucco building in which thirty staff members are responsible for six hundred students.

One of those six hundred youngsters conspicuously avoided joining the prayer circle on that Monday morning. Fourteen-year-old freshman Michael Carneal had been attending the school only two months. The boy had frequently been noticed standing in the lobby's periphery during the previous week, observing the prayers. With a small fringe group, he joined in taunting the participants of the circle. No one paid much attention to any of the vocal critics, including the small, thin, curly-haired Carneal.

Exchanging gibes is an age-old tradition among teenagers. Several of the jocks from the Heath Pirates' football team, which had recently ended its season, liked to tease the awkward lad. So did a few members of the prayer group. Ben Strong, seventeen, a defensive end for the team who had organized the morning prayer sessions, would later admit to good-natured "messing around", but said he never took the insults seriously.

461

Any anger Carneal might have felt about the teasing remained concealed. Perhaps his tendencies to disrupt classes with silly attempts to be funny or wear shirts printed with outrageous, attention-getting mottos were manifestations of internalized fury. Still, most people ignored the printed messages—Authority Sucks, or the satanic symbol 666—emblazoned on Carneal's black T-shirts. Teachers agreed that Carneal had been blessed with intelligence, but wondered when he would use it more productively. For the most part, he didn't seem to fit in with social groups. His main extracurricular activity consisted of spending time with a small coterie of skateboarders, some of whom responded to teasing from the athletes with verbal barbs of their own.

Among Carneal's few other friends, Nicole Hadley, fourteen, played clarinet in the school band, and often spoke congenially with Michael, who struggled with his tuba-like instrument, called a baritone.

If Carneal had a problem blending in, it certainly couldn't be blamed on a poor childhood. Indigent youngsters are usually the ones shunned by popular kids. But Carneal was the son of an affluent lawyer, the grandson of a well-known entrepreneur who had acquired extensive real estate, and the relative of a former elementary school principal in the same county.

The principal of Heath High later commented, "I knew the young man had some immaturity problems." But no one, in wildest imagination, could have conceived of the tragedy that was going to take place just a few weeks before Christmas. Only later would the senior, Ben Strong, recall that Carneal had previously sought him out and muttered a cryptic warning. The big athlete had no idea what motivated the smaller boy to suggest that the senior stay away from the prayer session on Monday morning. Carneal reportedly said, "Something big is going to happen." Another football player overheard the remark, and laughed with Strong, suggesting that Carneal probably intended to pull some goofy practical joke. Tossing it off, Strong said good-naturedly, "I'll beat you up if you do."

Michael Carneal's sister drove him to school on Monday morning. She noticed the bundle he reportedly brought with him, but couldn't see the two rifles and two shotguns wrapped in a blanket. *It's probably for some school project,* she thought. Allegedly, Carneal carried the bundle into a classroom and hid it, then made his way to the lobby.

As the prayer group assembled and quietly held hands in the circle, Michael Carneal stood about twenty feet away. He allegedly pulled earplugs from his pockets, inserted them with slow deliberation, then reached into his backpack and pulled out a semi-automatic .22 caliber handgun. With legs braced wide apart and arms outstretched, the boy reportedly gripped his weapon in both hands, just as a movie cop might. Sharp, popping noises startled the assembled group of about forty students. One witness observed that the shooter appeared to be taking careful aim with the first three rounds, and then he commenced pulling the trigger as fast as he could. Blood spurted. Screams filled the lobby. Young people ran in all directions, scrambling for safety, while others dropped to the floor. Another witness said, "I saw one of them go down, bleeding from her head. That's when I started running."

"You could see the fear on everyone's faces," a senior recalled.

"I heard ten shots in a row," said a grim-faced boy. "I didn't know they were gunshots at first. Then I heard a kid yelling, 'Hit the floor.' "

One of the first slugs slammed into the head of Carneal's fourteen-year-old band chum, Nicole Hadley.

Kayce Steger, fifteen, collapsed in a bloody heap.

Jessica James, seventeen, fell nearby, bleeding profusely.

Five other teenagers sustained injuries, including Missy Jenkins, sixteen. A bullet pierced her left shoulder, ripped into her spinal cord, and spun out, leaving a bloody exit wound. She became paralyzed from the waist down.

In the first instant, the thought reportedly flashed through Ben Strong's mind that Carneal was playing some stupid joke, but the athlete quickly recognized the serious danger. Discarding any concern for his own safety, Strong rapidly closed the short distance separating him from Carneal. According to newspaper accounts, Strong confronted the shooter and shouted, "Put the gun down! Why are you doing this? Don't shoot anybody. You gotta' stop!"

Not resisting, wearing a confused expression, Carneal allegedly let his arms drop and released the gun, which clattered to the floor. It had only one round left in the magazine. Strong pinned him against a wall near the sports trophy case. The athlete would recall, "He said, 'Kill me now,' or something like that."

Someone else thought they heard Carneal moan, "I can't believe I did that."

The school principal took custody of Carneal and guided the compliant boy into his office, where he held him for the police.

Forty-five minutes after the bloody carnage Kayce

464

Steger died in the emergency room of a Paducah hospital. Jessica James fought valiantly for her life during extensive surgery, but succumbed to her wounds. Nicole Hadley lasted several hours on life support systems, but slipped away from this life that same evening.

The ensuing investigation revealed that Carneal had allegedly stolen the arsenal of rifles just a few days earlier, on Thanksgiving day. In that robbery, he reportedly also took the handgun, six hundred rounds of ammunition, and one hundred shotgun shells.

Two more disturbing revelations also turned up during the police probe. First, according to police reports, they learned from interviewing Carneal's classmates that he might have been planning the attack for some time. The informants all said they hadn't taken him seriously. Second, it appeared that Carneal might have been influenced by watching a 1995 movie. Allegedly, Carneal had seen *Basketball Diaries,* a film starring popular actor Leonardo DiCaprio, about heroin abuse and violence in a New York Catholic school. In the movie, the star has a fantasy about vengefully murdering classmates. According to newspaper reports, when asked, Carneal admitted seeing the movie, and suggested that it may have been "a factor" in his mind.

President Bill Clinton, informed of the Paducah tragedy, broadcast a statement on radio in which he characterized the victims as America's "beautiful daughters." Saying the deaths were an "insistent, angry wake-up call," Clinton commented on the need to study teenage murder in schools. "We know more about the overall patterns of car theft in America than we do about the harm that comes to our children at school. . . . One thing we must do

465

right away is to gain a much clearer view of the problem.''

At the huge Bible Baptist Heartland Worship Center on the following Friday, a mass funeral for the three murdered students attracted thousands of mourners. Classmates, relatives of the victims, and their heartbroken friends sobbed softly to the strains of "Amazing Grace". As they passed the caskets they left touching notes expressing how much the girls would be missed. One said, "This isn't good-bye. I'll see you soon." Ben Strong, the son of a pastor, who had been hailed as a hero for stopping the massacre, spoke. "It hurts to see them go. . . . they were praying. As soon as they said, 'Amen,' they saw the face of God.''

Missy Jenkins, paralyzed from the waist down, is praying to walk again one day. If she can, she says, she will become a physical therapist.

Michael Carneal will face trial as an adult in Kentucky. His attorneys have announced they will use a "mental health" defense, in an attempt to convince a jury that he "suffered from a diminished mental capacity at the time of his offenses.''

If Carneal is convicted he will not face the death penalty, which is prohibited in that state for anyone under sixteen. Prosecutors have said they will seek a sentence of life in prison without the possibility of parole for at least twenty-five years.

March 26, 1998,
Jonesboro, Arkansas

An issue of *Time* magazine from April, 1998, contains a child's posed photograph that eerily mirrors the image of a teenager who became a killer two years earlier. The photo portrays a little boy, perhaps three or four-years-old, wearing a black cowboy hat and boots, a black and white flannel shirt, ammunition belt, and a floor-length duster. His right hand clutches a double-barreled shotgun, the muzzle tilted to the floor. The outfit nearly duplicates the apparel worn by Barry Loukaitis, fourteen, dressed in black cowboy clothing as he gunned down a teacher and two students at school in Moses Lake, Washington, on February 2, 1996.

On the magazine's cover, the same child is pictured at an even younger age, wearing "cammies," a miniature version of military olive and green combat uniforms, with a matching combat hat. He smiles happily while his tiny hands cradle what appears to be a child-size assault rifle.

The boy's name is Andrew Golden.

His pal, Mitchell Johnson, is portrayed on the cover with a smaller photo and in the inside article. His round face—freckled, cherubic, smiling—is also the picture of innocence.

That innocence is the reason that the nation reeled in confused anguish and horror when the news media made a stunning announcement about the two boys on March 26, 1998. Having grown a good deal since the photos were taken, Mitch Johnson, thirteen, and Drew Golden, eleven, were accused of using rifles to murder four schoolchildren—all preteen girls—and a female teacher. Nine more children and another teacher were wounded during the incredible assault at Westside Middle School in Jonesboro, Arkansas.

As the shock of yet another schoolyard massacre reverberated across the nation, the issue of appropriate punishment for children who commit murder dominated headlines and discussion circles everywhere. Nineteen states do *not* allow a child under fourteen to be tried as an adult. Arkansas is one of them. According to officials, Mitchell and Golden, if held responsible for the killings, may be incarcerated in juvenile facilities for no more than a few years. It appears likely that they will both be free by the time they reach the age of eighteen.

Located in the northeast corner of Arkansas, Jonesboro is larger than the other sites of teenage killings, with a population of approximately 50,000. It's a Bible Belt town, where camouflage clothing is commonly worn by young men, especially in seasons when they hunt turkey or deer in the wooded rural areas of that region.

Mitch Johnson had migrated in 1996 to Jonesboro from Kentucky with his divorced mother. Born in a small Minnesota town, Johnson reportedly hid a dark secret about events which allegedly took place during his early years in the land of lakes and hard winters. A relative would later reveal to interviewer Barbara Walters on the ABC television show *20-20* that the child had been sexually molested in Minnesota, more than once.

Other relatives said that Johnson suffered deep wounds over the split between his parents. His behavior changed after that, becoming aggressive and argumentive. He seemed to have a deep anger beneath his benign, chubby, almost sweet exterior. He allegedly once brandished a knife at school during a dispute with a classmate. When he reached the first stages of puberty he exhibited the normal preoccupation with girls, but reacted with unusually deep emotion if he felt rejected by them. For a boy who tried to project a macho image, Johnson seemed to burst into tears easily.

In September of 1997, Johnson developed a deep

468

interest in religion. A Jonesboro Baptist minister said that the newly converted lad ostensibly took comfort in the faith, and actively participated in church activities. Worshipping the Almighty seemed to strengthen Johnson's emotional makeup. But he suffered a setback at school when the target of his amorous feelings, an eleven-year-old girl named Candace, told him that she wasn't interested. Johnson allegedly reacted angrily and made threats, causing the girl to worry about what he might do.

Away from classes at Westside Middle School Johnson appeared to have few friends, but had started hanging around with eleven-year-old Andrew Golden.

Golden, whose parents were postmasters in separate U.S. Postal Service offices, owned his first gun at the age of six. He became proficient with it, and learned to enjoy accompanying adults on hunting expeditions. At a local shooting range the boy earned high marks for his accuracy at a fifty to seventy-five yard range. Not a shy or reticent child, Golden reportedly liked video games, especially those in which shooting was important, and had tried to become involved in martial arts. A neighbor said he usually wore military style camouflage clothing. A classmate would later reveal that Golden had spoken of a desire to take over the school.

On Tuesday morning, March 24, Mitch Johnson complained of a stomachache and did not go to school. He and Golden, wearing "cammies", allegedly broke into relatives' homes, stole ten handguns and three rifles, and made off with hundreds of rounds of ammunition. They loaded their loot into a van belonging to a relative of Johnson, along with sleeping bags, hunting knives, food, and other camping gear. Classes had already started when

Johnson, accompanied by Golden, drove the van up a steep gravel road and parked on a tree-lined knoll above the school.

They carried the high-powered, semi-automatic rifles to a vantage point high in the brush, from which they could easily see down across the manicured lawn and playground behind classrooms.

According to one report, Drew Golden then made his way to school, attended a class, and asked for permission to go to the bathroom. Just after 12:30 that afternoon, in the hallway, he allegedly pulled a fire alarm. As the jangling bell alerted teachers and students, Golden sprinted about seventy-five yards back up the hill to rejoin Mitch Johnson. In classrooms, excited children welcomed the break from books and studies. Laughing and chattering, they spilled through building exits, led by a group of young girls from a music class.

Without warning, a series of popping noises from the hill echoed across the schoolyard. As in previous shootings, most of the kids thought it sounded like firecrackers, until bloody wounds made them realize the situation was lethal.

Among the fifteen people hit by flying lead, ten sustained various injuries. Five died:

Paige Ann Herring, twelve,

Natalie Brooks, twelve,

Stephanie Johnson, twelve,

Brittany Varner, eleven, and

English teacher Shannon Wright, thirty-two. In trying to herd the students into the adjacent gymnasium for safety, Wright saw that an eleven-year-old girl stood frozen in the direct line of fire. The heroic teacher moved quickly to place her own body between the shooters and the child, thus shielding her. Slugs tore into the woman's chest and abdomen, killing her instantly.

One of the wounded who survived was Candace, the girl Mitchell Johnson had chosen to be his love, and who had rejected him. Another teacher also fell from the sharp sting of a bullet, but wasn't seriously injured. All of the victims except one were females; only one boy received wounds. No one but the shooters knows if the targeting of females was deliberate or accidental.

Twenty-three rounds of ammunition fired from the hill slammed into children, teachers, and buildings, in a span of about four minutes.

When the explosions ceased, the two shooters rose and ran toward the parked van. But the noise and rising smoke from the rifles had caught the attention of men who worked at a site behind the hill. They summoned the police, who arrived just in time to head off the fugitives.

Deputy Sheriffs John Varner (no relation to victim Brittany Varner) and John Moore, who had headed up the gravel road that deadends on the hill, spotted two boys wearing camouflage clothing. Each of the youths carried a rifle as they ran toward a gray van. Both deputies jumped from the cruiser and shouted for the runners to stop and lie flat on the ground. Varner recalled, "The youngest one dropped real quick. The older one hesitated." When the pair capitulated and lay supine, the officers snapped cuffs on their wrists and searched them. They found two hundred rounds of ammunition stuffed in their pockets.

In the van, the deputies discovered ten handguns, including revolvers, semiautomatic pistols, and derringers. "Each weapon was loaded to capacity and cocked."

When Varner asked the pair why they fired at schoolchildren and teachers, the deputy shook his head in disgust at their answers. He recalled, "Both of them just said, 'I don't know. I just don't know.'"

Neither Golden nor Johnson spoke any more during the ride to jail.

Ambulances carried away the wounded and the dead from the scene of bloody carnage. The news spread rapidly, and worried parents rushed to the school, desperately hoping to find that their children were safe.

Relatives of the two accused boys couldn't believe the nightmare. They would soon be subjected to hate mail and threats. Some of the messages they received expressed hope that the shooters would be raped or killed in prison.

At the next day's hearing Golden and Johnson no longer wore their cammies. Instead, they sat at a table dressed in the usual orange jumpsuits of jail inmates. The younger one, Golden, appeared sullen and stoic, while the older boy, Johnson, cried.

Andrew Golden and Mitchell Johnson will probably face a trial for capital murders. But because Arkansas does not allow children under fourteen to be tried as adults, they will not face capital punishment, nor long-term imprisonment, if convicted. Officials are guessing that both boys will be released when they are eighteen.

President Bill Clinton, awakened at midnight during a trip to Africa and informed of the latest schoolyard killings by young boys, couldn't get back to sleep. In a public address, he said, "We do not understand what drives children, whether in small towns or big cities, to pick up guns and take the lives of others. We may never make sense of the

senseless, but we have to try. . . . We have to understand that young children may not fully appreciate
the consequences of actions that are destructive but
may be able to be romanticized at a twisted
moment.'' He paid tribute to the victims, mentioning
each of them by name.

Analysts of the problem point out that in nearly
every case the young killers gave advance warnings,
by speaking to friends or classmates, of an urge or
fantasy to invade their schools, take control, and
perhaps to kill certain people. Unfortunately, no one
seemed to be listening. Serious study of the tragic
incidents could possibly reveal clues to be used for
the development of preventive measures.

Nationwide, while arguing the merits of extreme
or light penalties for young teenage killers, people
expressed the hope that such tragedies among young
people would stop. But it didn't. . . .

**April 24, 1998,
Edinboro, Pennsylvania**

Students of James Parker Middle School, Edinboro, Pennsylvania, gathered on Friday night, April
24, 1998, at a banquet hall, eagerly anticipating the
eighth grade graduation dance. The theme they had
chosen, ''I Had The Time of My Life'', reflected
their optimistic expectations. Dressed in gowns and
suits, two hundred and forty young people embraced, laughed, and partied with that special joy
which comes only in lives of teenagers. It was a
night of celebration, fun, and tenderness. No one
expected it to end in violent tragedy.

Science teacher John Gillette accepted his usual role as a chaperone at the dance. At age forty-eight, he'd spent twenty-seven years teaching in the General McLane School District, and had served as a student council advisor for much of that time. He cared deeply for the kids, and had helped organize the dance. The former football coach had recently been considering retirement, but hesitated to leave his fulfilling job. Less than twenty miles from Lake Erie, the middle school and the small town offered a safe and comfortable environment for Gillette and his family.

When the final song of the night played, couples swarmed to the dance floor. They all recognized "My Heart Will Go On", from the megahit movie, *Titanic*. Observed by chaperones, they swayed in locked embraces to the romantic music, not wanting the night to end. John Gillette could hear it from the patio where he stood.

Suddenly, a short, spectacled youth standing near Gillette allegedly raised his arm, pointed a handgun, and with no hesitation pulled the trigger. A loud "Boom" interrupted the music. John Gillette fell to the floor with a bullet in his head.

The young shooter, reportedly strode calmly through the door and into the dance hall and began firing the .25 caliber weapon again. The slugs grazed one boy, fourteen, across the abdomen, and ripped into the foot of another boy, the same age. A female teacher felt hot metal singe her flesh without doing any serious damage. As pandemonium broke out, teenagers scrambled for safety. "It was pretty horrible," one of them later cried. "We were all scared and crying and praying."

Still wielding his gun, the shooter allegedly rushed outside and loped across a vacant field. The owner of the dance hall, standing in his office, reportedly saw the fugitive, grabbed a shotgun, and ran after him. He caught up, ordered the boy to freeze, and held him at gunpoint until the police arrived.

When the emergency call for medical help came to the Edinboro Volunteer Fire Department at 9:40 P.M., the fire chief's heart nearly stopped. He heard the report of "multiple gunshot victims" at the dance hall, and prayed that his own daughter, fourteen, was not among the dead or injured. When the chief arrived on the scene he found his daughter safe, but his relief was tempered by the sight of the dead teacher.

After the police handcuffed the suspect and took his weapon, they allegedly found a small amount of marijuana in his pocket. Television pictures flashed across the nation showing the alleged shooter sitting in the backseat of the police vehicle, still wearing his glasses. His expression at first appeared blank. Then he stuck out his tongue, and grinned as if the whole thing were a joke.

The suspect, Andrew Wurst, fourteen, lived in a trailer house in the nearby town of McKean with his parents, and attended Parker Middle School. Acquaintances described him as a quiet loner who often dressed "sloppily." No one could recall Wurst ever talking to the victim, John Gillette, or having any conflict with him.

According to two boys who said they were Wurst's friends, he had threatened to "kill people and commit suicide." Of course, the witnesses insisted, they didn't believe Wurst when he made such outrageous comments. "He'd laugh when he said it. You couldn't really take him seriously."

Pennsylvania has no minimum age at which a

suspect charged with murder can be tried as an adult. Officials charged Andrew Wurst with criminal homicide, three counts each of aggravated assault and reckless endangerment, and then tacked on gun and drug charges. His trial is pending.

Until society can learn to listen, to understand the depths of rage and frustration that froth and boil in the minds of teenagers, to identify the common threads of these tragedies, and to act upon them, the tragic slaughter will probably continue.

APPENDIX

"Shotgun-Toting Teen Terror!" *Inside Detective*, November, 1992.

"He Torched Tom With Kerosene!" *Official Detective*, August, 1992.

"The Young & the Wasted," *Official Detective*, November, 1991.

"The Half-Naked Teen Was Sliced to Bits!" *Master Detective*, November, 1992.

"I'm Going to Kill Three Tonight . . . Then I'm Going to Kill Myself!' " *Master Detective*, July, 1993.

"Bullet-Riddled Bodies in the River!" *Inside Detective*, July, 1992.

"Lust-Crazed Teen's Flaming Vengeance!" *Inside Detective*, July, 1993.

"Shortcut to a Deadly Run-In!" *Inside Detective*, July, 1993.

"Blonde Was Bathed in Blood at Zuma Beach!" *Official Detective*, June, 1993.

"Rampage of the Teenage Bonnie & Clyde" *Master Detective*, September, 1992.

"Housewife was Ravaged, Then Strangled" *True Detective*, April, 1992.

"Murdering for Six Years – And Was Still a Teenager!" *Front Page Detective*, November, 1981.

"Freaked-Out Teen Murdered, Then Raped a Woman of 90!" *Official Detective*, August, 1993.

"Did the Teen Terror Toast the Slaughter of Three?" *Master Detective,* January, 1990.

"They Robbed, Rapped & Shot Pretty Lois Under 'Suicide Bridge!' " *Official Detective,* August, 1993.

"Teenage Serial Killer Who Claimed Five!" *Front Page Detective,* June, 1989.

"Throat-Slashed Virgins Took 15 Minutes to Die!" *Official Detective,* April, 1992.

"All-American Kid Slit Lisa's Throat with a Boy Scout Knife!" *Front Page Detective,* April, 1993.

"Was the Coed Killed by a Ghoulish Teen?" *Front Page Detective,* December, 1989.

"Demented Teen Virgin Raped/Murdered a Girl of 7" *Official Detective,* February, 1993.

"Massacred a Family of 3 with a Sledgehammer!" *Offiial Detective,* April, 1992.

"Raped, Shot, Doused with Gas & Torched in the Street!" *Front Page Detective,* September, 1993.

" Christie Chrome' Blasted 'Smiley' in the Gut!" *Front Page Detective,* August, 1993.

"Shawn Novak: Lured Two Innocents to Their Grisly Death!" *Master Detective,* December, 1992.

"He Stabbed Kim 95 Times . . . Then He Left the Blade in Her Skull!" *Official Detective,* April, 1992.

HORRIFYING TRUE CRIME
FROM PINNACLE BOOKS

MORE MUST-READ HORROR
FROM PINNACLE TRUE CRIME

TRUE CRIME AT ITS BEST
FROM PINNACLE BOOKS

From the Files of
True Detective
Magazine